The Colonization of Names

The Colonization of Names

Symbolic Violence and France's Occupation of Algeria

BENJAMIN CLAUDE BROWER

Columbia
University
Press
New York

Columbia University Press
Publishers Since 1893
New York   Chichester, West Sussex

Library of Congress Cataloging-in-Publication Data
Names: Brower, Benjamin Claude author
Title: The colonization of names : symbolic violence and France's occupation of Algeria / Benjamin Claude Brower.
Description: New York : Columbia University Press, [2025] | Includes bibliographical references and index.
Identifiers: LCCN 2024056005 (print) | LCCN 2024056006 (ebook) | ISBN 9780231216029 hardback | ISBN 9780231216012 trade paperback | ISBN 9780231561099 ebook
Subjects: LCSH: Algeria—Relations—France | France—Relations—Algeria | Algeria—Colonization—Social aspects | Names, Personal—Social aspects—Algeria | Onomasiology—Algeria—History—19th century | Algeria—Social conditions—1830–1962 | France—Colonies—Africa—Administration
Classification: LCC DT287.5.F8 B76 2025 (print) | LCC DT287.5.F8 (ebook) | DDC 929.40965/09034—dc23/eng/20250313

Cover design: Chang Jae Lee
Cover image: Daoudi, "Arbres généalogiques." FR ANOM Aix-en-Provence 9377//14-Touts droits réservés.

GPSR Authorized Representative: Easy Access System Europe, Mustamäe tee 50, 10621 Tallinn, Estonia, gpsr.requests@easproject.com

To my family and the memory of Robert Claude Brower

Contents

Acknowledgments ix
Note on Translation and Transliteration xiii

Introduction 1

1 What Is in a Name? 15

2 "Tell Me Your Name": Precolonial Naming Practices in Northwestern Africa 40

3 "Wherever the Flag Flies": The État Civil in Algeria: Conquest and Sovereignty, 1780s–1830s 66

4 "Am I That Name?": Algerians Make Their Names Known, 1827–1840 96

5 In Others' Names: Making the Algerian Name French, 1850s–1870s 128

6 A Colonial État Civil 160

Conclusion: Remember Their Names 201

Notes 211
Bibliography 285
Index 329

Acknowledgments

My idea for this book originally took shape in a summer split between Salon de Provence, France, and Sidi 'Amar, Algeria. Neither place has the reputation of being a stimulating intellectual haven, although they were for me. They are decidedly off the beaten track of artists, writers, and researchers. Salon attracts a few tourists looking for the medieval prophet of doom Nostradamus, but the town is dominated by its air force base, hospital, and working classes. For its part, Sidi 'Amar is a farming hamlet in the Oued Chelif valley. Denizens of the Algerian capital routinely mock this region for its rustic ways. However, the cities are fed by the families who farm here, many of them working ancestorial lands reclaimed in 1962 when European settlers finally left. Sidi 'Amar has a handsome mosque, well-stocked private library, and clinic, but it is a small, unknown place. Indeed, the first official road sign for the village appeared only in the summer I was there, quite mysteriously to all.

Both places taught me a lot. If this book provides some clarity to the questions it addresses, this will show the truth of a proposition Étienne Balibar once made: It is from the margins that one best understands the center. Ibn Khaldun himself recognized this centuries ago, writing that "nobility originates in the state of being outside . . . in a base, humble station." This observation came to him while writing in the fourteenth century in the Algerian steppes not so far from Sidi 'Amar. I am immensely grateful to Amor Taboubi and Djamila Drihem for the gracious hospitality they extended me in Salon, and to the Khouidmi family in Sidi 'Amar for their generosity and friendship. I felt neither an outsider nor on the margins under their roofs that summer.

This book was long in writing. Friendships dating back decades sustained my work. A very special word of thanks goes to Tracie Matysik, Judy Coffin, Yoav Di-Capula, Sabine Hake, and Joan Neuberger, who made up a Friday writing group at the University of Texas at Austin (UT). They read many iterations of this book, and without their support, it might have never been written. My dear friends Federico Finchelstein and Sofian Merabet also read many parts of the manuscript and provided crucial feedback, criticism, and advice, as did my brother, M. Brady Brower. Julie Hardwick skillfully read several chapters and engaged me in a lively conversation on them. Bertrand Rouziès-Léonardi faithfully guided me through some of the most arcane aspects of the French language, and the Rouziès-Léonardi family have been steadfast friends since childhood. I would also like to thank Arslan Talbi, Fouad Abrouk, Mouloud Haddad, Daouda Gary-Tounkara, Mary Gayne, Jocelyne Dakhlia, Ahmed Oulddali, Dalila Rebhi, Fatiha Sifou, Lahouari Addi, Eliot Tretter, and Moula Bouaziz. Danielle Porter Sanchez, once a gifted student, is now a valued colleague and trusted friend. Enzo Traverso and Magali Molinié have been supportive friends and models of what it means to be an intellectual, based on their brilliance, humility, and kindness. Steve Kaplan, Dominick LaCapra, John Weiss, Eric Tagliacozzo, and David S. Powers have guided me professionally and personally over many decades. Hamou Amirouche stands in my mind as the epitome of human generosity. I treasure his memory. I could not ask for more steadfast friends than Bert and Brenda Gay of Blackfoot, Idaho.

Institutional support and funding came from The University of Texas at Austin, including a vital Provost Author's Fellowship that sustained me during the isolation of writing in the Covid pandemic. I thank my friends and colleagues who were part of my fellowship group that year, Erika Bsumek, Kirsten Cather, and Eric Drott, for their support and feedback. The Institute for Historical Studies (IHS) at UT provided funding and essential course releases, as well as a hospitable forum to workshop my writing. Its directors over the years have been immensely supportive, including Julie Hardwick, Seth Garfield, Miriam Bodian, Jorge Cañizares-Esguerra, and

Mark Ravina. A special thanks to my friend courtney meador who has administered the IHS for more than a decade, in good part making it the brilliant center that it is today. Among the many excellent chairs of the Department of History at UT who have provided support, I am especially grateful to Alan Tully for helping me get this book across the finish line.

I worked out various parts of this book in many talks and conferences. I am happy to thank my hosts, commentators, interlocutors, and friends at these events. They include Osama Abi-Mershed, J. P. Daughton, Priya Satia, Emmanuelle Saada, Mohammed Hachemaoui, Elizabeth Foster, Michael Goebel, Mary Lewis, Todd Shepard, Bob Parks, Laryssa Chomiak, Karim Ouaras, Nelida Fuccaro, Rasmus Christian Elling, Etty Terem, Emma Kuby, Ismael Montana, Durba Ghosh, Sandra McGee Deutsch, Tobias Hof, Margaret Andersen, Adriane Lentz-Smith, Slimane Hachi, Hosni Kitouni, the late Zeineb Benazzouz, the late Abdelmadjid Merdaci, Mériem Merdaci, Fouad Soufi, Ouarda Siari-Tengour, Patricia Lorcin, Daniel Schroeter, Sarah Abrevaya Stein, Susan Slyomovics, Hervé Tchumkam, Jill E. Kelly, Dayna Oscherwitz, Jeffrey J. Byrne, Sung Choi, Hina Azam, Samy Ayoub, Emily Drumsta, Mél Lamotte, Valerie McGuire, Lyazid Benhami, Nils Anderson, Aïssa Kadri, Arezki Ighemat, Ronen Steinberg, and Jennifer Sessions.

Other parts of this book took shape in conversations and correspondence with many brilliant scholars. I would like to thank Noureddine Amara, Joshua Cole, M'hamed Oualdi, Augustin Jomier, Ramdane Touati, Jean-Philippe Bras, Tarik El-Ariss, Mark Metzler, Joan Scott, Joshua Schreier, James McDougall, Fouad Mami, Judith Surkis, Jim House, Jan Jansen, Sumit Guha, Indrani Chatterjee, Tatjana Lichtenstein, Daniel Foliard, Sonia Dayan-Herzbrun, and Lucette Valensi.

The reviewers who evaluated the manuscript for Columbia University Press deserve a special expression of my gratitude. They include Judith Surkis and Owen White, who reviewed the full manuscript, and J. P. Daughton and Will Hanley, who reviewed the proposal and initial chapters. Reviewing a book manuscript requires a tremendous amount of time, a commitment that is barely recognized and hardly renumerated in our field. Saying yes to such a task requires a leap of faith, as well as a deep commitment to the profession. My reviewers provided invaluable critical feedback, strengthening this book. Moreover, when these reports arrived near the end of the pandemic, they felt to me like answers to a message in a bottle sent by a castaway on a deserted island. Senior editor at CUP Caelyn Cobb assembled such skilled readers, and it has been an enormous pleasure to work with her and assistant editor, Emily Simon. I would also like to thank copyeditor Anita O'Brien for her meticulous work preparing the manuscript.

My thinking on colonial violence has developed in dialogue with many cohorts of extremely talented graduate students at UT. They are too numerous to thank by name, but I would like to acknowledge my intellectual debts to Alex Lang, Mónica Jiménez, Charalampos Minasidis, Dillon Savage, Ahmad Agbaria, Abikal Borah, Jocelyn Wright, Isabelle Headrick, Lior Sternfeld, Jimena Perry, Erin Kelleher, Spencer Rapone, Marion Foster, Knowledge Moyo, Jeff Moe, Camille Bossut, Carter Barnett, Denise Gomez, and Itay Eisinger. Estefanía Valenzuela Mochón provided priceless assistance understanding Algerian names handwritten in Arabic script, sharing both her expertise and her good humor. Hashem Alrefai has been a stimulating interlocutor since I first met him shortly after he arrived in the United States as a student charged with an ambitious intellectual agenda. Many groups of UT undergraduates have proved delightful companions to my thought as it is worked out in this book. I particularly valued my time with UT undergrads Lorena Ríos, Anthony Paultanis, Iman Berrahou, Ashleigh Pearce, Adrián Fernández, and Alexis Partyka.

Although I mention them in the fewest words, my greatest thanks go to my family. This includes my mother Franca Brower (née Bradish) and the memory of my much-missed father, Robert Claude Brower, my brother Brady, Amy, Stella, and Henry, my aunts Nancy and Betty Jo, my daughters Claudia, Hanan, and Sana, and my wife Sakina. Through Sakina I am joined to an Algerian family, Saad Drihem and Fatima Larit, Djamila, Nassera, Azzedine, and Nanou. This book is dedicated to all of them.

Note on Translation and Transliteration

Although writing a book on the harm that can be done through names and to them as they cross languages and writing systems, I do not attempt to correct or recover names in this English-language book. This task is best left to others. Names appear as I found them in the sources. When a name is written in Arabic script, I will privilege this version, transliterating it into Latin letters according to the *International Journal of Middle East Studies* guidelines. Although the Arabic language does not have uppercase letters, I have added these to transliterated names and text titles to aid the reader. I have not found any examples of the Tifinagh script in the état civil archive used to write Tamazight- or Berber-language names. In the absence of standardized rules for the transliteration of Tamazight in English, I have used the spellings of these names as they appear in the original sources. Algerian names found only in French letters appear in this book as in the original source unless otherwise noted. In some cases, when a name appears in both French and Arabic in the documents, I alternate between them based on context of iteration and the particular sources being used. Estefanía Valenzuela Mochón helped with transliteration and paleographic analysis of archival sources in Arabic, and Sofian Merabet and Daiyan Zakaria aided in the transliteration of Arabic. Unless otherwise noted, all translations are my own, as are any errors.

The Colonization of Names

Introduction

There's something I find stunning, and it's that nobody—not even after Independence—nobody at all ever tried to find out what the victim's name was, or where he lived, or what family he came from, or whether he had children. Nobody. . . . Who knows Musa's name today?

—Kamel Daoud, *The Meursault Investigation*

Colonialism forces people it dominates to ask the question constantly: "Who am I in reality?"

—Frantz Fanon, *The Wretched of the Earth*

Erasing names: France, 2005

This book about nineteenth-century Algeria can begin with an episode that took place in France in the early 2000s. The idea was to counter racism by taking away a person's name. It took root in the aftermath of the protests that swept across France in 2005, the year of the banlieue uprising when thousands of people took to the streets night after night in October and November. While the riots' causes are still debated, many thought that the problem lay in identity and assimilation. To open society's doors to young French people labeled *issues de l'immigration*, those who might burn cars and otherwise run amok, ways would have to be found to work around the fears or hatreds of employers regarding their religion and race so that they might be brought fully into French society. The riots seemed to say that the ideals of *Bleu-Blanc-Rouge*, the colors of the French flag, could not be found in *Black-Blanc-Beur.* This second triad had been important to events seven years earlier. It referred to the skin colors and ethnicities of the national soccer team that earned France a spectacular victory over Brazil in the World Cup final in 1998 and led the country to an equally spectacular moment of national unity. The Algerian flags that celebrators unfurled along the Champs-Élysées in the spontaneous mass rally that followed the game read not as a provocation but as an affirmation of a France that could live and even thrive together. A name that might have sounded distinctly foreign to "French" ears, "Zinedine Yazid Zidane," became, "Zizou!," a French name chanted by hundreds of thousands, if not millions, across the country that night.

The effervescence of that moment of solidarity soon passed. A few years later, in the notorious France-Algeria exhibition match of 2001, expressions of *Algérianité* (Algerianness), along with whistles sounded out during the playing of the French national anthem, resonated as an affront to the Republic. So, the *black-blanc-beur* would not be so easily accepted as French after all, as the riots two years later would confirm. From the perspective of the arbitrators of Frenchness, these marks of difference had to go or be effaced. This began with the names on job applications. A new *CV anonyme* was proposed. Article 24 of the Law for Equality of Opportunity (31 March 2006) hoped to inaugurate a new era by bringing job candidates into the market without names.[1] This meant redacting first names like Houria, Mokobé, and Najate, along with the superior patronymic, such as Bouteldja, Traoré, and Naït Ali, all names hailing from France's former colonies in North and West Africa. In this way, the racialization of names would no longer hold people back in the job market. The novelist Alexis Jenni dubs this problem the "sound of color" (*couleur sonore*), an expression that deftly captures how personal names can be heard in France's soundscape in distinctly racialized tones.[2] Calling out a person's name, as for a child in the classroom or across the playground, interpellates that person racially, as powerfully as skin color, clothing, or accent. By erasing names, "people hoped that, through silence, violence would go unspoken," Jenni wrote. In doing this, that part of society that Michel Wieviorka long ago called *la France raciste* might accommodate itself to diversity, its racism tricked, as it were, rather than censored or actually sanctioned by the law.[3] It was, of course, only a philosopher's trick reprocessed by those looking for a quick fix. In this respect, effacing names served as yet another way to efface difference, rather than provide a legal right to it.[4]

What is in a name?

The French wrote their names across Algeria after 1830. They rebaptized some towns and many streets to honor French heroes, remaking the country in their image, but they also targeted the personal names of Algerians. They could not understand these names or make them fit into their administrative documents and legal institutions. An Arabo-Islamic name like "Slīmān" was not replaced by a culturally French name like "Simon," but rather by "Slimane," an Arabic name converted to French letters.[5] Colonized Algerians did not need to be assimilated in their names in the sense of joining a community of citizens or a French nation. The doors to this community hardly opened to them at the time, and few chose to enter. Instead, the French state needed a way to identify and interpellate Algerians as distinct individuals, so that they did not remain anonymous or free of control. For example, a woman named "Fāṭima bint Muḥammad ibn 'Ali ibn Khālad Awlād al-'Aīdūnī" was renamed in the 1880s as "Fatma Kroualedi."[6] This woman's original, multipart Arabo-Islamic name referenced her Islamic faith (the Prophet's daughter, Fāṭima), as well as multiple rings of social belonging referenced through her father's name, that of her family's founding ancestor, as well as the name of her tribe. Together these names imbedded her in a highly meaningful web of social, cultural, and historical relations. By contrast, her French name, "Fatma Kroualedi," left only her given name intact, to which was added an invented family name, both written in French letters. It stands as an extremely stark example of onomastic brutalism.

During the nineteenth century, Arabic and Berber names were transcribed and transliterated to French in a rough and often arbitrary fashion, which often made it impossible to convert a name back to its original language. Moreover, the French overlaid existing names with new categories and conferred an entirely new name on them, a French-styled permanent patronymical surname called the *nom* or *nom de famille*. This was done in an effort to make names available to the offices of French governance, as well as the ordinary clerks, mayors, and department heads who ran them. Few of these people understood the local languages or the intricacies of Algerian onomastics, nor, for that matter, as I will show, did many of them seem to care. Among French institutions, that which most needed the name was the *état civil*, a state registry of vital statistics that an 1882 law extended to Muslims.[7] The état civil officialized a person's name at birth and fixed it for life. It also added other data to a person's records, such as age and family relations (mother and father, spouse, children) and biological sex, all of which were recorded at birth. Within this apparatus of modern governance and law, names produced an individual subject in words and paper on which French law might act.[8] As one source framed the name's importance: "For the security of [social] relations and business, [and] on behalf of families, does not society itself have an interest in seeing to it that each one of its members bears a name which belongs to this one person alone?"[9] Represented in the état civil through their name, a subject could be claimed by French sovereignty, and the vital records carefully measured this subject's civil being on which the law could apply or withdraw itself.[10] In the simplest of terms, the name anchors power to people.[11]

In France and for French citizens in Algeria, these officialized names and state records can give a coherent sense of self. The état civil confers a past, a heritage, and a genealogy. For Algerians, however, the age-old question famously posed by Shakespeare, "What is in a name?," asks itself in a distinct form. The most emphatic answer comes from voices in Algeria today, little heard outside of their own country. Contemporary Algerian specialists of names, linguists and geographers for the most part, have framed their work as responding to colonial erasure. Farid Benramdane deployed the term *onomacide* to express the violence of the colonial transformation of names.[12] This neologism combines the Greek word for name, *onoma*, and the Latin suffix *cide*, for killing. In this view, Algerians suffered an attack on their names that went alongside the French-led massacres of people. Cameroonian historian Achille Mbembe offers a useful expansion on the notion of onomastic alienation and erasure, one that gets to the name's central role in legal regimes and private property that are so important to the history of colonial names in Algeria. Mbembe dubs this "disappropriation," writing that this "process refers, on the one hand, to the juridical and economic procedures that lead to material expropriation and dispossession, and, on the other, to a singular experience of subjection characterized by the falsification of oneself by the other."[13] The Algerian writer Kamel Daoud used the colonial erasure of names as the basis for his novel *The Meursault Investigation*, in which he gives a name to the unnamed Arab killed on the beach by Albert Camus's character Meursault in *The Stranger*.[14] Algerian historians have pointed out the painful impact of French-conferred names.[15] Before Daoud, the historian Abdelkader Djeghloul discussed his own family name as case of colonial dispossession like the other forms of oppression that he studied as a scholar. A French administrator imposed this name on his grandfather, who knew himself to be "Benchergui" (bin Sharqī) or "son of the Easterner."[16] Likewise, the specialist of Amazigh culture and the Tamazight (Berber) language, Salem Chaker, notes that his family, the Chaker in Kabylia, knew themselves as "Ijlili(ten)" before this Tamazight name was recorded as "Chaker" in the état civil.[17]

The Algerian government recognized the importance of personal names to decolonization almost immediately after independence in 1962. Reclaiming names represented an act of sovereignty, as important as taking down one flag and putting up another. The Algerian president, Ahmed Ben Bella, signed some of the first decrees in September 1963 changing the names of individual Algerians. The first case was a particular one, concerning three minor children of a French mother, born Jacqueline Netter, who had divorced her French husband (Minne) in 1951 and remarried an Algerian man, Abdelkader Guerroudj. As the legal guardian of her children, she petitioned the government to confer her second husband's patronymic name on her children, as she had adopted it as her own in marriage. Thus, in a decree of 18 September 1963, signed by the president, seventeen-year-old Claude Minne took the name "Tewfik Guerroudj," sixteen-year-old Catherine Minne became "Nassima Guerroudj," and twelve-year-old Gilbert Minne took the name "Djawad Guerroudj."[18] (An older sister, born Danièle Minne, separately changed her name to "Djamila Amrane-Minne," having also married an Algerian.) The reader familiar with the Algerian Revolution will recognize Jaqueline Guerroudj and Abdelkader Guerroudj's names as those of the FLN militants who worked with Fernand Iveton to sabotage an Algiers gasworks in 1956 (an act for which a French court sent Iveton to the guillotine, although there was no loss of life or injury, and the Guerroudj couple to death row). Djamila Amrane-Minne, Jaqueline's daughter, is the name of the young FLN soldier who placed bombs during the Battle of Algiers. She went from a French prison to become the first historian of women in the FLN.[19]

Although the sovereignty of the Algerian state stood secure in 1963, the first Algerian name changes like these proceeded under French-style laws that dated back to the French Revolution (law of 11 Germinal, year XI), laws that subsequent administrative acts and decrees made by the Algerian Republic modified and translated into the institutions of the new state. This was capped by a presidential decree in 1971, which established Algeria's own legal procedures for changing one's name.[20] A steady stream of name changes ensued. In the first fifty years after Algeria's independence in 1962, it is estimated that Algerians made some thirty thousand applications to officially adopt new patronyms, a small but not insignificant number among a total population that numbered about fifteen million in the mid-1970s.[21] Examples published in the government's *Journal officiel* in the 1970s and 1980s include changing the patronymics Khamedj (Khāmaj, Ar.), which means "dirty"; Boukhenouna (Bū Khanūna, Ar.), which can mean "snot-nosed man"; and Boudjeroua (Bū Jarūa, Ar.), which means "man with the puppy," for new names.[22]

Some have argued that the damage done to Algerian names is irreparable. This finds confirmation in Algerians' sense of having been constituted as modern subjects in an estrangement from themselves. With the French having made something of a tabula rasa of names, many Algerians feel their colonial-era names stand as signs of otherness and alienation. *Nomen est omen* (the name is a sign), goes the old Latin saying, and if there is a codetermination of signifier and signified in the personal name, or if name and person exist in a constitutive relationship as many intellectual traditions hold, then semiotic questions become ontological ones. Algerian historian Hosni Kitouni gave a telling account of the problem when he asked:

> How to repair the lost genealogies, the broken filiations, the dislocated fraternity? How to repair the immeasurable humiliations suffered by those who have had to bear names that are abusive, defamatory, coarse, scatological . . .? . . . How can one establish a family's identity on such

> words? This crime—because that is what it truly is—can never be concealed or erased: no legal dispositions, no excuses, no repentance, no amnesty.[23]

Kitouni's pain expressed in this passage is palpable.

Violence and the name

What to call the violence of the name? Violence causes harm and extends power in many different ways. Best known is physical violence, meaning the wounds and deaths inflicted on living bodies. However, violence also exists in symbolic forms, such as language, individual words, and beliefs, all of which can do harm and even kill. The impact of colonial naming is not measured only by a body count. Not a single person was shot by colonial authorities as they went across the country in the 1890s imposing new names on Algerians and recording them in official registers. No one was arrested at this time, although some later were. While most of the violence of this renaming was invisible, it did not go unfelt. In as much as a name decides one's sense of self and place in society, imposing new names distorted and even destroyed Algerian identities and social institutions. Upon this destruction the French state extended its reach, using these new names to interpellate colonized subjects before its laws and commands.

At the time of Algeria's independence, many thinkers understood this sort of violence in terms of its psychological wounds. Listed among the founding principles and objectives of Algeria's first constitution (1963) is "the elimination of every vestige of colonialism," and this encompassed the problem of *dépersonnalisation*.[24] The drafters of the constitution imported this term from psychopathology, where it denotes feelings of disassociation from the self.[25] Combatting Algerians' sense of exile and loss, then, would be a central task of decolonization. Albert Memmi, Mohammed Harbi, and especially Frantz Fanon all wrote about the alienation and despair suffered by colonized people in northern Africa, blending their voices with much of the world attempting to throw off colonial rule in a meaningful and thorough way.[26] In a letter in 1956, Fanon stated that the "Arab, permanently alienated in his own country, lives in a state of absolute depersonalization," and he likened his political efforts to secure Algeria's independence (the letter announced his resignation from a psychiatric clinic to join the FLN) to his work as a psychiatrist to heal and "enable individuals no longer to be foreign to their environment."[27] Repairing this depersonalization, doing the work of restoring Algerians to themselves, meant that decolonization extended to the new country's symbolic system, its languages and its names. Finding the answer of colonized people to their question "Who am I?" necessitated finding themselves a proper name, a sign under which they might constitute an integrated subjectivity.[28]

Should this violence of signs and language then be called "symbolic violence"? This concept is best known through sociologist Pierre Bourdieu, and it enjoys considerable currency, even if it strikes some as an oxymoron.[29] Bourdieu used symbolic violence (and sometimes "symbolic power") to refer to subtle techniques of force and coercion—"gentle and often invisible violence," as he put it using a characteristic combination of counterintuitive words—which sustain social relations of domination.[30] With words functioning like cards in a stacked deck, carefully arranged to one player's advantage, symbolic violence makes social inequalities appear natural and within the legitimate order of things. Bourdieu wrote that this is "the power of constituting the given through utterances, of making people see and believe, of confirming or transforming the vision of the world and, thereby, action on the world and thus the world itself, an almost magical power which enables one to obtain the equivalent of what is obtained through force (whether physical or economic)."[31]

Working from Bourdieu, researchers have used symbolic violence to describe the practices by which the powerful maintain their dominant position by having the social and historical causes of their ascendency misrecognized or concealed. This concept has had uneven reception in different fields, and it has made only limited entry into Middle East studies and colonial historiography in English. Writing about Egypt, Timothy Mitchell defines symbolic violence thinly as a "system of deferential practices, appropriate behaviors, and patterns of modesty" practiced by lower classes towards village notables.[32] Algerian onomastic researchers also use the term but most often leave it undefined. The fact that the main agents of symbolic violence are also its victims makes it a difficult fit in the thinking of some. Bourdieu traced his ideas on symbolic violence as originating in his research in Kabylia and the active role that he saw Kabyle women playing in maintaining patriarchy.[33] He explains this in the following passage:

> Symbolic violence is the coercion which is set up only through the consent that the dominated cannot fail to give to the dominator (and therefore to the domination) when their understanding of the situation and relation can only use instruments of knowledge that they have in common with the dominator, which, being merely the incorporated form of the structure of the relation of domination, make this relation appear as natural.[34]

This further distinguishes symbolic violence, blurring the lines between perpetrators and victims in a way that many find objectionable.

When considering the case of the colonized name in Algeria, however, something about Bourdieu's symbolic violence does not quite work. As Bourdieu stated, for symbolic violence to function, a shared field of norms and cognitive structures must exist between dominated and dominator. While these arguably existed *within* the Kabyle society Bourdieu saw, such shared beliefs can be difficult to establish *between* colonizer and colonized inasmuch as in any colonial society many different systems of values and languages coexist, sometimes containing mutually incommensurable elements. This was not a question Bourdieu himself addressed even though he undertook his research in the midst of the Algerian War and Revolution. Here the formative work of historians of South Asia like Ranajit Guha has shown how during the Raj no single shared idiom united colonizers and colonized. Working through the political philosopher Antonio Gramsci's notion of hegemony, which is close to Bourdieu's symbolic violence, Guha argued that the British failed to universalize their values and had to rely on physical violence and coercion among colonial subalterns (as distinct from elites) rather than consent. This left India's colonial governance as "dominance without hegemony," as he famously put it.[35]

In this book, I put forward language as the most important component of symbolic violence. This frames symbolic violence in the sense that psychoanalysis gives the "symbolic," namely, that space where subjectivity is constituted in language.[36] Jacques Lacan called this *parlêtre*, a French neologism that stresses how one's sense of being or subjectivity emerges through the word and the intersubjective speech act. A psychoanalytically informed understanding of symbolic violence is especially useful to understand colonialism and a historical context where one did not "speak one's self" easily, even if one succeeded at times, but where it was more typical in official situations to be "spoken by an other," specifically in an other's name. Benramdane argues as much when he writes that the colonial experience of naming is one of "*j'ai été dit*" (I have been said), i.e., interpellated in an other's name and its attendant violence.[37] I believe that this adds a new dimension to Bourdieu and the related Gramscian notions of hegemony, one that gives symbolic violence greater analytical traction in the historical sources in colonized places such as Algeria.[38]

Whereas many historians will point to the loss of life and land to explain the crisis experienced by Algerian society in the colonial era, postcolonial onomatologists seek answers in the loss of names. As Brahim Atoui writes, "In the loss of its name [the tribe] loses its identity, its solidarity, because individuals no longer recognize themselves together in the same eponymous ancestor and no longer feel themselves united."[39] *The Colonization of Names* takes as its point of departure decades of research undertaken by scholars in Algeria, much of which has not been recognized by those writing about Algeria from North America and Europe. I acknowledge my debt to these Algerian researchers here. Specialists like Farid Benramdane, Brahim Atoui, Ouerdia Yermeche, and Foudil Cheriguen, among many others, have undertaken a painstaking project to inventory names, trace their changes over time, and standardize their modern form. This is a substantial project in Algeria, where a single town might have several different names or spellings of names, or even no officially recognized name at all, as was still the case only a few years ago for some small villages, almost fifty years after independence.[40]

Algerian researchers have also tried to give a more rigorous and systematic form to Algeria's onomastic decolonization, using linguistics to weigh in authoritatively on the sort of authentic names that might replace those conferred by the French. This is difficult work, to say the least, with many moving pieces, politics, word morphology, as well as the political project of the state and popular usage, which often clashed. In the research of Mohand-Akli Haddadou, this entails not only undoing the effects of French colonization but also pushing back against an Arabo-centric epistemology by uncovering an original Berber etymology for countless toponyms.[41]

The Colonization of Names contributes to this project by using history and the colonial archive. The French state attempted to assert a symbolic monopoly over the Algerian name. I examine how this seizure of power worked, reconstructing the project of name reform as well as how officials executed their work on the ground. I simultaneously weigh the impact of these policies on Algerians, several of whom appear as compelling characters in this book. The story of the colonization of Algerian names is not a straightforward one in which a powerful colonizer exerts its will on a less powerful colonized. This history is not as simple as retelling Thucydides's Melian Dialogue, wherein France plays the role of the powerful Athenians able to "do what they have the power to do," and the Algerians are cast as the weak Melians forced to "accept what they have to accept."[42] Nor for that matter is it one of noble resistance, sly civility, or the weapons of the weak. Rather the historical sources show a process occurring in language in which cultures, societies, and people became mutually imbricated—as is typical in history—but one that stands as distinct for its violence.

Outline of chapters

The six chapters in this book unfold chronologically and thematically. They alternate between, on the one hand, understanding personal names in themselves and, on the other, examining the institutions that harnessed names to do political and legal work. The most important of these institutions was the état civil, a system of vital records that produced an official identity and calculated an individual's characteristics before the law.

The first chapter serves as a thematic and theoretical introduction to the book, sketching how names and power intersect. It begins with an invitation to the reader to reexamine their understanding of the name, which is frequently approached as a sign through which one gets to something else, as in an index or database. I point instead to the constitutive power of names. The chapter finishes by working through these questions in the sources, resolving a long-standing point of confusion in the historiography: What is the proper name of France's territories in Algeria? I use a close reading of the official and quasi-official texts to show some surprising twists in what the French state called Algeria in the 1830s, denominations that historians have frequently mistaken for names. This section highlights the stakes when the name is withheld or erased.

Chapter 2 reconstructs the Algerian personal name before its conversion to French norms. Names have served as a primary sign of identity, delineating boundaries between communities while binding these groups to a larger society. I explain how the personal name functioned, focusing on practices that might seem counterintuitive to readers today. Rather than a sovereign, centered sign of the self, a person's name belonged to others—family members, neighbors, even people in the street—meaning that the name intersected many different social contexts. My sources in the chapter include nineteenth-century Arabic-language publications edited by French Arabists (grammar books, dictionaries, translation guidebooks, and bilingual manuals), which I examine alongside the findings of modern specialists—historians and linguists—as well as the research of well-informed amateurs who documented naming practices in their own communities. The chapter gives the reader an introduction to the classical Arabo-Islamic name, which served as a normative model for the region, and traces different iterations of personal names used by local Arabs, Berbers, and Jews. The chapter seeks to establish a rough baseline for precolonial names, before their transformation under the French.

The third chapter examines how the modern French system of vital statistics, the état civil, promulgated in Revolutionary-era France in 1792, worked beyond French borders in pre- and early colonial Algeria. It starts with the first extant French vital records in Algeria from the 1780s, in order to show how the registries became harnessed to the conquest of the 1830s, a time when sovereignty in Algeria remained undecided. French officials extended their government's claims on certain classes of people in Algeria and excluded others, using the registers as a gatekeeping device. In this way, the état civil attacked the remnants of Ottoman sovereignty and shored up that of France. The exercise followed a controversial path first laid by Napoleon Bonaparte, who claimed that recording the vital acts of French soldiers in occupied foreign lands, or "wherever the [French] flag flies," was a sovereign prerogative of his conquering army. After working through the legal debates around this stance, the chapter takes the reader into the first état civil registries in two different Algerian cities occupied by French troops to show how this worked in practice.

In chapter 4 I double down on the understudied 1830s to consider the circulation of Algerian names in the first decade of colonial rule. In this chapter I focus on a particular iteration of the name, the signature. These put people into texts as distinct individuals, binding identity and agency. I examine Algerian signatures as they appeared in Arabic-language petitions addressed to French authorities. The chapter turns to focus on one individual who succeeded in making his name known, Aḥmad bin Ismāʿīl Abū Ḍarba (d. 1865), or, in French, Ahmed Bouderba. Using his case, I work though questions of identity, agency, and language, centering my attention on a unique doubled French and Arabic signature that he used at different moments in his life. I approach this doubled name from literary and feminist theory, including the seminal question posed by Denise Riley, "Am I that name?," with which she interrogated the category "woman." I restage Riley's question with regard to Abū Ḍarba's signature and then pull a fine-toothed comb through the archive to locate his answer to the cultural and political questions posed in the dangerous first decade of the colonization of his country.

Chapter 5 moves forward to the mid-nineteenth century, when French Arabists first systematized the conversion of Algerian names into French. Like the previous chapter, this one is devoted to personal names in their own right. It briefly tells the history of the modern French name, which emerged from the Revolution narrowed to two parts, a given *prénom* and a second patronym or *nom*. Lawmakers at the end of the eighteenth century also established rules for the choice of names, which had to be culturally French. While Algerians did not have to take these French names, they had to have names that were *technically* French. This meant the truncation of existing names to conform to the two-part French model and the Romanization of their letters. This produced demonstrable ruptures in Arabic and Berber names. Pejorative names also appeared at this time. I investigate their origins in a special type of surname that property owners were required to take in the 1870s. These used the names of farmlands for people, a tactic that reformers thought would best distinguish Algerian landowners from one another in property titles. Many culturally abject words were used to name farms in Algeria, which were offensive when used for people. Although officials were barred from using obviously offensive words, the archives suggest that some French registrars maliciously shifted between languages to turn Algerian names into a vicious inside joke. I conclude that the extremely crude system that French administrators forged at this time to convert Algerian names to French letters meant, in fact, that the joke was on them.

The book's final chapter follows the registration of Algerian Muslims in the état civil as it occurred from 1882 to about 1914. French registrars recorded millions of people at this time within a secular civil registry system originally established for citizens during the French Revolution. In an initial moment, registration of Algerian Muslim in the état civil, with names appearing in the records alongside those of white citizens, risked compromising the system of legal exclusion by which colonized Algerians had been made French but were excluded from the rights of citizens, a problem I explore at length. The chapter then turns to the impact of the état civil on social institutions like the family. French officials employed names to break up extended families by barring them from using a common patronym, which would have symbolically connected extended kinship groups in an emerging field dominated by French norms. Moreover, the patronym determined a family's relationships to property in French law. French officials presented this policy to Algerians as a beneficial device so that their families would not become confused, with the separate patronyms precisely mapping family relationships. Those who designed the rules, however, clearly understood that in cutting entire branches from the family tree into different names, they compromised the power and security that came with a robust array of social relations. Some families availed themselves of an option to combine branches of their family in a shared patronym, while others used the French civil records to deliberately cut out unwanted members of their families in the interests of inheritance. Records in one Algerian village suggest a systematic effort on the part of local families to exclude adult women from the new French records as part of ongoing strategies to disinherit them and maintain property among male members. Finally, I examine cases in which Algerians took a great deal of care to ensure that the names they received in the état civil suited them. Algerians did not go into the état civil in silence: Many of them went to extensive lengths to ensure that their French-conferred names corresponded to their own sense of identity, history, and family, even if these new names appeared in foreign, French letters that many of them were never able to read.

1

What Is in a Name?

And when a name comes, it immediately says more than the name.

—Jacques Derrida, *On the Name*

Fellag is not a stage name. It means bandit or highwayman. The French gave names in the civil registry as they pleased according to the character or the reputation of the person who came to register a birth . . . over time, my name merged with my role in life.

—Mohand Saïd Fellag, *Djurdjurassique Bled*

"Name's Stamp, Stamp Paid." So one of the characters in Toni Morrison's novel *Beloved* introduces himself.[1] A formerly enslaved man living in Ohio, Stamp Paid helps those seeking freedom through the Underground Railway. Like many of the names Morrison uses, this one is deeply significant. As she lets the reader know in later pages, Stamp Paid's name does not refer to the bill of sale he received after buying his own freedom. Rather, it marks the price he paid in the humiliation suffered when the master's son raped his wife. "Whatever his obligations were, that act paid them off," Morrison writes. Escaping to the North, Stamp Paid helped other people to freedom, their debts to the world, like his own, fully paid in the misery endured in their previous enslaved lives.[2] Novelists devote much attention to names, building out the name's semantic density as a way to develop their characters.[3] "If God the Father had created things by naming them," as Marcel Proust famously wrote, "it was by taking away their names or giving them other names that Elstir [i.e., the writer] created them anew."[4] Just as they give life to characters in a novel, so too names can inflict death, even in real life. Sociologist Orlando Patterson highlighted this in his classic study, *Slavery and Social Death*. Among the rituals of enslavement he discussed was conferring a new name, one that cut a person off from their past life. "The slave's former name died with his former self," Patterson writes.[5] Historian Martin Klein confirms this practice in his research on slavery in western Africa (Senegal and Gambia), where he writes that the "Wolof have a saying that a slave has no name."[6] Conversely, when emancipated, former slaves in Africa embraced new names symbolizing their freedom.[7] In all these cases, the name is understood as a special sort of word, one that contains symbolic power that reflects or produces the person, rather than a sign that simply denotes them. If one knows the name, one knows the person, with the name and the person in a mutually determinative relationship.

Names and the practice of history

Like novelists, philosophers and linguists have long labored on the name, and this part of speech also caught the attention of literary theorists for a moment in the second half of the twentieth century. By contrast, few historians seem interested in names. Only a small group tackled the personal name head-on in a subfield that reached its peak decades ago.[8] Of course, historians do not use names like a novelist does, but at the outset of this book it is worth considering the name's importance to our work. At the most basic level, proper nouns of all sorts are necessary to find structure in a text, and the personal name serves as an especially important starting point for archival research. Some of these names have achieved relative fame in the historiography, especially among microhistorians and those researching otherwise obscure individuals. "Menocchio" is one example well known to my generation.[9] Carlo Ginzburg wrote at the beginning of *The Cheese and the Worms*, "what I knew about him was only his name: Domenico Scandella, called Menocchio."[10] Armed with this name, Ginzburg navigated the labyrinthine archives of the Inquisition and reanimated a forgotten episode of popular religious thought. Personal names also figure centrally within the biographies of historically marginal individuals. Less famous than the Italian miller, but well known to historians of northwestern Africa, is Mardochée Naggiar, a Tunisian linguist and merchant who first appeared to history as a name, Mordecai Naggiar, in the 1826 journal of a Protestant missionary read by Lucette Valensi. Like Ginzburg, she used this name as a sort of North Star to navigate an otherwise lost world inhabited by a man who wrote little about himself and left only scattered traces in the archives. "To name is to extract from the anonymous mass, to call out that man *there*, pointing him out, forcing us to notice him and interrogate him," Valensi writes.[11] Or there is Jean-Baptiste Capeletti. Fanny Colonna used this name as a sort of spade to dig this man and his Algerian (Shāwī) wife out of the cave in eastern Algeria in which they lived for a time in the early twentieth century. In a society marked by the colonial-colonized divide, Baptiste, as he was known, was accepted by the local Shāwī, who did not forbid his marriage with one of their own even though he had not converted to Islam. Indeed, according to Colonna, they even gave him an uplifting sobriquet, the "Lion of the Aurès," which he proudly used, even if this origin story strikes me as containing a distinctly apocryphal note.[12] Another example of an unknown historical individual made known through the name is Louis-François Pinagot, a French clog maker whose name was chosen at random by Alain Corbin, who used it, what he called a "social atom," to work through the archive in an effort to "reverse the work of the bulldozers" of the passing of time.[13]

Although we are told that these people led "anonymous" lives (Corbin titled his book *The Life of an Unknown*), the research that immortalized them would not have been possible without the name.[14] The name makes human existence *proper*, and its ability to mark the separate and the particular lets the historian identity individuals among the millions of words found in their sources. Without the distinction offered by the name, the archive remains a vague and undifferentiated body of paper and words, leaving the historian with few means to attribute authorship, identity, and agency. By contrast, once one has a name in hand, police reports, court records, nominative censuses, passenger lists, travelers' accounts, land titles, and signatures become historically meaningful. In their names, "unknown" people become known. In this sense, an archive without personal names might be thought of like Ferdinand de Saussure's "swirling cloud" of thought before the introduction of linguistic structure: "Without the support of signs we would be incapable of distinguishing ideas in a clear and constant fashion."[15]

Thus, personal names go a long way toward dissipating the confusion that would otherwise envelope the archive. That the name serves this purpose is generally taken for granted by historians in their day-to-day work. We look for names in inventories and indexes, library catalogs and documents, even electronically, carefully placing them in quotation marks so that internet search engines can exactly sift through the memory banks of the World Wide Web to identify a single person out of millions (or, in many cases, churn out an overwhelming number of homonyms). We do this without much reflection on the origins of the name or how it has changed over time. In short, historians tend to take these signs for granted, giving them no more thought than admonishments to our students and colleagues to get the spellings of the names of historical figures "right." Even this presupposes that names exist in a fixed form like words in a dictionary, or in fact that we accept how they are given in dictionaries of national biography and official records as unproblematic and final. Although they might conveniently fix names, these types of authoritative sources do not yield an innocent or neutral name but are themselves hegemonic and interested texts.[16] Tools for historians, names are themselves the product of history.

So, I call on readers to ask the age-old question anew: What is in a name? This chapter will give some answers, or frame some questions, that will set up the chapters that follow.

Sovereign names

The main concern of this book is understanding the name's relationship to power. Many points of entry to this question exist. The insights of feminist theory, deconstruction, psychoanalysis, and postcolonial studies most closely inform my reading of the sources. At this point, however, I would like to introduce the question with some larger reflections of the relationship of words to power. The creation narratives of the three monotheistic traditions give an idea of this relationship. Judaism, Christianity, and Islam all highlight Adam's knowing the names of earthly things and tie this knowing of names to Adam's power in the world. Reading the biblical tradition, the German philosopher Walter Benjamin put it this way: Adam "is lord of nature and can give names to things."[17] Expressed differently, the names used by Adam were the extension of God's word, and they were how beings could be both known and ruled by Adam, the first "lord of nature."[18] Benjamin presented this reading in an essay from 1916, "On Language as Such and on the Language of Man," the text that started his theoretical work on language.[19] He developed his belief that language was not a tool subordinate to thought, but a medium of creation. "*En archēi ēn ho logos*" (in the beginning was the word), Benjamin would later write, citing the biblical line in Greek.[20] As many commentators have noted, his arguments hinged on the individual elements of language: It was the word rather than the sentence that fascinated Benjamin.

Among all the words and the different parts of speech, the name had a special place for Benjamin as it represented the starting point for signification. "The name is that *through* which, and *in* which, language itself communicates itself absolutely."[21] Thus in the names bestowed at the beginning of time, Benjamin saw a link between God's creative word and undifferentiated, nameless things and beings of the world. The name brought them into a universe of language, distinct and identifiable, and thus within the realm of human knowledge.[22] The name is both ontological and cognitive.[23] It might be said, therefore, that Adam *names* these things into existence out of the primordial soup of sameness. Even if Adam's naming did not have the same creative and absolute powers as the word of God, the names he conferred bound these things and beings to him, making them knowable and governable.[24] Or as Benjamin wrote, the "proper name is the communion of man with the *creative* word of God."[25] Further clarifying Benjamin's argument, the philosopher Max Pensky offers that "Adamic naming constitutes the translation of spiritual essences of divine nature (that is, the language of things) into the ordered realm of names, and in this sense constitutes the idea of knowledge, establishing Adam as the first and true philosopher."[26]

Benjamin's essay belonged to a growing appreciation of the relationship between language and power as constitutive of social being. This relationship was all too evident in the midst of the First World War when belligerent states used their domination of language to define self and other and transform a vast field of overlapping identities into bifurcated categories, friends and enemies. As subsequent chapters will show, the same power of official language was present in colonial practices that presumed an exclusive right to establish social relations through names. In the end, Benjamin's reflections were not abstract. Like Adam, language itself fell, and its fall told the story of modernity for Benjamin, a German Jew who witnessed fascists' manipulation of language that proved fatal for millions, including himself.[27] Or, as Benjamin's colleague Max Horkheimer put it, at the root of fascism was "something rotten in language itself."[28]

References to religious texts abound in Benjamin, but he apparently did not read the Qur'an, even though a German translation had recently appeared in the "Universal-Bibliothek."[29] The canon of European philosophical concerns did not include Islam and Muslim thinkers at the time. European philosophers sufficed themselves with what Jacques Lacan later embraced uncritically as the "the Judeo-Christian tradition."[30] But if, following the inspiration of scholars like the Algerian philosopher Mohammed Arkoun, we include the Qur'an in the library of theory, we can see that it nicely completes Benjamin's line of thought. The Qur'an's creation story appears in the second sura, al-Baqara (The Cow), and it differs significantly from the version of Genesis known to Benjamin. Whereas in the biblical tradition Adam himself has the power to name (albeit using language given by God), in the Qur'an the names originated with God, who taught them to Adam, "all of them."[31] Adam duly learns these names, grasping the connection between word and being. The relevant passage tells the moment when God reveals to the skeptical angels that he has chosen Adam, a human, to rule them. Adam's power over them derives not from physical force, but through his mastery of names. To make his point to the angels, God set up a contest asking Adam and the angels who can give the proper name for all creations.

> He taught Adam all the names [of things].
> Then He put them [these things] before the angels, and said,
> "Tell me the names of these if you are truthful."
> They said, "Glory to You.
> The only knowledge we have is what You have taught us.

You are the Knowing and the Wise."
He said, "Adam! Tell them their names."
And when he had told them their names, He said [to the angels],
"Did I not tell you that I know what is Invisible in the heavens and the
earth
and that I know what you disclose and what you have been hiding?"
And [recall] when We said to the angels,
"Prostrate yourselves to Adam";
and they [all] prostrated themselves.[32]

In the many centuries since this sura was first revealed, commentators have given various interpretations on the range of the Qur'an's naming project, debating if naming included abstractions such as languages and ideas.[33] (One name was not given to Adam: a single proper name of God, which was concealed behind the "veiling name" (*hijāb al-ism*) and the ninety-nine "most beautiful names" (*al-asmā' al-ḥusnā*) that the faithful can repeat in prayer.[34]) Without going too deeply into this literature, one can see that the Qur'an communicates in a higher degree the political process of naming that Benjamin saw in the Bible: Whereas Genesis asserts that "he is lord of nature and can give names to things," the Qur'an says that *he can give names to things and thereby is lord of nature*. This expresses a causal relationship linking the name and power, rather than an associative one.[35] In the Qur'an the name comes first, before power. The power of names allows Adam to rise above the angels, who, ignorant of names (including their own), must bend down in submission.[36] Reading this story through the lessons of the ninth-century mystic Manṣūr al-Ḥallāj, Louis Massignon explains: "The proper names designate to man the creatures whom he can command, as long as he has been granted use of them. They present the creatures to him as different from himself, separate from God, and distinguished one from another; in short, as individual, interdependent existences."[37] The Quranic name thus offers two sorts of knowledge applicable across many contexts. On the one hand, it differentiates, delimits, and distinguishes in a system of differences, and, on the other, the name associates, links, and constitutes relations, making social beings and lending them a coherent form.

In this sense, the Qur'an expresses how the name offers understanding in order to act, yielding a world governed by symbolic structures.[38] These lessons are shared in contemporary scholarship. French sociologist Pierre Bourdieu brought attention to these qualities of the name, writing: "By structuring the perception which social agents have of the social world, the act of naming helps to establish the structure of this world."[39] In other words, the name establishes the subject's existence and positions this subject within a larger symbolic order. According to Bourdieu, this positioning "create[s] the world" or at least "helps to construct the reality of the world" in the sense that it both limits and enables political strategies and social relations.[40] This power can be monopolized. Those who know the names possess the name's power, and they can act like Adam. Thus, through names God endowed Adam with sovereign worldly power, making him the first of God's earthly *Khulafā'* (deputies).[41]

Like Adam, a modern state needs names: a name for itself, a name for its territory, and name(s) for its people. A coherent sense of self, beginnings and ends, comes from these names. The name of a state's place (toponym) and the name of its people (ethnonym) mark boundaries and borders, and with them comes the all-important delimitation of sovereignty. Names also serve to instantiate laws, which are enacted "in the name of" some sovereign entity, such as God, a monarch, or the People. The name is thus a fundamental element of state building, as important as the police, the courts, and the army. These classic agents of the monopoly of *physical* violence by which European states constituted themselves, however, had lesser-known accomplices responsible for the state's monopoly of *symbolic* violence. They include the arbitrators of language, ranging from the "great" grammarians in the academies to lowly teachers, secretaries, surveyors, and copyeditors.[42] Coining and controlling its names, the state exercises its monopoly of symbolic violence.[43] Moreover, a name makes what is a politically and socially fragmented body, like a nation, appear whole, complete, and seamless.[44] If a state (or a movement hoping to found or control a state) lacks these names, or if they are not recognized by others, its power will not resonate. In German, this would be a case of *namenlos* (adj.), literally "nameless" or outside of discourse.[45]

A candidate to the order of modern states must make a name for itself. It needs to know the names of other states and make known its name to its peers. For this name to carry full power, the state's name typically must be its *own*, an "endonym," and not one coined by others from the outside, an "exonym." For example, on 25 September 1962, independent Algeria's first constituent assembly officially named the new state. What had been known in the first months of its existence as the generic État Algérien (Algerian State) became the République Algérienne Démocratique et Populaire (Democratic and Popular Algerian Republic).[46] Later, the country's first constitution in 1963 gave this name officially in Arabic, al-Jumhūriyya al-Jazā'iriyya al-Dīmuqrāṭiyya al-Sh'abiyya, and it made Arabic the state's formal language.[47] Could this Arabic name be translated into other languages or writing systems? Would it become a dreaded exonym?

Because proper nouns are understood as a special class of words that have a single referent, some argue that a name cannot be translated.[48] While a common English noun like "dawn" is easily enough translated as *aube* in French, one would not normally translate the personal name Dawn. Dawn is Dawn and not Aube, regardless of the language. Likewise, one would not translate the French name Pierre into Peter, and certainly not translate it literally as "Rock," based on the meaning of the common French noun *pierre*. But other cases are not so clear-cut. Is the French name Londres adequate to the English London, or does the old English spelling of Peking properly render Beijing?[49] Jacques Derrida sums up this thinking when he writes: A "pure signifier to a single being," a name like " 'Peter' . . . is not a translation of Pierre, any more than 'Londres' is a translation of London."[50] Derrida makes this point, one that is best known through the work of the linguist Georges Kleiber, by way of developing a different argument about the mutual imbrication of languages and the (im)possibility of translation.[51]

Derrida's argument about the translation of names could have been illustrated more easily had he taken the example of the name of the country of his birth, Algeria. Its name has appeared in many different languages, belying the notion that names are untranslatable. What remains important to modern understandings of sovereignty, however, is that the translation of a name must come from within. As it entered into world affairs, Algeria gave its name in many different languages, including Chinese, English, Russian, and Spanish, along with Arabic and French.[52] The importance of endonyms to sovereignty has been taken seriously enough that the United Nations convenes a special committee, the Group of Experts on Geographical Names (UNGEGN), which over the last sixty years has labored to produce a standardized toponymy for the world that privileges endonyms written in Roman script.[53] By their view, "the unauthorized changing of geographical names that have already been established by a legally constituted entity and are nationally recognized" might "lead to the loss of cultural and historical heritage."[54] Exonyms also put at risk a state's legitimacy, as well as the stability of the international state system, which depends on proper, self-same names. This accounts for the stress UNGEGN places on names that come from the official national representatives of a given country, who have the right to name their country.[55] By extension of this logic, it can be expected that failing to fix a country's name from within opens it to potential acts of expropriation, as well as contributing to general symbolic confusion resulting in lawlessness. In this understanding, inasmuch as a state's sovereignty depends on maintaining a monopoly of physical violence within its borders, so too a state's symbolic monopoly must not be encroached on by "exonyms," names coming from the outside.

To colonize, to name

If the name serves to legitimate sovereignty and instantiate a legal order, what happens when things are left unnamed? If names typically establish truth, what happens when they deceive? It is in the nature of colonialism to rely on exonyms, importing and imposing names. This problem is perhaps best grasped in toponyms, the names of settlements, countries, and geographic features. Although this book is focused on personal names, examining colonial toponyms helps unpack the name's power. Here the schemes of colonization should emerge in a clear form with the colonizer conferring a new set of names to mark their power. In the case of France in Algeria, however, the record does not reveal wholesale renaming. One might expect that having arrived in Algeria, France would have created a sort of "New France" by conferring a series of French-language toponyms symbolically remaking the colony in its own image.[56] In this scenario, names would act like so many flags planted across the landscape by victorious soldiers. While French imperialism certainly used names strategically across northwestern Africa, it did not erase existing toponyms wholesale.[57] The major Algerian cities continued to be known by their precolonial French renderings derived from Arabic like "Constantine" for Qusanṭīna, "Oran" for Wahrān, "Bône" for Būna, "Médéah" for al-Madiyya, "Tlemcen" for Tilimsān, and so on. Each one of these names, which had entered into French usage well before the conquest, was less a threatening exonym than part of a long-standing practice of converting Arabic names to make them usable in the French language. Indeed, when the military began the project of mapping Algeria, they paid special care to preserve existing toponyms. In 1831 the minister of war gave detailed instruction on the matter. After requesting that the names of every important feature be included on the military's maps ("every village, farmhouse, café, shrine, [and] tomb"), he asked "to have these names in Arabic in order to place them on the map."[58]

These efforts to preserve existing toponyms shaped French practices throughout the decade and beyond.[59] In the case of an 1836 map, cartographers went so far as to include the original names in Arabic script alongside their rendering in French letters.[60] Abel Malo, of the Malo brothers workshop in Paris, produced the engraved letters for the map, and presumably he inserted the Arabic script so that cartographers could check later transliterations against the original. The orthography of Algerian place names in French letters was still in flux, and French Arabists themselves had not settled on a system of transliteration. Likewise, Algeria's mountains, deserts, springs, and rivers continued to be known by their existing Arabic or Berber names (often derived from Punic, Greek, or Latin words). Historian Hélène Blais argues that the preservation of existing names expressed the experiences of French cartographers in Algeria, where "a foreign language came to join itself, almost naturally, to a 'bizarre country,'" so that seemingly exotic names captured the French feelings toward northwestern Africa.[61] Perhaps as important as this logic of othering, however, was the fact that using existing names helped French writers fix toponyms in a single form. This avoided the problems caused when Arabic words were converted to French letters or other European alphabets unsystematically. The most common method of converting Arabic to French was to write out words as they sounded to a French ear, seeking phonetic equivalents. But this frequently led to multiple spellings for the same name. Napoleon's expedition to Egypt in 1798 had already confronted this problem, and eighteenth-century orientalist the Comte de Volney pointed it out when he lamented how European travelers mangled the spellings of toponyms in Syria and Egypt. "By conveying the words of one language in the characters of another, they have so disfigured them as to render them difficult to be known."[62] Thus, in the interest of standardization, prevailing names were privileged.

On the other hand, where new French settlements appeared, or when large influxes of Europeans settled in existing Algerian towns, they received French names. These celebrated officers who had led the battles against Algerians—Bugeaud, Mac-Mahon, Saint-Arnaud, Randon, Clauzel, and Canrobert. In other towns, names referenced events from France's European history, such as the town of Valmy, found in the department of Oran, which received its name referencing the famous Revolutionary victory; or Palestro, named after the battle that led to Austria's defeat by Franco-Italian armies in 1859. In addition, names for new settlements came from generals of the Revolution and Napoleonic era (Carnot, Kléber), writers and artists (Condorcet, Littré, Rabelais, Tocqueville, Horace-Vernet), politicians (Carnot, Colbert, Félix Faure), and canonized French kings (Saint-Louis). In a few cases, names yielded rare mixed Algerian-French names like Saint-Cyprien-des-Attafs, an appropriate hybrid name for a town that was home to a small community of Muslim converts to Catholicism.[63]

And yet these names did not always emerge out of a straightforward name-as-flag effort to impose French sovereignty. Narrower Franco-French political interests and ordinary bootlicking influenced some choices. These included names that high-level officers selected to ingratiate themselves with their superiors. Notably King Louis-Philippe d'Orléans (r. 1830–1848) exploited the Algerian conquest initiated by his Bourbon predecessor to garner public support for his crown.[64] Thus, when Governor General Valée sought to name a coastal settlement in 1838, he proposed "Philippeville" (today's Skikda) after the reigning monarch. "The town that I propose to your Excellence to give the name of Philippeville, will extend upon the green mountains, the peaks of which are occupied by our works (*ouvrages*)."[65] This gesture pleased the king, who returned the favor by instructing Valée to name one of the city's forts after himself.[66] The same thing occurred in the case of El-Esnam (today's Chlef), transformed into a French town under the name "Orléansville." In announcing his plans for El-Esnam in the spring of 1843, Valée's successor, Governor General Bugeaud wrote to the Ministry of War with plans to rename the town Orléans-ville to honor the royal family.[67] Nothing much came of this first effort, however, and Bugeaud continued to use the existing name (El-Esnam) in his subsequent correspondence. This changed a few weeks later when the king's son, Henri d'Orléans, an officer in the French army, won a major victory over the formidable 'Abd al-Qadir (a battle known in French as the *prise de la Smala*, 16 May 1843). Bugeaud seized the moment to propose again the king's family name for the town, implying that his troops had spontaneously coined it in their celebrations. "This news made my little camp burst into rapturous joy."[68] When Bugeaud arrived in the town two days later, he replaced "El-Esnam" with "Orléans-ville" in his letter's dateline and used the new name systematically from that point forward (with the hyphen later dropping off).[69] So in these cases, officers' ambitions to advance their careers played an important role in colonial toponyms, giving a more muddled picture of the relationship between naming, power, and sovereignty.

The most aggressive effort to symbolically remake Algeria's toponyms can be found within Algerian cities and the names given to streets and squares, what historian Jan Jansen has called a "conquest by names."[70] Only two years into the occupation of Algiers, the French recognized only twelve remaining Ottoman-era street names among the more than two hundred named streets originally recorded in the 1830s.[71] By the first part of the twentieth century, the names of the military heroes that had predominated in cities gave way to locally important civilian figures such as politicians and explorers, and they joined the standard repertoire of street names found in metropolitan France, such as Victor Hugo, Austerlitz, Gambetta, and, after World War I, 11 novembre.[72] Together these French names virtually obliterated the formal and informal street names derived from Arabic, Turkish, or Tamazight that typified Ottoman Algeria.[73] This was a timid project inasmuch as street names did not carry the same political weight as city names. As is often commented on, however, the French street names were some of the most enduring onomastic legacies of the colonial era, with Algerians continuing to use them into the twenty-first century, although with much different meanings.[74]

A colony without a name, Algeria 1830–1845

When did the French government name "its" Algeria? The French name "Algérie" took shape in a convoluted process that merits telling in detail, especially inasmuch as it remains the object of substantial misinformation. The date when this word was officially used as a name for French territories in the former Ottoman province has long captured the attention of amateur and professional historians alike. Today, uncovering the first colonial usage of Algérie is a favorite pursuit of Europeans who formerly lived in Algeria and left at the time of the country's independence. These people, who self-identify as Pied Noirs, debate the question in social media and print magazines aimed at their community.[75] The tone of much of this writing is openly revanchist, with discussions of proper nouns serving to contest the legitimacy of the independent Algerian republic. But the stakes of these discourses go beyond idle chat of disgruntled white settlers. They claim that the Algerian state is, in fact, a French creation, as is Algeria as a country. The argument is an old one. It appeared most infamously in President Charles De Gaulle's speech in 1959 on auto-determination, when he attacked the very existence of an Algerian nation. Speaking on television, he said that "since the beginning of the world there has never been any true Algerian unity, far less any Algerian sovereignty."[76] He built on previous discourses that reached their high point in 1930, the centenary of French Algeria. In celebrating one hundred years of France's achievements in Algeria, writers put forth an unrelenting claim to French sovereignty using a highly instrumentalized reading of the name Algeria. Thus, at about this time a historian of ancient North Africa, Stéphane Gsell, wrote: "Algeria! A name that we created and that only became official in 1838. It is a piece of land arbitrarily cut out of North Africa during the Turkish period, and which then took on its approximate present-day limits. In sum, [precolonial] Algeria had a contrived unity which France has made, as much as she could, a real unity."[77] By this logic, if the name Algeria meant nothing before the colonial era, as Gsell claimed, then France's sovereignty here rested not only on the act of military conquest but on *onoma nullius*, the names equivalent to the empty lands (*terra nullius*) claims made by European empires the world over.[78]

When procolonial writers claim that France coined the name Algérie, they imply that France fashioned this country ex nihilo. Recycled today, this colonial-era claim serves a double function. First, it discredits Algerian nationalists who understood their mission as the *restoration* of an Algerian state and sovereignty usurped by France. By the revanchist reading of the name, there was nothing to "restore" in Algeria after the country's independence in 1962, except the sovereignty of Algeria's "true" founder, France. If France named or "invented" Algeria, then the country, along with its name, somehow belonged to it, like a French trademark or copyright. This camp will accuse historians who use "Algeria" (or "Algerians") before the beginning of the French era of anachronism. As one pied noir commentator wrote in 1998: To say "French Algeria would be a dangerous error because it implies that there was another Algeria before. This is why 'Algeria, French creation' is the preferred term."[79] President Emmanuel Macron repeated the trope in 2021, asking: "Was there an Algerian nation before colonization?"[80] Some professional historians seem to agree with at least part of this reasoning. Guy Pervillé wrote in 1997 that historians should avoid using the term "Algerian" to refer to Muslims living in the country before independence. Taking issue with Algerian scholars like Daho Djerbal, Pervillé justified his position according to the historical sources that reserved "Algerian" for Europeans in Algeria, a term they used to legitimate themselves and distinguish themselves from French citizens of the metropole. To write of "Algerians" for Muslims before 1962 was to "systematically contradict" the vocabulary of the primary documents, he argued.[81] I will leave aside the deeply problematic aspects of this position, which stands on a sort of "born-again positivism," to simply point out that Pervillé himself does not abide by the strict rules he lays out when he addresses other (European) nationalities and ethnonyms.[82] For example, he writes unselfconsciously of "Italians" with respect to the parents of the notorious antisemite Max Régis, who migrated to Algeria at a time of the Risorgimento, when Italy itself remained officially unnamed as a country.[83]

In fact, Algeria had been frequently used as name well before 1830, most notably in the French language. In an important body of research undertaken in 1960s and 1970s, historian Guy Turbet-Delof uncovered the many names used in the early modern era. "Barbaric" was the most common name used in French to refer to the entire coastal region of northwestern Africa, a name that had passed into modern European languages with its pejorative connotations from the ancient Greek.[84] (Medieval Arabic also had the word *al-barbar* to refer to local people, although commentators fashioned an etymology that broke it free from its pejorative Greek connotations.[85]) However, "Algérie" also appeared frequently in precolonial French texts. The name was not a French invention. "Algérie" entered

French from the Arabic name of Algiers, "al-Jazā'ir" (the islands), which had been used to refer to the city and surrounding lands going at least back to the medieval era.[86] It referenced the islands that sat in the bay of the port city. The Ottoman province that fell to France in the nineteenth century knew itself as "Cezayir-i Garp" (western islands), among other names, taking up the Arabic name in Ottoman Turkish for the capital city and using it for the entire province.[87] Like the Ottomans, the Spanish Hapsburgs used these islands as a name, dubbing their short-lived sixteenth-century fort built on them the "Peñón d'Argel" (Rock of Algiers) as part of their failed expansion into northwestern Africa. Algérie appeared as a country name in French texts around the seventeenth century. At this time French geographers and lexicographers followed the custom of using the name of the city, "Alger," synecdochically to refer to country itself. Thus Alger did double duty as "the city and the kingdom of Africa," as one geographic dictionary of 1694 put it.[88] This definition was repeated in the Baudrand geographical dictionary of 1701, which amended it with the mention, "one of the Barbary States in Africa."[89] When it served as an ethnonym, the word's morphology changed to *algérien* (adj.)/Algérien (n.). Turbet-Delof found sporadic use of this ethnonym in literature spanning the seventeenth century, such as the *jeunesse algérienne* (children of the leading families of Algiers) mentioned by a priest in his account of ransoming captives.[90] As a proper noun, the ethnonym "Algériens" first appeared in the work of the French friar, Pierre Dan's *Histoire de Barbarie* (1637), and it spread to become a commonly used name in literature, journalism, and official iterations by the end of Louis XIV's reign.[91] Government officials themselves used this term also. For example, on the eve of the French invasion of 1830, the author of French war plans found it useful to talk about the country and the state, such as in his reference to France's enemy, the "Algerian government."[92]

Thus, the argument of Algérie being a French creation does not hold up to even a cursory reading of the precolonial sources. What is true, however, is that in the 1830s, the first decade of occupation, the Algerian name nearly disappeared in French texts. Once the Ottoman dey in Algiers surrendered on 5 July 1830, Algérie dropped out of official or semiofficial usage, replaced by "Barbarie," "Afrique," "Régence," and "Alger."[93] Each had a slightly different connotation. Of these, the long-used Barbarie fell by the wayside fairly quickly. Colonial writers found it attractive in double entendres to decivilize local people as barbarians, as it had long done in

French texts. Nevertheless, it lacked the necessary specificity for France's geopolitical interests inasmuch as it designated the entirety of the Mediterranean's southwestern shores rather than the Ottoman province that France conquered.[94] Afrique was likewise an overly open name, referring to an entire continent, even if it appeared frequently. In particular, the Ministry of War used the Africa name consistently in the first years. Thus, the invading French military force was named the "Army of Africa," and the most important French authority in Algeria in the 1830–1834 period was the "commander in chief of the Army of Africa" or "the commander in chief of the occupation corps of Africa."[95] Likewise, policymakers wrote about "our possessions in Africa," in a specific sense of the territory held by French troops.[96] However, Régence, the long-standing French name for the Algero-Ottoman state in Algeria, appeared most commonly in the first four years. Those authors who wished to create a year zero significance for 1830 and make explicit France's political ambitions called it "ex-Regency" or the "former Regency." This was done, for example, in the important decree of 9 September 1830 establishing a provisional legal system for French Algeria. The moniker reappeared later in a series of decrees by which the Ministry of War and its commander in Algiers pushed other ministries in Paris, which had just come to power after the Revolution of 1830, to permanently occupy Algiers.[97]

Names and claims of sovereignty went together. For the first four years after taking Algiers, the French government left the legal status of the occupied territories undecided.[98] This changed in 1834 with the royal ordinance of 22 July 1834, which formalized French rule. The historian Charles André Julien once called this law the "veritable birth certificate" of French Algeria, and most historians have subsequently accepted this as fact.[99] The edict stated that France would rule Algeria. It established the monarchy as the ultimate site of governing power and established the institutions through which the crown's power would flow. The edict thus resolved the question of a French evacuation or power sharing with other states, which had been on the table in various forms since the expedition was first conceived. It also specified a system of administration, law, and public order. In short, the ordinance in 1834 consecrated France's annexation of the Ottoman province of Algeria as a colony.

The French government, however, did not yet play the role of Adam: The ordinance stopped short of giving French Algeria a name. Indeed, no proper name appears in the 1834 ordinance at all. Instead, it deployed a group of common words: "French possessions in the north of Africa," or, as it appears in French, *possessions françaises dans le nord de l'Afrique*. As in today's English, the upper case marks the proper noun in French, meaning that "Africa" is the only true name in this expression.[100] This might be one of the most curious denominations up to this point in the history of French empire. It has deceived many historians (myself included) who mistook it for a name and changed the case of the first letter to "Possessions," thinking they were silently correcting errata in their sources. But there were no mistakes made in the original text, printed in the government's official newspaper, *Le Moniteur universel*, on 13 August 1834.[101] The designation appears twice, in the first and fourth article, of this relatively simple seven-article edict:

> Art. 1. The general command and the high administration of the French possessions in the north of Africa (former regency of Algiers) are entrusted to a governor general.

> Art. 4. Until further notice, the French possessions in the north of Africa will be governed by our ordinances.

In the first case, it was necessary to include "former regency of Algiers" so that the reader would know the exact extent of French claims, whereas by the fourth article, when the edict makes its unambiguous claim of control but not outright sovereignty, the term can stand on its own.

The full critical history of France's legal claims in Algeria has yet to be written, but this curious pseudo name merits explanation.[102] Not only was *les possessions françaises dans le nord de l'Afrique* exceedingly vague, it was also out of place for its time. Prior to this moment, other overseas territories came under French control with an official name that conformed to recognizable naming practices. For example, French Haiti had had a proper name since the beginning when "Saint-Domingue" was established by the Treaty of Ryswick (1697); so too did France's important island in the Indian Ocean called variously "Isle Bourbon"/"Isle Reunion"/"Isle Bonaparte," a three-part evolution dictated by the political upheavals of the Revolution. For its part, Corsica entered under the authority of the French crown with a proper name, the "Isle de Corse," coined by the Treaty of Versailles (1768).[103] Compared with these examples of proper names, *les possessions françaises dans le nord de l'Afrique* stands out as decidedly odd.

One historian has observed that French Algeria began as a "colony without a name."[104] But one might also say that it began with a "paranym," a name that disguises or misrepresent the truth. The ordinance's language is worth a close reading. It came out of the various designations used in the deliberations of two governmental commissions convoked in 1833 to provide policy recommendations. The commissions met at a time of rising costs and growing uncertainty as to the feasibility of continuing Algeria's occupation. The king charged members with developing a long-reaching plan, asking them directly, "What must we do with Algiers?"[105] The government did not pack the commission with partisans of any single policy position. There were those who were sympathetic to the idea that the national interest was best served by withdrawing troops, while others supported expansion and settlement. The first commissioners arrived in Algiers in September 1833, and they worked in the country collecting information and debating questions in twenty-nine meetings that ran until mid-November. They drafted eleven reports which they addressed to the king, summarizing their research and making recommendations on issues as varied as types of government to management of Muslim religious endowments. The government then called a second commission in December and asked members to provide final recommendations. By the spring of 1834, reporters and clerks had transcribed months of discussion and drafted the final versions of dozens of reports. When they came back from the printer, the materials numbered well over a thousand pages.[106] They provided all sorts of information about Algeria at the end of the Ottoman era. This ranged from population numbers (estimates ranged from a low of two million to a high of ten million) to the Ottoman legal and taxation system. In all, it represented France's attempt to produce a sort of Great Survey for Algeria, mobilizing knowledge in its pursuit of power.

In spite of commissioners' efforts to make Algeria transparent, their reports show a tendency wherein "the shadows were stronger than the light," as one historian has written astutely.[107] The most salient shadow is the name of Algeria itself. Throughout their discussions and reports, commissioners struggled with what to call this place. They had to come up with something to serve as the grammatical subject and object in their sentences. But "Algérie" was taken off the table at some point. In long hours of deliberations, commissioners did not once use it (or if they did, it was expunged from the printed record). In its place they spoke of "Alger,"

"Afrique," "Régence d'Alger," and "ex-Regence," among several common nouns. The ethnonym "Algérien" and the adjective "algérien" appear in the deliberations, but rarely, with the first proper noun used for the people of Algiers alone. Another common term used in the place of the name Algeria were expressions based on the word "possessions," which appears nearly one hundred times between the two reports. These included "our possessions in Africa" (as in "our possessions in Africa will become a vast and rich colony") as well as "possessions of the northern coast of Africa" (as in "the interests and honor of France command it to conserve its possessions of the northern coast of Africa").[108]

Some have argued that the use of "possessions" reflected metropolitan indifference to, or ignorance of, Algeria.[109] By this view, "possessions" was a generic geographic term that served to label a territory that few considered a proper country on a little-known African continent. However, "possessions" had a specific legal meaning, one that was particularly important in international law and imperial acquisition.[110] In property law, "possession" signified property relations that were ambiguous and stopped short of legal title. Having possession of something was sufficient grounds to claim exclusive use and enjoyment of it "as if" one were its owner.[111] This meant that possession was not calculated by legitimacy but on fact, as in the common saying that possession is 9/10 of the law. This left the door open for possession of property to be had by usurpation or theft, which the law might eventually recognize in some circumstances. As one French legal reference put it slyly in 1902, the thief "is the most resolute among possessors."[112] The concept of possession came to French code from Roman law, and while French jurists tried to rein in its corrosive threats to the regime of private property, states found it supremely useful for territorial acquisitions and empire building.[113] Historian Lauren Benton and classicist Benjamin Straumann argue that the concept of possession played a key role in the early modern era as part of the "scattershot" rationales and justifications used by European states to claim territory using Roman terms.[114] Alongside the notion of *res nullius*, which effaced the legal rights of non-Europeans, *possessio* legitimated the claims of European empires against each other. In particular, possession of non-European territory dispensed with legitimacy: "The possessor did not have to prove title, which was absolute, in order to keep possession—he merely had to show that his claim to the thing in question was better than his contestant's claim." This meant that "inquiring about possession did not involve inquiring about the rightfulness of acquisition," Benton and Straumann conclude.[115] Possession was so useful to European empires that it became synonymous with "colony" in the language of French diplomacy and international law.[116] By the end of the nineteenth century, even a legal scholar like the Argentine Carlos Calvo (d. 1906), who is best known as a protector of small-state sovereignty in an age of Euro-U.S. hegemony, recognized this understanding of possession as a principle of international law in his important French-language study in 1885.[117] He recounted the consensus that if possession lasted long enough and was not contested by other states, then it yielded a claim to territory that had "a force equal to that resulting from a formal contract or positive international law."[118] Lawfulness of acquisition was not at stake. Territorial acquisitions made by states could be considered valid even if, as Calvo remarked, "possession was originally accomplished by violence and in defiance of the law."[119] The ultimate sovereignty of a conquering state in this scenario was judged permissible if it established order in its possessions and a consensus emerged among other states that the acquisition did not threaten international security.[120] Notably, the "consensus" Calvo described did not include the consent of conquered people.

Used for Algeria in the 1830s, "possessions" concealed as much as it revealed. It designated a liminal space wherein questions of legitimacy and law (understood as moral rules and principles) receded, giving pride of place to the fact of possession. Lawmakers did not discuss publicly the legal substance of the concept of possession in their deliberations leading up to the ordinance of 1834. However, some obviously recognized the term's significance. In May 1834 the parliamentarian Élie Decazes publicly reassured French settlers in a speech at the Chambre of Peers that the government would move forward with colonization and not evacuate Algeria. As part of his glossing of settlers' concerns, he played on the semantic and legal differences between occupation and possession. Those who had staked their fortunes on colonization reported to him that they feared that "the government did not anticipate keeping Algiers, that French leaders only wanted to militarily *occupy* it and not *possess* it. They thought they saw in the previous acts of the government a refusal to recognize France as a *possessor* and to declare its sovereignty. They demand that the government openly declares that Algiers is a *French possession.*" Turning to his colleagues,

Decazes pointed to the reports drafted by the Africa Commissions, again drawing attention to the language they used to designate Algeria. He noted that "possession" appeared prominently in these documents and that the term had spread to other official texts. "The ordinance drafts, printed following the reports that have just been distributed to you, were written for the judicial organization . . . in the *French possessions on the north coast of Africa*. The commission deliberately chose this denomination in agreement with the Minister of War which leaves no doubt about the intentions of the government."[121] This revealed, he concluded, the government's steadfast intentions to claim Algeria as a French colony, even if it would not state so openly.

Some in the chamber that day saw things differently in a long debate about the power of words. For Decazes's colleague the Comte de Montlosier, the problem was the word "colony," which he argued was the cause of all the violence and disorder witnessed thus far. This word led European settlers and soldiers to believe that "Algiers was a territory that belonged to them, [and] that the natives were barbarians they could expel." By contrast, when "Louis XIV conquered Alsace he did not call it a colony. When Corsica was joined to us, it was not called a colony. . . . The word colonization, I repeat, is the source of all the disorders that have arrived in Algiers."[122]

While the government's use of "possessions" cleared up Algeria's status for Decazes, indicating a quasi-official bid to the territory, this clarity did not echo in the texts. Many writers adopted the "French possessions in the north of Africa" label with hesitancy. It served in the title of the newly created governor general position, but writers in Algiers still used the old terms even in official texts, and they appeared in the state's quasi-official newspaper in Algiers, *Le Moniteur algérien*.[123] Likewise, French maps published up through 1840 continued to refer to Algeria as the "Régence d'Alger," while some started using "Algérie" alone as early as 1838.[124] Among the many maps produced at this time, I have only found one using the *possessions françaises dans le nord de l'Afrique* moniker.[125]

Even when the new terminology was adopted, people struggled with how to write the case of the words: should "possessions" be capitalized and turned into a name? Clerical staff, administrators, editors, and printers worked against their better judgment to get it right. *Les possessions françaises dans le nord de l'Afrique* had all the appearances of a name, and it functioned as such in their texts. Therefore, many put the first noun in the upper case, upgrading it into a proper noun as "Possessions." This appeared with some frequency in *Le Moniteur algérien* newspaper up to 1838, which transformed the 1834 ordinance's term into a name repeatedly. For example, in a decree of 22 December 1834 printed in the paper, the governor general pronounced himself as the "Governor General of French *Possessions* in the north of Africa," the first among many errors appearing in the *Le Moniteur algérien*.[126] Internal handwritten government reports also turned "Possessions" into a name. For example, this occurred in an 1835 summary of French policy, which stated that the problem of what to do with Algeria was solved in 1834, when "the ex-Regency of Algiers received the name of French Possessions in northern Africa (sic.)."[127] Much later, editors of legal dictionaries and directories of the legal code took it on themselves to change the word's case when they reprinted the early documents, upgrading the common noun used in the original 1834 ordinance to a name.[128] How could this word be anything other than a name when viewed retrospectively and with the received wisdom that Algeria was born in the July 1834 ordinance? A "birth certificate" for French Algeria needed a proper name.

By the end of the decade, it became increasingly obvious that French Algeria could not remain unnamed much longer, nor did it have to be. Algérie had already begun to reappear in various official or quasi-official documents later in the 1830s, with one notable occurrence being a royal ordinance of 31 October 1838, which restructured the administration, placing French governance on new organizational footing.[129] However, the name Algérie did not stick at this point. Hoping to put the matter to rest, the next year the director of African affairs within the Ministry of War wrote the governor general stating that Algérie needed to be used exclusively as the colony's name. The text and its errata are worth quoting in full:

> Monsieur Maréchal, to this date, the territory we occupy in North Africa has been designated, in official communications, either under the name of French Possessions [*sic*] in North [*sic*] Africa, or under that of the former Regency of Algiers, or finally under that of Algeria. This last designation is shorter, simpler and at the same time more precise than all the others, [and it] seems to me that it should prevail from now on. It has already been sanctioned by constant use in documents distributed to the legislative chambers and in several speeches from the throne. I

> therefore invite you to prescribe the necessary measures so that the various authorities and generally all the agents who, in any capacity whatsoever, are attached to the civil or military services of our colony, thus in their official correspondence, and in any acts or certificates that they may be called upon to deliver, to substitute the word *Algeria* for the denominations previously in use.[130]

I quote this 1839 document at length not to set the record straight and give those looking for origins the founding text they need, but rather because even here the author confused proper and common nouns. Like other writers, he upgraded "Possessions" to a name even as he discarded it as inadequate because it was not one. And as the official pretended to exchange one name for another, "Algeria" for "Possessions," the colony could not be named officially for the simple reason that an internal directive like this did not have the authority to officially coin Algeria's name. It was only six years later, in the ordinance of 15 April 1845, which finally ended the administrative regime established in 1834, that an official name appeared.[131] The governor general could now bear the title "Governor General of Algeria."

If this were a contest of names, as God laid out pitting Adam against the angels, France failed miserably. It did not know what to call its new territory, or it dared not speak its true name. This episode points attention not only to the links between the name and power, but between the name and law (or lack thereof). Words that passed themselves off as names such as "possessions" produced power that worked outside of the law. Compared with Adam, who in the Qur'an took power through names openly, justly, in clear view of the supreme lawgiver, France worked itself into the symbolic fabric of Algeria surreptitiously, using quasi-names alongside the military conquest. Whereas the name is generally something that resolves ambiguity, like those used in international treaties or even Proust's character-revealing names, France's early names for Algeria produced confusion. Thus, it took fifteen years before some semblance of semantic stability took shape around a rediscovered name, Algérie, that had already been in use for a very long time.

It is useful to think about names not as possession but *dis*possession. The best-known example is *Robinson Crusoe* (1719), the urtext of European colonialism. Crusoe never properly named his island, which is known in Daniel Defoe's book only as "the Island of Despair." Thus, while Crusoe enjoyed supreme power, saying "I was King and Lord of all this Country indefeasibly"—a concept of sovereignty that might have been cribbed directly from the pages of Jean Bodin—this power exercised itself in isolation and therefore did not have occasion to speak itself.[132] But on the island Crusoe was not alone, and his power over his fellow human being announced itself in names. Thus, Crusoe quickly dubs his only rival on the island with a proper name, "Friday." With this name, Crusoe enslaved his neighbor.[133]

This chapter began with the question: "What is in a name?" Considering a colonial context at the end of the chapter, the answer comes in this story of taking another person's freedom.

2

"Tell Me Your Name"

Precolonial Naming Practices in Northwestern Africa

Tell me your name, and I'll tell you who you are.

—Jean-Pierre Makouta-Mboukou, *Les Dents du destin*

Name. Names? What's in a name? What name am I in?

—Samuel R. Delany, *Babel-17*

Colonial names were not pure inventions.[1] Certainly, France imposed its onomastic norms on Algerians, officializing and fixing their personal names and converting them to French letters. But like the name of the country "Algérie," this was not done ex nihilo. In this chapter I sketch personal names before their transformation in the second half of the nineteenth century. Names across northwestern Africa, Algeria included, bear the imprint of around a dozen different languages, making a proper linguistic and historical study of personal names a herculean task that would detour this book considerably from its main concerns. The reader who has knowledge of the dynamic ways that people use names in this region will no doubt be able to add their own experiences to the lacunae of this chapter. I draw this part of the book in admittedly broad strokes, glossing the prevalent practices among people speaking Arabic and Tamazight (Berber), Muslims and Jews. The investigation I pursue here has no pretensions of recovering cultural forms and practices destroyed by colonialism.[2] Rather, I stress how the personal name functioned within society, highlighting practices that French name reformers found particularly problematic.

The classical Arabo-Islamic name

I begin by introducing the "classical" Arabo-Islamic name.[3] Actual names came in many shapes and sizes, but in the medieval era writers formalized a series of rules that became standards.[4] Specialists today use these rules to decode the Arabic names they find in their sources, even as the rules might best be understood as ideal types that do not determine every iteration of a name. No institution fully monopolized names, and personal names remained quite fluid and unfixed before the French took hold of them.

The classical Arabic name consists of five parts.[5] At the name's core stands two components, the *ism*, a given name consisting of a single word or combination of several words, and the *nasab*, a genealogical name consisting of "ibn"/"bin" (son of) or "bint" (daughter of), which establishes a patrilineal lineage. Families conferred these two names on a baby at birth, and they served to individuate the child as well as embed the new arrival within the family. Other names came to a person during their lifetime, some even after death. These include the *kunya*, either an honorific name or a "teknonym" by which a child's name serves as a name for the parent, as in "Abū"/"Umm," (father of/mother of) followed by the name of a child; the *nisba*, a name referring to tribe, origin, residence, trade, or place of study; and the *laqab*, a nickname referencing personal traits or physical characteristics that might be honorific, prophylactic, even pejorative.[6] Occupations often figured directly after a person's name, and these might turn into names, as occurred with Khūja (secretary), Shāūsh (bailiff), and Khaznadār (treasurer).[7] Sequenced in a specific order (*kunya, ism, nasab, nisba*, and *laqab*), these five names contextualized an individual, making this person not only distinct and identifiable, like any proper noun, but socially legible, marking association, networks, bonds, and hierarchies.

Scholars of Arabic onomastics invite their readers to think of the classical name as an abbreviated life history. Jacqueline Sublet writes that the "name is itself a story, a biography that does not finish writing itself until the moment of death, [when the] veritable 'author' of the name [dies]."[8] Personal names convey markers of gender, ethnicity, and race, as well as social status, education, and profession. Richard Bulliet writes that the Arabic name is both a "cornucopia of information" and a "biographical puzzle" for the scholar to solve.[9] Historians have put names to good use. When they find a large collection of names, like those appearing in registries, tax records, and legal documents, they can write a prosopography of a place in time, decoding names to draw social profiles, even the portrait an entire society.[10]

The puzzle of the name has to be solved carefully, however. Although names offer a window on the past, there are many things that cannot be learned from them. For example, degrees of relations do not reveal themselves easily in the name. Brothers and sisters of the same father have matching nasabs, but collateral relations disappear. Occasionally, large extended families shared a name in common, but generally only influential families had one. To find extended relations for ordinary people, one has to look outside of the person's name and the single chain of descent given by the nasab, an exercise that requires metadata, such as genealogical narratives, oral archives, and family trees.[11]

The Arabo-Islamic name worked best in stable, face-to-face relations. In socially ephemeral situations it did not reliably identify and individuate. This became a central concern for French specialists seeking standardization, but Muslim writers commented on it over the years. The limits of the classical name are well illustrated by a humorous anecdote of misrecognition told by the eleventh-century historian Abū al-Faraj al-Muʿāfā ibn Zakariyyāʾ al-Nahrawānī that occurred during his pilgrimage (*ḥajj*). Moving within a large crowd of pilgrims gathered outside Mecca, he hears the first part his name, his kunya, called, but he hesitates to respond because it is so common. He therefore waits until the other many parts of his name are called, each in turn.

> I heard a crier calling, "O Abū l-Faraj!" I said: "Perhaps he means me." Then I said to myself, "Among the people are a great number named Abū al-Faraj," so I did not answer. When he saw that no one answered him he called, "O Abū l-Faraj al-Muʿāfā." I intended answering him, but then I said, "Perhaps he is calling someone else." When he saw that no one

> answered him, he called, "O Abū l-Faraj al-Mu'āfā ibn Zakariyyā al-Nahrawānī." I said, "There remains no doubt after this; he mentioned my name [*ism*], my by-name [*kunya*], my father's name [*nasab*], and my town [*nisba*]." I said, "I am that man. What is your wish?" He said to me, "Are you perhaps from the Nahrawān of the West?" [a different town by the same name as his own]. I was amazed at the coincidence of the name, by-name, patronymic, and name of the town, but I knew that in the West there is a town named Nahrawān [whereas I come from the one in the East]. This is an unusual occurrence.[12]

Al-Mu'āfā's telling of the story, in which each part of his name is called out in turn, builds suspense, ending in a resolution when at the last moment he realizes that the call is for someone else in the crowd. Even if it were told in a deadpan voice, the story would have easily brought a smile to those who had found themselves in similar circumstances. The medieval anecdote made its way into French Orientalist texts in the 1840s, where, stripped of its humor, it served to illustrate the technical shortcomings of Arabic names for modern identification purposes.[13]

The mother generally disappears in the classical name. While she may be named after her child in her own kunya, she leaves no trace on her child's name except in the rare cases of maternal nasabs.[14] Likewise, names do not convey a person's marital status: a woman does not change her name upon marriage, taking a name from her husband's family, nor, generally, does anything in a husband's name indicate his marital status or links to his wife's family. Historians have observed exceptions to this rule, however. For example, Abraham Marcus writes of an eighteenth-century Aleppo case where a social climber adopted the name of his wife's, higher-status family, as a way to burnish his own meager capital.[15]

Among the classical name's parts, the genealogical nasab merits special attention. It has been called nothing less than "the most fundamental organising principle in Arab society."[16] The nasab establishes a patrilineal line, linking daughters and sons to their father, and then to grandfathers and so on in chains of nasabs (*silsilat al-nasab*). The chain metaphor exactly conveys how the nasab functions: The name of one's father (*ism al-ab*) joins itself to the name of one's paternal grandfather (*ism al-jadd*) and then to the name of one's paternal great-grandfather (*ism ab al-jadd*).[17] At the heart of the name, the nasab reveals the fundamental importance of lineage, which the name constitutes out of a system of traces, wherein names of people reference other words and other people. This point is suggested in several well-known hadiths, and blunt expression of it comes in an often-cited medieval-era saying, "Whoever does not know lineage does not know people, and whoever does not know people is not considered one of mankind."[18] In other words, one's very humanity is at stake in this name. While the name's other parts designate an individual person, they cannot complete an autonomous and unique self. This self is constituted, rather, in its relationship to ancestors, like the meaning of a word that emerges in its relationship to other words.[19] In addition, the nasab represents cultural and political capital.[20] Genealogies can be finessed, even invented to maximize a family's stature, with the most prized genealogical line leading back to the house of the Prophet.[21] When a devoted student wrote a biography of the modern Egyptian reformer al-Ṭahṭāwī (1801–1873), he introduced his master with a dizzying fifteen-line list of nasabs, which took al-Ṭahṭāwī's family back a thousand years, from his father born in the late eighteenth century to the "daughter of the Prophet of God, our Lord al-Muṣṭafā Muḥammad," born at the beginning of the seventh century.[22] Holders of this noble lineage, going back to the house of the Prophet, enjoyed important advantages, including tax exemptions in some societies.[23] And even in cases when it was not appropriate to list every known ancestor, a robust chain of names in the nasab measured the density of one's social capital. For example, a seventeenth-century biographer of the Algerian poet Sīdī Aḥmad bin al-Ḥajj (d. ca. 1524) listed six separate ancestors in the poet's nasab, "bin Muḥammad bin Muḥammad bin 'Uthmān bin Ya'qūb bin S'aīd bin 'Abd Allāh."[24] In most contexts, people used only one part of the name.[25] While the poet himself would not have used this full name in his daily life, it communicated nicely Sīdī Aḥmad's steeped familial tradition of scholarship and notability.[26]

Precolonial naming practices across northwestern Africa

From the classical rules, I turn to some actual historical practices.[27] Attempts to understand the precolonial name must account for specific forms based on religion (Jews and Muslims), language (Berber and Arabic), and important regional variations.[28] The names of Arabic-speaking

Muslims in the central Maghrib included the five elements that made up the classical name, but in the Maghrib they might be composed and ordered differently, depending on social rank and the circumstances of a name's iteration, among other factors.[29] Algerians conferred the given name, the *ism* (also known in the *'alam*, meaning the "sign" or "mark"), near the seventh day after a child's birth in a celebration that marked the baby's arrival (known variously as *sāb'a*, *subū'*, *'aqīqa*, or *walīma*).[30] Choosing the given name was a collective affair negotiated among the child's family, invited friends and notables, and community members. In its public aspect, as known to the outside observers who recorded the event, men decided the ism, but it is safe to suspect that women played a role, even deploying "veiled sentiments," to use anthropologist Lila Abu-Lughod's felicitous term, to influence the choice of a baby's name.[31] The Algerian novelist Mouloud Feraoun (1913–1962) noted in his semiautobiographical book, *The Poor Man's Son*, that his grandmother, the most influential person in his family, named him.[32]

Isms typically reflected the baby's birth order and his or her relationship to other members of the family. A standard name for a first-born boy was "Muḥammad," after the Prophet, and "Fāṭima al-Zahrā'" for a first-born girl, after the Prophet's daughter Fāṭima, known as "al-Zahrā'," or "The Splendid One." While these names drew on a common heritage and reflected the many hadiths, or sayings of the Prophet, which encouraged Muslims to use his ism, actual usage marked family and regional particularities. For instance, mothers living today in Figuig, on the Moroccan side of the border with Algeria, are entitled to having their first-born son named after the Prophet, even if their husband had previously fathered a son named Muḥammad with another woman (i.e., a man who was divorced, widowed, or polygamous).[33] Names circulated within a family over time as part of commemorative strategies that expressed respect of elders and solidarity. The name of a deceased grandfather might be chosen for a first born boy if no other child already bore this name. In this way, the name provided a mnemonic device to assure the family that the memory of its lost patriarch would perpetuate itself in memory by his name. Although the sources do not comment on the practice, one suspects that the same held true for grandmothers and beloved aunts. Likewise, if a family had previously suffered the death of a child, a newborn might be given the name of this dead child. Some names were regionally specific. Locally respected saints provided a good source of these. " 'Abd al-Raḥman" was a common ism for boys in Algiers, commemorating the patron saint of the city, the medieval scholar, Sīdī 'Abd al-Raḥman al-Th'ālibī (d. 1468/69); "Hūwārī" was common in Oran and other parts of western Algeria, after Oran's patron saint, Sīdī Muḥammad al-Hūwārī (d. 1439); and "Ghawthī" was common in Tlemcen after the great Sufi shaykh, Sīdī Abū Madyan (d. 1198) (known as "al-Ghawth," for his "succor"), who died near the city while traveling to Marrakech. Naming children after saints linked them to the saint's blessings (*barakāt*) and marked their origins. Saints also provided health and reproductive care: if a couple successfully overcame infertility thanks to the intercession of a saint, the resulting child might carry that person's name in recognition of their role. Finally, the Islamic calendar served as source for names, with a baby's ism coming from the month or holiday, or even day of the week, on which she or he was born.[34] This accounts for common isms like "Ramḍān" (the ninth month, a sacred month of fasting), "Rabī'" (Rabī' al-Awal, the third month and the month of the Prophet's birth), "Mawlid" (the Prophet's birthday), and " 'Īd" (masculine) or " 'Āīda" (feminine) (meaning "holiday"). By the same logic, a boy born on the Friday of 'Āshūrā' might be named "Bū Jumu'a," adapting the kunya into part of a proper ism, which literally translates as "Father of Friday." Thus, in all these cases, families selected their child's ism with words that expressed their gratitude to God and love for the child, as well as the need to place the child within a larger web of social relations.

Like many proper nouns, some Algerian names derived from common words, nouns, adjectives, and verbs.[35] Generally speaking, isms originated in words with meanings that expressed piety. Not surprisingly, therefore, propitiatory and theophilic names appear frequently.[36] The repertoire of pious names began with those of the Prophet, who has been known to Muslims by many different names, collectively called the Nobel Names (*Asmā' al-Sharīfa*).[37] Of these, which number up to a thousand in some traditions, Algerians generally favored a half dozen, including "Aḥmad" (the Prophet's heavenly name), "Muṣṭafā" (chosen), "Ṭāhir" (pure), "Bashīr" (bringer of good tidings), "Qāsim" (distributor), and "Ḥabīb" (beloved friend).[38] The names of the Prophet's immediate family and his most famous companions (*ṣaḥāba*) also figured routinely among Algerians' names. The Prophet's wives (especially Khadīja and 'Ā'isha) and daughters (Fāṭima) appeared commonly among girls' names. Other names joined this core onomastic stock. They included words that expressed positive notions, valued objects, and words that God might find pleasing, like " 'Azīza" (cherished), "Sa'īda" (happy), "Faḍīla" (virtue), and "Lu'lu'a" (pearl).[39] Boys could also be given names from this group, such as "Malīḥ" (handsome), "Ashraf" (honorable), and "Rābaḥ" (prosperous).[40] Along with piety, given names could signal ethnicity, kinship groups, or geographic location. For example, some families in the city of Constantine favored isms that evoked Turkish heritage, like "Muṣṭafā," "Khalīl," and "Sulaymān."[41]

The same name might have different spellings or pronunciations. These demonstrated both regional variations as well as affective and familiar forms. In some cases, tensions emerged between a name's spoken and written form. For example, Khadīja could also be "Khadāūj," "Khaddūja," "Dūja," or "Khadāwaj"; and Idrīs could also be "Īdris," by shifting the placement of the long vowel.[42] Likewise, Fāṭima could appear in many different iterations, ranging from "Faṭṭūm," "Faṭṭūma," and "Fīṭma" to "Ṭūma" or "Ṭaītma," or even simply "Faṭma" or "Fṭīma."[43] An extreme example is the name Aḥmad, which had at least twenty-six different morphological variations in nineteenth-century Algeria.[44] Some forms were common to specific regions. Aḥmad tended to be "Ḥammū" in Oran, "Ḥamī" in Tlemcen, "Ḥamūda" in the east, and "Ḥamīdūsh" in the center of the country.[45] The celebrated Companion 'Umar's name also had at least two different forms: the standard spelling, " 'Umar" (عُمَر), and the variant, " 'Amr" (عَمْر)[46] The former prevailed in cities and the latter in the countryside.[47] A special case was the Prophet's ism, which could be written in at least two different forms depending on the vocalization of the minor vowels. The Arabic language writes out only the consonants and long vowels; the short vowels might appear in some texts as diacritical marks where exactness was crucial, such as the Qur'an, but common texts left them unmarked or "unvocalized." This meant that the exact pronunciation of a word might not be apparent in writing. And in some cases, even the long vowels, which have their own letters and are crucial to proper spelling, might be omitted. This was the case with the Malikite mufti of Algiers, Sayyid Aḥmad bin Ibrahim bin Mūsā, whose name appeared in a petition in 1831 addressed to French authorities (see chapter 4). His nasab, "Ibrahim," is written without the long vowels (*ʾalif* and *yāʾ*) that were used generally to spell this name, yielding ابرهم (Ibrahim) instead of the standard ابراهيم (Ibrāhīm).[48] While this might be a scribal error, it points to a thornier problem in Arabic onomastics concerning homographs and homophones, something that occupied previous generations of scholars and biographers who authored specialized reference texts to sort things out.[49] The standard Muḥammad (مُحَمَّد) existed along with the variant "Maḥammad" (مَحَمَّد) or "Mḥammad" (مْحَمَّد), each forming a separate name.[50] For example, in some families the first-born son bore the standard version, while his younger brother would be called Mḥammad. This last case, with its shifts in vocalization common to northwestern African pronunciations, posed challenges.[51] While it is unlikely that this subtle variation caused people to pause when they heard it pronounced, with the ear easily enough sorting out the differences, in writing it risked creating errors. Like most other written words, names were customarily left unvocalized, meaning that the short vowels, the "u" and the "a" of these two different names, did not appear in the written text. Scriveners solved the problem by writing out in their texts "M[u]ḥammad with the *ḍamma*" (short u) and "M[a]ḥammad with the *fatḥa*" (short a), thereby preserving the name's integrity while not contravening the standard spelling. A case in point is an 1856–1857 (AH 1275) judgment of a majlis appeals court in which two parties were both named محمد. The scribe writing out the proceedings included the men's nasabs, which might have effectively identified them as separate people, but he took pains to ensure that the precise differences between the men's isms were used by writing out "Muhammad with the ḍamma ibn Sa'īd" for one and "Mahammad with the fatḥa ibn Musṭafā bin 'Arīsh" for the other.[52]

Titles often preceded the names of Algerians, and they became part of the name in legal documents and things like bills of sale, as well as in signatures.[53] The honorifics "Sīd," "Sī," "Sayyid," or "Sīdī" were common. Although these are often translated as the equivalent of "Sir" in English, they had a precise meaning. As recently as the seventeenth century, "Sayyid" applied only to individuals who could trace their lineage back to the Prophet's family, as well as to religious and legal scholars, and a few secular elites.[54] By the mid-nineteenth century, many classes had adopted this title, and it could be found as a prefix to names of those who practiced lowly professions as barbers or in bathhouses, suggesting a loosening of the rules. But those who used this title inappropriately risked censure, like that found in the proverb, "A ['Sayyid'] who does not know how to read is like an untrained dog."[55] Like men, women of stature might be addressed with an honorific such as "Sayyida," "Wālīya," and "Lālla" (equivalents to

"Mistress"), or "Amat Allāh" (which translates to "servant of God").[56] These titles expressed respect, such as when addressing religious notables or when younger people spoke to older women. Lālla appeared so widely for religious figures that it became a constituent element of these women's name. Thus the head of the Raḥmāniyya Sufi center of El Hamel was known to all as Lālla Zaynab, whereas the full articulation of her name, including her nasab and laqab, is Zaynab bint Shaykh Muḥammad ibn Abī al-Qāsim bint Ṣāliḥa (or "virtuous daughter," d. 1904).[57] Another common honorific title was "al-Ḥajj" (masc.)/"al-Ḥajja" (fem.). Those who made the pilgrimage to Mecca carried this title, and it had considerable prestige. Families even recorded the pilgrimages of fathers and grandfathers in the nasab of their descendants (e.g., ibn/bint al-Ḥajj + ancestor's ism). Children born in the period when pilgrims returned home might have "Ḥajj" as an ism in this way.

As for the kunya itself, Algerians often used it as a sobriquet or metonym, along with the standard honorific usage as "father of/mother of," as had long been common in the classical tradition.[58] As sobriquets, kunyas took metaphorical meanings such as the "man with" or the "possessor of," in addition to serving as a teknonym. The classical sources include flattering kunyas of this type, such as "Abū Liḥya" (man with a beard), "Abū al-Faḍā'il" (man with merits), or "Abu l-Maḥāsin" (man of good qualities). A notable kunya for women in medieval Egypt was "Umm al-Banīn" (mother of the many sons), which was given to baby girls in anticipation of a fecund family life.[59] In Algerian or Maghrebi sources, "Abū" was often abbreviated to "Bū," and one finds kunyas made from less straightforward words, such as "Bū Kurā'a" (man with the hoof), "Bū Jamā'a" (man of the congregation), or "Bū Thalja" (man of snow).[60] While these kunyas might strike us as a strange way to honor somebody today, they likely stemmed from an original interpellation made by someone who did not know this person's proper name. As described by Muḥammad Ibn Aḥmad al-Ibshīhī (d. 1446), a widely read reference, this practice fell into the class of the address of strangers wherein one hailed a person based on outward characteristics, such as "O faqīr!" (poor person) for the shabbily dressed, or "O faqīh!" (legal scholar) for a man of educated appearance.[61]

Names might change from one context to another. Some of these changes reflected the moment of recording and the norms that governed this occasion.[62] But place and context also mattered. Nisbas indicating origin illustrate this well. As a rule, a nisba such as "al-Qusanṭīnī" (from Constantine) made sense only when used outside of the city's walls. Likewise, a nisba such as "al-Jazā'irī" (the Algerian) or "al-Maghribī" (the Moroccan or the Maghrebi) served outside of northwest Africa, such as in the Arab East and other parts of the Islamic world. However, in Constantine itself, nisbas from neighboring cities or places appeared in the documents. Among the many names of outsiders found by historian Fatima Guechi in her research on Constantine is a woman named Faṭṭūm bint Muḥammad bin 'Azzūz al-Jayjalī. She appeared before a judge to give over her part of an orchard and farmland to her brother in AH 1215 (1800–1801 CE). Like other people with roots outside of the city, Faṭṭūm entered into the record with her nisba, referencing the town of Jījal (Djidjelli) some one hundred miles away. The nisba ensured the name's ability to distinguish her exactly in the written documents.[63]

Names identified individuals, making their bearers distinct in what set them apart from other individuals, even as names also attached people to families, lineages, professions, and places. In this sense, they functioned as names have long done and continue to do today. However, the Algerian name in the precolonial era was unfixed and shifted according to context and idiomatic variations. Thus, one can find the same name used by different people, and different names used by the same person.

Malicious names

Names could be used maliciously. A source none other than the Qur'an anticipated the problem by expressly forbidding pejorative names: "Do not find fault with another, nor insult each other with nicknames" (Q49:11).[64] Nevertheless, this appears to have occurred throughout history, especially in the laqab sobriquets, which split between the beautiful or flattering laqab (*al-laqab al-jamīl*) and the pejorative one (*al-laqab al-sū'*), which could be full of irony, even spite.[65] For example, one undated Arabic document used in a colonial-era language manual refers to a certain 'Alī ibn al-Ā'raj, who came before the cadi for disorderly conduct.[66] 'Alī's full name suggests that his physical condition might have had something to do with his crime. "Ā'raj" translates into "lame" or "limping," suggesting either that 'Alī had a disabled father or perhaps that he himself suffered from lameness and had been forced to beg. The fifteenth-century writer al-Ibshīhī stated that by his era scholars had come to a consensus to permit nicknames that were not intentionally malicious, and he explicitly gives the example of al-Āʿraj as permissible, along with "al-Aʿmā" (the blind), "al-Afṭas" (the pug-nosed), and "al-Aqraʿ" (the bald), among many others.[67] Enemies conferred names as well, however, and they proved to be important sites of struggle. The best known comes from the community of the first Muslims. The Prophet's favorite wife, 'Ā'isha bint Abi Bakr, acquired many different sobriquets during her life, notably "al-Mubarra'a" (the vindicated) and "al-Ṭahira" (the pure). While these might appear as simple compliments for this esteemed figure, historian Denise Spellberg notes that they are in fact highly politicized names given by her defenders after a controversy risked compromising her reputation.[68] Another of the most preeminent early Muslims, 'Ali ibn Abī Ṭālib, the Prophet's son-in-law and fourth caliph, suffered slander in the names used by his enemies. In his case, it was the kunya "Abū Turāb" (literally "father of dust" or "dusty man") that did him dishonor, insinuating uncleanliness. But the meaning of these types of names could change over time, and later traditions argued that Muḥammad coined the Abū Turāb name, guaranteeing its good intentions.[69] Although the kunya serves in the classical tradition a sign of respect, friendship, and honor, it could diminish its bearer as well as elevate him or her. Another example of the semantic instability of the honorific kunya comes with those based on animals. Al-Ibshīhī argued that kunyas based on animals were perfectly legitimate. As evidence, he cited a tradition of the Prophet conferring "Abū Hurayra" (Man with the Kitten) on one of his trusted companions because he saw him playing with a cat.[70] The Prophet's use canonized this name and legitimated the practice, but the fact that al-Ibshīhī felt it necessary to clarify the question, using it as a teachable moment so to speak, shows up ambivalences people felt and the need to contain slippages.

Making sense of the name's turns of meanings, some of them made with the skill of the jester, is not easy. There are dangers in a "straight" reading of names, which is to say that names do not always convey a singular voice or meaning, however obvious it might appear. A skilled reader of the medieval sources like S. D. Goitein could tease out the fact that a laqab like "al-Faylasūf" (the Philosopher) might not mean that its bearer is actually a philosopher but might be an uneducated person or even a pretentious idiot. Likewise, Goitein finds that the onomatopoeic name "Baqbūq" (sounds like "gurgle") might not work literally to evoke the pleasant sound of water bubbling from a spring but figuratively to denote "the prattle of a chatterbox."[71] The original context of enunciation decided a name's meaning, and the passage of time makes it virtually impossible to capture irony. Moreover, intonation, pronunciation, and physical gestures at the moment of pronunciation shaped a name's inflection, none of which can be decoded from the written sources.

A name's slippages in meaning could be exploited, and irony could turn overtly malevolent. This became a problem especially when names crossed languages and cultures, offering an interstitial space for those seeking to do harm.[72] This can best be observed by shifting periods forward into the colonial era to consider several well-documented cases. By the mid-nineteenth century, the personal names of Algerians frequently appeared in French texts. While French authors treated widely recognized names as such, converting a name like Mas'ūd (fortunate) into "Masoud" without translating its meaning, the common nouns that served in kunyas or laqabs might be translated. For example, French authors literally translated the meaning of the name of Bū Sitta ("the man with six"), an enslaved man captured with his Tuareg master in the 1880s. His name denoted a polydactylous deformity that left him with six fingers on each hand and six toes on his left foot.[73] After his capture, Bū Sitta was taken to Paris by the colonial scholar Émile Masqueray, who displayed him at the Universal Exposition in 1889, an ethnographic exhibit that historians have called a "human zoo." Giving the meaning of his name, French authors redoubled Bū Sitta's victimization, using it as an occasion to mock him. (Bū Sitta had the last laugh, however, escaping later from a French prison.[74])

Another case showing how an Arabic name could be used maliciously in French is that of a man known as Muḥammad ibn 'Abdallāh, who led an important uprising in the mid-1840s. Algerians called him by his kunya, "Bū Mā'aza."[75] "Mā'aza" means goat in Arabic, and local people conferred the kunya for the goat that reputedly accompanied him, an animal they understood to have been sent by God as a sign that he was the chosen one.[76] For their part, French authors used it to denigrate Bū Mā'aza, translating his name as the "Father of the Goat," framing him as a rustic mystic and charlatan.[77] Novelist Alexandre Dumas even used it in his travel account of North Africa, comparing Bū Mā'aza to the heroine of *The Hunchback of Notre Dame*, Esmeralda, known for the goat that accompanied her. "The father of the goat, this poor prophet, who like the shining Esmeralda, owed his prestige to the goat which paraded around him."[78] Dumas produced a clearly sardonic effect in this juxtaposition of the two figures, with Quasimodo, the tragic, simpleminded hunchback of Hugo's story, lurking in the margins of his readers' minds.

In another case, an officer in the Arab Bureau in Algeria boasted about how he conferred a kunya on a local man to mock him, a name that produced a particularly negative effect in the crossing between the French and Arabic languages. The officer was irked by the long-windedness of a local man, Moustafa Ben Ali, who talked too much in the meetings between notables. The man happened to be blind in one eye, and at the end of one of his particularly long speeches, the French officer made a joke: "While God only gave you one eye, he gave you two tongues."[79] Moustafa Ben Ali was then saddled with the kunya "Bou Lessanin" (Bū Lisānīn), or "man with two tongues." In French, "two tongued" (*deux langues*) roughly gets across the meaning of long-windedness. In Arabic, however, *lisānīn* means deceitful, an especially harmful accusation when made in the context of a meeting with the French officer, where reputations were especially vulnerable.[80] One can imagine a tense silence or nervous laughter descending on the meeting when the Frenchman made the joke in his heavily accented Arabic, which probably left some wondering if they had understood him correctly, forced to read between the officer's facial expression and intonation announcing a friendly joke and his actual words that delivered a cutting insult. While he gave no indication that he knew that he knowingly maligned the man, the officer wrote with apparent pleasure that the kunya stuck, and that Moustafa Ben Ali considered it particularly humiliating and asked him to stop using it.

In cases where French authorities sought good relations with Algerians, they approached the polysemy of names differently. At the end of the nineteenth century, French troops moved deep into the Sahara. French success here depended on cultivating local partners as well as crushing enemies. One potential ally was a man the French knew as "Mohammed ben El Hadj Ahmed Gaga." He emerged as a key player at one point in the 1890s, when the government's support for desert conquests waned, alarming pro-expansionist leaders in Algiers. The governor general, who was committed to claiming the Sahara, discreetly floated a plan to invest this man with a mandate to rule, a project that would commit Paris to a Saharan protectorate.[81] But before the wildcat plan could proceed, it needed a larger circle of support, which meant revealing the man's identity to other French leaders. The surname "Gaga" posed a problem here. This name, probably a laqab nickname, might have come from several different Arabic or Berber words, most likely either the Arabic *jājā*, a call made to camels to drink, or *ja'jā'*, a word meaning "clamorous" or "blustering," as in a "loud-mouthed person."[82] The governor general had no sense of the name's original meaning, but he warned off his collaborators from using it. In French *gaga* meant senile or "imbecile," as in the "ga-ga" of a baby.[83] Pronouncing it at a committee meeting risked provoking ridicule and sinking the project. In a postscript to a letter sent to a confidant, the governor general wrote, "It will be good to no longer call Gaga anything other than Mohammed ben el Hadj Ahmed. Do you not think that the way that the French are, that the very name of 'Gaga' would be enough to ridicule this man, to destroy his importance and doom us?"[84]

With the exception of "Two Tongues," these examples do not show that people who were the butt of French jokes actually knew or cared about what the French called them. Ahmed Gaga probably did not know the French language, and he was not invited to any of the meetings. In the case of Bū Mā'aza, while the French mocked his name, those who actually mattered to this resistance leader, the men and women who answered his call to arms, saw his kunya as a credential, the confirmation of his special status. The *mā'aza* (goat) was the sign of the redeemer, so too the *baghla* (donkey) and the *ghazāl* (gazelle).[85] But the meaning of names can shift over time, even in the same language. A postscript to the Bū Mā'aza story shows this nicely. In 1988 a journalist wrote an article for an Algerian military magazine about an exhibit featuring statues of anticolonial leaders. "This glorious era is completed by the bust . . . of Mohamed Ben Abdellah (1845–1847) . . . whom the colonizer named 'Bou-Maza.' "[86] Ill at ease with the literal meanings of the kunya and unaware of its actual origins, the army journalist blamed it on the French and, in an ironic turn, privileged a form of this man's name that would have fit into the modern French naming system. By this time, a "proper" name for a hero had changed considerably.

Onomastic heteroglossia, Tamazight names

Northwestern African society was neither exclusively Arabophone nor Muslim. Tamazight-speaking people lived across northwestern Africa. And smaller but significant communities of Jews also lived here, among other minorities. Arabic held an ascendant status as a liturgical language for Muslims, as well as the language of the law, scholarship, and formal education in the Islamic sciences. Arabic was not exclusive to Muslims. Jews in northern Africa used a distinctive form of Arabic, Judeo-Arabic, as their primary vernacular language. In its written form, Judeo-Arabic is immediately recognizable by the use of Hebrew script to write Arabic words, a distinctive intersection of the spoken and written language. When spoken, Judeo-Arabic contained a series of distinctive features, word choices and pronunciations, that helped mark its speaker as a Jew.[87] Thus, language, like food and clothing, set social boundaries while providing the means to cross them.[88] Alongside Arabic, Berber is the other most important language in northern Africa. Its dialects dominate in many regions in Algeria and Morocco, and to a lesser extent in other northwestern African countries. In Algeria, Berber was the primary language in Kabylia and was spoken widely in the southeastern Aurès region, as well as in many Saharan communities. The people speaking Tamazight were overwhelmingly Muslims (although Berber-speaking Jewish communities have existed over time). Berber-speaking people adopted Islam beginning in the seventh century when the first Arab Muslims arrived in northwestern Africa, and many used Arabic for liturgical purposes while continuing to use their own tongue as a spoken, vernacular language. An entrenched prejudicial understanding of Berber that has existed for centuries sees it as a low tongue suitable only for daily life, whereas classical Arabic was the exclusive high language of Muslims.[89] New scholarship has shown conclusively that Arabic did not monopolize high cultural expression, nor was Tamazight only a spoken language.[90] Authors and copyists wrote Tamazight in Arabic script (as well as using the Tifinagh alphabet in some cases), a practice that dates back to the eighth century CE.[91] In the later medieval era, written Berber appears in many different sources, ranging from law manuals to scientific treatises on medicine and astronomy. Religious texts also appeared in Berber, including manuals of religious instruction.[92] Moreover, Tamazight oral texts served for high cultural expression, including poetry, fables, and proverbs.[93] Berber commanded wide cultural prestige through the sixteenth century, and it enjoyed an especially high status during the period of Almohad rule (twelfth–thirteenth centuries), when it served both political and liturgical purposes for this Berberophone dynasty. (Berber even shed its prejudicial "Bar-Bar" name in some Arabic-language texts at this time, when writers referred to it with a more prestigious moniker, "*al-Lisān al-Gharbī*," or Arabic for "the western language."[94]) Arabic and Tamazight are not neatly compartmentalized languages. Each occupies a separate branch of the Afroasiatic language family, but they share a number of similarities and have mutually influenced each other over the centuries in significant ways, such as sharing words and mutually shaping pronunciations.[95] Thus Arabic and Tamazight share a long and intertwined history, as do the people who use them. Looking at the medieval-era sources, historian Ramzi Rouighi even argues that "the Berbers began to be a people in Arabic," in the sense that Arab scholars approached Berber-speaking people, who understood themselves as distinct from each other, and fit them into their own epistemologies to fashion them into single people like themselves.[96]

The other languages appearing over time in northwestern Africa that affected names included Turkish. The Ottoman administration employed it both for practical uses and to establish the identity of its political and military elites, affirming their attachment to the Sublime Porte as separate from local people.[97] Sub-Saharan African languages including Hausa or Kanuri resonated among enslaved people and free people of color, who, even if they knew Arabic, used their own languages among themselves, such as in the Bori societies of Tunisia.[98] Local people also used Romance languages, such as the Italian dialects used by the Livornese Jews living in Tunis or the Spanish and Portuguese influences that circulated among the exiles, Muslims and Jews, who relocated to the western Maghreb after the expulsions from Iberia starting in the late fifteenth century. Finally, standing outside all these languages was the Mediterranean's Lingua Franca. This Romance-based language allowed people otherwise foreign to each other to communicate without identity claims, making it a practical tool of communication or a "no man's language," as historian Jocelyne Dakhlia has argued in her rich study.[99]

It can be difficult to understand the names Berber-speaking people have used historically through the existing scholarship. Part of this has to do with the instrumentalized ways the Tamazight sources have been read and produced; part of it has to do with the sources themselves.[100] There are few accessible early written documents, and when they exist, Berber names are written out in other languages or scripts. This can efface the distinct features of Tamazight names. As linguist Salem Chaker notes, the sources "for Berber onomastic studies are only accessible to us most often through the filter of dominant foreign languages . . . and not through a direct knowledge of Berber sources."[101] This means that Berber names bear the trace of phonetic and orthographic transformations of these languages. (The colonial-era conversion to the French language further transformed Berber names, as discussed in chapter 5.) These effacing forces have shaped the priorities of researchers. Most work on Berber onomastics has addressed the recovery of Tamazight names, which scholars publish in onomasticons to ensure their preservation.[102] Moreover, while linguists have produced useful synchronic studies of personal names, a historical understanding of Berber naming practices changing over time does not exist in the same way that it does for Arabic.

That said, Berber-speaking people have named their children from a similar repertoire of names as their Arabophone neighbors, using an analogous name structure. Tamazight names included a given name, a genealogical name, and a name formed from toponyms and/or ethnonyms such as a tribe's name, itself generally taken from an eponymous ancestor. These names were expressed in Berber words or Berberized Arab words.[103] Thus, the Arabic names of the famous early Muslims appeared in Berber forms: the Arabic "Muḥammad" was adapted to Berber as "Muḥend," "Māmat," or "Ḥammū"; "Aḥmad" rendered itself in Tamazight as "Ḥend" or "Ḥaddu"; and the Arabic "Ā'isha" became "Tā'yašt."[104] Other common Berber names appearing over time include "Ziri," a Berber word meaning moon; "Gellid," meaning king, or "Zemmur," meaning olive/olive tree. Verbal expressions in Tamazight also formed names such as "Ifren" (he is chosen) and "Izmerten" (he will endure). In the nineteenth century, families frequently named daughters "Tasaεdit" (Fr. Tassadit), meaning good fortune, a meaning shared with the Arabic "Sayyida."[105] As in Arabic, esteemed animals often appeared in Tamazight names. Thus, a boy might be called after the Berber word for elephant, "Ilu," while the turtle served to name Berber girls called "Tamilla." The Tamazight language also provided common nouns and adjectives that served as names, such as "Mokrane" (great), and verbal forms of names such as "Yidir" (*y-idir* or "he lives") "Yezmer"/ "Tezmer" (he/she can). There was also a Berberization of the genealogical name corresponding to the Arabic nasab. The Arabic "ibn" (son of) could be expressed in Berber as "ag," "w"or "u," whereas "bint" (daughter of) appeared as "welt."[106] An analogue of the nisba formed this way also, as in "u Tmazirt," or "son of the country." Likewise, collective names used the plural "ayt," as in "ayt Moussa," meaning "sons/children of Moussa," an eponymous ancestor. Like with Arabic, parts of a Berber name might drop off depending on the context, and name choice also reflected regional preferences. In the mountains of Kabylia, given names like Aklī, Meziane, and Qāsī predominated, whereas 'Addūn, Bakīr, and Zakrī were typical to the Berber-speaking people of the Mzab region in the Sahara.[107] In addition to the names of the early Muslims, common Arabic nouns made their way into Berberized forms to be used as names like the Arabic *farūj* (chicken), which became the Berber name "Ferruja," or the Arabic word *jawhar* (gem), converted into the Berber name "Juher."[108] Some people had names that mixed the two languages, and some had names based on words common to both languages, meaning that they could be converted back and forth easily. For instance, the name of a medieval-era Almoravid notable mixed Arabic and Berber, with one name "Yaḥyā" using the Arabic equivalent of John, and a second name "Ang^{w}mar" using a Berber word for hunter.[109] In these ways, names helped Amazigh societies to mark their distinctions as well as imbricate themselves within Islamic society where Arabic had a special place.

As names particular to a language traversed several tongues, so too they crossed between the written and spoken forms of these languages. Berbers and Arabs likely understood each other's names as they heard them. This might entail a moment of mental translation to find the equivalent name in one's own language or to grasp the sounds of a new word, including that of hearing one's name spoken back with a different accent. This would be analogous to the experience of an English-speaking person named "Joan" hearing her name pronounced in Arabic as *jooaan*, with the Arabic speaker reproducing the sounds of the original name in the speech sounds available in Arabic. On the other hand, writing names between languages presents greater challenges. Joan can be converted according to a strict phonetic logic, which would yield a name written in Arabic characters as جوان (Jū'ān), a name that does not otherwise exist in the language, to my knowledge. Or it can be written in the Arabic version of the same name, يونّا (Yuwannā), which would effectively assimilate it to Arabic and compromise its specificity and its ability to serve as a cultural marker of Joan's English-language name. The Joan example is relatively simple, a word puzzle solved by finding equivalences between different languages, but it opens onto a rich, shifting world that exists between the written and spoken language, and between different cultural and language systems. Converting Berber phonemes into Arabic letters risked turning a distinct Berber name into an Arabic one, especially in those cases where the Berber name had an Arabic origin, as the examples show was common. Moreover, there were technical problems. The Arabic alphabet did not have exact equivalences for every Tamazight phoneme.[110] Berber is a consonantal language, with only three underlying vowels, but with a rich set of consonant phonemes. In Tamazight pronunciation, the consonants of words shared between the languages stand out while the vowels, which figure so prominently in the Arabic pronunciation, fade away.[111] Thus, the back-and-forth of names between languages did not function like the pistons of a well-oiled translation machine, smoothly turning out onomastic equivalences between languages.

Berber names in between: Ibnou Zakri

Moving between languages and between their written and oral forms carried high stakes, especially for Tamazight-speaking people living in a world where Arabic norms claimed ascendency. Considerable cultural capital permeated the name. An example worth close attention is the case of a man we know as "Mohammed Saïd Ibnou Zakri" (d. 1914), a colonial-era Algerian scholar studied by historian Kamel Chachoua.[112] Ibnou Zakri published a well-known *risāla* (epistle) in 1903, which called for educational reform in Kabylia as well as ending the discriminatory aspects of customary law toward women. He came from Kabylia, but his career took him away from his home to the capital, where he served as mufti and madrasa instructor. This rise from comparatively humble beginnings to the top ranks of the country's religious scholars (*'ulamā'*) meant that Ibnou Zakri lived his life between different identities. He was a colonial functionary, a scholar of the Islamic sciences, and a member of a rural family. Each of these roles came with a corresponding language: French, literary Arabic, and Berber. Of these languages and subject positions, Chachoua tells us that Ibnou Zakri felt most urgently the tensions between his upbringing in Kabylia and his Tamazight mother tongue and the elite world of Arabophone scholars in Algiers. He was proud of his home region but had to face urban stereotypes that saw it as a provincial outlier to the world of Islam and its high culture. During the colonial era in particular, Berber-speaking people in Algeria had to contend with those who saw them as eternal newcomers to the faith. French writers are best known for having spun the myth that Berbers were somehow exogenous to Islam, but Ibnou Zakri himself may have felt the prejudices of his fellow Muslims most immediately.[113] Ibnou Zakri existed, therefore, in what Chachoua has called a "trap" that cages many Kabyles even today who are considered (and consider themselves) "Berber by language but Arab by religion."[114] The ranks of Algiers' scholars were relatively open, but outsiders had to abide by norms centered on Arabo-Islamic orthodoxy and urban culture. Ibnou Zakri compensated for his rural origins and paucity of cultural and social capital (he had not gone abroad to study with prestigious teachers) with an excellent command of the Arabic language and an ability to write in a refined style that echoed that of the Qur'an. Nevertheless, in Algiers he felt "like a rustic in the city, a Bedouin in the medina, in short, an intruder," as Chachoua writes.[115]

In this context, Ibnou Zakri's original Tamazight name was a liability. What if he converted it to Arabic?[116] In his village, people knew Ibnou Zakri in Tamazight as "M'ḥend Saɛid," a common name in Kabylia that combines the diminutive, Berberized version of the Prophet's name with a Berberization of "Saʿīd," the Arabic name that comes from the word for the happy or fortunate one, as in *najm saʿīd*, or "lucky star."[117] Chachoua notes that Arabic speakers would have struggled to reproduce properly the Kabyle pronunciation of M'ḥend, or refused to do so. He also notes that a sticking point for Arabs, particularly scholars concerned with orthodoxy, would have been that this name deviated from the canonical form of the Prophet's name, using the shortened Berberized form, on one hand, and adding a second name, "Saɛid," on the other hand. This reflected a common Kabyle practice of adding a second given name to that of the Prophet, something that Arabic-speaking Algerians avoided. Thus, within the high standards of the urban scholars, Ibnou Zakri bore the "stigma" of his

Kabyle origins in his name itself. However, this stigma might be lifted when his name appeared in written Arabic. Arabic-language texts give Ibnou Zakri's full name as "al-Shaykh ibn Zakrī Muḥammad al-Sa'īd al-Zawāwī," as it appears in a side note to an authoritative Arabic-language biographical dictionary of religious scholars published in 1906.[118] Apart from the ism that doubled the Prophet's name with another, this name otherwise conforms to the norms of the classical Arabic name, with the title of a scholar ("al-Shaykh"), a nasab ("ibn Zakrī"), and a nisba referring to his Kabyle origins ("al-Zawāwī"). This conversion conveys Ibnou Zakri's assimilation to the Arabic-centric norms of his profession, as well as something of Arabic's capacity as a universal language for Muslims, here taking a name from a different language and seamlessly rendering it in Arabic, or so it seems. Ibnou Zakri freely used this Arabic name in his life, even on occasions when he might have used a different script or language. So when he signed the birth certificate of his son before a French civil servant in 1893, Ibnou Zakri choose to sign "Ibn Zakrī Muḥammad Sa'īd bin Aḥmad" in Arabic characters, even though his two witnesses, both Muslim Algerians, signed their names in French letters (as was common in these documents).[119] But not all parts of Ibnou Zakri's Berber name had Arabic equivalents, particularly his original genealogical name. Chachoua speculates that his Arabic nasab "Zakrī" actually came from a similar-sounding but different Berber word, such as "Aveskri." No matter the original name, Ibnou Zakri converted it to Zakrī to maximize cultural capital. In this sense it nicely bridged the two languages. More important, it suggested that Ibnou Zakri held a prestigious pedigree. Through this name, Ibnou Zakri implied that he descended from a famous fifteenth-century scholar from Tlemcen, who was also named "Ibn Zakrī" (Abū al-'Abbās Aḥmad b. Muḥammad b. Zakrī al-Maghrāwī al-Tilimsānī d. 1494).[120] In this manner, as Chachoua concludes, "Ibnou Zakri the Berber 'invented' ibn Zakri," his Arab self.[121]

Cultivating difference, Jewish names

North African Jews also used names both to bridge and to mark linguistic and social divides. Anthropologist Joëlle Bahloul writes that names "expressed the choice of Jews to fit into their local social context and within the forms of communication specific to their prevailing milieu."[122] Maghribi Jews thus continued a long-established practice of "naming like the neighbors" that historians trace to the Roman era.[123] Jewish names showed the same concern for piety, marking lineage, and elevating and protecting the named person as did the names of Muslims.[124] Many different languages influenced these names, including the Romance languages (Portuguese, Spanish, Italian) common to Sephardi names, along with Hebrew and Berber.[125] Arabic may have been the primary influence. An amateur scholar of Jewish studies working in Algeria in the 1930s estimated that 45 percent of Jewish family names had an Arabic origin, followed by names based on Romance languages at 17 percent.[126] Hebrew and Arabic are cognate languages facilitating the conversion of names.[127] For example, the Hebrew name "Hayyim" (life) coverts to "Ya'īsh" in Arabic; while "Halfon" (substitute) expresses itself in the Arabic "Khalfūn" or "Khalīfa" or "Makhlūf."[128] Along with these words that connected easily between the languages were the many biblical names of figures shared by Jews and Muslims, a list that runs literally from A (Ayūb/Iyov) to Z (Zakariyyā'/Zechariah).[129] For someone like Abraham Isaac Laredo (1895–1969), who wrote an important study of Maghrebi Jewish names, these did not represent *translations* of Jewish names into Arabic. Rather, he saw these names, taken from sources common to Abrahamic religions, as proper to both communities. Jews did not have to seek "either the assimilation or the translation of their names" to fit into Arabo-Islamic society.[130] In other cases, Jews simply adopted names from Arabic words.[131] In modern Tunisia, Jews and Muslims shared given names like "'Ashūr" and "Ṭāhir," as well as the surnames that later became family names, like "'Arīsh" (from *'arsh* or "tribe") and "Gharbī" ("Westerner" or Moroccan). Berber words also served Jews as names, such as "Amzalak"/"Amzallag," a family name that means "maker of necklaces/strings."[132] The Moroccan Jewish names studied by Laredo had multiple parts like the Arabo-Islamic name. This included a given "circumcision" or "cradle name"; the genealogical name of patrilineal descent marked by "ibn" or "bin"; and various surnames, reflecting professions and trades, as well as origins. Some prominent families bore a family name held in common, formed from any one of the typical surnames that functioned to reference the family's eponymous ancestor.[133]

Just as Jewish names bridged religious and ethnic divides with neighbors, they communicated the community's claims on the person as one of their own. In other words, while names linked Jews to Muslims, they did so in a way that marked boundaries. In this respect, personal names figured as part of larger strategy by which North African Jews "cultivated difference" from Muslims, as historians Abraham Udovitch and Lucette Valensi have argued based on their study of the Jewish community of Jerba (Tunisia) in the late 1970s.[134] The divide between communities had to be carefully drawn and continually redrawn to ensure that the lines stayed distinct. To the untrained eye, there was little to distinguish Jews and Muslims. When French colonial observers first considered the question, they dubbed Algerian Jews "Arabs of the Jewish Faith," an expression that historian Joshua Schreier adapted into a title for his book considering changing relations between Jews and Muslims during the early colonial period.[135] Precolonial Jews had been bound to rules separating Jews from Muslims in a legally subordinate position, but dress, speech, and social practices were strikingly similar, and it took an informed reading of the codes to reveal differences. Names provided guideposts. Predictably, Jews did not adopt the names of the high canonical Muslims, such as the Prophet Muḥammad, his famous companions, and the illustrious early Muslim women.[136] And in the case of shared names, pronunciations might mark divisions. For example, listening to the Jerban Jews, Udovitch and Valensi found that pronunciation provided the most common way that names parsed themselves: "A Brahem (Jewish) cannot be taken for an Ibrahim, nor a Mushi for a Musa, nor a Yushif for a Yousef."[137] Things might become tricky in writing, however: Written in Arabic letters, the names might appear identical. In some cases, devices might be inserted to resolve ambiguity. A telling example would be Jewish men named Ibrāhīm (Abraham).[138] Jews and Arabs both consider Ibrāhīm as their common progenitor, but with a separate lineage through his two sons: Ismāʿīl (Ishmael) is considered the father of the Arabs, and Isḥāq (Isaac) is understood to be the father of the Jews. To mark their own specific genealogy, some Jews named Ibrāhīm took the kunya "Abū Isḥāq." This did not mean that they themselves had a son named Isaac. Instead, this kunya functioned allegorically to reference the biblical father, who was in this case "Father of Isaac" and progenitor of the Jews. In this way, the kunya handily served Jews to mark their side of the Abrahamic family.

Jewish names divided themselves into different classes according to gender. Jewish girls had names that expressed their family's love, such as

"Mas'ūda" (fortunate) and "Ḥabība" (cherished). However, girls often received names based on vernacular languages, such as Judaeo-Arabic, whereas boys typically bore Hebrew names. As Bahloul explains these gendered divisions, "the sacralized and ritualized naming of boys could only be done in the sacred language."[139] In Laredo's work on Moroccan Jewish names, he gave examples of how names expressed prevalent attitudes about the gender composition of the family with the preference for boys. This could be expressed ironically. He recounts an anecdote about a baby girl named Faḍīnā (فضينا) born in Fez. One day, Laredo relates, a rabbi paid a visit to his friend on the occasion of a birth in the family, a baby girl who had not yet been named. Given that the family had many daughters, the rabbi "suggested to the parents that they name the newborn Faḍīnā."[140] "Faḍīnā" is a word with a double meaning: Its root in Arabic can mean either "conclusion," as in the last of, or the precious metal "silver," depending on the part of speech it occupies. As Laredo tells this story, a piece of onomastic folklore given in the form of a rabbi joke, the visiting rabbi put forward the first meaning, "conclusion," in his conversation with his friend. This name would "put an end to the prolific feminine tide and thus provoke the birth of boys" he promised.

While names could be tongue-in-cheek, this chapter shows that naming represented serious business. The precolonial Algerian name occupied a multidimensional symbolic space open to many different signifying practices and social interests, as it did in many societies before the modern era. Although religion was the dominate force shaping names, no one institution fully monopolized the name. It was a highly dialogized word, carrying the traces of many different cultures, languages, and interests. This is especially true of the name's acquired parts, surnames and nicknames, which changed according to both stance and circumstance. Even with respect to the given name or ism, there was an overlay of powers. While the family exercised the greatest amount of influence in choosing this name, the public ceremony ensured that it did not decide the name alone. Through the name, the family attested to its affiliation to the larger community by performing its norms faithfully. In this respect, one did not easily "make a name for oneself"; rather, names belonged to others. In this sense, the name did not reflect one's social position and identity in a static taxonomy, as much as it created them in a dynamic sociolinguistic situation involving many parties. In this context asking, "Tell me your name, and I'll tell you who you are," as the epigraph from novelist Makouta-Mboukou opening this chapter put it, was an open, dialogic, or "writerly" statement.[141] A name's meaning came only when read in relation to other names, and by negotiating the social values and cultural norms that expressed themselves within it. Names tied society together and made it intelligible to itself. For individuals named this way, the experience might have been different. Such a person certainly had occasion in their lives when they sought some symbolic control over their name and identity. The Kabyle Ibnou Zakri did this successfully as he negotiated his career as a scholar of Islam in colonial Algiers. However, the ever-changing name might have been maddening for others who bore it, as the Samuel Delany line from *Babel-17*, also opening this chapter, suggests. Called out in names decided by others, they might have asked themselves on any given day, "What name am I in?," as did Delany in his novel exploring the power of language.

When the French turned to the question of the Algerian name in the mid-nineteenth century, they did so with the aim of destroying this dynamic symbolic environment by establishing the French state's monopoly on the names of its colonized subjects. They did not intend to grant these people sovereignty over their name and identity, allowing them greater control. They did, however, try to "emancipate" the individuals from their families and society in the hopes of giving rise to actors who would better participate in a capitalist economy. The colonization of Algerian names aimed to make them transparent, easily decipherable, and useful to colonial law and administration. This meant fixing names according to French rules and interests, and then turning this newly monopolized sign into a tool. In these names, France attached Algerians to the colonial project, making them pay taxes, serve in the military, sell their land, and stand before French law. Inasmuch as this project was successful, which was not always the case, Algerians saw their names turned against them.

3

"Wherever the Flag Flies"

The État Civil in Algeria: Conquest and Sovereignty, 1780s–1830s

Among the many ways that France exerted its power in Algeria stands an easily overlooked politico-legal technology used to register vital events—births, deaths, marriages, and divorces. This registry is known in French as the *état civil*. At its core, the état civil calculates the individual political and legal subject. On one hand, this is the "ability to exercise rights guaranteed by civil law," or a person's civil status, which is how the term is typically translated into English.[1] And on the other hand, the état civil refers to the actual documents that produce this status, a modernized registry of vital statistics. This part of the état civil is made of volumes known as the matrix registers (*registres-matrices*), and they take hold of the person at birth and calculate that person's capacity to act within the law and how the law will act on them during the course of their life, based on sex, age, filiation, and marital status. Although the état civil enabled individual agency and decided a person's capacity to act in public life, it represented a vast array of symbolic powers that the modern French state monopolized and used toward its own ends. Normally, the power of the état civil was exercised only within French borders, but in the early nineteenth century it was mobilized to advance France's claims to people and even territory outside of the hexagon.

France's état civil had its forbearers in the early modern European parish register. These recorded major life events like baptisms, marriages, and deaths. In addition, they spelled out names in an official form (or the closest approximation of this at the time) and established a record of age and family relations. When combined, this information produced a distinct form of identity, more abstract and dependent on the written word than the previous forms based on lived face-to-face relations.[2] The earliest registers appeared in fourteenth-century Italy, where the clergy sporadically kept lists of baptisms. The Catholic Church formalized these practices during the Reformation, and Protestant pastors also started keeping records on their congregations, expanding the range of information in some cases to include levels of religious instruction.[3] In this sense, the parish registers fit into a process by which powerful institutions calculated populations, a practice that included surveys like the census.[4] As the sixteenth-century political theorist Jean Bodin wrote, the "most high, absolute, and perpetual power" of the sovereign depended on carefully calculating and ordering a state's human and material wealth and "disciplining and reprimanding the subject."[5] These same powerful institutions sought to define the individual and the family in their own terms. For example, the religious officials who initiated the registers used them to regulate marriage and shape the family's composition. Most importantly, the Catholic Church sought to enforce its prohibition against the marriage of kin and end privately celebrated "broomstick marriages."[6] States also used vital registries for the leverage they provided to transform social relations at the ground level, legally defining institutions like the family and who might belong to it. So too vital registries could be used to decide other forms of legal belonging, like who belonged to a national community and who did not.

The wide powers available in the vital registries made them a sovereign concern. In 1792 revolutionary lawmakers wrested control of the registries away from the Catholic Church and placed them entirely in the hands of the state.[7] They explained this move as asserting the prerogatives of the state vis à vis the church. As one politician debating the legislation put it, "the sovereignty of the nation was shamefully bent to the harness of priestly usurpation," referring to the previous era when church officials held responsibility for the registries.[8] The undivided power of the state was certainly at stake, but the état civil was not a simple matter of secularizing institutions and freeing the state from the church. The 6 sections and 103 articles of the état civil law (decree of 20 September 1792), consisting in large part of dull clerical procedures, served as a tool to restructure key social institutions so that they might better support a new form of politics and give life to popular sovereignty.[9] Nationalizing the vital registers threw into the air many pieces of a complex puzzle of interlocking social, legal, and political relations. Changing the ways that people registered vital events provided the opportunity to remake politics and society.

Historians of modern France have studied the état civil's role in the social and political upheavals caused when France moved toward a legal regime of codified laws and rights and a political system based on popular sovereignty. For example, Suzanne Desan showed how the état civil enabled fundamental changes to the family, like civil marriage and legalized divorce. She writes: "The seemingly mundane matter of how to record and regulate marriages in parish registers placed the matter of marriage squarely onto the agenda of the National and Legislative Assemblies."[10] Likewise, historians of popular sovereignty and citizenship like Gérard Noiriel have shown how revolutionaries looked to the état civil to distribute political rights, in effect creating the politically active citizen. The état civil then became the point of access into a sovereign nation. Noiriel writes that upon enrolling in the état civil, one "became a member of the civil community, just as baptism marked entry into the community of Christians."[11] Read from this angle, the lists of names, dates, and places in the registers served as so many signposts on the path toward the *sacré du citoyen*, an electoral body founding modern democracy.[12] Finally, there are historians like Joshua Cole who study the état civil's role in the nineteenth-century population sciences. Demographers and medical professionals gleaned numbers of births, marriages, and deaths from the registers and then compiled them into large sets of data. When doctors were called on to verify deaths for the état civil, as they were in some cases, they could record the causes of certain deaths, such as homicide and contagious disease, providing material to better understand life processes.[13] Cole's attention then centers on the état civil's biopolitical function.

> If the état civil gave the appearance of a commitment to an egalitarian individualism, the procedures for registering information about individuals in these records created the possibility of a new kind of aggregate thinking, based on distinctions of sex, age, profession, wealth, and regional identity. In other words, the principle of equality in membership, once established in the état civil, opened the way for population

> researchers to search for a new evaluation of every individual's function and value to society.[14]

Therefore, while the architects of the original état civil saw it as a way to empower individual citizens—linking "the citizen to the fatherland, and the fatherland to the citizen," as one lawmaker put it in 1792—Cole shows how it could simultaneously manage a population at large, a project stripped of democratic intent or emancipatory results.[15]

Public institutions relied on the état civil to function in this new era of civil society, but the état civil also operated beyond French borders. This chapter looks at how the état civil served the early contest for power in Algeria, where it did work not typically associated with vital records. As it happened, Napoléon had once proposed an imperious role for the état civil registries that went well beyond officializing names, recording dates of birth, and establishing family relationships. He sought to harness them to his army in its conquests. Napoléon's suggestion came in a meeting in 1801 of the committee that drafted France's new civil law, the Napoleonic Code, which was promulgated a few years later. The committee had to decide if the original legislation from 1792 sufficiently addressed how to handle the vital acts of troops stationed outside of France.[16] For the original lawmakers, the oversight was understandable. They approached their work primarily in terms of forging a French citizenry and establishing the secular state's normative monopoly on the family without much thought to how it might affect French men and women abroad. They gave even less attention to interstate relations and the fact that recording vital events became something of a sovereign act once the church lost its hold on the registers and their control fell exclusively to the state. Could French agents officiate over the births, deaths, and marriages of French citizens living in foreign countries without encroaching on local sovereignty? Did French people risk civil erasure at home if they recorded their vital acts with foreign authorities? How to maintain France's prerogative on its citizens when they crossed borders and made and remade their families in foreign lands beyond the reach of French law? By 1801 these questions could no longer be easily ignored. Most pressing was the fact that in addition to ordinary expatriates, France had troops waging war around the world. Along with their conquests, these soldiers married, had children, and died far from France. Although the French flag flew above the soldiers themselves, marking their side of the battlefield, the territory they occupied was often of uncertain status.

As Revolutionary-era France built a new empire, primarily in Europe, the government in Paris did not follow a consistent course concerning the politico-legal status of the territories and people that fell under its power. Some places were annexed outright based on ideas concerning France's "natural frontiers" or in acknowledgment of the expressed wishes of local people to join France.[17] These people became French, and their lands were annexed as French departments, as happened with Avignon (a papal enclave until 1790) and Nice, as well as larger territories like Belgium and the Rhineland. Such too was the fate of the Ionian Islands off the coast of Greece, which became noncontiguous parts of France as three departments in 1797.[18] In other cases, newly born revolutionary states might be embraced as "Sister Republics." These were allied to France but with their own constitutions that, while following the French example of government, did not formally cede their own sovereignty, as happened with the Batavian Republic in Holland in 1798.[19] Most of the countries that eventually made up the Grand Empire first formalized their status in this manner; however, their sovereignty eroded rapidly under the effects of French interference. This included French-fomented coup d'états and military interventions, which were often preceded by invitations from local leaders who sought to use French troops against their rivals. The practical realities of the system became clear when Napoleon callously divvied up thrones to his family members, negating previous arrangements. Outside of Europe in Ottoman Egypt, Bonaparte dispensed with even a veneer of legality when he invaded and militarily defeated the ruling Mamluks, leaving the country under an undefined form of military occupation between 1798 and 1801. The status of French authority wavered between some sort of expression of the sovereignty of the Egyptian people, whom Bonaparte claimed to liberate (without consulting their opinions), and that of the Ottoman Empire, whose interests in Egypt France improbably claimed to defend against the local Mamluk rulers.[20] All these arrangements upended existing models of deciding sovereignty over territory and people and pushed these questions into an indistinct, gray zone.

Despite the novelty of this era of revolutionary empire, one lawmaker (Antoine Thibaudeau) proposed simply extending the existing procedures used for French civilians living abroad. These followed the principle of *locus regit actum* (the place governs the act). Although French diplomatic personnel might officiate vital acts for their own subjects abroad, they typically left the task to the foreign authorities.[21] By constituting their acts under foreign law, French subjects living abroad deferred to this law's hold on them, which was in turn recognized by the French state, even as it did not relinquish its own sovereign claims on its nationals.[22] An oft-cited metaphor in the literature, coined in the eighteenth century, held that "the juridical act is a child, citizen of the place where it is born which must be dressed in the custom of its country."[23] By this measure, a vital act was bound to the law where it originated, but it could be "re-dressed" and made legally valid when it crossed borders. For example, a marriage act written for a French subject by Prussian authorities could be translated into French and used to establish the validity of this marriage back in France.[24] So too, foreigners in France could have access to French officials to constitute their vital acts for use in their home country thereby expressing the "solidarity" that sovereign states owed each other. Legal commentators typically explained this arrangement as an example of how French law accommodated itself to the complex ways in which people actually lived their lives.[25] But, most important, *locus regit actum* ensured that the movement of people did not threaten a state's sovereignty and prevented hollowing it out from within. It left existing state-to-state relations untroubled, maintaining the principle of reciprocity between states on which the existing European state system depended. The territoriality of the law and prevailing concept of sovereignty confirmed themselves in this arrangement. As one manual of civil law put it: "Having its roots in the soil, sovereignty [makes of] man nothing more than a sort of accessory [of itself]."[26] Governed by *locus regit actum*, vital acts could cross borders seamlessly, and they thereby contributed to the stability of the whole system rather than threatening it. By the end of the nineteenth century, legal commentators hailed this principle as a "maxim" of international law.[27]

Napoleon rejected this arrangement for the vital acts of his troops making war outside of France's own sovereign territory. In the civil code deliberations of 1801, he declared that "the soldier is never on foreign soil when he is under the flag: wherever the flag flies, there is France."[28] This extremely controversial statement, which implies that the act of military occupation liquidates the occupied state's sovereignty, requires some unpacking. Its origins lay in the notion of embassy exterritoriality, which had solved the problem of Reformation-era diplomacy, allowing diplomatic missions to practice their own faith within the embassy's chapel, shielded from the heresy laws in their host country.[29] Napoleon's comment implied extending this sovereign enclave to the barracks, the military camp, or even the battlefield, a dangerous innovation. "Wherever the flag flies" suggested that a state's sovereignty existed in a coterminous relationship with its army, accompanying it on its campaigns.[30] Invading armies do not exist in the same legal and political space as diplomats or ordinary people. Enjoying an effective monopoly of violence, occupying soldiers had the means to enforce public order, introduce new laws, or even bring their own laws with them and impose them on otherwise foreign lands and people.[31] An example of where this type of thinking can lead is found in an argument from 1866 in favor of consular extraterritoriality tellingly told in the relationship of violence and sovereignty:

> In all the foreign countries where they are established, consuls are armed with the right of police, and, in the Ottoman ports, with a right of jurisdiction on the French who reside in these countries. However, the right of police and the right of jurisdiction necessarily derive from the right of sovereignty, and sovereignty can only be exercised over territory. It must therefore be admitted that the consular residence, where the consul or the court sits and which the national flag protects, is considered as a portion of French territory where the laws and authority of France reign.[32]

The fact that this author referenced rules prevailing in the Ottoman Empire is not inconsequential, as I will discuss shortly. Within the context of the Napoleonic wars and the undecided status of conquered territory, this sort of thinking matched with "wherever the flag flies" to harness the état civil to conquest, using this ordinary administrative procedure to encroach on a defeated state's sovereignty and tip a military occupation toward territorial acquisition, freed from some of the burdens of the negotiations, treaties, constitutions, and the justifications that would have typically been necessary for territory to pass hands legitimately and be accepted by other states.[33] Simply recording soldiers' vital acts in occupied lands, the French state acted as if these lands were part of France. To express this in Napoleon's own language, the emperor could look out from under the French flag, his soldier's bayonets, and the open pages of the état civil registers and say, "There is France."

Napoleon made his totalizing "wherever the flag flies" claim within the context of a rather (judging by the minutes) mundane moment within a committee meeting devoted to hammering out civil law. In this context, it might be read as a hyperbolic assertion blurted out by a man out of his concerns for the legal well-being of his soldiers, such as the need to record their deaths within the chaos of battle so that surviving families benefitted from the full protection of the law. Fears about French soldiers entering into private marriages with local women, leaving behind wives and children in France, might also have motivated the issue.[34] Ultimately, the drafters of the Napoleonic Code chose a mixed response. They affirmed *locus regit actum* for civilians residing abroad declaring plainly: "Any act of the état civil for French people as well as foreigners concluded in a foreign country will be valid, if it was written in the prevailing forms of that country" (art. 47).[35] However, in a less clearly worded article, the code reserved the possibility for French consular officials to act as an agent of the état civil in their posts abroad, effectively breaking with the *locus regit actum* principle (art. 48).[36] Moreover and most important, it granted the military the right to use its own agents to record the vital acts of French soldiers (and accompanying civilian agents) outside of French territory, as Napoleon had requested.[37]

The implications of "wherever the flag flies" should not be overlooked, even if those sitting in on the meeting with Napoleon on that day in 1801 seemed to have done so. While it fit into the soon-to-be emperor's general indifference to legality in building his empire, subsequent French legal scholars revisited this episode decades later and eyed it with horror.[38] Writing in the aftermath of the Franco-Prussian War, in which France lost significant territories annexed to Germany, one French jurist denounced Napoleon's understanding as extremely dangerous to international law:

> We rely on the fiction that the State, as a juridical person, as a metaphysical being, moves with its army, or, as Napoleon expressed it, on the fact that: "The soldier is never on foreign soil when he is under the flag: wherever the flag flies, there is France." But this is only a fiction, and it is impossible to draw juridical lessons from it. Because if one must consider that the army is always and everywhere a representative of the State, it does not follow that the laws designed for the interior of the country must be equally applied abroad. Such an extension can only happen through the legal sanction of positive law.[39]

Like-minded French scholars also rejected Napoleon's comment as a menace to the principle of territorial sovereignty.[40] Writing in 1870, another French jurist used the blunt force of civilization or barbarism rhetoric to denounce the "wherever the flag flies" principle, which risked, he wrote, bringing the world "back to the savage barbarism of the Huns and the Mongols."[41] Indeed, only German writers stepped forward at this time to defend Napoleon's precedent.[42]

It is useful to recall that all this occurred at a time when norms and principles surrounding war making and conquests underwent a significant reconsideration. Even as French troops swept across Europe, the Middle East, and the Caribbean during the Revolution, their actions stood contrary to emerging ideals, which frowned on wars of territorial expansion.[43] Five years before Immanuel Kant penned his seminal essay *Perpetual Peace*, the French government issued the decree of 22 May 1790, known as the "Declaration of Peace to the World." Often forgotten by historians of French empire in light of what followed, it stated: "The French nation renounces the undertaking of any wars aimed at conquest, and will never employ its forces against the liberty of any people."[44] The declaration, subsequently incorporated into the constitution of 1791, did not exactly mean that France had abandoned war, nor that it limited itself to defensive wars. Rather, it held that war making rightly belonged to the people, not monarchs, and that the people would use war virtuously as tool of emancipation rather than domination and aggression. Waged in solidarity across borders, a people's war targeted tyrants in order to emancipate their oppressed subjects, who could then realize their vocation as a sovereign nation. Briefly, French armies would no longer "conquer," they would "liberate."[45] Those who continued the old project of empire as domination and conquest had to square it with the new principles or simply blur the facts.

The beginning of the état civil in Algeria

While the registers of the état civil never became weapons of conquest in their own right, the "wherever the flag flies" episode shows up the stakes when the état civil functioned abroad where it might erode local sovereignty. A look at the history of the first decade of the état civil in Algeria shows how Napoleon's logic realized itself. If the act of conferring names serves to claim power in the classic models sketched in the first chapter of this book (and withholding them obscured these claims, as in the case of France's "possessions" in North Africa), then the personal names inscribed in the état civil might be understood as a different modality of the same process of symbolic conquest. Officiating vital acts represented a sovereign prerogative, particularly viewed from the French side, even if the registers themselves might appear as a less dramatic order of sovereignty than a coronation, the signing of treaty, or even an execution.[46]

France's état civil in Algeria built itself on a vital records system that predated the conquest in 1830, with the extant records going back at least to the early eighteenth century. Well before French soldiers planted their flag above Algiers, vital registries served as the "guardian of social relations" of French men, women, and children living in this North African port, as they did in France.[47] Until the secularization of vital records in 1792, the responsibility for keeping the French registries fell to the local clergy. Algiers had been home to an apostolic vicariate since the seventeenth century, and Catholic authorities kept records that they shared with the French king's consul for the government's use. French men and women living in Algiers appear in the registers when they died or gave birth to children.[48] For example, on 4 January 1782 a baby boy named Jean Louis Vanture was baptized by a local priest, having been born to Anne Chais, a woman "of the French nation," and an undeclared father.[49] The child soon died, and church officials recorded his burial in the local Christian cemetery. Many of the entries concerned French captives, people held as slaves across Algeria and other northwestern African ports in the corsair campaigns of the early modern era.[50] The heyday of corsair activity came in the late sixteenth and seventeen centuries, but it remained ongoing throughout the eighteenth century, with the warring sides changing frequently depending on diplomatic arrangements and the whims of the corsairs themselves. The Vanture baby was brought to the priests for baptism by an enslaved Frenchman named Claude Véroelé, and he and another French captive witnessed the baby's burial a week later. Even though dwindling numbers of French men and women were held in Algeria as slaves by the latter half of the eighteenth century, some were still plucked from the high seas by Algerian corsairs or otherwise found themselves in Algiers and denied their freedom. Apostolic records keepers also recorded the adult baptisms of French Protestants who chose to convert to Catholicism.

This was the case in 1782 for three Protestant captives originally from the reformed community near Nîmes in southern France. After multiple years in Algiers, they were all baptized by the pro-vicar on 14 July 1782.[51] It is likely that these people saw conversion as a way to freedom. Louis XVI was putting together plans to ransom French slaves at the time, after decades of indifference to their fate.[52] While he did not end up excluding people based on their faith, earlier repatriation campaigns had barred Protestants, and the converts of 1782 might have seen the advantages of moving into the arms of the Catholic Church in Algiers to ensure their return home. Sometime after passage of the 1792 secular état civil law, Catholic officials relinquished the registries to France's consul in Algiers. Along with the French citizens appearing in the registers are people who worked in the consulates of other European states, such as those in the Low Countries and the Italian states. The état civil did not decide a person's nationality in itself, and the French registers in Algiers were not closed to foreigners. The consul's recordkeeping work was not heavy at this time. In the 1810s and 1820s there were only a few acts recorded each year, and in some years none at all.[53]

France was not the only country keeping records in Algeria. Ottoman officials, along with Algerian religious and legal authorities, presided over some vital acts, and while others emerged out of unofficiated verbal agreements that had the force of law. They were made known through witnesses, as or through many other sorts of formal and informal practices such as marriage contracts and funerals, or in the baby-naming ceremonies discussed in chapter 2. So, there was not a single state or religious office that officialized vital acts where foreigners might go to register their live events on the model of *locus regit actum*, even if Algeria had a system of vital records, contrary to colonial-era claims that society lived in civil anarchy before the France introduced the état civil.

However, the rules for vital acts and their relationship to sovereignty were different in Algiers than in Europe. When the French consul recorded vital events, he did so with the acquiescence of the Algerian deylik, according to special legal powers the consul enjoyed under bilateral treaties signed between the French and Algerian governments, as well as separate agreements between France and the Ottoman Empire. This speaks to the varied understandings of vital acts and sovereignty. Ottoman political and legal concepts did not converge neatly with the territorial model of sovereignty that France came to take as the norm, nor did Ottomans have the same understanding of legal subjectivity and jurisdiction.[54] In schematic terms, one can say that Ottoman law attached itself to people as much as territory. It calculated jurisdiction not according to which side of a border one stood on but rather on the religion of the concerned party and other measures determining community. This yielded many different legal domains within the sultan's single sovereign field of power.[55] For their part, European foreigners in Ottoman territories benefitted from this pluralism in an extraterritorial legal regime known as the capitulations. In general, European subjects living in Ottoman lands could not be prosecuted in Ottoman courts for criminal matters or brought before them for civil disputes. Instead, legal powers in their cases devolved to European diplomats who operated their own consular courts.

This system provided the basis for the French consul's jurisdiction over vital events in precolonial Algiers. Compared to Europe's *locus regit actum* model, these extraterritorial powers might appear to have let the French flag cast a longer shadow in the Muslim Mediterranean than in Europe.[56] And indeed, by the late nineteenth century this is how the consular powers worked, when they became an "effective stalking horse for imperialism," as one historian has noted.[57] In precolonial Algeria, however, the dey did not see his government's prerogatives compromised when the French consuls or Catholic clergy presided at baptisms, marriages, and funerals, even though these events occurred on his territory.[58] Even if foreigners put down roots in Algeria through such acts, this arrangement ensured that they remained outsiders, safely enclaved from Ottoman law by their own exceptional status.[59] Moreover, when push came to shove, the dey could encroach on French jurisdiction himself. For example, when France found itself weakened by the revolutionary wars of the 1790s, the dey forced the consul to defer to him in many legal matters concerning French citizens residing in Algeria, cases where consular courts should have had authority. He influenced cases like those of the émigrés who had fled revolutionary justice in France to his protection.[60] Overall, then, while the French consul exercised great powers in keeping the vital registers, these powers were bracketed by the capitulations regime itself and how it made French residents legally exogenous to Algeria. In other words, a "wherever the flag flies"-style affront to Ottoman sovereignty was not possible as long as the état civil registers remained within the confines of the French consulate, whose very presence in Algiers stood as a sign of France's recognition of the dey's authority and the good relations existing between the two countries. And of course, the état civil was no threat as long as France did not have an army there.

The war that precipitated France's invasion of Algeria first broke out in 1827, nominally sparked by a diplomatic incident regarding debts France owed the deylik. At this time the French consul shuttered his office and left Algiers. When French troops victoriously entered Algiers and deposed the dey in 1830, a new consul accompanied the troops and reopened the diplomatic mission.[61] This odd posting spoke volumes about France's unsure status in Algeria in 1830. Normally a consul served as the French government's representative to a foreign government, but Algeria no longer had a government that France recognized in any meaningful sense. The dey had surrendered, and the French forced him to leave the country without a replacement, but no treaty decided Algeria's status, as normally would have been necessary to transfer sovereignty.[62] Even in a formal sense, France did not assert a claim to exclusive and permanent authority in Algeria until 1834, and this was tentative, as discussed in chapter 1. No international congress decided France's claims, nor did the Ottoman Empire concede its own rights in Algeria to France.[63] Prussia and Russia had previously acquiesced to Charles X, when the last Bourbon king originally announced his intentions to invade Algiers (and they did not require precise clarification of what would happen next); however, the Bourbon king fell in the Revolution of 1830, a few weeks after his victory across the Mediterranean. Moreover, Britain stood resolutely opposed any lasting French designs in Algeria under any government.[64] Already in March 1830, months before French troops landed, British authorities summoned the French ambassador in London to explain Paris's goals, and they made clear they would not accept a "war of extermination founded on the debris of Algiers's government."[65] In other words, Britain would not tolerate a war of conquest or regime change.

The Ottoman Empire had largely been excluded from the international order at the Congress of Vienna in 1815, leaving it isolated with regard to the Algerian–French war.[66] The relationship of Istanbul with Algiers had evolved significantly from the early sixteenth century when the central Maghrib originally entered into the Ottoman Empire. Like leaders in Ottoman Tunisia, Tripoli, and Egypt, Algeria's governors, or deys, enjoyed a great deal of autonomy, namely, in their ability to conduct foreign relations in the western Mediterranean. But Algeria was a valuable part of the empire that the sultans would not abandon, even if they did not go to war with France to defend it.[67] The Ottoman government had opposed the various plans offered by France in the lead-up to the invasion in 1830, plans that included Muhammad Ali of Egypt invading Algeria and ruling the country on his own. Instead, Istanbul had tried to negotiate a solution to the crisis between France and the dey, sending an envoy to the region, efforts that the French government rebuffed and blocked. Subsequent Ottoman initiatives also failed, with one Ottoman diplomat writing in exasperation of the general indifference of the great powers toward the violence of the French conquest that if "the European states are not caring about the sins committed [by France] in Algiers, . . . [it is] because they do not see [the Muslims] as humans," a prophetic observation uncovered in the research of historian Ozan Ozavci.[68] Ottoman refusal to officially accede to French rule in Algeria remained a persistent feature of French–Ottoman relations in the 1830s and beyond.

In the absence of a consensus and a formal agreement among the leading powers, France's aspirations faced a looming question mark as far as the international order was concerned.[69] Also weighing in were France's domestic political upheavals caused by the Revolution of July 1830. Revolutionaries severed the Bourbon royal line, placing a new king on the throne, Louis-Philippe, duc d'Orleans, whose own father had voted with radicals to behead Louis XVI in 1793. Taking the crown offered to him by revolutionaries in August 1830, Louis-Philippe had to sort out carefully what to do with the French army in northern Africa and the victories of its generals, many of whom had been appointed by Charles X.[70]

In short, the French government could not just declare victory in Algeria and unilaterally announce its claims on this land and its people. Even if it was obvious that France had serious and lasting designs here, a minimum of discretion remained important among French planners lest unforeseen events lead to their country's isolation. Revealing of this concern is the onomastics record discussed in the first chapter of this book: Although the king claimed quasi-sovereign powers in Algeria in 1834, he stopped well short of giving a name to it, using instead the moniker, "*possessions françaises dans le nord de l'Afrique*," These common words could not properly name French Algeria nor announce France's claims to the rest of the world.

In this context, the état civil provided a tool for France to begin attaching Algeria to itself. The état civil served the conquest by both appropriating sovereign rights over the officialization of vital acts and binding a select group of people living in Algeria to French law and authority. The état civil rooted French law in Algeria through its very operation once the dey had left the country, and with the unshared prerogatives it claimed over certain legal subjects. In 1834 France abolished the capitulations of all countries in Algeria, ending any sharing of legal powers with other European governments.[71] Algerians still had recourse to their own codes to decide the civil cases through their own courts decided by their separate personal status (Jews and Muslims), but French law stood as superior, and the king established his prerogatives over the local confessional courts. The sovereign right to kill and to pardon was placed in the hands of the French king and the head of the French army in Algeria.[72]

Colonization and the état civil

The état civil worked itself into lives of people in Algeria subtly and at different paces for different groups. It opened its registries widely to those whom it identified as a privileged part of the colonial project; tolerated the inclusion of some; and excluded others outright. As it did in France, the état civil could parse the individual legal subject according to sex, age, and marital status, but in Algeria registries also classified people according to religious, ethnic, and national groups. As I will discuss, some people were allowed to enter the registers only as racialized subjects of greatest interest when they died, with administrators using the état civil as a source of demographic data to calculate the successes and failures of colonization's population goals.

These factors can be seen in looking at the implementation of the état civil in the capital of Algiers and in the eastern port city of Bône (Būna, today's Annaba). In the first six months of the occupation of Algiers, the city's vital registers were kept according to the system used under the deys. This setup was abolished by a decree issued by the occupying military authority on 7 December 1830, which shifted responsibility for the registers from the consul to a newly established office of royal commissioner. The royal commissioner served as the *officier de l'état civil*, recording births, deaths, and marriages in the vital registers.[73] Most significantly, the move announced that the role of a French consul had become superfluous. With France's victory over the dey and his expulsion from the country, Algeria was not foreign land. Its relations with France no longer had to pass through the Ministry of Foreign Affairs and the consul. The new royal commissioner performed vital acts, verifying deaths and births and officiating at marriage ceremonies (including those of soldiers). He kept the registers for French civilians living in the city and delivered copies (*extraits*) from them when people needed proof for legal or administrative purposes. By the next year, some of the acts began appearing in the pages of the quasi-official French newspaper in Algeria, *Le Moniteur algérien*, printed alongside the laws and decrees by which France expanded and officialized its hold on the country. This included the marriage that joined Jean-Stanislas Grégoire, forty-two years old, a musician in the French army, and Françoise-Catherine-Virginie Perez, twenty-one years old, a seamstress living in Algiers.[74] Appearing under the headline "Legal and Judicial Publications" on 10 April 1832, this marriage stands as a milestone of sorts, the first published act of colonial Algeria's état civil.[75] By midcentury, when France's claims were more or less assured, a decree fully regularized the état civil in Algeria, implementing the invaluable ten-year alphabetical tables so that the records could be used with the same ease and in "the same manner as in France," as one legal manual put it.[76]

Many European civilians accompanied French troops or already lived in Algiers, and not all of them were French.[77] France's abolition of the capitulations in 1834 meant these people no longer had access to their country's consular courts: All civil matters concerning people from other parts of Europe, mainly Italians, as well as people from Malta and Spain, had to be judged in French courts.[78] While foreigners might use their own country's documents with the French officials according to the reciprocity of *locus regit actum*, the only place left in Algeria to officiate new vital acts in most cases was now the état civil officer. Even before the capitulations officially ended, foreigners recorded their births and celebrated their marriages under French officials according to French law.[79] For example, on 10 October 1833 Enrico Giovanné, a Sardinian national who worked in a French military hospital, presented himself with his newborn daughter to register her birth. The man's wife, Catharina Pallicière, had given birth to the child the day before, and the couple named her Henriette Marguerite.[80]

Earlier the same month Octavio Caprioli, a domestic servant from Milan and a subject of the Kingdom of Lombardy-Venetia, recorded the arrival of a son, Joseph Charles, born to him and Marianna Angioli.[81] While foreigners started reporting their newborns to French officials quite early, it was some time before they officialized their marriages, the most consequential act of the état civil. Recording a marriage in the état civil meant that it was contracted by the terms of the French civil code, requiring that in most cases the couple would have to abide by its prescriptions, including those concerning inheritance, the ban on divorce, and matrimonial rights. In other words, foreigners living in Algeria would have to submit to the normative provisions of France's civil law and its vision of the family, even though they were not French nor living in France itself. To ensure that all parties understood the contractual nature of marriage, passages of the French civil code were read aloud at the ceremony. For example, a couple from Malta who married in Algiers on 26 September 1835 listened, along with their four witnesses, as title 5, chapter 6, of the civil code was read aloud. This section stated fatefully that a woman lost her capacities as an autonomous legal agent to her husband upon marriage, as well as giving him the authority to manage her property.[82] Language posed a problem in some cases. Neither the groom, Joseph Aquilina, who was born in 1811 in the Maltese capital, Valletta, nor the bride, Magdelaine Bartolo, born in 1815 in Cospicua, had sufficient capacities in the French language to understand the text. Therefore, an interpreter translated it into Arabic, the language closest to their own mother tongue, so that that they could enter knowingly into the terms of French civil law. Couples of mixed nationalities also contracted their marriages under French law. This was the case with Ambrosio Laguerra, a sailor from Genoa, and Marie Joséphine Victoire Bénavente, a subject of the Spanish monarchy from Cordoba, whom a French official married on 28 January 1835, this time without the services of a translator, as presumably someone in the marriage party could translate the French, or the couple themselves understood the language.[83]

In all these cases, people who were not French became tied more closely to France. Having a French état civil did not have an immediate impact on one's nationality; however, it did serve to better assimilate one's legal subjectivity to French law. In practical terms, life in Algiers would be facilitated for those couples who could produce a French marriage certificate in their encounters with the authorities.[84] This might have served a more immediate purpose for the Italian sailor, Laguerra, mentioned above. He was born in the last years of the Republic of Genoa's existence, a state that disappeared in the Ligurian Republic and was not revived at the Congress of Vienna. While being stateless at this time did not carry the immense risks that it would in the twentieth century, not having a nationality had consequences. A document like a French marriage certificate would help place Laguerra on what historian Jessica Marglin has aptly called a "spectrum of legal belonging" that took shape in the complex political and legal terrain of the nineteenth-century Mediterranean.[85]

Colonial names: Becoming French in Algeria

The names foreigners chose for their children sometimes signaled a desire to assimilate to France in a cultural sense. This history echoes the sort of onomastic choices seen in chapter 2, dealing with Tamazight, Arabic, and Judeo-Arabic names, and the topic is worth revisiting here in regard to Euro-French names and their crossings between languages. Many Europeans in Algiers who were not French conferred French *prénoms* on their newborns. These include the cases of the Italian babies mentioned earlier, Henriette Marguerite and Joseph Charles, who carried two sets of solidly French names, among many other examples in the registers. This practice is common among people traversing political and cultural boundaries, but it had its own iterations at this time that reflect the particular linguistic and onomastic contests of French empire in the entire Mediterranean region. Examples include the people who accompanied Napoleon's army returning from Egypt in 1801. Forming a community of about a thousand people, most of them initially settled in Marseille. These new arrivals to France regularly registered their vital acts in Marseille's état civil from the 1790s to 1830, a strong signal of their plans to stay. They stand out in the documents in their distinctive names, which adopted a latinized Arabic name for the patronym while using something more conventionally French for the child's given name. Beyond the easy equivalences that Frenchified an Arabic name, such as "Joseph" or "Marie," both of which could be converted to French from the Arabic "Yūsūf" or "Mariyam," they also chose French names without clear Arabic equivalences, such as "Françoise" or

"Laurent."[86] These Francocentric names effectively curtailed the possibilities for these people to live across languages: "Françoise" could be converted to Arabic script, but it could not be translated by finding an equivalent in Arabic. Some of these eastern Mediterranean peoples went from Marseille to work in Algeria, accompanying the French military administration as translators. One of them was the Cairo-born interpreter Joanny Pharaon, who was part of the Pharaon dynasty of interpreters and Arabists. The fact that the family, originating in Damascus, were Melkite Christians facilitated their assimilation to French society, as did their ambitions, which converged with new opportunities as France's interests increased across the Arabic-speaking world.[87] In 1825 Joanny married Thérèse Eyriès, from a family that included an important geographer, a union that facilitated his assimilation.[88] But his was not a seamless story of becoming French, nor one without ambivalences on his part. Having moved with his wife to Algiers, Pharaon declared the birth of a son in April 1833, naming the child with a four-part given name, Marie Joanny Charles Faruq.[89] This name did not last long. Once he had seen it written into the record and heard it pronounced by a French registrar, Pharaon had second thoughts about "Faruq," the last given name. This high-standing, Arabic name (Fārūq), meaning one who can distinguish truth from falsehood, is struck through in the état civil record. In its place stands a corrected new name, "Shiré," which appears in the marginal notes reserved for corrections, alongside Pharaon's signature and that of the other witnesses officializing the change. The name is an adaption of Pharaon's mother's name, Chéhiré, which is a French spelling of an Arabic name, Shahira, meaning well-known or famous. The Arabic origins of "Chéhiré" concealed themselves well in French, where it pronounced itself easily, much more seamlessly than obviously foreign "Faruq," with its hard to pronounce final throaty *qaf*. (In the twentieth century the name Chéhiré even made its way into the standard reference for French names, the venerable Dauzat guide, before subsequent editors found the error and removed the name.[90]) Pharaon's own names had been Gallicized in equally revealing ways. The shared family name Pharaon was "Fir'awn" in Arabic, the word for Pharaoh. As the large family branched out around the world in its nineteenth- and twentieth-century migrations, they adapted its spelling to the languages where they settled.[91] Joanny's given name, what would have been his ism in an Arabic name, was "Yaḥunā," the same name as "John" in English. But rather than using the French equivalent, "Jean," someone—either his family, a French administrator, or Joanny himself—adopted "Joanny," which was the diminutive form of "Jean" in spoken French. While Joanny Pharaon risked being infantilized by this name as an adult, he might have found it attractive because its first two syllables echo "Yaḥunā's" Arabic pronunciation. In this way, it served nicely as a crossover name, or one that stood at the threshold between two languages.[92] In sum, Pharaon, the interpreter, knew well how one word could hide behind another. The meaning of such a word could conceal itself in sounds and letters, revealing itself only to those who, like himself, could read the expertly hidden story.

European settlers also brought old names that took on new resonances within the symbolic contests of French colonialism. Even if they do not reveal the same sort of esoteric plays on meaning and identity as the Pharaon case, they can be read as markers of the ups and downs of the colonial project itself. For example, on 27 November 1830 a girl was born to a Spanish mother, Maria Rosario Borgos, who had come to Algiers from Cadiz to open an inn along with her French husband, Joseph Thon.[93] The couple named their child "Louise Elisabeth Africa" and recorded her birth in the état civil, with a French army surgeon standing by as one of the witnesses. While "Africa" did not become a popular name among the settlers in Algeria, those from Spain occasionally used it to name their girls.[94] Names join people to places, and places to people. The Thon baby was only the third child with French nationality born in Algiers since the invasion, meaning that her christening inevitably took a political significance, standing as a measure of this family's connection to their new home, and this child's place as one of the first Algerian-born settlers.[95] However, neither the child nor her name lasted long. Dying in 1832 at less than two years of age, she went to her grave deprived of her Africa name, which her father failed to report among her *prénoms* when he declared her death. Her parents had spent two years caring for this child in this new place, a Mediterranean port that was like and yet so different from their previous home in Europe. In the end, Africa was not a fruitful place for the family. The couple never had another child in Algeria. Judging by their own disappearance in the civil registries, they left the country shortly after the death of their child, never to return.[96] If the names recorded in the état civil stood as an expression of French sovereignty in Algeria and gave a record of the rooting of French colonialism in its births and marriages, they also told stories of its many failures.

Jews and Muslims in the first registers

While recording the vital acts of settlers helped assimilate Europeans to France and French colonialism, a different politico-administrative environment faced Algerians Jews and Muslims. In the 1830s these people did not have a clear legal status. In effect, French law viewed Algerians as foreigners in their own country. Normally—that is to say in France's European territories—civil law and much of its regime of rights extended to foreigners living in the country. The principle of state-to-state reciprocity ensured liberal access to French law.[97] This posed a problem for the Algerians. While non-French Europeans made their way easily enough into France's civil law and the regime of rights based on reciprocity, Algerians had no government representing them that France recognized. The Ottoman Empire still claimed them as their subjects, but Algerians would have to travel outside of their country for this recognition to have any effect, meaning they could become Ottoman subjects in Egypt or the Hijaz, for example. Within an Algeria controlled by France, Algerians were essentially stateless at this time.[98]

This state-centered perspective on the question of rights provides a slightly different understanding of Algerian disenfranchisement than typically used by historians looking at political, cultural, and economic factors. It highlights the stakes of state erasure even at the very beginning of the modern era. Algerians maintained a separate and diminished civil status based on confession, what was known as their personal status (*statut personnel*). This downgraded the legal importance of the état civil for them. They were not French, nor did most French civil law apply to them. Decisions regarding the most urgent issues, such as formalizing and publicizing family relationships and managing inheritance, were made by Jewish and Muslim authorities using their own laws, categories, and norms, along with the formal and informal public practices used by lay people.[99]

Some adapted to the new situation, using the vital registers as a tool to make a way forward for themselves. The decree of 1830 that regularized the état civil's procedures did not formally forbid Algerian enrollment, nor did it require it. While no rules demanded it, the names of some Algerians appear in the earliest état civil records. The Jewish community of Algiers in particular appears frequently in the registers, having started declaring their births, marriages, and deaths to French authorities in the mid-1830s. For example, a father who appears in French records as David Filus, who worked as jeweler in Algiers, registered the birth of his son, Isaac, with the royal commissioner in 1834. The spelling of this man's name and the fact that his wife, Rosine Calfon Aboccaja, had a family name more common to Tuscan Jews, suggests that their families were of European origin, although they might have lived for generations in northern Africa. Nevertheless, he went into the état marked as "Algerian" by the recording officer, making this record one of the earliest appearances of Algiers's Jewish community in the état civil. It also shows how the état civil defined and reified the boundaries of communities and confessional law regimes, based on its own categories.[100] Over the next few years, Jews appeared regularly in the état civil. Their acts were sometimes included in the registries' pages alongside those of French people, and sometimes they were placed in a separate section devoted exclusively to Jews, making them easier to identify and calculate as a distinct population. In 1838 the Jews of Algiers recorded a total of 261 births, whereas Europeans recorded 429 births in that year.[101] (For reference, the total population of Algiers was figured at 26,000 people at this time, split between 6,100 Jews, 7,600 Europeans, and 12,300 Muslims.[102])

Why did Jews in Algiers choose to report the births of their children? The sources do not give a clear answer. Like the Italian settlers, they may have decided that having names and family relationships that were understandable to the colonial administration along with a legal subjectivity assimilable to French norms were important ways to manage their place in the new regime. Property owners in particular had an immediate incentive to clarify themselves to French law through the état civil to protect their holdings from the sudden upheavals to property law and its submission to French interests, which occurred almost immediately with the arrival of French soldiers. The people of Algiers had to negotiate a complex campaign of title verification with immense stakes. Failure to produce a "proper" title placed owners at risk of having their holdings appropriated by the French state. Unsurprisingly, the problem of incommensurability and the lack of equivalences between the French and Algerian systems of property tenure and identity worked against local people, as historians Isabelle Grangaud and François Dumasy have shown.[103] Entering into a Eurocentric regime of "propertied abstractions," a problem confronted by colonized people the world over, was facilitated in Algeria by having an official name and family relations recorded in the master registers.[104] Jewish authorities recognized this fact. Well before Algerian Jews ascended to French citizenship with the Cremieux Decree in 1870, their leaders encouraged their community to register in the état civil.[105]

And yet, many of the Algerian Jews who first recorded their vital acts had little property and occupied humble stations in life, leaving few obvious material incentives to explain their decision. Moreover, it took a lot of work for these people to enter the état civil. And when they went before French authorities for acts like marriages, they exposed themselves to risks given the French laws governing marriage.[106] For example, in 1836 Messaouda Tabet, a sixteen-year-old daughter of a peddler, came before the état civil officer to marry Joseph Zeraffa, a twenty-year-old fishmonger. Although they came from working-class society, the couple and their families had invested much planning, time, and effort preparing the necessary paperwork for French authorities. This included documentary proof of the couple's births, including their ages and names, as well as the ages and names of the four parents, along with death certificates for the two parents who had previously passed away. In all, this represented a substantial dossier of documents. Many questions certainly came to their mind; perhaps the most important was: Why did they have to put on French papers what everyone in the community already knew? The grand rabbi of Algiers stepped in to draft some of the necessary documents in the form of affidavits, which the municipal interpreter translated into French. Without this assistance, it would have been impossible for the couple to marry before French officials: Neither the bride, the groom, nor his mother (who had to represent her son because he was not yet of the age of majority) could write or read.[107]

After completing their file, the couple went before the officer of the état civil for the ceremony. They heard the relevant passages of civil code read to them. As was the case with the Maltese couple discussed earlier, an interpreter converted the relevant passages of French civil code into Arabic so that all parties understood. Verbally expressing their consent, this couple had completed a French civil marriage. It is not clear what this new-style marriage entailed for the couple over the long run, nor what they hoped to gain by going before French authorities. Unlike the European foreigners who married according to the French civil code, Jews normally would have been subject to the terms of mosaic law according to their separate personal status.[108] Nevertheless, a French civil marriage obscured the separate legal spheres of personal status based on confession, and it came with significant liabilities. In 1836 the exact boundaries of jurisdictions had not revealed themselves, and French jurists debated the question of the ipso facto application of the French civil code in cases of the civil marriage of Algerian Jews through to the 1860s.[109] The fact that the French code forbade divorce at this time, which many Algerians, Muslims and Jews alike, saw as an essential fail-safe against barren marriages, would have been especially worrisome for the Tabet and Zeraffa families.[110]

Algerian Muslims faced a different relationship to the état civil at this stage, albeit one that reveals itself with difficulty. I have not found a single Muslim appearing in Algiers's état civil in records from the 1830s available to me. This leaves the historian with a dog-that-didn't-bark problem: Is this absence itself a significant fact? Although Muslims in the capital had nearly identical social and economic interests as Jews with regard to protecting their property, they were distinct by history, culture, and religion. Politically and economically, they were far and away Algiers's largest and most consequential community. It may have been that the French registers were deliberately closed to them, reflecting beliefs among officials that they were not assimilable (while Jews might be), or the city's Muslims themselves may have kept their family acts off the books and steered clear of the French administration as much as possible. It might also have been a question of available sources, with the registers of Algiers's Muslims recoded in separate volumes (like some of the registries of Algiers's Jews) that have been lost or are unavailable.[111] The idea that Muslims refused registration favors an explanation based on Algerian resistance. It is difficult to explain, however, how not a single person broke ranks based on their own particular situation, as did many in the years ahead, people who individually chose to register the vital acts of their family well before an

1882 law made it mandatory. Indeed, at the end of the century, many Algerians would come to see opportunities to leverage French institutions for their own purposes.

Death and race in Bône's état civil

While Muslims do not appear in the état civil in Algiers in the 1830s, they do in other cities. The particular way that registrars recorded them in these cases signals another role for the état civil. Indeed, the special attention they gave to the racial composition of the Muslim community reveals how the état civil might manage a population according to the priorities of colonial demographics. This privileged the lives of white settlers while seeking signs of decline among Algerians. The case of Bône, a strategic eastern port city, offers a good example of this approach. The recording of Bône's état civil began within weeks of the city's occupation in the spring of 1832, undertaken among a myriad of other urgent tasks.[112] As with Algiers, Bône's registrars privileged European settlers, and the acts of several Algerian Jews living in the city also appear in the registries. Among the three types of vital acts—births, marriages, and deaths—Muslims appear regularly only in the death registers. The city's état civil does not include a single Muslim marriage for the 1830s, and even birth records show very few Muslim entries, and these declined precipitously over time.[113] In 1833 four children born to Muslim parents appear alongside a total of eighteen births recorded in the city; whereas in 1834 only two Muslim babies were recorded for the sixty-one European births. The next year registrars recorded only one Muslim baby among a total of more than sixty births, and in 1836 the last Muslim baby to appear in the état civil record for this decade was registered, a girl named Fatma, who was born to Aïcha and Mohammed Babaï.[114] She died the next morning. By contrast, deaths in this community appear in the registers in great numbers. For example, in 1833 Muslims accounted for 116 of 198 total deaths in Bône (the remainder were 62 French, 16 Europeans or British subjects from Malta, and 4 Algerian Jews). Registrars paid careful attention to deaths for the next five years. Death records for Muslims appear frequently from 1833 up to 1838, when they abruptly disappear from the books.[115]

In working through this problem of why Bône's Muslims appear only in the death registers, it is useful to first consider registration from the perspective of the interests of those who appear in it, as with the Jews of Algiers. Clearly, having a French death act had extremely limited value to the Muslim families of Bône. It did not document a contract, like a marriage, nor did it establish family ties as a birth record did. Anyone could report a death, and the formula did not require disclosing spouses, children, or parents. This meant that it could not serve as a legal record of a family's members. Those appearing in Bône's death registers show no signs of possessing any wealth, people who might have had complex estates to settle in which French records might be useful even if they would have been decided by a Muslim judge. In fact, many of these people were like the short-lived baby Fatma, people who had barely begun their lives before death took them. Their families had little if any interest in reporting their deaths to French authorities in regard to the typical sort of legal interests associated with the état civil. This was the case with two young girls who died in Bône in 1834, two-week-old Halima and four-year-old Fatma.[116] There are also deaths of those at the very margins of society. For example, in 1834 the death records include a thirty-year-old woman with a single name, Mabroka, who died at the caravanserai at Bône's Constantine gate.[117] She had no family in in the city, and her passing was reported by an interpreter (Angel ben Abu) working for the municipal government. Mabroka had been born in the Bornu Empire (centered on Lake Chad), and she was almost certainly an enslaved woman who had been forced across the Sahara to be sold in North Africa. (While France had presented its conquest of Algeria as a mission to end white slavery in 1830, it was not until 1848 that it abolished slavery for Africans of color.[118])

When viewed from the French perspective, however, some possible answers emerge. Indeed, while some Algerians declared deaths in their families to French authorities on their own initiative, the fact that the municipal interpreter felt compelled to report the death of Mabroka, a stranger to the city, shows that colonial authorities themselves took the initiative to include as many Muslim deaths as they could. The civically generative part of the état civil did not concern these administrators because it clearly did not apply to colonized people nor to those like Mabroka forced to the extreme margins of society. As a subsequent account put it, the results of these early efforts of an état civil for Muslims were "pretty much zero" as far as legal identities were concerned.[119] Nor can the recording of Muslim deaths be explained as an effort to advance French claims through a logic of sovereignty, conventionally understood.

France faced a challenging situation in eastern Algeria in the 1830s. Whereas all the other Ottoman governors had capitulated by this time, the eastern governor, the Ottoman bey of Constantine, Ḥajj Aḥmad Bey (d. 1851), refused to put down his standards. He inflicted a stinging military defeat on France in 1836, and he enjoyed local and international support. In a situation like this, where there were competing claims to sovereignty over local territory and people, the état civil registries might have served to solidify French claims. For example, some sort of French protégé status might have been put forward for the Muslims of Bône, throwing the French flag over them provisionally to offset the claims of the bey.[120] It made no sense, however, to claim these people as French charges at the moment of their deaths. So, while French sovereignty was at stake in Bône's état civil, it was of a considerably different sort.

The type of sovereignty at work in these records appears most closely related to the irresistible, final, and "sovereign" laws that many at the time argued governed biology, health, and demographics.[121] One clue to understanding why registrars produced vital records for Muslims is the way they drew the death records, giving metadata that was not required in the état civil, nor even mentioned in the official guidelines.[122] For example, next to Mabroka's name, the état civil officer wrote "Negress" clearly across the top of the page. For other nonwhites, he indicated that they were either "Moor," "Negro" [*nègre*], "Israelite," or "Turk," writing out the ethno-racial label next to the person's name at the top of the record. In all these cases, racial typologies were of great concern.

This modification of format changed what the registers could do. The regular format of the vital records did not lend itself to data miners. France's état civil at this time comprised entries written out by hand as a transcript of what was a lengthy verbal locution of a legal act. Marriages acts, for example, spread over several pages, and birth dates and sex were buried within the lines of a much longer, handwritten text. Even the numbers for dates had to be deciphered from the longhand, with numerals banned from the records for fear of fraud. Although there were prescribed styles of script for the état civil, the reader is inevitably at the mercy of the registrar's handwriting. Only the decadal, alphabetized registers, designed as a reference tool to find acts for individual people, easily yielded total numbers of vital events in a given district. The registrar in Bône produced a different type of document. Placing race and ethnicity in the act's header ensured that it appeared immediately. This became even more manifest than the names themselves. A reader of the registrars quickly tallies the number of deaths in the town precisely parsed by race.

Deaths in Algeria, European and Algerian, were of paramount interest to colonial authorities. The young child Louise Elisabeth Africa Thon, mentioned earlier, was not the only European to live a short life in Algeria. While the overall number of settlers climbed steadily year after year, reaching 100,000 by 1847, up from 8,000 in 1833, they suffered from what were thought to be dangerously elevated death rates for the first four decades of the colonial period.[123] Looking at this situation with unease, health specialists worried that Europeans could not adapt to northern Africa's climate and diseases.[124] Commentators wrote openly of an insurmountable population crisis in the colony, arguing that there was no future for Europeans in Africa. They feared that only a massive pool of immigrants could constantly replenish their numbers.[125] In this respect, commentators argued that the high morbidity and low fertility experienced by settlers represented as menacing an enemy as any army or rebellion.[126] Reflecting on these challenges in the 1860s, one French general wrote: "the cemeteries are the only colonies always increasing in population in Algeria."[127] The foremost French specialist on the question of health and population at the time, Jean-Christian-Marc Boudin, the chief physician to the army, expressed himself in alarming terms about the inability of Europeans, and especially French, to survive.[128] "In each of the years studied, more or less without exception, and in each province, deaths exceed births. From this we can conclude that the growth of the European population relies entirely on the arrival of new immigrants, and that without the support of this element, the European population, in current conditions, would be threatened by disappearance."[129] The menace of cholera, which swept the country in 1835 and 1837, drove home these fears and intensified efforts to expand population data collection.[130]

In these discussions, demographic questions appear as a zero-sum game pitting Europeans against Algerians. For example, the early tallies of the population published by the Ministry of War appeared under the column headings "gains" and "losses," as if these figures were a scoreboard of their success.[131] When another demographic study showed growth for urban Jews, the author warned that "the time is perhaps not far off when . . . the cities of Algeria will be populated only by Jews."[132] The logic of settler colonialism encouraged this type of thinking, wherein the declining numbers of Algerians measured France's successes. Reflecting on data for Muslims, one planner wrote that "the only positive things that we have been able to observe in this population are . . . the frequent departures of Muslims and an ever-increasing poverty among those who remain."[133] Ideally, white settlers would be self-sustaining in numbers and self-sufficient in labor one day. Some argued that the solution to population crisis lay in expelling Algerians or pushing them toward demographic collapse. Boudin, although extremely pessimistic on the possibilities of European settlement, looked at the rates of death and emigration for Algerians and asked if it were not the confirmation of auto-genocide, or as he put it, "this mysterious law by which certain inferior races seemed destined to disappear when they contact superior races."[134] Others wrote with optimism that "the decline of the Muslim population in Algeria seems a certain fact."[135]

This sort of thinking, then, welcomed the poor showings of Muslims in Algeria's population figures. A high death count among them was cause for optimism. A doctor in private practice, Eugène Bodichon, openly envisioned an Algerian genocide in the 1840s. "If we want a durable colony we must achieve the following: Ensure that there are no more Arabs on the surface of northern Algeria."[136] These plans never found an enthusiastic reading among actual decision makers (in spite of the fact that Bodichon provided only a scientific apparatus to frame what the French army already practiced on the ground).[137] Yet Bodichon's ideas intrigued colonial demographers, and their significance should not be underestimated. The more influential and mainstream authority, the army doctor Boudin, for example, cited one of Bodichon's most hateful passages in a phosphorescent footnote: "Without violating the laws of morality, we could combat our African enemies by powder and iron, internal divisions, war, by alcohol, corruption and disorganization. . . . Without spilling blood, we could, every year, decimate them by attacking their food supply, cutting the fig trees and the cacti across Algeria."[138] Placed at the end of a passage wherein Boudin crunches the numbers of Muslim births and deaths in Algeria's cities, which showed the "considerable excess of deaths over births," Boudin's citation of Bodichon serves as an effective endorsement of the genocidal doctor's vision to the reader, even as the cautious demographer Boudin states in his own voice that he lacks sufficient data to draw a final conclusion.

The type of sovereignty that motivated the officer of the état civil in Bône to record Muslim deaths by race was part of a broader focus on colonial demographics. This field's understanding of sovereignty as it related to vital records was of a different sort than that envisioned by Napoléon "wherever the flag flies" model of surreptitious undermining of sovereignty through the mechanisms of legal belonging. It was much closer to the emerging modern theories, which gave precedence to race over nation in determining belonging. As the influential British racial theorist Robert Knox wrote in a section of *The Races of Men* (1850) focused on Algeria, nationality was itself nothing more than a "legal fiction," one of the era's "human contrivances." Instead, it was race that decided the "great laws regulating the living organic world."[139]

Over the next decades, the registration of Algerians' vital acts made only fitful advances. Efforts to include Muslims focused on reporting their births and deaths as part of a rough population count, rather than enrolling them in the état civil itself. Already the decree of 7 December 1830, which had originally taken the état civil out of the hands of the French consul and regularized it as a mark of French sovereignty, contained an article requiring burial permits for Algerians in Algiers. These permits amounted to a sort of death certificate, which provided the data necessary for demographic studies without civil registration. Beginning in 1838, Algerian midwives and cadis were charged with reporting births to the municipal government every ten days, giving the name, age, profession, and address of the father and a single name for the mother. This order was respected only sporadically in the cities, with towns like Mostaganem, Oran, and Bône generating more complete records than larger cities like Algiers.[140] In rural areas no records were kept for either births or deaths. France could muster only an estimated head count for Algerians, estimates that many scrutinized carefully for signs of a population collapse that would seal the demographic supremacy of Europeans.[141] For many, this was all the information about Algerian life processes they needed.[142]

4

"Am I That Name?"

Algerians Make Their Names Known, 1827–1840

In general, political and legal power needs to know names to take hold of people. These names can be learned or conferred. However, a history of the colonization of Algerian personal names includes several paradoxical stories of the "undiscovery" of names. While knowing the names of Algerians would allow France to root its power in precisely the way the first chapter of this book has argued—using names within a larger language of symbolic violence—it took some time before French policymakers interested themselves in the names of actual Algerians. Indeed, they initially ignored many of the names they already knew.

This chapter begins by examining how the colonial naming project created a sense of onomastic rupture around 1830. While counterproductive in the short term, this established practices and attitudes for the rest of the nineteenth century and beyond. Much as happened with forgetting the country name "Algérie," the forgetting of personal names created ruptures that served France's particular style of rule through violence. Policymakers ceased to write out the names of individual Algerians, people they certainly knew, relying instead on vague ethnonyms. This symbolically reduced Algerians to amorphous groups and downplayed their capacity for political thought and action. Algerians, however, had their own names, and they used them as part of a short-lived early effort to shape policy through direct lobbying of the French government. The story of this Algerian-led project to make their names known focuses on a unique iteration of the name, the signature, attached to their letters and petitions. The chapter examines the possibilities for asserting agency in the first years of the occupation through these names as they moved between Arabic and French, interpellating people and constituting colonized subjects. The case of a bilingual merchant from Algiers who signed his name in several ways as he tried to assert a voice in his country's affairs will illustrate how this struggle played itself out. Viewed by his signature's different iterations, this man had occasion to ask himself, as others have done when considering their name and their sense of self: "Am I that name?"[1]

Onoma nullius: Unnaming the Algerians, 1827–1832

In 1827, when war first broke out between France and Algeria, the policymakers who turned their attention to the crisis learned only a few Algerian names, a handful of those belonging to the political elite, and none particularly well. Most telling in this respect is the paucity of individual names that appear in documents at this time, a tendency that ran into the early 1830s. Crudely transliterated names like "Abdelcader-ben-Het-Nedjar" appeared in exceptional circumstances when it was necessary to individuate Algerians. In this example, the occasion was a report of the death sentence passed on this man in April 1832, published in the quasi-official French newspaper.[2] "Abdelcader" was one of the first Algerians executed by a public legal judgment, convicted of murdering a French soldier during a robbery. In most cases, however, French texts referred to Algerians without names. They deployed hazy terms like "an Arab" from such-and-such a place, or such-and-such tribe, if they wrote of Algerians as individuals at all. There is no obvious explanation for this onomastic indifference. While knowing the proper names of others can signal respect and concern, even functioning as the basic acknowledgment of their humanity, at its heart the name is a potent political technology. Names rationalize and differentiate people so that they can be acted on. Moreover, knowing names would have facilitated the diplomatic projects that preceded the invasion, when officials scrambled to court potential Algerian friends and identify likely enemies. The complexity of the full Algerian name might have warned some off from any attempt to know properly everyone's names.

The formal study of Arabo-Islamic onomastics did not begin in France until the mid-nineteenth century, so the ability to read the multiple parts of the name for a person's affiliation, status, profession, origin, and lineage would have been impossible for all but a handful of Orientalists. Nevertheless, given that "there is no state-making without state-naming," as scholars have argued, France's initial indifference to names merits close reading.[3]

Algeria clearly did not lie in a far-off black hole to France, even if the texts of the late 1820s and early 1830s made it seem as if it stood entirely unknown to France. This epistemological void had a recent origin. Only when war was declared and French planners looked toward invading the country did Algeria become a "primitive and frightening African wilderness peopled by wild barbarians," as historian Ann Thomson has written.[4] Algeria had, in fact, always been quite accessible to France. Sailing vessels starting out from Marseille could lay anchor off North African shores after a few days at sea, and frequent travel and exchange ensured that many in France knew Algeria and its people well, even intimately. Much of this knowledge was dispersed and not immediately available for war planning in the tight time frame of 1827–1830. The sea raiding of Algerian corsairs had effectively collapsed around 1806, meaning that few could report about their captivity experiences in Algiers, a significant source of intelligence in previous eras.[5] When Napoleon Bonaparte pondered invading Algiers in 1808, he had to send a spy to get information about the city's defenses.[6] The knowledge of the free laborers, artisans, and sailors who worked in Algeria likely circulated only by word of mouth among circles not readily accessible to the government.[7] However, the Ministry of Foreign Affairs, which planned the 1830 invasion in conjunction with the Ministry of War, had ready access to its own diplomats and a deep archive of knowledge. These people had developed long-standing contacts in Algeria, living in the country and working alongside its government's officials in a continuous and dense history that dates back at least to end of the seventeenth century.[8] In addition, French commercial and diplomatic agents lived in several trading stations along the Algerian coast, concessions originally established in the mid-sixteenth century. They came to know Algerians well, depending as they did on them for their food and safety.[9]

Emblematic of these old Algerian hands was Pierre Deval, who headed the French consulate in Algiers during the Restoration. Descending from a family of French dragomans and diplomats (his mother gave birth to him in Istanbul), Deval spoke fluent Turkish and Arabic. He studied these languages formally in Paris and perfected them in diplomatic service in Aleppo, Alexandria, and Baghdad, as well as a decade of political exile he spent in Istanbul during the Revolution.[10] Named consul in Algiers in 1815, he spent a dozen years there. He became so familiar to Algerian officials that they had taken to warning each other about the Frenchman's bad breath, according to some accounts.[11] Deval fell ill and died during the invasion's planning phase, meaning that his accumulated knowledge was confined to the archive of his correspondence and reports. But others could replace him. His own nephew, Alexandre Deval, occupied important consular posts in Oran and Bône in the 1820s, and he drew on this experience when the government called him to replace his dead uncle. Outside of the Deval family were others, people like Florent Thierry-Dufougeray, a young diplomat who wrote plans for the invasion based on his time in Algiers (he also knew Tunis well). He could converse with local people in Arabic or Italian along with French, and he possessed detailed information earned from the period beginning in 1825 when he arrived as the *élève consul* in Algiers, and later in 1826 when he served as the diplomatic head of the trading station in La Calle (al-Qāla). A final example of the sort of experienced agents available to the planners was Jean-Dauphin Raimbert, called to lead a secret mission to eastern Algeria planned for spring 1830, just prior to the French landings. Raimbert had lived in Bône off and on with his family since the late eighteenth century, overseeing the French trading stations. His responsibilities included monthly meetings with local Algerian tribes who helped assure the defense of these posts.[12]

All these people—and many others—knew Algeria well, and their knowledge served in the expansive, if rushed, intelligence-gathering that laid the groundwork for the 1830 invasion. When called on to identify Algerians who might be won over as allies, however, these officials wrote about local people not as individuals or separate tribes that might harbor distinct political tendencies—potential friends or enemies—but in wildly schematic terms, using ethnic categories as collective names.[13] For example, in one report, Thierry-Dufougeray did not parse the political terrain by discussing the many Algerian leaders he knew personally or by reputation. Rather he wrote about various ethno-linguistic groups and pinned political typologies to them.[14] Thus his report highlights the "Cobaïls" (Kabyles) who were "of a gentle disposition, sober and easy to please," "Arabes" who would show themselves to be "fairly moderate," and "Maures," a name that French authors used to refer to denizens of the cities and who he figured might be an "obstacle." While ministers solicited Thierry-Dufougeray precisely for his expertise, he chose to write in the very terms used by superiors who knew nothing of the country, ventriloquizing their ignorance. The same clichés reappeared in the orders for Raimbert's 1830 mission. Raimbert and two other men (Prosper Gérardin and Louis Philibert Brun d'Aubignosc) were tasked with traveling secretly to eastern Algeria and dissuading leaders in the Constantine region from marching west to defend Algiers once French troops landed.[15] The Ministry of War drafted the mission's orders, instructing the team to convince people that the fall of the Ottoman dey in Algiers would be to their advantage. Raimbert's team was to see "leaders of the Moorish tribal bands [*peuplades*]" and tell them that "in joining their arms to ours, the Moors will advance the day of their deliverance; [whereas] fighting the French will lead to certain ruin."[16] In at least one case they had authorization to go beyond loose promises and make concrete offers. In particular, the mission was instructed to meet with Bey Aḥmad of Constantine and tell him that if he supported France, the government would recognize him as a "king."[17] In other cases, General Bourmont, who led the invasion forces, made pointless suggestions about how Islam might be mobilized in negotiations, writing, "it is said in the Coran that the Mahommedans must treat Christians as their brothers and friends, and these words of the Prophet must first apply to the French."[18] Certainly, more useful to the secret mission would have been a list of local contacts. Oddly, this type of detailed information appears only in anonymous notes written in the margins of a report signed by Gérardin, a man who knew virtually nothing of the Maghreb but who had been recruited because he had served in Senegal and was thought able to blend in among Africans. These marginal notes, most likely written by Raimbert, sought to clarify things by stating, "in giving the generic name of Coubails [Gérardin means specifically the tribes named] Beni Abès and Beni Djébar." For his part, the mission's third member, D'Aubignosc, also provided the names of tribes near Béjaïa and the name of one leader based on his own knowledge.[19] However, none of these names recirculated from the report's margins to be incorporated into other planning materials. The task of identifying individual Algerians who might prove important to the success of the invasion was, in effect, a neglected side note within the larger project itself written in stereotypes. Indeed, except for Ḥusayn Pāshā, the last Ottoman dey in Algiers, few if any of the personal names of Algerian officials and notables appear in the mass of crucial documents generated in anticipation of the invasion.[20]

It did not take long before colonial authorities grasped the importance of Algerian names. By the second or third year of the occupation, the names of people with whom the French worked, as well as those of some enemies, began to appear regularly.[21] In addition to identifying individuals and enabling political relations, these names eventually served to organize the colonial archive itself. By the 1840s, rather than filing them into folders marked "Kabyles," "Arabs," or "Jews," clerical staff sorted letters and reports according to the names of specific tribes and individuals, a practice that archivists reshuffling the documents over the years have followed, showing how important these names are to the archive's very intelligibility. Designations provided by the personal name also served to organize letters Algerians sent to the French at the time, most of them written in Arabic. When these arrived in the hands of government translators, they wrote the authors' names in French letters across the top of the page to ensure that the original was not separated from the translation as it passed across the desks of administrators who could not decipher a single letter from the Arabic script. In this way, Algerian names came to serve, as one might expect, as a simple but crucial tool organizing a system of information.[22] By the 1850s, knowing the names of individuals became the sine qua non of the newly flourishing practice of writing biographical notices for important Algerians and short histories of influential families.[23]

Quasi-names: Violence and language

While the French started using proper names for Algerians quickly enough, ethnonyms continued to play a major role in the genre of administrative writing, which rose above day-to-day tasks to discuss long-term policy recommendations. Here "Moor," "Kabyle," "Jew," "Muslim," "Turk," "Arab," or "Bedouin" did the work of naming Algerians, along with common nouns like "inhabitants," "populations," and "natives." These words served in the place of "Barbaresques" and "Algériens," two names that disappeared almost entirely from the colonial lexicon after 1830, never to reappear in the nineteenth century. "Barbaresques" had taken the place of the narrowly pejorative "Barbares" in French texts at the end of the seventeenth century but had outlived its role by the nineteenth century.[24] On the other hand, "Algérien," which had commonly appeared in official French texts to denote both the people living in Algiers and those in other parts of this Ottoman province, was an obviously problematic term after about 1830, implying as it did the unity and common purpose among local people, even an Algerian nation, which served at counter-purposes to colonial planning.[25] Although the political motives of this sort of symbolic erasure of these names are obvious, substitutes had to be found so that sentences could function grammatically. Common nouns served nicely in the place of names. "Inhabitants" (*habitants*) and "natives" (*natifs* or *naturels*) emerged as preferred terms, appearing almost as if a copyeditor had struck through "Algérien." These quasi names could be used in situations when the French state directly addressed Algerians, as occurred notably in the Arabic-language proclamation intended for circulation before the French troops landed. In this document, General Bourmont, addressed himself "to inhabitants of Algiers and people of the tribes" (*'ilā sukkān al-jazā'ir wa ahālī al-qabā'il*).[26]

What might have been the political impact of these sorts of denominations? Or, to ask the question differently, what was the impact of France's signifiers on the signified? Ethnonyms and collective nouns served colonial planners to sketch Algeria in broad stereotypical strokes. Thus, Arabs were predisposed to such-and-such political behaviors, Berbers another set, Jews another, and so on, with the various common nouns like "inhabitants" and "natives" writ large to lump them all together. Language calls out and positions the subject, and these words served as keystones of the discursive and political edifice by which France sought to impose its power on people it had otherwise unnamed and made strangely unfamiliar. Unsurprisingly, this failed to fix the political dispositions of actual people. These words, however, were not irrelevant to historical outcomes. They gave colonial writers the parts of speech they needed to write, and, in some cases, ordinary words might be fleshed out into proper names. As names tend to do, these more fully decided their bearer, even if only in the mind of the person who used them. This was the case with *indigène* (native), a word that increasingly appeared in the upper case as time went on to become the predominate French name for Algerians up to World War II.[27]

In the case of French thinking and policymaking, this is a clear situation where a word did what it said, making Algerians the appropriate raw matter for colonialization.[28]

Great violence could be done through these names. This is evidenced in texts where they functioned as linguistic supports for visceral hatred. Such documents fill the colonial archive, as even a casual reader of French sources for this era knows. Four lesser-known examples suffice. In 1833 or early in 1834, an army interpreter, Henri Rémusat, wrote of Arabs and Kabyles in these terms:

> They are cruel, vindictive and deceitful to the supreme degree, traitors by principle, murderers by habit, and fanatic by religion. Woe be it to anyone who trusts them, woe to the stranger who gives oneself over to them, even if he is their best friend . . . nothing can snatch him from death. In the plains, that is to say among the *Arabs*, he will have his head cut off. In the mountains, that is to say among the *Kabails*, he will be burned alive and always after having suffered through a very long series of the usual cruel tortures.[29]

Second, there are the words of Abbé Dopigez, a chaplain who accompanied the first French troops into Algiers in July 1830. He wrote the following about the city's people:

> When one finds oneself amongst these half naked people who circulate in the city, when one sees these hideous Jewish populations, these women always veiled with only black eyes peering out, and these silent coffeehouses in front of which a *Frenchman* crossed on the day of the conquest without attracting a single glance, one feels an inexpressible impatience and disgust; a great malaise seizes the heart, and one makes haste to leave this city of slaves to breath purer air.[30]

(This passage is especially noteworthy for its complexity, mobilizing disembodied gazes, metaphors, indirect terms, and lesser parts of speech to designate local people, with "Frenchman" being the only proper noun.)

In a third example from 1837, "Bedouin" is the chosen term used by a doctor, Jacques Cognat, in an unsolicited letter he wrote to the government laying out a plan of action: "The *Bedouins* are as follows: if you spare them, they think that you are afraid, and they despise you. If you retreat, they think that you are in difficulty, and they rally to annihilate you. All reasoning does not destroy the facts. . . . One can understand why gentle methods which succeed at home have always failed in Africa."[31]

Finally, "natives" (*indigènes*) serves an author, J. Sabbatier, who wrote an open letter to parliament in June 1836 describing his plan to advance colonization. "It is possible to plow in Africa with something other than the sword, and even to enrich the *natives*, instead of slitting their throats; but it was necessary to start by making them submit."[32]

In these examples, one sees how ordinarily innocuous words—"Bedouin," "Arabs," "natives," "populations"—served to inflict injury. They constructed Algerians as dangerous people to be approached with weapons in hand. Any violence done to them would necessarily be justified, with the hate and racism infusing the word with which they are named, absolving the perpetrator of responsibility. The prejudicial name contains in itself the explanation for the colonizer's violence. Indeed, such names allow for a politically useful confusion of cause and effect, offering an explanation for colonial violence that displaces its origin from colonizer onto the colonized. The scenario of interpellation then becomes a thing of immediate risk for colonized Algerians. The enmity embedded in these words positioned their referent directly in the line of French fire, people whom the French killed claiming self-defense.

Historian Jocelyne Dakhlia has argued that this sort of radical othering, or the cultural and epistemological "shock" of contact found in the post-1830 French sources, was new to the western Mediterranean, just as it accurately translated the sorts of violence that ensued. The theme of rupture in the early texts, or the "savagization" (*ensauvagement*) of Algerians, served as the precondition of colonialism. She writes: "The colonial relationship can justify itself only by a strong, even radical alterity, posed as its precondition."[33] This symbolic othering carries with it important material effects. Rémusat, Dopigez, Cognat, and Sabbatier underscore the importance of understanding physical violence in terms of its symbolic dimensions. Signs wound bodies, and these bodies in turn become signs in their own right, sending a gruesome warning to others (as well as a confirmation to the perpetrators of their own righteousness).[34] These examples give some sense of how names work in these cases, with words serving as weapons that inflict physical violence. In the case of "Bedouin," the term used by Cognat, it served him to detail a draconian plan to "pacify" Algeria through extreme cruelty and mass killings.[35] He recommended that in cases of revolt, half the tribe should be executed, their "*cheic*" impaled, and survivors forced to pay a tribute equal to five years of taxes. If it revolted a second time, the tribe would be simply annihilated: Half would be killed on the spot, and the other half sold into slavery. Summing up these outcomes in series of brutal clauses, he wrote, "Either the Bedouins will submit, and pacification will be accomplished; or the Bedouins revolt in part, and the rebels will be forced into submission and pacification will be accomplished; or the Bedouins will revolt [in toto], and they will all be cut down and decimated and pacification will be accomplished." This gruesome scenario, outlined in a forgotten letter by an unknown doctor, realized itself in countless large- and small-scale massacres that swept across the country. Indeed, the term "pacification" echoed across the decades ahead in colonial discourses as a euphemism for what was in fact violent conquest, death, and destruction. These examples underscore how words can be made to do what they say. Here an otherwise inoffensive name serves to symbolically construct Algerians as the object of enmity. The conclusion that logically follows from Cognat's letter is that France must either reduce the Algerian "Bedouin" to some subhuman state, such as slavery, or exterminate them outright.

Cognat wrote about the "Bedouins," but there is also the case of more commonly used name, "Native" (*Indigène*), which, unlike the proper ethnonyms, appeared first as a common noun, a part of speech grammatically ill-suited to the task of calling out specific people. Made to do the work of the name (although left as a common noun) in the 1836 example cited earlier, *indigène* functioned in what its author presented as a benevolent option: Making Algerians submit to French authority will spare them having their throats slit. The "submit or else" ultimatum exposes the author's false humanitarianism easily enough. More interesting is how *indigène* strips Algerians of their humanity at least two times over. First, described as "*indigènes*," Algerians fall out of the world of states, nations, and civilization they had occupied under names like "Algérien," and it places them indifferently alongside the world's many different indigenous peoples that European and Euro-American writers had slated for disappearance according to the theories of autogenocide that proliferated in the eighteenth and nineteen centuries. As I argued in the previous chapter, these likely influenced the état civil registrar in Bône, who so eagerly racialized and recorded Muslim deaths in his city, hoping to find evidence of the demographic collapse of indigenous people. Second, designating people by a common French noun like *indigène* thrusts them into a lesser class of living things, part of the "native" flora and fauna to be mastered and used, rather than the singular, or at least separate, world of human beings. When applied to Algeria, the special charge of the French word opened a symbolic space for erasure. An 1832 open letter to a procolonization newspaper succinctly summed up the thinking for this position when it declared of French relations with Algerians (here named "Bedouins"): "We must act on the country as if they did not exist."[36]

Algerians and their names in the resistance dialogue

While French commentators anticipated their destruction in the very names used for them, Algerians planned for the future, weighing how to respond to the dangers of French rule with the possibilities that came with the end of the Ottoman era. To understand their story as it played out in names, it is useful to begin by revisiting how names functioned in the colonial interpellation of Algerians, as well as in Algerians' own efforts to make a place for themselves in their colonized country. This requires some theoretical unpacking. In the previous section, I pointed to the logic of practice contained in certain names, names that did what they said, and how they enabled extreme violence. *Indigène* legitimated in French minds the physical violence that could be done to them through this name. This sort of naming is not fully coterminous with the act of interpellation—calling one into a certain subject position—but to better understand the predicament Algerians faced, it is useful to think of naming and interpellation together. In his well-known model, Louis Althusser taught that interpellation, the "hey, you there!" called out by the police officer in the street, always hits its target, no matter how scattershot the dispatch.[37] The hailed person, preconditioned by ideology, recognizes themselves as the object of the officer's imperative call ("he means me!"), and in this moment of self-recognition this person assumes their proper subordinate position before authority.[38] Importantly, interpellation does not happen through an external application of physical violence. The officer uses words, not a truncheon to stop the subject dead in their tracks. Moreover, the officer does not need to use a name but relies on only a formal "you" (*vous*), which is the simplest of French pronouns, undifferentiated by gender or number. This sort of interpellation produces a very generic subjectivity, but one that sufficed to call out a single person. Althusser used this example to ground his critique of the self-conscious subject who seems to act autonomously rather than through the power of ideology, as he argued is actually the case. However, interpellation can take place though social categories, like "woman" or "queer," among others that have a deterministic or essentializing effect. These common nouns can function in some instances like names, as in the case of *Indigène*, Arab, or even *ahālī al-qabā'il* (people of the tribes), as used in the 1830 proclamation to Algerians.

Althusser's critique of liberal notions of individual agency leaves little room for an interpellated subject like the *Indigène* to speak back. And yet, names, like any other word, are subject to slippages in meaning, as shown in chapter 2, and these can be exploited or manipulated to resist interpellation. Althusser's experiences with his own name give a good example of refusing names, along with questioning and self-questioning, that otherwise disappear in his canonical model of interpellation. His personal struggles are especially apropos here inasmuch as they touch on the French philosopher's underrecognized history with Algeria. Althusser's paternal and maternal grandparents immigrated to Algeria to work in the state forestry services in the last decades of the nineteenth century, with his father's side fleeing from their home in Alsace after its annexation by Germany following the Franco-Prussian War.[39] His father, Charles was born in Algiers in 1888, and he worked his way up in a banking career, rising from messenger boy to director of several local offices, eventually relocating his family to metropolitan France. The parents of Althusser's mother originated in Burgundy, and they raised several daughters in Algeria who prepared careers as teachers, before retiring in France.

As he told the story of his growing up, Althusser did not simply submit to the implacable interpellative force of names. In particular, he did not fall into the role laid out for him by his name. His first name, "Louis," was the stickler. It was the name of his mother's sweetheart, the first Louis Althusser, whom she had planned to marry before he died in combat during the First World War. She then married his surviving brother, the man named Charles. The son born to the couple, Louis the philosopher, then bore the first name of a dead man his mother had loved, but who was not his father, while his patronymic came to him from a different man who had actually fathered him. This was a complicated psycho-onomastic heritage for the boy, to say the least.[40] For a time, Althusser had tried to go by "Jacques," rather than respond to a "*dead man's name.*"[41] (Apparently, taking a Muslim or Jewish Algerian alias did not tempt him.) Of course, in one way or another, all names are those of the dead, but the name "Louis" left him with profound feelings of estrangement. "My mother whom I loved with all my heart loved someone else through and beyond me, using my physical presence to remind her of a person who was absent, or rather seeing his presence though my absence," he wrote in his memoirs.[42] This led him to ask emphatically: "How could I make my mother love me, since it wasn't actually me she loved?" Respite came for Althusser when he left Algeria at twelve years of age. He was sent to France, where he spent a year with his retired maternal grandparents, eventually relocating permanently in the metropole. Living with his grandparents, he found a new name, and with it some peace. People in the town called him by his mother's maiden name (Berger), which they used to assimilate this young outsider to their local community and its lineages. The future philosopher found that he recognized himself easily in this name, enjoying a proper, coherent sense of self for the first time in his life.[43]

Althusser's psychoanalytic story of overcoming the name's alienation told in his memoirs differs significantly from his arguments on interpellation and its totalizing mandate. In the name "Berger," a patronym that came from his maternal grandfather, he escaped the symbolic authority of his father, and this name also freed him from his mother's morbid desire, or rather his projection thereof. In it he found his own place in the social and symbolic relations of metropolitan France, making this place his home.[44] Indeed, he tells this as a story of self-mastery and sovereignty, however improbable it might be given his views on ideology. I will leave it to others to decide how this personal victory squares with Althusser's theory of interpellation, as well as untangling the psychocultural politics of his biography and relationship with Algeria and settler society. (Later in life, Althusser had virtually nothing to say about the country of his birth, returning only once for a daylong layover en route to Morocco.[45]) I offer it here because it opens useful perspectives to consider defying the name's symbolic power.

How then to read the historical sources and the real challenges faced by Algerians in the 1830s? What stands out at this time are Algerians who tried to have their original names known to the French. They attached these names to their proposals and criticisms of colonial policies. For a short period in the 1830s, Algerians attempted to play a meaningful role in governing their country. This produced a movement that historian Abdelkader Djeghloul has dubbed the "resistance dialogue."[46] Led initially by Algiers's urban notables (generally known as *ḥaḍarī*, in Arabic, or separately, *maures*, in French), it used the press and personal lobbying to shape French public opinion, influence the government, and transform colonial rule. Letters and petitions took prominent place in these efforts. Notables wrote frequently on a variety of issues, which ranged from protesting the destruction of buildings and the confiscation of religious endowments; to attesting to the innocence of people wrongfully arrested by the French military; to welcoming incoming administrators, a courtesy extended to select French leaders known for their honesty and sense of fair play.[47] Some letters came from Algerians who had been invested by France in local leadership positions, known as *caïds* and *aghas*. They wrote on behalf of people they represented to demand the return of stolen property or offered information about French prisoners taken captive in battle. Best known in the 1830s, this correspondence actually ran the course of the nineteenth century, as historian Fatiha Sifou has shown in her careful study.[48] Although French leaders dubbed the Algerian writers the "Moor party"—as if they were a secretive cabal—in fact they undertook their campaign in the plain light of day. Authors openly affixed their names to their efforts, either as an author's printed name in a publication or more often in the form of a signature appended to letters and petitions. Although select individuals drafted their correspondence in French and converted their signatures to French letters, most protests came in Arabic, with their names converted by interpreters to French. In this way, Algerians made a name for themselves in the emerging colonial system, even across language barriers.

The name as signature

The signature is a special sort of name. Generally speaking, it establishes a person's presence in a written document. This understanding holds true both in Europe and in the Middle East and North Africa, notwithstanding the fact that the signature is not exactly homologous between these two societies at every historical moment.[49] Like the Arabo-Islamic name, an autographed signature reveals a good deal about a person's education and other markers of identity, such as gender, age, and class, all of which the trained eye can distinguishable through handwriting and the types of names and titles included. Signatures, therefore, put people into texts as distinct individuals, giving shape to their person and providing proof that they had been once physically present with the document. Legally speaking, this allows an authentic embodied voice to speak through the written word. In all, a signature makes a person concrete within the confines of an otherwise abstract and inert piece of paper. In his study of modern Yemeni court documents, anthropologist Brinkley Messick calls signatures "the summary scripts of human presences."[50] In northwestern Africa, the signature was known as the *khaṭṭ al-yad* or "hand stroke."[51] It bound together identity and agency and enabled the written word to affect life off the page. The French standard of the autographed signature, a particular form in which the named person writes their own name in a unique stylized form, was not foreign to Algerians, although it was not necessary for the signature to do its work.[52] Within the epistolary rules that governed the nineteenth-century Arabic letter in Algeria, for example, the name of the letter's author is not always set apart in an autographed signature at the bottom of the page but incorporated into its final lines in the terms of a formal salutation, followed by that person's occupation and the date. A generic expression of this type reads: "Greetings from the one who has written you these words, your student and your son," followed by the sender's name and the date.[53] In this way, the name itself functions as a signature, ascribing an authorial voice to the text, even if it might be written by the hand of another person, such as a professional letter writer, clerk, or notary.[54]

The signature expands the politics of the name considerably from the names called out by a police officer or written down by a government agent on an ID card. While signatures can be forged or coerced, they stand as testament to a person's ability to speak, communicate points held in common with an interlocutor, and, in some cases, authorize opposing views and a call for change. A case in point is a document dated 15 Sha'bān 1246

FIGURE 4.1 Document dated 15 Sh'abān 1246 (28 January 1831). Note: signatures in preface and margins. FR ANOM. Aix-en-Provence 1h1-*Touts droits réservés.*

(28 January 1831, see figure 4.1) that a group of notables from Algiers wrote in Arabic and collectively addressed to French authorities with their signatures to voice their support for a man named Abū Ḍarba and vouch for his good character and leadership skills, as a way of stating that they had chosen him to represent their interests in dealings with the French government.[55] It can be understood as a type of petition or effort to consult with French authorities. Abū Ḍarba was on his way to Paris to seek restitution for properties illegally confiscated or destroyed by the military, and more generally to present the notables' recommendations on Algiers's governance and the future of Algeria.

Twenty-four signatures appear in this document, and they merit scrutiny. Four names are written into the preface that begins the text, and the names of another twenty people appear in the document's right margin, continuing across its bottom. Most of these are not autographed signatures, properly speaking. Analysis of this document by the specialist of premodern Arabic Estefanía Valenzuela Mochón reveals several different hands writing out the signatures so that the twenty-four names appear in five different groups, each group distinguishable by distinctive handwriting.[56] Only a single name is written in its own style, suggesting that it is an autographed signature. (Some of the names within each group might have been signed by one member, who then wrote the names of his immediate colleagues.) In addition to the names, properly speaking, formal titles precede nearly every name. They include " 'Abd Rabbi" (Servant/Slave of God), "al-Sayyid" (indicating noble status derived from descent from the Prophet's family), "al-Ḥajj" (typically someone who has made the great pilgrimage to Mecca), or titles of education (" 'Ālim" and "Kātib").[57] These mark the person's piety or their status as scholars of the Islamic sciences. In some cases, occupations and former occupations follow the name, such as "Malikite mufti" and "Hanafite qadi," titles that convey important social and cultural capital. The signatures in the petition use a compact form of the name, i.e., the birth name, or ism, and a single nasab referencing the person's father, along with their own profession. (The only exception to this is Aḥmad bin Ibrahim bin Mūsā, a Malikite mufti, who includes a two-generation nasab, using the name of his father, Ibrahim, and grandfather, Mūsā.) Leaving off other parts of the name allows these signatures to fit into the document's margins. While this compact name leaves off important information, as signatures they do the necessary work. They placed signatories within the text, attesting to their agency.

The writers of the letter knew that only a handful of those in the French administration could read their Arabic. This text had to be converted to French once it was received, a task performed by an anonymous interpreter.[58] The French translation paraphrases the original document's content, and at the end it provides a list of the names, written in their French approximation. No standards for the conversion of names from Arabic to French existed at the time, nor for that matter had a uniform system of transliteration of Arabic in French letters been decided on by French Arabists (a project discussed in the next chapter). The translator sounded out Arabic names and provided an approximation for their phonemes in the closest equivalents in French letters. The task was not an easy one, and its challenges were compounded by the imprecise handwriting in which the names appear, making it nearly impossible in several cases for an outsider to determine their original spelling exactly. The translator therefore had to make some educated guesses in converting the names into French. Beyond the inevitable errors of this type of exercise, the translator took considerable liberties in deciding the final form of the names in French and in editing their components. These changes reveal important divides that separated what the French administration sought in the Algerian name and that which Algerians themselves valued and wished to convey. For example, the translator left off all the " 'Abd Rabbi" titles as well as "al-Sayyid," both important markers of status within an economy of signs and social hierarchies that French officials apparently rejected. The one exception is the fact that the translator carried over the "Ḥajj" titles of those who had travelled to Mecca for the pilgrimage. The job titles given in the original Arabic were for the most part carried over; however, the translator added several occupations that do not appear in the original signatures, such as *propriétaire* (property owner), *négociant* (merchant), or, in the case of one man ('Abd Rabbi-hi Yūsuf bin 'Ammār), head of the silk weavers' guild. The translator must have worked from his own knowledge and filled in the blanks in anticipation of what his superiors would want to know about the petitioners. This shows that French understandings of what constituted power and influence departed significantly from those of the Algerian signatories themselves. The latter made sure that the religious sciences and their faith figured prominently in their signed name, but they did not include indicators of monied wealth and secular professions.[59] These two documents, the original 1831 Arabic letter and its French translation, begin to show several yawning gaps that separated Algerian names across language.

Aḥmad Abū Ḍarba/Ahmed Bouderba: A name à *contre-voix*

Arabic remained the preferred language for Algerians petitioning the French administration until the end of the nineteenth century.[60] Many of these documents went untranslated or unread, or were ignored, which turns out to have been the Shaʿbān petition's fate, as we shall see at the end of this chapter.[61] Some Algerians, however, wrote their letters in French. Appearing on a colonial administrator's desk in French, these documents had a better chance of being read at their word, given the haphazard translations interpreters might otherwise subject them to. Moreover, by using the colonizers' own language, Algerians expected recognition as legitimate interlocutors on questions of policy, rather than serving passively as native informants or intermediaries. In particular, when they wrote in the French language, these people claimed a place for themselves on the page of modern political discourses concerning emancipation, rule of law, and government by consent. "Ahmed Bouderba," among other spellings, was one Algerian who used the French language in this way.

He was born Aḥmad bin Ismāʿīl Abū Ḍarba (d. 1865), and at this point I will call this man Abū Ḍarba, shifting to French spelling below based on context.[62] He came from a family of well-established merchants (*tujjār*) and administrators in Ottoman Algiers, some of whom had worked in commerce across the western Mediterranean since at least the late eighteenth century. The family owned several urban properties in the capital, and, as most monied families in Algiers, they likely held agricultural estates nearby. In the early months of the occupation, the French records show that one of their apartments housed a Swiss family who had relocated to North Africa.[63] Like other notables in Algiers, the Abū Ḍarbas carefully cultivated their social capital by intermarrying with other local elite families involved in commerce and government service.[64] In the early 1820s one of the Abū Ḍarba sons, Aḥmad, left for Marseille to work with his uncle Muṣṭafā trading between France and Algeria.[65] Contrary to the established practice in his family, he married a French woman, Célestine Durand. She gave birth in France to their son, Ismāʿīl/Ismaël, in January 1823, cementing the couple's relationship. Little is known about Durand or the reasons why she and Bouderba (under his French name) chose to marry across the boundaries of religion, nationality, and race. A fictionalized and prejudicial French narrative written at this time presents her as a pretty woman from Avignon, although the municipal archives in the city have no record of her birth.[66] More telling is this source's claim that she was *une jolie grisette*, a French expression current at the time to denote the sexually accessible, poor women of bourgeois fantasies. Within the French grid of race and class used to assess Abū Ḍarba's standing, Durand the *grisette* is made to appear like a knock-off product of a woman of beauty and class whom a wealthy but unsophisticated Arab would mistake for the real thing. In fact, other, less prejudicial sources suggest that while she was not born to the high houses of merchants or diplomats and could not pretend to be the social equal of her husband, she did not come from poverty either. She was likely from a family of either artisans or lawyers, living somewhere in the lower Rhône valley. One branch lived in Aix-en-Provence, onetime home to the provincial parlement of Provence, just inland from the port at Marseille.[67] If she did not bring a large dowry to the marriage, Durand was an attractive partner to Abū Ḍarba, in her nationality, native language, and intelligence alone. He did not add to his wealth through her property and connections, but he had occasion to appreciate her cool head and excellent judgment. Indeed, she probably saved his life at a critical juncture later in Algiers, as I will discuss.

Although Abū Ḍarba had married and started a family in Marseille and lived well there for years among a small group of expat Algerians merchants, he did not put down even rudimentary roots. Marseille had built its fortunes on colonial and Mediterranean trade, and it faced an uncertain future after the Revolution and Haitian independence.[68] Moreover, the city had not shown itself particularly hospitable to Muslims and those of other faiths from across the southern Mediterranean. Among these people, Tunisians and Algerians in Marseille had enjoyed privileged status because they came from powerful states and thus benefited from the principle of reciprocity that governed interstate relations before 1830. A letter from their government gave them ample leverage if they had problems with local authorities. For example, in 1775 the dey of Algiers responded to complaints from his subjects in Marseille about access to a Muslim cemetery by intervening directly with the French king, who in turn pressed the case with local authorities, stressing the crown's treaty obligations with the deylik.[69] These arrangements did not always go smoothly, however. During the Revolution, early enthusiasm to enlarge the boundaries of citizens to include Muslims faded, and merchants from Algiers, both Muslims and Jews, faced the hostility of authorities, which led to the confiscation and sale of their property.[70] At the end of the revolutionary era, rioters in Marseille attacked the local community of "Mamelouks," people, like Joanny Pharaon, who came to Marseille with French troops evacuating Egypt in 1801. A dozen of them died at the hands of a local mob in June 1815.[71] While the Algerians and other North Africans in Marseille apparently escaped this violence, having no relationship with the hated Napoleon, they soon faced their own problems when the newly restored Bourbon kings refused to honor debts the previous French governments had contracted with Algiers and relations between the countries deteriorated to the point of war. In retaliation, the dey forbade his subjects from repaying their own debts to French creditors. Abū Ḍarba himself appears on a list of Algerian subjects ("Hamet Bouderba") who collectively owed creditors in Marseille a half million francs in 1830.[72]

This liminal status of Algerians might account for why Abū Ḍarba and Durand did not register either their marriage or the birth of their son with the municipal authorities in Marseille.[73] The omission is telling. Without an état civil to document these relations, the couple lacked the foundations for a civil life in France. Abū Ḍarba, like the other Maghribi merchants in Marseille, did not seem to have been interested in registering his vital acts. This set the community apart from other Ottoman subjects living in France, like the people from Egypt who regularly recorded their vital acts in Marseille's état civil. For a mixed couple like Durand and Abū Ḍarba, the fact that their union had no état civil might mean that they chose to forgo legally constituting their marriage, a not-unheard-of decision, but one that put their family and whatever property they owned in France at risk. Or it might mean that authorities at the city hall turned them away. Abū Ḍarba was a foreigner, and municipal agents might have interpreted the état civil's rules and procedures in their own way. Although foreigners had the right to register their vital acts in the official records, there were some gray zones. For example, a local registrar might have deemed Durand ineligible because French law expected that the wife of a foreigner assimilate to her husband's nationality (an expectation that carried the risk of apatride for certain women whose husband's country did not allow for easy naturalization of spouses).

Abū Ḍarba left Marseille in the early months of 1830, and at the beginning of July he was in Algiers, then under siege by the French army. As the tide of battle turned irrevocably against the Algerians, he presented himself to French officers and offered to negotiate the city's surrender. He helped draft the document by which the Algerian dey put down arms in return for French guarantees for the physical safety of the people of Algiers, as well as promises to protect property and Islamic institutions.[74] Known as the Convention and signed on 5 July 1830, the document stated: "The exercise of the Muslim religion will remain free. The liberty of the inhabitants of all classes, their religion, their properties, their commerce, and their industry will experience no harm. Their women will be respected."[75] In the months ahead, Abū Ḍarba emerged as the single most important Algerian working between the occupation authorities and the people of Algiers. He served various roles in the municipal administration, including president of the interim municipal commission and then as a Muslim adjunct to the French mayor. Other members of his family also held powerful positions, such as the head of the most important religious endowment in Algeria, which managed properties devoted to the annual pilgrimage to Mecca.[76] He enjoyed the trust of people on both sides, with his French wife and cultural skills serving as guarantor of his fidelity to France, and his powerful and respected family making him a logical candidate to represent the denizens of Algiers. Thus, at about the same time as local notables expressed their confidence in Abū Ḍarba in the Shaʿbān letter of 1831, a sympathetic French officer wrote that he was "animated by an equal zeal for his country and for France."[77]

The French knew Abū Ḍarba as "Bouderba" (a name I'll shift to in this section devoted to his French-language texts). It is in this name and the French language that his place in history is known. What baggage came with his use of the colonizer's tongue? Scholars typically understand expressing oneself in an other's language to be a fraught exercise with regards to identity and agency, with northwestern Africa figuring as something of an epicenter for this question, given its long history of polyglotism.[78] For his part, Bouderba must have felt at home in at least the domestic idioms of French. It was the only language he shared with Durand, and he used it frequently with their son, who grew up fully bilingual. His French interlocutors commented on Bouderba's excellent French skills, even if he was a nonnative speaker. Nonetheless, he likely encountered language prejudices.[79] Bouderba protested difficulties using French in formal discourse, which were corroborated in the historical record. The texts he authored and transcripts of his spoken testimony show an excellent, but not perfect, command of the language. For example, Bouderba prefaced an important address he made to a parliamentary commission in 1834 by stating, "I begin by asking for a thousand pardons of the reader for my style [which reflects] my ignorance of the French language, and leaves me unable to find or discover beautiful phrases."[80] But in the same text, he spoke with great fluidity on key questions, such as explaining the deep attachment Algerian Muslims felt for Islam and the need for the French to contain their own religious (or anticlerical) beliefs in the interest of good order. In this respect, the following passage from Bouderba's speech is worth considering in full in a literal translation from the original French text.

> The authorities must do all that is possible not to change anything, not in their [i.e., Algerian] customs, nor in their practices or habits, especially not religion, which is the primary base that must be solidly established with the Muslim, without ever thinking to violate it in any instance; instead, the French must adopt proper conduct, by giving good examples, acting with justice, faithfulness, and moderation, and not harming anyone in their beliefs or in their practices. Acting in this manner will introduce true civilization: Seeing your wise and fair conduct, the natives on their own accord will seek to change their customs and habits. I can say without offense to anyone that up to now the natives who have known the French only in Algiers have a very poor opinion of this magnanimous nation, because the overwhelming majority of the French who have gone to this country act without morals and without any beliefs, even in the existence of God, so much so that when an Arab, a Bedouin, or an inhabitant of the city, when they go before an authority to submit a complaint, if they have the misfortune to pronounce the name of God, and call on him, they are immediately heckled in the most revolting manner, some

> abandon their legal complaints so that they might not hear these insults cast upon the supreme Being.[81]

However roughly Bouderba's French reads in this text, with its difficult syntax and challenging structure (although native writers and speakers of French could do much worse), it should be remembered that this was originally a speech, which a clerk transcribed before handing it off for copyediting and punctuation.[82] Had the secretary properly repunctuated Bouderba's address and ironed it out for the written word, the results would have been much different. Therefore, given Bouderba's relatively expert command of French, one imagines that his apologetic preface had more to do with his accent, which when matched to his race, and perhaps clothing (there are no sources indicating how Bouderba dressed in France), risked marking him as an outsider to his audience of upper-class, white politicians. In this case, Bouderba might have felt himself required to perform an exercise in humility. Regardless, no one could fault his command of French philosophical idioms nor his fine grasp of religion in French politics.[83] Bouderba precisely invokes ideologically weighted terms like "supreme Being," central to the French Deist tradition, and he enlists principles like "justice, faithfulness, and moderation" that anchored the Enlightenment's reaction to the fervor of the Reformation and the religious violence that consumed France in the sixteenth century, as well as the country's recent political violence of the Revolution. Moreover, Bouderba finely tuned his terms to the particular context of France in the 1830s under the July Monarchy. At this time the sort of rationality and universalism that served as a hallmark of the Enlightenment was mitigated by the need to find political equilibrium or compromise, a project that writers dubbed the *juste milieu*. Moderation was its byword, and pragmatism took priority of place.[84] Bouderba clearly expressed his belief that enlightened, sober elites could best lead in France, and so too, he argued, Algeria needed these people to govern. Countervailing the racialized expectations of his audience, Bouderba argued by his own example that Algerians like himself might best serve as these leaders, rather than the rough-shod Frenchmen who were attracted to life across the Mediterranean. Bouderba made this claim when he redeployed the emerging key term of modern French imperialism, "civilization." Regardless of his accent or appearance, he professed his own membership among civilized leaders, set apart from others. Addressing an elite audience of statesmen in Paris, the Algerian plays up their fears of the lower classes by presenting the settlers and soldiers in Algeria as a godless, uncouth population, who act "without morals and without any beliefs." He did not, however, try to ingratiate himself with his interlocutors by repeating any of their denigrating views of Algerians, as often occurs in such situations when self-degradation is the price of admission to the elites. The problem facing France in Algeria is not Muslim fanaticism, Bouderba states, but the normlessness of an unfortunate French rabble who had themselves gone astray long before arriving in Africa. Both he and his French interlocutors could agree on that, he implied.

In this instance, Bouderba modeled his own subjectivity according to French norms, and he thereby invited his audience to join him above the fray as a clear-sighted leader interested in public order and the common good.[85] And yet, he had to contend with his interlocutors' views of him. The Enlightenment's universalism was predicated on exclusions, the most important of which in this context was Islam. These had been recently updated for nineteenth-century French imperialism by writers like the Comte de Volney, who cast Islam as France's most formidable opponent in the Mediterranean.[86] Bouderba never hid the fact that he was a Muslim, nor did he take distance from his faith by voicing any of the era's Islamophobic tropes to ingratiate himself with the French. This refusal to meet the French in their prejudices likely doomed his efforts. In the end, Bouderba failed to connect with his (idealized) enlightened audience. French leaders did not respond to his call. Already in 1831 some in the administration had started calling Bouderba a "crafty moor," and they later turned his proximity to French culture against him.[87] While some would see his bilingualism and embrace of French values as a valuable resource, to others these signaled an intrigant and a person who could change sides too easily.

A name in a loophole

I would like now to return to Abū Ḍarba/Bouderba's name as he fashioned it into a signature to understand how he negotiated these problems of language, subjectivity, and agency. The name Abū Ḍarba originates in an Arabic word *ḍaraba*, which means to strike a blow or fight for something.[88] Paired with "Abū," it formed an honorific name or kunya of a family ancestor known as "the man who fights," or someone who had proven himself in battle. The Abū Ḍarba family had adopted this as a shared family name dating back at least to the 1780s, and likely centuries earlier. In northwestern Africa, it evokes the old struggles against the Spanish Reconquista, and Muslim efforts to defend Islam. Adapted to French, "Bouderba" served the family throughout the nineteenth century and beyond.[89] But the specific cultural capital of the Abū Ḍarba name fell away in French. It was not until 1902 that a French journalist and amateur orientalist took an interest in the family name and decided that Abū Ḍarba meant "the scarred man," writing that it referred to an ancestor whose nose had been cut off.[90] In this French account, the name became a sign of humiliating facial disfiguration rather than bravery.

For his part, Abū Ḍarba had evident pride in the Arabic version of his name and ensured that it did not disappear as his name made its way across Arabic and French. This can be seen in the distinctive autographed signature he used at different points in his life. Overall, Abū Ḍarba drew his name with what would have been called confidence, meaning his letters show the steady lines, continuous angles and loops, of a well-practiced hand. When writing to French authorities, he most often signed his name in its French version, using French letters. The name's orthography differed over the years. In 1833 he signed his name "Hamid Bouderba," and later in 1837 he wrote it as "Achmed Abouderba." By the 1840s he took to signing "Ahmed Abouderba." As the spelling of the name changed, so too did the handwriting in his signature, which appeared sometimes in tight and angular letters, and others in a more open, rounded form with carefully flowing cursive French letters.[91]

Of the greatest interest are several documents in which Bouderba signed his name twice over, once in French and a second time using Arabic script and the Arabic spelling.[92] He first did this in 1831. After signing his name in French letters, written from left to right, he shifted to write his Arabic name from right to left, with separate flourishes drawn from the end of each name extending underneath and ending in two loopholes (see figure 4.2). In later iterations, he enlarged the loopholes and wrote his Arabic name "Aḥmad" and then "Abū Ḍarba" within them.[93] In this way, his French-language name was echoed underneath in the loopholes in its original Arabic letters.

Bouderba's doubled signature is not unique. Many of those who lived between Europe and the Maghrib also used different versions of their

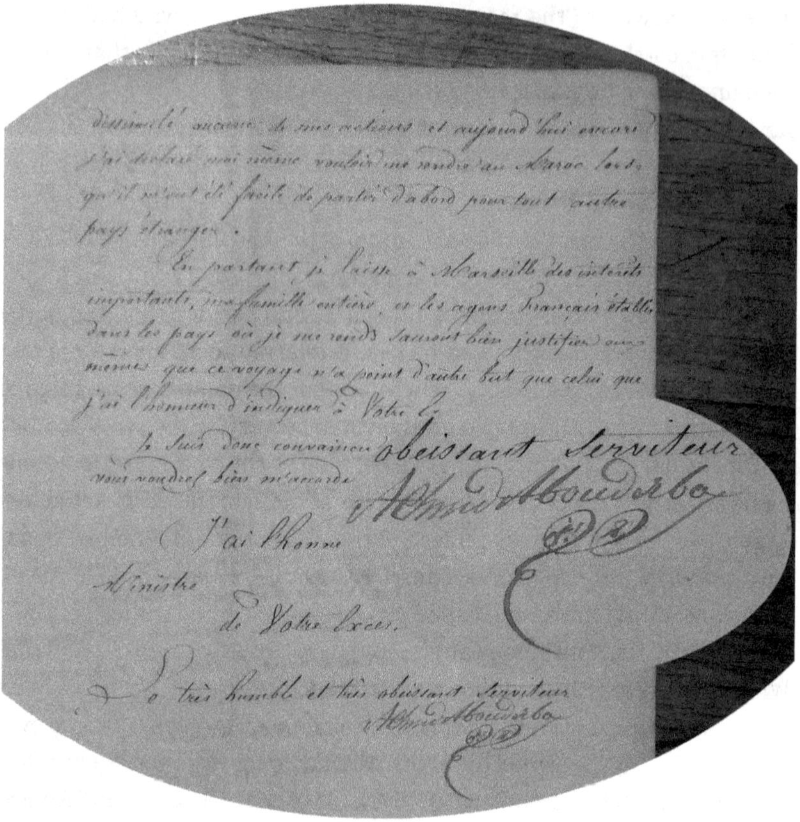
desservi le succès de mes actions et aujourd'hui encore
j'ai déclaré moi-même vouloir me rendre au Maroc lors-
qu'il m'eut été facile de partir d'abord pour tout autre
pays étranger.
En partant je laisse à Marseille des intérêts
importants, ma famille entière, et les agens français établis
dans les pays où je me rends sauront bien justifier eux-
mêmes que ce voyage n'a point d'autre but que celui que
j'ai l'honneur d'indiquer à Votre Ex.
Je suis donc convaincu
vous voudrez bien m'accorder
J'ai l'honneur
Ministre
de Votre Excel.
le très humble et très obéissant serviteur
Ahmed Abouderba

FIGURE 4.2 Abouderba/Abū Ḍarba handwritten letter in French to minister of interior, Marseille, 4 April 1846. FR ANOM. Aix-en-Provence 1h1-*Touts droits réservés.* Detail: Arabic name within loophole flourishes below magnified signature.

names across languages. Most famous is the sixteenth-century Moroccan geographer known as Leo Africanus. After converting to Christianity as a slave in Italy, he signed his works with both his new Christian name and his original Arabo-Islamic name.[94] There are also lesser-known people uncovered by historians in places like precolonial Tunisia, such as the general Ḥusayn ibn 'Abdallah (d. 1887), studied by M'hamed Oualdi, and the Tunisian linguist Mardochée Naggiar (d. ca. 1840s), whose biography was written by Lucette Valensi.[95] Each of these men either hybridized their signatures between Latin and Arabic letters (Ḥusayn formed the first letter of his name by combining a Latin "H" and an Arabic *ḥa* in a single sign) or signed their names twice in two different languages. Natalie Zemon Davis reads Leo Africanus's doubled signature as a way that he negotiated "the entanglement of values, perspectives, and personae in his life in Italy."[96] In this respect she sees his signature as confirmation of the autonomy and integrity of the self and its capacity for agency even under coerced conditions. In the case of the two precolonial Tunisians, one sees in their doubled or hybridized signatures less the work of violence and European domination than the influence of North Africa's multiple cultures and overlapping languages, wherein the name served to both cross divides (a name for each language) and mark divides, as names have long done.

A doubled signature stands as an especially interesting site to interrogate the questions of this chapter, such as the name's relationship to sovereignty and subjectivity, dispossession and alienation. Abū Ḍarba was a colonized subject, although he did not recognize what this meant at first. In Algeria after 1830, the type of onomastic crossings made in the precolonial era became increasingly fraught. The old contests for meaning, self-definition, and the definition of the other that had historically played themselves out in the name changed under the colonial era's hardened forms of identity and subjectivity, struggles in which France and the French language held a hegemonic position.[97] Bouderba/Abū Ḍarba tried to navigate these in his talks with the French to the advantage of the notables of Algiers like himself, and his French signature reads as an extension of these efforts. Written in a careful hand after a valediction, his French name assures his reader of familiarity, serving as something of a semantic bond made in the French language across the colonial divide. In this respect Bouderba did not write his Arabic name, Abū Ḍarba, as a provocation. Indeed, the untrained French eye might easily misread the Arabic script in the loophole as some of the flourish that frequently appeared at the end of French signatures of this era.

What to make of the man in the loophole? For Abū Ḍarba, the "man who fights," this Arabic name obviously held deep significance. The fact that he split or doubled his name suggests insight into how he responded to the basic question of interpellation and the name. To the question "Am I this name?" his French name, "Bouderba" answers in the affirmative, affirming that he shared the same language and values as his French interlocutors, whereas when he writes "Abū Ḍarba" into the loophole, he also says "I am not only that" or "this is actually something of me, down here." Such an equivocal answer to colonial interpellation suggests that he would not give a final account of himself to his French reader on that person's terms. In this respect, his signature became a "word with a loophole," literally enacting Mikhail Bakhtin's trope best known in literary theory.[98] Like the novelistic characters that Bakhtin studied, who used loophole words to manage the outside forces that split them and obliged them to betray their own intentions and violate their sense of autonomy, Abū Ḍarba/Bouderba's doubled signature offered him the possibility for what Bakhtin called "the retention for oneself of the possibility for altering the ultimate, final meaning of one's own words." In this sense the doubled name responded in ambiguous and indeterminate terms to the French insistence that Abū Ḍarba/Bouderba's signature establish his amenability to their interests. However, the agency seemingly afforded by the loophole was limited by the fact that it was bound to other's language, meaning that it must take "into account internally the responsive, contrary evaluation of oneself made by another."[99] As Bakhtin suggests, the literary character who spins out multiple definitions of the self risks losing sight, not so much of some sort of stable true self—the "who am I" question—but of who it is who ultimately controls the back-and-forth of identity. Is it the hero's own self-definition or that of the other? For Bakhtin, this means that "the loophole makes the hero ambiguous and elusive *even for himself*. In order to break through to his self the hero must travel a very long road."[100]

The loophole closes for Abū Ḍarba

Abū Ḍarba died far from home in the Moroccan port of Tangier in 1865. Twice he had been expelled from Algeria, first in 1832 and then in 1836, when he was permanently barred from Algeria (and all French territory for a time) after an arrest and imprisonment on baseless political charges.[101] He returned only once to his homeland to my knowledge, in 1837, when the French government granted him exceptional entry so that he might meet Amīr 'Abd al-Qādir to work out terms with this man who led the most formidable armed opposition France faced at the time. Otherwise, the door to Algeria closed permanently to him. In 1838 he settled in Marseille, this time in exile, living on the rue Curiol, not far from the port. Here he tried to revive the family's business, shifting its commerce from Algeria to Morocco.[102]

Hard-line army leaders expelled him from Algiers, people who dominated policy, often at the expense of the government itself. They argued that France was not bound by the Convention of 1830, and they rejected outright the premise of shared or consultative governance with Algerians. When Algerians addressed letters or petitions to these authorities, it was taken as a dangerous violation of the proper relationship between colonized and colonizer. French authorities used the signatures of Algerians fixed to these documents to identify and track down their enemies.[103]

Already by the occupation's second year, Algerians saw they had entered a time of unprecedented troubles. French troops massacred about eight hundred people in Blida in 1830, and in April 1832 around one hundred people of the Ūfiyya tribe (Ouffia, Fr.) were slaughtered wantonly by French-led troops in their camp immediately outside of Algiers as they slept. Soldiers took bloody loot from the massacre and sold it openly in the city's markets. The severed head of an 'Ūfiyya man was put on public display.[104] A climate of lawlessness and emergency descended on the city that fateful year.[105] Massive demonstrations numbering about ten thousand people took to the streets to oppose arbitrary rule. In particular, the demonstrators sought to protect the city's congregational mosques, the largest and most splendid places of worship. Even though the Convention of 1830 had expressly guaranteed their protection, they were being threatened with confiscation. At this point, the Muslims of Algiers maintained control of only four of the thirteen major mosques (*jāmi' masjid*) where they had made the public Friday prayer before 1830.[106] In a last-ditch effort to save the beloved Katshāwa (Ketchaoua, Fr.) mosque in late 1832, thousands of people barricaded themselves inside it. French authorities had chosen to seize Katshāwa and convert it into a Catholic church in time to celebrate Christmas mass, leading to a standoff that almost ended in a bloodbath for the Algerians. Abū Ḍarba led efforts to save Katshāwa. In the committee meetings leading up to the confiscation, he tried to hold France accountable to promises made in 1830, inviting its leaders again to live up to their professed principles of civilization and moderation, even offering lesser mosques that might serve as a church. Failing there, he interposed himself on the mosque's steps on the day of the standoff along with several interpreters who hoped to defuse the crisis. Looking down the French bayonets, he was nearly killed in the stampede that ensued when gunshots rang out.

This was the second time Abū Ḍarba escaped death that year. Before the Katshāwa mosque standoff, in February 1832, he narrowly avoided arrest by General Savary (the Duc de Rovigo), the feared commander of the French army in Algeria. The general suspected Abū Ḍarba of conspiring against him and wanted to silence the Algerian once and for all. The suspicion and hostility of a man like Savary alone put Abū Ḍarba's life in jeopardy. The French general had served previously as Napoleon's minister of police (1810–1814), when he earned a reputation as a particularly ruthless man. He also fought in Egypt and led French troops in the brutal war in Spain. As the head of the armed forces in Algeria, he spread terror through summary executions and the arbitrary imprisonment of suspects, many of whom died mysterious deaths.

Abū Ḍarba narrowly avoided this fate thanks to the intervention of his wife, Durand. The general agreed to meet the Frenchwoman and hear her plead her husband's case. Savary turned the meeting into an interrogation, however.[107] In the letter he personally wrote to the minister of war, the only record of the encounter, Savary displays evident pleasure in telling how he browbeat, threatened, and cajoled Durand in an effort to get her to let slip some incriminating detail that he could use against her husband. "[T]his woman was terrified," he wrote with satisfaction, describing his impact on her. Reading between the lines of Savary's account, one can see, however, that Durand played her cards well, giving the French general nothing that could be used against Abū Ḍarba. In the end, she succeeded in getting Savary to guarantee her husband's safety as long as he would temporarily leave Algeria.

Names evidently figure in Savary's account of this meeting. They include the names of Abū Ḍarba and his supposed Algerian co-conspirators. Bouderba is written as "Abouderbach," along with "Ben Zamoun" (i.e., al-Ḥajj Muḥammad bin Zaʿmūm) and "Sidi Said" (i.e., al-Ḥajj Sīdī al-Saʿdī.) However, two names are conspicuously absent. The first is Durand herself. Savary identifies her only as a "Marseillaise, speaking very good French." Why he thought it important to note that Durand spoke French well is surprising, when it was, after all, her native tongue. Was this an inside joke he shared with the minister, suggesting that a Frenchwoman risked losing her ability to speak proper French when she married an Arab, or an attack on her southern accent? In any case, Durand appears in this letter like the unnamed "Bedouins" and "Kabyles" that frequented French documents of the era, referred to only by her place of origin. The second absent name, or rather set of names, relates to one of Savary's accusations against Abū Ḍarba. Along with the charge of anti-French conspiracy, Savary held that Abū Ḍarba had lied about his role as a spokesperson for the notables of Algiers to the French government on his mission to Paris in 1831. This "man dominated by the need to intrigue" had falsely presented himself in the French capital as having a mandate from local people, Savary wrote. Of course he did have that mandate. Somewhere in his office lay the Sha'bān letter of 1831 whereby the capital's notables officially endorsed Abū Ḍarba as their representative. The twenty-four signatures affixed to this document effectively disappeared, with Savary simply ignoring them.

Graphologists have a lot to say about signatures and what they reveal about a person's character and mental state. Accordingly, a readable signature marks courage, a large signature is a sign of vanity, a rising signature reveals ardor, and a series of dots after the name equals defiance.[108] By contrast, a signature that crosses itself out is said to signal an act of self-negation, and it often appears as a precursor or metaphor for suicide.[109] Abū Ḍarba never struck through his signature outright. But around this time, he stopped double-signing his name in French and Arabic. He first had used a doubled signature on an 1831 mission, when he still had an optimistic outlook. In the French capital, Abū Ḍarba received an audience at the Ministry of War, where he was invited to share his proposals for Algiers's future, with a French secretary sitting by to write them up, twenty-one propositions in all, which were later considered at the highest levels of government.[110] He signed this document in his own hand, first in French, with a carefully drawn "Hamid Bodarba," and then, underneath in Arabic, he jotted out "Aḥmad Bū Ḍarba." It would be nine years before he would reproduce this doubled signature again. The government ended up giving his 1831 proposals a hostile hearing, and the escalating violence the next year in Algiers effectively closed opportunities for Algerians seeking to participate in their own governance. With them, the "loophole" in Bouderba's signature also closed.[111]

5

In Others' Names

Making the Algerian Name French, 1850s–1870s

> The name turns everyone into a letter within an immense, potentially endless alphabet, which would be the human species.
>
> —Michelle Grangaud, *État civil: Inventaires*

Modernization of the French Name

Personal names in France underwent fundamental changes beginning with the Revolution. With these changes, the state hitched the name to new techniques of statecraft and law. Before this time, French names roughly resembled the ways precolonial names worked in northwestern Africa. They were unfixed and variable and responded primarily to the needs of the people who used them in face-to-face relations. In this era, single baptismal names and various sorts of surnames and sobriquets circulated freely to signify an individual and fulfill the social functions of naming. These distinguished individuals as such and marked the social associations that linked them into families and communities. Some models promised greater structure. Far in the past lay the three-part name used in the Roman Empire, the *Praenomen* (personal forename), the *Nomen* (kinship group), and the *Cognomen* (acquired nickname).[1] This naming model was reworked, forgotten, and rediscovered over the centuries as no institution stood ready to monopolize the name. The Catholic Church gained some ascendency with its control of the baptismal font and the names conferred there.[2] For the most part, however, local custom decided the form of names, and there were few widely followed rules.[3] The use of hereditary family names began to spread from a small group of elites to the rest of society in the late Middle Ages and early modern era.[4] But even these names lacked fixed forms, and people passed them through the family in idiosyncratic ways. Between the sixteenth and eighteenth centuries, modern French naming practices began to take shape. At this time the state started drafting some formal rules even if it did not have the will or the means to impose them.[5]

During the French Revolution, the state seized expansive powers over the name, including deciding fundamental questions about what constituted an appropriate word for a name. A law of 1790 forbade seigneurial names (*nom à particule* or *nom de terre*) and titles (comte, baron, marquis, etc.), seeing them as vestiges of the abolished feudal order.[6] Two years later, the 1792 decree that established the secularized état civil laid out rules for a new, standardized name. The given name(s) became the *prénom*, a nod to the Roman term, and the family name became the nom, a fixed patronym. This was followed by a decree that forbade adding sobriquets, fixing the name into the état civil for all usages, or, as the law put it "no citizen may bear a surname or first name other than those expressed in his birth certificate."[7] This ended the way that names had previously evolved during the course of one's life, and it raised the stakes of the état civil records themselves, which effectively tethered a person to their birth name for their entire life. In short, names became officialized and immutable, standing as an essential part of a person's public subjectivity. By 1824, one important reference expounded on the name in ontological terms: "Our proper name is ourselves . . . nothing can separate our being from it."[8]

Having fixed the name's form, revolutionaries asserted the state's right to decide what were acceptable names.[9] In the early years of the Revolution, people enjoyed great latitude to change and choose their own names with a simple declaration at the city hall. This encouraged revolutionaries to express their political values in new names. They included a former nun born Angélique Goux, who married an ex-curé with a new name, "Liberté."[10] Others dropped names associated with the Old Regime in favor of new names, as did Louis-Philippe le duc d'Orléans, who abandoned his ducal title and took "Égalité" as his family name.[11] The name then became a sign by which one's revolutionary ardor announced itself. Those who carried names considered out of synch with the times faced censure. A humorous anecdote told in a nineteenth-century name manual showed up the stakes. The case concerned a man named M. de Saint-Cyr, who had been convoked before a revolutionary tribunal.[12] When this man pronounced his name, the judge heard the "de" preposition in his name, a marker of noble status, and said "there is no more nobility." The man removed the "de" and said, "My name then is Saint-Cyr." The judge, still not satisfied, replied, "The reign of superstition and that of the saints has passed," a comment that the man recognized was directed at the canonical title in his name. "I'll call myself Cyr, then," he stated. But even this truncated name did not satisfy the judge. "Cyr" derived from the Greek word for master and lord, and the judge took it for more aristocratic pretensions. Exasperated, the accused tried to turn the increasingly absurd situation against the court: "Since I have no name, I escape the law, because I am no more than an abstraction, you'll find no law condemning an abstraction. I must therefore be acquitted!" The tactic worked, and the man was sent out the door as "Citizen Abstraction."

The funny story made an important point, a sense that the implausible demands made on names had gone too far. To contain the name as a usable sign, as well as mark the era's own conservative turn, a law in 1803 revoked the right to change one's name easily.[13] It also limited the repertoire of available names, stating that "only names appearing in various calendars and those known in ancient history can be accepted as first names in the civil registers."[14] Although no master list of permissible names emerged (the recording état civil officer himself decided if a particular name met the requirements), the rule stated that names must reflect prevailing French cultural norms, centered on a Christian and classical Greco-Roman heritage.[15] The government imposed such norms on minorities. A decree in 1808 obliged French Jews to adopt a patronym while prohibiting them from using Old Testament names, allowing an exemption only for families who had already established a biblical patronym.[16] This ostensibly served identification purposes because it was felt that the limited repertoire of biblical names produced too many homonyms among Jews, a view that ignored the proliferations of homonyms within culturally Christian names.

More important, it reflected the view that Jews must assimilate as individuals. A "French" patronym name helped "to better aggregate these heterogeneous molecules into the social body," as one commentator put it.[17] Thus, names appeared that a French-trained ear found harmonious. Abrand replaced "Abraham," and Lévy became "Léon."[18] The names of other minorities were Gallicized, as occurred with Breton names, rooted in the region's Celtic language, a process that mutilated many people's names.[19]

The keystone of the modern French name was the patronym or nom. Derived from the father's surname, the patronym passed automatically to his natural or legitimate children upon their birth. It established a firm and unambiguous identity for the individual. The nineteenth-century sources proclaimed that the patronym enshrined the individual at the center of law and rights. As one legal reference stated: "The name (*nom*) is the characteristic and distinctive sign of the individual. It is inseparable from the person of which it constitutes an essential element, in the same way as honor and freedom. These rights are absolute."[20] In this view, the patronym promoted autonomy, moral integrity, freedom, and equality. But the identity it conferred expressed less one's "freedom and honor," than the father's central place in French law and society. The legal historian Anne Lefebvre-Teillard writes that the patronym is "a sign of attachment to the father, the one who 'naturally' stands at the head of the family and in whom domestic power lies."[21] So the patronym makes an individual's identity a function of the father's power as well as the ties of filiation imbedded in his name. French code gave extensive powers to the father, including, paradoxically, the ability to deny that he was the father of children he had had with women other than his legal wife. Such children had no right to inheritance, nor could they claim to belong to his lineage.[22] They could not bear his name. Within the confines of the patriarchal family, they suffered the equivalent of civil death. If illegitimate children used their biological father's name as their own, they would be treated like thieves, with the law considering the name as a form of property that must be protected against usurpers.[23] As the sources put it, the patronym determined the destiny of the individual. To put it more exactly, this person's ability to exist as a legal subject was an effect of the patronym as sign. This name anchored social relations within the family, which were themselves given the force of law and made concrete in the name. In this sense, then, one can say that the reality of the family emerged from the patronym as a sign and the way that actual laws and social practices used it.[24] Whereas the personal names of premodern France amply fulfilled social needs, the new name introduced during the Revolution produced a political subject useful for the state and the law.[25]

Algeria: Modern names, modern rights?

The early colonial administration expressed little interest in name reform for Algerians up to 1865. When local caïds started reporting births and deaths in the 1840s and 1850s, they could use existing names written in Arabic.[26] Most of these sporadically collected records went untranslated, and they had little impact in the French system. This reflected the prevailing indifference to the legal status of Algerians.[27] An exception to these piecemeal efforts was a civil registration drive undertaken in 1856 in the city of Constantine. This responded to an earlier decree (8 August 1854) requiring Algerians living in territory under civilian authority to register their families as a first step toward regularizing their vital records. This created some support for changing Algerian names to meet French standards, and at the same time it revealed the challenges before such a project. At first the registration drive floundered because no municipal employee knew enough Arabic to ask people their names.[28] But when the task was turned over to Charles Dolly, an assistant in the departmental Arab Bureau who could read and write Arabic, it moved ahead quickly. He worked with Algerian forest guards, agents of religious endowments, and local caïds who lent the lone Frenchman their influence and skills decoding names. Dolly posted orders in neighborhoods requiring heads of households to present themselves and register their family members by name. Some feared that registration aimed at conscripting troops for the Crimean War, or that it had something to do with taxes. Most, however, complied. At the end of several months, Dolly succeeded in registering six thousand individuals, a number that represented about 40 percent of the city's Muslim population. There were numerous errors, errata, and lacunae in these records, but the effort was considered a success. The official reporting on the work concluded: "A new step [has been] taken by Arab society on the road to European institutions and this represents further proof that civil fusion . . . can be brought to a successful conclusion, without outside assistance and without violence."[29]

"Civil fusion" in this context meant making Algerians assimilable to French civil law, with an identity attested to by official, state-drafted records. This sort of legal assimilation became an urgent concern in the next decade. In 1863 Napoléon III announced his so-called Arab Kingdom project, which claimed to turn the page on previous harsh approaches toward Algerians and adopt a more liberal stance.[30] The emperor claimed: "We have not come to Algeria to oppress and despoil them but to bring them the benefits of civilization. And in fact, the first condition of civilization is the respect of everyone's rights."[31] To fulfill this claim, Napoléon III had to resolve two outstanding questions that had left Algerians' status in limbo: property rights and nationality. A law of 22 April 1863 issued by the emperor (a type of law called a "Sénatus-Consulte") addressed the first problem by recognizing the historic land rights of Algerians as valid. This law protected large sections of valuable farmlands that had been under constant threat of state seizure since the 1830s.[32] A second Sénatus-Consulte of 14 July 1865 resolved Algerians' nationality. It formally claimed them as French subjects, making them French from a legal perspective. The laws narrowly lived up to the liberal claims of the Arab Kingdom by carefully circumscribing the types of rights Algerians might enjoy.[33] The 1865 law conferred French nationality on Algerians while barring nearly all of them from the rights of citizenship. It contained a bridge to citizenship, but crossing it required abandoning confessional family law and one's personal status, which many Muslims viewed as an act of apostasy (see chapter 6). Whereas the earlier 1863 law granted Algerians the right of private property, this single modality of rights came disassociated from the important link property had had to political rights for French citizens for the first half of the nineteenth century.[34] Commentators who supported settlers saw Algerian land rights narrowly as the "right" to sell their property to Europeans

These changes gave newfound importance to Algerian names and the need to transform them according to French standards. Even as the Arab Kingdom barred Algerians from rights, it brought them closer to French law than they had ever been. For things like French-conferred property rights to function, Algerians had to have a legal subjectivity recognizable to French institutions. The state's vital registries or état civil provided much of the information that yielded this legal subjectivity (known as the *sujet de droit* in France), such as age, sex, occupation, and family filiation. Although some Algerians had appeared previously in various registries, like the dead people recorded by the official in Bône in the 1830s or those recorded by Dolly in Constantine two decades later, few had an official name and an état civil. The Constantine civil registration drive had shown up the problem. While it produced thousands of French-language records, it contained only approximate versions of names. The rules Dolly used said nothing about how to resolve the complexity of Algerian names nor how to make them legible to French personnel who, unlike himself, could not decipher Arabic script, let alone read or write the language. It simply called for Arabic documents to be "transcribed" into French at the city hall. If the French-produced records hoped to fix identities for legal purposes, names had to have fixed spellings. Uniform standards for converting Arabic script to French letters were only emerging at this time. Moreover, existing names did not contain the all-important French-style patronym.

A decade after the Constantine registration, a report in 1866 addressed the problem. Algerians needed to have a fixed patronymical surname, and names needed a standardized spelling in French letters. This name alone could do the fine-tooled work of, as the report put it:

> designat[ing] each family in society and each individual in the family. . . . We know, in fact, that most of the natives do not have a family name. Moreover, they use a very limited number of first names. This is a source of incessant confusion. Even in their everyday life within the tribe it is a problem, and the difficulties will be inextricable for all those who will be called upon to participate in the complexities of European life and for all those who seek the advantages of the Sénatus-Consulte.[35]

This put the problem in a nutshell. Algerian names had to fit French standards in order to assimilate Algerians to the colonial economy and administrative institutions. Those responsible for standardizing names knew they faced significant obstacles, perhaps the most important being ensuring Algerian cooperation. They called for a gradualist and less coercive process than that used in France during the Revolution. In particular, they ruled out imposing names on Algerians as they had been for Alsatian Jews in 1808, which had allowed them only three months to adopt a patronym. Algerians would not be forced to adopt new names in mass. But little by little, it was thought, they would recognize the advantages of a new name and chose to adopt one. As the 1866 order put it, individuals would embrace their new names, "stimulated by the progress of our political mores, the sheer force of things, and the free impulse of individual interests." It was in fact a much more arduous process, one that took another thirty years.

Converting Algerian names to French letters, 1850s–1860s

Anticipating this new era, experts in the 1850s and 1860s had already started working out a conversion system. The government's assimilation project accelerated these efforts and revealed the problems. Many of these problems were technical in nature. In a letter of 25 June 1865, Napoleon III wrote:

> Arab names make for difficult transcription in French characters. Writing them by ear, as one thinks one hears them pronounced, not everybody spells them the same way. Everyone follows their own, very different system of transcription. Thus, the same name figures sometimes in one way, sometimes another, in the registers of the état civil, on the tax rolls, property inventories, in court files, or in the clerk of the court and municipal records. A rigorously uniform spelling of names is indispensable for acts of the état civil.[36]

Hardly a linguist, the emperor reported what experts had told him for some time: The name troubles represented only one part of a larger problem of converting Arabic words to French letters. A decade earlier, the governor general in Algeria convened a commission of interpreters to address this issue. The team included top Arabists, people like Marcelin Beaussier and Louis-Jacques Bresnier, the holder of the first public chair of Arabic in Algiers. They began by regularizing the spellings of toponyms and tribe names in French, a project that did not get very far based on the extant documents.[37] Napoleon III's 1865 order resuscitated their efforts and turned the project toward personal names. Specialists compiled lists of names written in French letters by gleaning published sources like newspapers, which reflected emerging standards for converting Arabic names to French letters, as well as sources that featured names written in their original Arabic script. The latter included lists of names solicited from Arab Bureau personnel working locally, who themselves were either Arabists or worked with their interpreters or Arabophone clerical staff. This preliminary work went to the preeminent colonial-era orientalist, William Mac Guckin de Slane, famous for his translation of Ibn Khaldun, and Charles Gabeau, who had served as interpreter for the resistance leader 'Abd al-Qādir during his imprisonment in France.[38] The Arabists faced many challenges, including the sheer amount of names in the list, each one of which had to have its individual spellings fixed in both Arabic and French and had to be arranged alphabetically for publication. No Algerians formally participated in this work.

Most of the scholars working on the project specialized in literary Arabic, and this shaped the way they approached their task. Only two members of the first team, Beaussier and Bresnier, had competency in dialectical Algerian Arabic.[39] The Tamazight languages came late to the interests of French orientalists, who gave concerted attention to them only when military leaders tried to conquer Kabylia fully in 1857. In the 1860s existing French understandings of Berber names were insufficient to the task.[40] This left the team ill prepared to deal with actual naming practices. They struggled under the weight of the many different languages and informal practices that had left their imprint on names. However, capturing the full nuance of people's names was not their goal. They only had to standardize spellings in French letters. To do this, the Arabists felt entitled to "correct" names, effacing local idiosyncrasies, pronunciations, and orthography. Faced with the plethora of Algerian names, Mac Guckin de Slane and Gabeau matched names to words in the high idioms of the Arabic that they knew well and used these as a starting point for their French versions and a standardized orthography. Effectively, this meant that they took local names and translated them first into Classical Arabic before converting them into French.

This Arabo-centrism had a particularly strong impact on names in Tamazight, a language that itself split into distinct dialects with their own onomastic practices. The rules established by the Arabists transformed the morphology and orthography of Berber names and stripped them of other distinct signs.[41] When agents in the field later tried to use the system in the registration drives in the 1880s and 1890s, they learned soon enough that Berber-speaking people used their names in ways not reducible to the classical Arabo-Islamic model.[42] For example, in 1890 a registrar in

Kabylia wrote to superiors in Algiers asking how to apply his instructions to the actual names people used. "In Kabyle territory, the word Naït [*n'ayt*] is used with the same meaning as the word Ben (*bin*) in Arabic but with more extension, . . . that is to say that it serves to hyphenate two names regardless of the degree of kinship linking those who bear or have borne these names. Can the état civil commissioner use this word Naït on the various civil status documents or must he absolutely replace it with the word Ben?"[43] Likewise, he continued, the "ou" (*w*) did not always denote actual kinship relationships. Some given names were prefaced by the "ou," or it served to form a compound first name without the sense of filiation of Arabic's "son of." In Kabylia, for example, it was understood that the name Ramdan *ou* Salem was a compound first name, not a nasab. If he changed it into "Ramdan *ben* Salem" based on Arabic standards, it would mean "Ramdan son of Salem," signifying filiation. Was that acceptable? he asked. In their response, this registrar's superiors emphasized the value they placed on actual family relations. This meant that Kabyle names had to appear in French in a way that did not obscure filiation as the French understood it. In other words, the registrar needed to privilege local Berberophone practices over rules based on Arabic in a case like this that risked confusing the family. This stands as a notable exception. Officials allowed it only to ensure that name reform did not entirely obliterate the tie between fathers and their children. In other cases, however, the rules developed on the Arabic model had to be applied, overwriting the Berber name as necessary to convert to French letters.

Mac Guckin de Slane and Gabeau's project was well-received when it first appeared in 1868. They produced a bilingual onomasticon with more than 4,500 names published in a reference book, the *Vocabulaire*. It laid out rules for converting Algerian names into French, and it gave fifty-three pages of specific examples of standardized orthography for Algerian names in French letters as well as in Arabic script. This appeared in alphabetical order and in neatly compiled columns.[44] The *Vocabulaire* went to city halls, interpreters, and offices of the Bureaux arabes across Algeria as the standard reference for Algerian names.[45]

However, problems emerged in the *Vocabulaire* soon enough. Many of these related to the technical challenges faced when going between Arabic and French, and these are worth unpacking in detail. Finding a method by which an Algerian name can be written in French letters is not easy.

Even today, specialists who deal with the problem in Algeria struggle to regularize names for the Algerian republic's own état civil, which uses both Arabic and French letters to produce two versions of the same name.[46] In the nineteenth century, European linguists had only begun to address their need for a universal set of letters that could be used to convert the world's languages into a single alphabet. The German linguist Richard Lepsius, responsible for the world's first standard alphabet (the precursor to today's International Phonetic Alphabet), wrote:

> The diversity of signs for one and the same sound in different languages . . . has at length become so great, that the translator of Oriental works, the Tourist, the Geographer and Chartographer [*sic*], the Naturalist, the Ethnographer, the Historian, in short everyone who has to do with the names and words of foreign languages . . . find themselves entangled in an intolerable confusion of orthographic systems and signs, from which each individual finds it impossible to extricate himself.[47]

Lepsius thought that only the Latin alphabet, rather than any of the world's other writing systems, resolved the problem posed by a nearly infinite world of signs.[48] However, it was not well suited to the task. In the case of Latin-based French letters used for Arabic, it made an imperfect fit. In the most basic terms, Arabic letters can be converted to French through either phonetic *transcription*, writing what one hears in the approximate sounds of another alphabet, or an orthographic *transliteration*, focusing on the written language and using a system of equivalences between letters. Moreover, most French Arabists at the time believed that Arabic was a diglossic language, meaning they had two registers to consider, Classical Arabic (*arabe classique*, Fr.), the high version of the language used primarily in written form following the rules of a formal grammar, and dialectical Arabic (*arabe vulgaire*, Fr.) which was primarily a spoken version of the language, although some believed it could be adapted for writing.[49] Specialists generally prefer transliteration because it provides a more exact conversion process, working from written letter to written letter. However, even if one puts aside the unique aspects of the Arabic alphabet (such as the *hamza*) and considers only written letters (graphemes) and the sounds they represent (phonemes), a basic problem emerges for transliterating Arabic in French: the shortage of letters in the French alphabet. The basic alphabet used in nineteenth-century French texts was rich in letters for vowels, and the use of distinctive French accents further expanded their range of graphic signs.[50] In schematic terms, one can say that Latin gives French six basic vowels letters (*a, e, i, o, u, y*), which French expands with a series of accents and diacritical marks. The *accent grave* modifies three letters, *à, è, ù*; the *accent aigu* is used with *é*; the *accent circumflex* yields five new letters, *â, ê, î, ô, û*; and finally, the *tréma* marks, *ë, ï, ü, ÿ*. There are also combined vowel letters called orthographic ligatures, which produce the æ and œ. Together these give French a total of twenty-one different letters for vowels. So, the French alphabet offers an ample number of letters for Arabic's vowels. Moreover, French letters can combine to produce the correct equivalent in cases of long vowels. For example, Arabic's long a, *'ālif* in the name Ḥanān, can be accommodated phonetically in French by adding a final *e*, or "Hanane," which elongates the second *a* to better match the sound of the Arabic vowel.

The French alphabet had an abundance of vowels, but it came up short with respect to Arabic's consonant-rich alphabet. The French alphabet had only nineteen consonant letters at this time, not counting the *w*, which had not yet officially entered the French alphabet, or the diacritically marked ç or *cédille*, avoided by Arabists because it printed erratically.[51] By contrast, Arabic has a total of twenty-eight consonant letters in its alphabet (not counting the *hamza* glottal stop), three of which, the ا, و, ي (i.e., *'ālif, wāw,* and *yā'*), can also serve as vowels. This alphabet is expanded by diacritical marks placed above or below the line to represent Arabic's three short vowels, collectively called the *ḥarakāt*. If we take the example of "Ḥanān" again, the problem reveals itself. While the long "a" vowel is easily accommodated in French letters, the name's first consonant, the *ḥā'* (ح), of Arabic's distinctive hard "h" consonant, poses problems. How to distinguish it (a pharyngeal fricative) from the separate letter *hā* (ه), Arabic's soft "h" (glottal fricative), when French has only a single letter *h*? Moreover, a French speaker risks pronouncing this letter as an aspirated or silent "h," as is common in French words followed by an "a," making for a drastically different sounding name. Given the limits of their alphabet, French Arabists would have to figure out a way to accommodate sounds that had no corresponding signs in their own alphabet.

To put all this simply, the French alphabet is several sizes too small for Arabic. Mac Guckin de Slane and Gabeau reckoned that eight or nine new letters would be needed to fully represent Arabic.[52] These sorts of technical problems are not unique to French's relationship with Arabic. Judeo-Arabic writers also had to contend with the fact that the Hebrew alphabet also falls short of sufficient letters to represent those in Arabic. Living in predominately Arabic-speaking societies, they solved the problem by adding a dot or slash to their Hebrew letters when writing out Arabic words.[53] By modifying their own alphabet, these writers guarded the orthographic integrity of the original Arabic word based on its written (graphemic) form. Another option would have been to base equivalences on the sounds (phonemes) of the spoken language. Some Judeo-Arabic writers used this option because it simplified their task. They did not need to know the original orthography for a given word but could approximate its written form based on what they heard. Insofar as Arabic speakers did not always respect the distinct pronunciation that separated certain consonants in their vernacular speech, Judeo-Arabic writers could put several different Arabic letters into a single Hebrew letter based on approximate sounds.[54]

Few native speakers of Arabic or Berber participated in these debates. In the early decades of the nineteenth century and earlier, native speakers like Joanny Pharaon played an important role in French orientalism. So too did a variety of others, including the Moroccan acrobats who taught the interpreter and consul Jean-Michel Venture de Paradis some Tamazight in the 1780s while performing in Paris. At a different level, the Egyptian scholar al-Ṭahṭāwī did some work with Antoine Silvestre de Sacy, the director of the École des Langues Orientales in Paris, while staying in the French capital in the 1820s.[55] The invasion of Algeria fundamentally changed the field, however, as historian Alain Messaoudi has shown. Native speakers, especially Muslims, thinned from the ranks of Arabists, and Frenchmen dominated the field for decades. An exception to this trend was the corps of military interpreters in Algeria, which included some native Arabic speakers, although by the mid-nineteenth century they were nearly all from eastern Christian families or Arabophone Jews. Ismaël Bouderba (d. 1878), the son of Aḥmad Abū Ḍarba and Célestine Durand, was one of the few Algerian Muslims to serve as a career interpreter at midcentury. Later, new state schools like the Collège Impérial Arabe-Français (est. 1857) and the École Normale Primaire d'Alger/Bouzaréah (est. 1866) expanded career opportunities for the few Algerian Muslims fortunate enough to complete a degree.[56] They taught Arabic and Berber in Algeria, and a few became scholars in their own right. Belkacem Ben Sedira (Muḥammad ben Qāsim ben Ṣadīra, d. 1901) taught Arabic and Berber at the École des Lettres d'Alger and published important studies of both languages in the last decades of the nineteenth century.[57] However, Algerian scholars educated in the French traditions, an extremely rare lot already, experienced marginalization.[58] Not until the early twentieth century did they make a name at the highest levels of academic study, led by Mohammed Ben Cheneb (d. 1929), who was the first Muslim to occupy a chair at the University of Algiers. There were, of course, Algerian scholars who had trained in the Islamic sciences, either in Algeria or at prestigious institutions like Zaytuna University in Tunis or schools further east. Few of them knew French, and they were not invited to participate with the French Arabists working in government circles. When Mac Guckin de Slane and Gabeau decided the rules for name conversion in the 1860s, they did not consult Algerian counterparts.

Before Mac Guckin de Slane and Gabeau completed the *Vocabulaire*, other French scholars working for the government established a rough set of rules to convert Arabic to French letters (see figure 5.1). Published in the third volume of the Scientific Commission's studies on Algeria in 1853 (a project modeled on Bonaparte's famous Commission of Sciences and Arts in Egypt), it combined transliteration and transcription, privileging phonetic equivalences as a workaround for the French alphabet's shortage of consonant letters. It thereby eschewed any major diacritical modifications to the French alphabet, using only an apostrophe in some cases after the French letter to extend it in another iteration.

The Scientific Commission's system privileged similar-sounding phonemes in an effort to find distinct graphemes that might exactly reproduce the original written language. This compromised its ability to fully represent the original Arabic. But as one commentator argued, this was the "least defective" option. The French reader unfamiliar with Arabic, he continued, could never fully access the original through its transcription anyway, given "the impossibility of representing to the eyes [i.e., reading a written word] sounds that the ear has not yet known."[59] The system relied on analogous letters rather than exact equivalence of signs to fill in the French alphabet's lacunae. For example, it combined two French letters to approximate the sound of a single Arabic letter, as in the French *kh* for the Arabic letter خ. The same happened when two French letters were combined as *dj* and used for Arabic's ج. In other cases, two similar-sounding but distinct Arabic letters were collapsed into a single French letter, as

Lettres.	Valeur.	
ا	A, Ė, I, O.	L'emploi de ces divers caractères est déterminé par la prononciation et l'accentuation de la lettre arabe.
ب	B.	
ت ث	T.	Ces deux lettres sont généralement confondues dans la prononciation.
ج	Dj.	
ح	H'.	
خ	Kh.	
د ذ	D	Généralement confondues.
ر	R.	
ز	Z.	
س	S, C, Ç.	L'emploi de ces trois lettres sera réglé de manière à conserver le son sifflant de l'S.
ش	Ch.	
ص	S', C', Ç'	Même observation que pour le س.
ض ظ	D'	Ces deux lettres sont confondues par tous les Barbaresques dans la prononciation et dans l'écriture.
ط	T'.	
ع	'	Apostrophe précédée ou suivie de celle des voyelles dont la prononciation nécessite l'emploi.
غ	R'.	
ڢ	F.	
ڧ	K', G, Gu.	Le *g* et le *gu* seront employés dans les mots où l'usage attribue au ڧ la prononciation gutturale du *g*; ex.: *Gafs'a*, *Guélma*.
ك	K.	
ل	L.	
م	M.	
ن	N.	
ه	H.	
و	Ou, Ô.	
ى	I, Ī.	

FIGURE 5.1 Arabic-French conversion table. Source: Ernest Carette, *Exploration scientifique de l'Algérie*, vol. 3: *Recherches sur l'origine et les migrations des principales tribus de l'Afrique septentrionale et particulièrement de l'Algérie* (Paris: Imprimerie impérial, 1853), n.p.

happened with the French *d'* (diacritically marked with a trailing apostrophe), which stood in for two different Arabic letters, the ض and the ظ. The same happened with a single unmarked French letter *d*, which served to render Arabic's separate letters د and ذ. Arabic's ث and ت were combined into a single French letter, *t*. The rationale for all this was that the differences between letters were purely conventional, as measured by Algerian pronunciation. So, compared to those Judeo-Arabic writers who used dots and slashes to expand their own alphabet, adapting Hebrew letters to Arabic sounds, the specialists on the Scientific Commission reversed the relationship and made Arabic fit French letters, which for their part remained unchanged. In sum, they put the two alphabets next to each other and decided that Arabic was so full of redundancies based on vernacular pronunciations that they could fix it by converting it to a "superior" French alphabet.

A decade later, when Mac Guckin de Slane and Gabeau converted names into French, this tendency to make Arabic fit French became even more extreme. The separate Arabic letters *al-tā'* (ت) and the emphatic *al-ṭa'* (ط) became the French letter *t* (dropping the trailing apostrophe used in the Scientific Commission's system); the hard h, *al-ḥā'* (ح), and the soft h, *al-hā* (ه), were rendered as the French *h*; *al-sīn* (س) and *al-ṣād* (ص) as *s*; *al-rā'* (ر) and *al-ghayn* (غ) became *r*; and *al-kāf* (ك) and *al-qāf* (ق) appeared as *k*. Finally, in the case of *al-dāl* (د), *al-dhāl* (ذ), *al-ḍād* (ض), and *al-ẓā* (ظ), Mac Guckin de Slane and Gabeau consolidated the four separate letters into the single French *d*.[60] In sum, fourteen Arabic consonants shared six French letters. This consolidation helped Mac Guckin de Slane and Gabeau alphabetize their list of names, with "Ahmed" in the A's and "Zinet" at the end with the Z's. Moreover, dispensing with new diacritics, the system made no demands on publishers who could use their existing print sets.[61] Beyond the reduced alphabet, Mac Guckin de Slane and Gabeau further simplified Algerian names by stripping them of any definite articles, along with the all-important honorific titles, like those carefully deployed in the Sha'bān letter in 1832, which the translator at the time had also removed in his rendering of the text in French.

Although Arabists did this work, people who understood the complexities of languages, they approached converting Algerian names as if they were cracking a code, reminiscent of the linguists who appear as characters in a spy or science fiction novel. They did not treat names as special words organized within a larger, unique language but as puzzles to resolve. They broke down the name, turning it first into a common noun, and then separated out the individual letters from this word and linked them to French equivalents. This simplified their task, which was one not of translation, properly speaking, but of converting one letter for another based on the assumption of good-enough equivalences expressed in a conversion table of letters. They produced what amounted to a codebreaking machine.[62]

Seemingly automatic, this machine did not yield reliable results in the hands of a nonspecialist. Reflecting on the insufficiencies of this first effort, someone in the office of Native Affairs in the Oran prefecture stressed his need for competent Arabists to actually do the work of registering Algerian names. Otherwise, he warned, we will have "truncated names, an assemblage of letters forming words that do not belong to any language. Even if we can pronounce them, they will in no way resemble the Arabic names that they are supposed to reproduce."[63] In other words, those following the rules would be like copyeditors running amuck in the draft of a text, introducing as many new problems as they fixed existing ones. For example, although they all begin with the French letter "*d*," the names "Daud" (داود), "Daïd" (ذايد), and "Demria" (ظمرية) do not begin with the same letter in Arabic. As mentioned earlier, the transcript/transliteration rules judged that it was acceptable to use the French *d* in all cases because pronunciation failed to distinguish between the different Arabic letters. Writing would follow speech. This might have worked for a few names inasmuch as some letters of the Arabic alphabet that people pronounced the same way were in fact related to each other in the written language, so that د (*al-dāl*) and ذ (*al-dhāl*) are visibly distinguished from each other only by the diacritical dot (*iʿjām*) above the second word's first letter. But the transcription system consolidated other letters that had no natural relationship to each other than how they sounded to a French ear, such as the *ẓā* in "Demria" (ظمرية), which was grouped with other "*d*" names. While they recognized that these changes made it difficult to convert from French back to the original Arabic, Mac Guckin de Slane and Gabeau reasoned that an "approximative painting of the sound" would suffice for governmental purposes.[64]

Along with the technical challenges involved in this project came significant political stakes. The question of privileging transcription and rendering names phonetically merits further explanation from this perspective. For colonial linguists, race and language intersected, and they used the languages they studied to create hierarchies among people, coming to predictably prejudicial orders.[65] A view popularized in the eighteenth century placed the French language at the pinnacle of languages for its supposedly inherent clarity and precision. This made French suitable as a universal language, and one that was uniquely serviceable for translation. People approached these problems, which otherwise concerned only savants, as an exercise in national greatness. They tested "the capacities and expressivity of one language against another," as one scholar has written.[66] Linguists working in sub-Saharan Africa extended these accounts of European language supremacy when they viewed social and cultural questions through language. They produced incomplete accounts of African languages and then used their own simplified evidence to argue that African society was itself simplistic.[67]

Language prejudices regarding the written and spoken word also played themselves out. French orientalists debated among themselves how to negotiate what they saw as Arabic's diglossia, or the differences between a high classical language and a low dialectical tongue (*classique* and *vulgaire*, Fr.). They had to decide which to privilege in Algeria as a modern, standardized language, or replace both with French. Some thought that the dialectical language, understood as primarily a spoken language, could be adapted and standardized for writing and print, and that it best suited modern education and official situations. In this view, classical Arabic, although primarily written, was an archaic language best left to the past. Moreover, because classical Arabic was the language of Islam, they feared it gave rise to "fanaticism," whereas the vernacular was more susceptible to secular usages.[68] Others scorned dialectical Arabic, the "*vulgaire*" language, as a debased and irrational tongue of the masses, lacking a formal grammar and distorted in usage from region to region. By this view, classical Arabic alone had the precision and depth necessary for the intellectual rigors of modern usage. Further complicating the issue were some Arabists who refused to reduce the diverse registers of Arabic found in Algeria to the diglossic concept. In an important early critique, Louis-Jacques Bresnier took aim at the prejudices that informed his colleagues who had developed the diglossia conceptualization of Arabic. Bresnier did some of the most important research of the era on the commonly used forms of Arabic in Algeria, approaching it as a living language rather than a dead, classical one. To show up the prejudices of the diglossia approach, he asked his reader to consider it in terms of French, which itself had many varieties. "What would we say if we learned that a foreigner, having studied our literature but having never laid eyes on even one of us, proclaimed that our laws, newspapers, novels, and letters were in dialectical French (*français vulgaire*) because they are not written exactly according to the rhythm of Racine's *Athalie* or in the epic style of Fénelon's *Télémaque*?"[69] In Bresnier's opinion, Arabic had to be studied as a complex but single language, not parsed into high and low versions. While Arabic-speaking people had their own views on these questions, their opinions do not appear in these discussions. By contrast, the French Arabists frequently mapped their own country's political struggles onto Algerian's use of Arabic. After 1848, for example, those who valued a democratic society argued that literary Arabic was the language of nobles and clerics, whereas dialectical Arabic had inherent egalitarian qualities.[70] Alongside these debates were those who simply argued that Arabic in any iteration was a language of reaction that needed to be abolished and replaced by French.[71]

Within their own work, the orientalists turned their nose up at transcription into French letters, preferring to reproduce Arabic script in their field's specialized publications. This reflected the influence of Silvestre de Sacy, whose Jansenist upbringing led him to give great importance to the original languages and their writing systems.[72] Others, primarily outside of the academy, refused this view and pushed for the Latinization of Arabic as a way to modernize it and give it a progressive, emancipatory potential. This included the Comte de Volney, a freethinker who, like Lepsius, sought a universal system of transcription. To promote the project, he endowed an annual prize for scholars whose research aligned with his interests.[73] In other cases, amateur scholars like Sophie Liet (d. 1891) lobbied for Romanizing Arabic. Inspired by the pedagogical method of Joseph Jacotot, the "ignorant schoolmaster" made famous today by Jacques Rancière, Liet argued that doing away with the Arabic alphabet would facilitate its mastery by European settlers in Algeria and open the country's literary masterpieces to the lay French readers, liberating them from the rarefied world of the orientalists.[74] Liet gave little thought to the integrity of the Arabic language, nor to the opinions of Arabic-speaking people and the millions of others who used the language for liturgical purposes. Instead, she saw Arabic as a dying, if not quite dead, language that only the Latin alphabet and French efforts could rejuvenate.

The relationship between the spoken and written word posed additional questions. Phonetics might be a good way for children to learn to write by what they hear, but the written language suffers.[75] Bresnier recognized as much with Arabic and French. In an instruction book, he signaled the problems of writing out Arabic in French letters based on the sounds of the spoken word. To show the effects of phonetic transcription, he used the example of the French word *monsieur* written out phonetically as *mocieu*. Likewise, he showed that the correct spelling of *ils disent* ("they say") writes out by ear as *il dize*; or the properly written *nous aimons* ("we love") becomes *nou zêmon*. Bresnier played on well-worn language prejudices in French.[76] Nonstandard pronunciations of the lower classes often appeared phonetically in print to ironic effect. The best-known example is Molière's *Don Juan*, which parodied the *patois* of the peasantry, a spoken language that Molière wrote out in mangled letters to great effect.[77] Oral-based dialects had been labeled "corrupted language" in the eighteenth century, and the growing powers of institutions like the school sought their eradication over the next two centuries.[78] Bresnier criticized the bifurcation of Arabic into high and low languages, making a case for the importance of dialectical Arabic. But this did not mean he thought spoken Arabic was a simple "good enough" language. Rather, he argued that a modern Algerian Arabic deserved the same care as modern French. He asked his reader: "In what method of learning French would one teach the *orthography* and the *syntax* of the coarse and colorful French of the rabble of Paris or Marseille?"[79] Bresnier did not aim his criticism at name reform, but his arguments cast a clear critical light on his colleagues' shoddy work converting Algerian names. Would they accept the same approach to French names? A colleague of Bresnier who shared these views put it as follows: To write out "the language of Algerian conversations would be to put oneself in the situation of a foreigner who, thinking to be writing in French, expresses himself in pure gobbledygook."[80]

The transcription of Algerian names changed the task of translation—rendering the text of one language into another—as it had been known, which was generally through finding equivalences across languages.[81] Today a translation is considered good when it is circular and dialogic—one language does not foist itself on another.[82] Moreover, a good translation shows up narrow-sighted notions about language purity, on one hand, and exaggerated claims of universal equivalencies or metalanguages, on the other.[83] This was decidedly not the understanding of translation held by those responsible for converting Algerian names to French. The Arabists privileged spoken Arabic to justify their extreme simplification of names. Their work went faster this way, and the resulting system made Algerian names available to ordinary French administrators who did not know Arabic or Berber. In other words, Mac Guckin de Slane, Gabeau, and others imposed French on Arabic, ensuring that French remained in the dominate position. This was true also of the separate transcription system for Arabic forged alongside the name project, which was itself slightly more sophisticated. In his painstaking history of colonial interpreters in Algeria, Alain Messaoudi argues that the Arabic-French transcription rules that emerged in midcentury marked a definitive shift in colonial language policy. Before, interpreters had thought of themselves as mediators "working for an Algeria that was equally Arabic and French." In the second half of the nineteenth century this changed, and they imposed French norms on Arabic. "The language of the colonizer, French, served as the only common reference from this point forward."[84] The scholars who converted Algerian names abandoned universal notions (such as the old ideal of a single natural language) and instead universalized their own particular idiom, a case that contemporary critical theorists call out for its violence.[85] In a fashion, as the French had ignored Algerian names in the first years of the occupation, they ignored them a second time over, paradoxically at the moment when knowing names first became a priority. This time around, however, these names were not simply treated as if they did not exist, but they were written over by French letters, which took hold of the names' original sounds and gave them back written out as "gobbledygook."

The *nom à particule*: Taking land, overwriting names, 1873

The fall of Napoléon III's regime in 1870 and the crushing of a major Algerian uprising, the Muqrani Revolt, the next year set the stage for leaders of the new Third Republic to decide colonial policy. These men turned economic liberalism and French property law into an overt weapon against Algerians. They passed the Warnier Law (26 July 1873), which required using French legal code in the most significant land sales and individuating property that families had held in common.[86]

Reforming personal names proved indispensable to producing an individual landowner.[87] The Warnier Law included provisions for a new family name as part of individuating land titles.[88] Rather than using existing names, a nasab, laqab, or nisba, the law called for a topographical surname by which people would be named after their fields and farms. In France this was known as the *nom à particule*, and it was a characteristic of the nobility. French politicians did not choose it for Algerian landowners to make aristocrats out of them but out of expediency as the simplest way to introduce patronyms and accelerate land markets. This occurred in two ways: One dealt with the division of power within the family, and the other related to the types of family names this new name yielded, which were often denigrating. Both cases require some unpacking in turn.

First, shifting the Algerian name's center of gravity away from existing names toward a French-coined family name compromised the historic function of names, which held people together. Certainly, it promised to serve administers and notaries by streamlining record keeping. The owner of a parcel of land needed only to exist in name to tie this person to the property that they were expected to sell. But each part of this person's original name did more than identify them on a bill of sale. These names *embedded* that person within a larger network of social relations and obligations, which themselves stood as a block to transferring land to outsiders. This was the greatest danger the Algerian name represented from the French perspective. Before 1873 Algerians successfully obstructed the sale of land outside of the family by using the multiple interests that overlapped a single piece of property to gum up the transaction.[89] The early French rules on bills of sales and contracts had neglected to address the problem posed by existing names, saying simply that the documents had to be written in the "language of the contracting parties."[90] By contrast, the 1873 law's proposed family name and its downgrading of the name's social function facilitated disentangling individual members from their larger family. Whereas existing Algerian names identified people in relationship to their family, the topographic surname identified them in relationship to a parcel of land.

To further grasp the social disarticulation promised by the Warnier Law's family name, it is useful to note what this name represented to power distribution within the family. Even if the family name of 1873 was not a true patronymic in the sense of the French nom, it reflected the French patronymic model, and with it the patriarchal social institutions it enabled. Within French law, the patronymic nom placed the father at the legal head of a compact family, and from this position the law afforded him extensive powers over his children and his wife, powers that notably extended to her property. Although the civil code did not quite make the man of the family an "absolute master" of his wife, as one legal guidebook was at pains to explain, it guaranteed him the wife's "obedience."[91] He decided where she would live, whether she could participate in court, and, unless prenuptial agreements existed, her ability to buy, sell, or give away property, including that which she possessed when she married him.[92] Summed up by one bluntly worded account, "the Code placed married women on no higher plane than minors and lunatics."[93] Of course, the civil code's rules on marriage did not apply to Algerian Muslims based on their separate personal status. While the Warnier Law's drafters certainly saw the advantages of the civil code's narrow, patriarchal type of the family as a way toward the birth of an Algerian Homo economicus ready to sell his property on the marketplace and maximize his individual interests, they could not impose French civil law outright.[94] Tampering with the separate legal regimes of personal status by extending the French civil code to the Algerian family threatened the whole legal apparatus of white supremacy (see chapter 6). Rather, the 1873 law, and the family name it proposed, endeavored to introduce selective parts of the French patriarchy, especially those in the symbolic realm where the impact might not be immediately apparent. Rather than the aged patriarch leading several family generations toward their common interests in respect of tradition, as in the (idealized) model of Muslim society, a husband and father ruled over a compact, rational, and efficient family. The new name granted Algerian landowners access to those parts of the patronym's symbolic powers that enabled modern private property relations, including independent action and patriarchal domination within the family, while ensuring that the full world of rights and agency fixed in the French nom remained closed. In this way, the new name promised to draw the Algerian landowner out of their extended family and into the French-dominated marketplace.

Second, the Warnier Law's new name targeted a family's cultural capital. This was more direct and immediate, although it is not clear that lawmakers fully understood the symbolic impact of their mandate. The 1873 surname based itself on the example of the French *nom à particule*, a name formed from the preposition *de* (from) followed by the name of the family's land.[95] In France the *particule* or "estate name" (*nom de terre*) had marked nobility, and despite attempts to abolish noble names during the French Revolution, it resurfaced in the nineteenth century (legally reestablished under Napoléon I, the Charter of 1814 confirmed noble names).[96] In France, the *nom à particule* elevated a family's cultural capital, with the idea that behind the name was a concrete place with a line of noble lords. "No seigneur without land, no land without a seigneur" went an old adage expressing the idea that noble status was inseparable from a landed property and the medieval fief.[97] Linking landownership and a family's standing was not unique to French culture and history; Algerians deeply valued their farmlands, to say the least. They did not, however, name themselves after their farms. Rather than elevating a family, when a toponym was attached to people it degraded them.

The names of Algerian fields and farms were quite distinct from those used for human beings. While an entire estate (*ḥaūsh*) frequently bore the name of the person recognized as its founder, individual fields often carried names based on their physical features or their history, as well as the type of soil or the animals that frequented the area.[98] Some of these might strike us as inoffensive, like a farm called "Ḥaūsh al-Rūmīliyya" or "Ḥaūsh Smara" (Farm of the Gorse Bush), or individual parcels of farmland dubbed "Ḍabbābiyya" (Foggy), "Blad 'Aīn al-Nasūr" (Field of the Eagles Spring), or "Muqsam al-Qanṭara" (Section by the Bridge).[99] In France, any of these might have served as a *nom à particule*. No one to my knowledge has complained about a patronymic like "Delafontaine" (meaning, "of the fountain") in history, and French patronyms originating in topographic surnames remain common. With the exception of some prestigious and beloved animals, however, Algerians did not use the types of words found in land names for the core part of their own personal names (i.e., the ism and nasab), even if they might appear in a kunya or as sobriquets. An officer in the indigenous affairs department clarified the problem in 1875:

> Few natives would accept willingly to leave their traditional Muslim names and take new ones coined from the plants, beasts, or accidents of geography that name their property. What luck would one have to see a

> native named after the Prophet and one of the leaders of Islam, [like] Mohammed ben Ali, accept a sobriquet taken from his field named Chabet el Kelb [ravine of the dog], Tobbet el Hallouf, [parcel of the pig], Quaa el Ousfan [bottomlands of the slave], etc. One would confront the extreme repugnance of people. [This situation is] comparable to our case when people rejected the Republican calendar and the names of Greek and Roman heroes that were imposed in 1793, [and saw] the substitution of the saint names used in the calendar with the names of vegetables or agricultural instruments.[100]

Others did not share this man's sensitivity. A case in point is a French official named Devauly, who worked in an office dealing with Algerian property. He wrote a sizable report in the mid-1870s outlining how to use the *nom à particule* model to form Algerian surname. While Devauly recognized that this would yield names that would "cover [Algerians] in ridicule," he sought a workaround.[101] He suggested converting these names into a sort of kunya by prefixing them "Abū/Bū." Devauly did not concern himself with the finer points of the actual kunya. He even proposed new prefixes such as "Moul" (*mūlay*, "master"), "Ahel" (*ahl*, "people of"), or "Arbab" (*arbāb*, "lords of").[102] Armed with these, administrators could look through their surveys and identify some distinctive word in the property description and confer it as a surname, preceded by one of his prefixes. What about properties named the "Farm of the Wild Pigs" (al-Ḥalālīf, an actual farm located near Collo) or "Ruqa'a Umm al-Aṣnām" (Plot of the Mother of the Idols)?[103] While these were acceptable names for land, no Muslim would knowingly accept them as a personal name. Devauly had enough sense to recognize that a field named after wild pigs was not suitable; however, in a list of other possible surnames, he gave "Arbab el Asnam" (Lords of the Idols) as an example.[104] He offered other choices that, while less insulting, were hardly flattering. They included "Arbab el Gueraba," meaning "Lords of the Shacks." Devauly argued that over time Algerians and the critically disposed Arabists in the administration would accommodate themselves to the new names. As he put it, "it is not a question of finding names so pure that they satisfy the Arabists, we need only find names such that one gets used to their apparent strangeness."[105] Considered only from French interests, the short-term priorities of the rapacious Warnier Law era—getting titles regularized and quickly bringing properties to the market—took precedence over long-term considerations. The latter included ensuring that Algerians would like these names and adopt them as their own.

Pejorative names

French law considered the personal name as property and protected it carefully. Not only did a name risk usurpation, but it could be harmed, and through it, the family who used it.[106] By this logic, misuse of a name in itself might inflict injury. Although the original 1803 French law regulating the types of names that people could use as *prénoms* ensured that this class of names was free of pejorative words, some unflattering names had made their way into the patronymic nom over time. By the twentieth century, these names made for a subgenre of practical jokes. Printed telephone directories of the era contained family names like Labitte (the cock/penis), Meurdesoif (dying of thirst), Lacuisse (the thigh), Cocu (cuckold), Trompette (rumor-monger, fig.), Nichon (boob/breast), Connard (asshole, fig.), and Bordel (whore house). These provided the materials for numerous prank calls, which at one point were featured in popular TV news programs.[107] The origins of these names are not well known. But having a "grotesque or obscene name" was one of the conditions by which one could petition to have one's name changed.[108] Historians have found that abandoned children in France were frequently registered in the état civil under stigmatizing patronyms, although these had been forbidden.[109]

In Algeria, pejorative names are the most controversial aspect of the colonial era's legacy of names. Historian Hosni Kitouni gives more than fifty examples of pejorative names that appeared in the état civil.[110] Some of his examples likely originated in a less than flattering original laqab and were not the work of French registrars, while others are of a scatological nature or originated in pejorative French words converted to Arab letters phonetically, meaning they could only have a French origin. Who did this and when? The archives provide only a few clues and little hard evidence. While the architects of Algerian name reform showed indifference to the integrity of names, the actual directives to French agents clearly forbade conferring derogatory names, a ban that was more emphatically stressed when full scale civil registration of Algerians began in the 1880s.

The common explanation for the origins of pejorative Algerian names is that malicious French administrators did it anyway, giving them to unsuspecting, illiterate people. This argument originated in a study of civil status written in 1909 by a jurist, Edmond Norès, and subsequent writers have repeated his cases, down to today, even if the original source is rarely cited, such has it become common knowledge.[111] Norès was working on a project to codify Islamic family law, and in his research in the recently established état civil records, he found at least four examples of what he took to be derogatory names: Djeriou (*jarw*, puppy), Ràs-el-Kelb (*ra's al-kalb*, dog's head), Chadi (*shādī*, monkey), and Talefraïou (the one who has lost his mind).[112] Of these four names, examples can be found for only two within the electronically indexed état civil database available to researchers, which stops in the early 1920s, meaning they may have not been common in this first period.[113] There is not a single Ràs-el-Kelb or any "dog head" variant in these records, and Talefraïou cannot be found in them either. This leaves Djeriou and Chadi. The état civil shows that men named Djeriou reported the births of their children on at least three occasions between 1858 and 1903.[114] There are three Chadi children in the birth records born to separate fathers with this name. These men were illiterate farmers, who signed their name with an "X." Not able to read the documents, they might have been vulnerable to the type of malicious administrator that Norès signaled. A procedure existed for changing erroneous or derogatory names (see the next chapter), but it required significant paperwork and skills, although even people of humble station like these men availed themselves of the opportunity to correct their names. The evidence of malicious naming is less compelling in the case of the Djeriou families. The fathers who reported these births had occupations that ensured a strong familiarity with the French language and the colonial administration. The first was Mohamed ben Djeriou, who in 1858 registered the birth of a son. He served in a spahis military unit stationed outside of Algiers. While he did not sign the birth document in his own hand, his military service placed him in close contact with the French and their administrative culture. Moreover, he was accompanied at the registration by an Algerian of considerable local authority, the French-named *cheikh* of Médéah, El Hadj ben Moussa bou Rouis, whose high position ensured that he had easy access to those with advanced French language skills, if he did not possess these himself.[115] The *cheikh* frequently accompanied Algerians going to the mayor's office in

Médéah to record births in their community at this time. Neither he nor the spahis fit the profile of someone who might be duped by a malicious French functionary. Rather, they were for all intents and purposes colleagues of the officer of the état civil seated before him, both working for the colonial administration. The second Djeriou father was a gendarme named Seddik ben Ahmed Djeriou who lived in a small town in eastern Algeria. He reported the births of two girls born to him and his wife in 1900 and 1903, named Zakia Seddik Djeriou and Louise Djeriou, respectively.[116] Seddik Ben Ahmed signed his name in well-drawn French letters. Like the spahi in Médéah, he also was accompanied before the état civil officer by men of some significance, two fellow gendarmes, both of them Frenchmen. Again, this man emerges from the archives as an unlikely victim of duplicitous naming. Moreover, as a police officer, he would have had easy opportunity to apply for a name change if he found the Djeriou name to be a problem. The fact that he conferred a French first name on the daughter born in 1903, an infrequent but not isolated case, further shows his proximity and comfort with French society. Its language and norms were not exotic to him.

These examples do not fit neatly in the scenario of abusive French administrators exploiting the ignorance of humble Algerians. They could just as easily be read as a case of shifting onomastic norms and the change in expectations and attitudes as names moved between languages and cultures.[117] Nevertheless, the record of pejorative names identified by Kitouni remains an important consideration, even if the archive does not contain a smoking gun documenting their origins. The Djeriou cases do not mean that the conversion of Algerian names at the end of the nineteenth century was free of malice, nor that the stigmatizing names that appear in the record came there innocently.

Digging further into the question, one can see that the 1873 Warnier Law's *nom à particule* offered opportunities to hide offensive Arabic words by first translating them into French. An anecdote told in an 1891 publication recounts how one (unnamed) administrator earned a reputation in the 1870s for translating pejorative Arabic farm names into French words, which he then used for Algerians who did not know French.[118] The source does not give any examples, but this would be like taking the Arabic word for puppy, *jarw*, and using the French *chiot* for a name, which would be unrecognizable to all except those who were bilingual. The possibilities for even more degrading names extend with this model, particularly if one exploited the differences between the spoken and written word as they emerged in two languages. For example, one can consider a hypothetical case with *nom à particule*-type of name based on the example of the "wild pigs" farm. The offending word, *al-ḥallūf,* would first be fit into an Arabic formulation like, *ahl al-ḥallūf* ("people of the wild pigs") as Devauly suggested, and then one could translate it into French, as *les gens du cochon.* The joke would be an open one to all francophones hearing or reading the name. Although advanced French skills were not common among the mass of Algerians, the language did not exist in an airtight world exclusive to the French (nor did any other language), meaning that it would not take long before Arabic- or Berber-speaking people figured out that a name had placed someone as the butt of a bad joke. However, if one took these French words and phonetically wrote them out in Arabic script as something like *Lizjun du Kūshun* (لزجن دوكوشن), the malice becomes much more difficult to locate. Only an attentive listener well versed in both languages might recognize the origin of the name when sounding it out. Otherwise, it represented only gibberish to an untrained ear. Moreover, the French words written as "لزجن دوكوشن" meant nothing in Arabic. If this expression were to be converted back into French letters, privileging the phonetic conversion system used for names, the result "*Lisjoun du Koushoun*" further blurred the offensive origins. Thus, going between languages and their written and spoken versions in this hypothetical exercise shows how difficult it can be to detect a pejorative name, which can bury itself as an insidious insiders' joke.

The question of intent is important in considering the question of malicious names. Algerian names had long been shaped by moving between languages and cultures. These movements could serve as a mild pun, as occurred with the baby girl in Morocco named Faḍīna (meaning "silver" or "conclusion") by her father, as discussed in chapter 2, an expression of gender prejudices that few questioned. This book has given many examples of precolonial Algerian names that might strike readers today as unflattering or pejorative. Long before the French arrived, baldness, physical defects, poor dress, and lack of intelligence served Algerians to name each other. However, these names figured within a specific part of the Arabo-Islamic name, the laqab. People knew that laqabs, conferred as a nickname, could be flattering or diminishing, and they expected as much.[119]

The name given to a child at birth, the ism, was much different, as was the genealogical nasab. These names, closest to a French prénom and nom, were arguably the most personal and intimate of names. For this reason, families typically chose uplifting and positive names for their children. When a starkly unflattering ism appeared, the intent was not to harm the child, but rather to shield them. For example, families suffering precarious conditions might select negative words as names in the hope that they would function prophylactically, turning malevolent forces away. Salem Chaker gives the example of a woman who, having had lost many children to illness, named a surviving baby Iẓẓan (excrement) in the hope that this offensive name would protect her child.[120] The origin of the commonly used Berber name Akli, (Taklit fem.) meaning "slave," "servant," or Black person, also comes from this belief, with the common association of dark skin color with slavery producing its negative resonance.[121] Although it represents an overworked subject at this point, the so-called evil eye or *'ayn* (Arabic) or *tiṭṭ* (Berber) was held responsible for the illnesses, accidents, and violence that made childhood so dangerous.[122] The glance of envy (*ḥasad*) had harmful effects, as summed up in the popular saying, "It puts the camel in the cooking pot and the man in his grave."[123] Against this glance, a negative name served the child like a barrier of thorny cacti planted around a prosperous house, cloaking its riches and provoking fear, pity, or even disgust. Therefore, intent matters in names. When French officials seized on a nickname that they found funny, even if it was translated to them by an interpreter and written into the record as a family name, it cannot be said that they were simply using names that already existed. This name would be taken literally out of context, removed from the special place reserved for it in the Arabo-Islamic name, and fixed to a family for generations.

French lawmakers introduced an actual patronymic nom for Algerians in 1882, a topic I turn to in the next chapter. Algerians came to call this new name either *naqma* or *naqwa*, words that today refer both to the family name and, metonymically, to an ID card.[124] The etymology of these words is unknown and remains a topic of debate, with some saying that *naqwa* used in this context is an Arabization of the French expression "*Tu es né quoi?*" (You were born [with] what [name]?).[125] For its part, the Arabic word *naqma* in standard usage means "vengeance."[126] Frantz Fanon wrote at length about the alienating effects of the French language on colonized people, especially how it split into a high version used by well-educated, generally white, speakers, on one hand, and the pidgin language for colonial subjects, on the other.[127] This sort of language prejudice gave itself over to full-blown racialized caricatures known by the extremely pejorative term *parler petit nègre*.[128] As Fanon observed, pronunciation, syntax, and word choice racialized the colonized subject, "classifying him, imprisoning him, primitivizing him, decivilizing him."[129]

Fanon's observations shed light on the colonization of names. The anonymous administer discussed earlier amused himself thinking that naming people after animals turned them into the butt of his jokes. However, the butt of certain jokes can be repositioned, turning it back on the person who makes it.[130] This works best if we put aside obviously malicious names to consider the majority of Algerian names that came out of the crude conversion system that turned them into French. In these cases, French officials spoke pidgin to Algerians in their new names, using a low, simplified version of an original Tamazight or Arabic word. From the perspective of native speakers, the Gallicized names looked strange and sounded ridiculous. Although the French reformers had the power to coin these names, they stood in no position to speak down to Algerians in them. After all, this time it was the colonizer who babbled out strange approximations of words from languages they failed to speak well. In other words, if pidgin French signaled a lack of education, culture, and even humanity from the colonizer's perspective, as Fanon identified, what might it mean for Algerians when they heard the colonizers pronounce their names?[131] When a colonizer names a colonized person in the equivalent of *parler petit nègre*, this certainly showed contempt, but did it not also signal more clearly the colonizer's own failures in Algerian languages that were not their own and they did not master?

My thoughts here are speculative but not divorced from ongoing discussions among Algerians about their names. In his hilarious standup comedy show "Le dernier chameau" in 2004, Mohamed Fellag turned the tables precisely in this way. Well known for poking fun at Algerian history, identity, and French stereotypes, Fellag did a sketch on colonial names. He plays the role of an Algerian peasant who has to explain to a French registrar why there are so many people named "Mohamed" in Algeria.[132] The peasant tells the condescending functionary that Algerian names are, in fact, quite logical, elegant, and precise. When the administrator signals his frustration that he does not understand or care about the peasant's tutorial, Fellag delivers his punchline. Affecting the accent of an uneducated peasant speaking French—the pidgin of colonial Algeria—Fellag's character asks the official: "You's sure, you speak good French, you?" (*Tu's sûr te'comprenez bien le français, toi?*)

6

A Colonial État Civil

> Woe to those who, to the very end, insist on regulating the movement that exceeds them with the narrow mind of the mechanic who changes a tire.
>
> —Georges Bataille, *The Accursed Share*

When farmers prune a fruit tree, they do so to better its health and to produce larger yields. Armed with shears or a saw, they look up into the canopy for dead or diseased branches and small suckers. Those that will not thrive need to be cut, so too weak boughs that risk breaking in the wind or under a heavy load of fruit. Pruning an olive tree follows its own principles. It rejuvenates an aged tree and extends its life. A Kabyle proverb makes this point by giving voice to an olive tree, which tells the farmer, "Make me poor in wood, and I'll make you rich in oil," a colorful image of nature playing on human greed to have people do its bidding.[1] Families also grow in trees. In Tamazight a family tree is called an *aseklu n timmarewt*, and in Arabic it is known as a *shajara al-nasab*. The health of a family tree is measured differently from that of those in the grove. An Algerian family's well-being resided not in compact, young growth but in the many generations of solid boughs and branches that stretched out from the main trunk, like a great ash tree (*dardār*) sheltering people and livestock from summer sun. These needed to be orderly but were otherwise encouraged to grow and expand. In these branches one measured the family's influence, resilience, and wealth. The genealogical tree's roots also contained valuable cultural and social capital. The Prophet Muhammad himself is reported to have encouraged people to carefully safeguard their families and know their lineages: "Keeping the ties of kinship encourages affection among the relatives, increases the wealth, and increases the lifespan."[2]

In the last decades of the nineteenth century, the French government went beyond previous desultory attempts to count Algerian births and deaths and moved to record everyone in the state's registries.[3] The law of 23 March 1882 established an état civil for Algerian Muslims.[4] The standard registries used in France since 1792 served as the model. The vital acts of Algerian Muslims and Europeans appeared alongside each other within the civil registries: The separate registers or sections used for Algerian Jews in Algiers in the 1830s and the racial classifications appearing in Bône's early état civil disappeared. Now the patronymic names stood out in the headers and margins of the registers, and their cultural codes alone set Europeans apart from the "Indigènes" who appeared in the same pages. However, the Algerians' état civil—called the "état civil of the natives"—differed in important ways from that of others in the French civil registry. Most significantly, Algerians entered the registries not as subjects of a rights-based legal system but as colonized subjects defined precisely by their debased legal status. Moreover, the first état civil for Algerians did not emerge in individual vital events, beginning with the declaration of a child's birth. Rather, a massive registration drive produced records for everyone, everywhere, at the same time. French registrars went to hamlets, villages, and towns to record names, ages, and professions of every Algerian Muslim and draw genealogical trees to establish their family's composition. That meant that the first master registers for Muslim Algerians look more like a census, a list of people organized by place of residence and family name, than an état civil's individual life events. Nevertheless, the "état civil of the natives" established a new legal identity, making these people legible to French law and the colonial administration, and binding them to these institutions. Most important, it imposed a patronymic modeled on the nom introduced in France during the Revolution. This name reified a family's boundaries, and it stood as its linguistic sign.

To finish the registration project in a single year, as was once envisioned, would have required processing ten thousand people a day, with registrars spread across hundreds of thousands of square kilometers. The queues, confusion, and backlogs of correspondence triggered by such hasty work did not come to pass. Beginning in earnest only in 1892, registrars worked village by village to ensure they missed no one.[5] They did not achieve this goal, but by the end of 1894, officials celebrated master registers in which they counted some three million people, covering, it seemed, nearly the entire population in Algeria's three departments.[6] The project cost one million francs.[7] This made the "état civil of the natives" one of the most ambitious legal-administrative projects undertaken up to the First World War.[8]

Historian Hosni Kitouni calls the 1882 law an "irreparable crime" for its impact on the Algerian family. "After having destroyed the tribe economically and dispersing its members, a triumphal colonialism went to the next step, shattering the family and erasing with one stroke centuries-old genealogies."[9] The violence Kitouni refers to did not rely on adoptions, boarding schools, deportations, or massacres. Certainly, Algerians suffered these types of attacks, as did colonized people throughout the world, but the état civil's violence occurred elsewhere. It did not take place "off the books," as might happen with torture or verbal commands for mass killings, which typically went unrecorded, but it appears clearly marked on the very pages of the colonial archives. Registration did the work of destruction.

The visibility of the names but the invisibility of their violence needs some unpacking. The état civil calculated family relations in a particular way. The rules for registration invested one person from the family, dubbed the *ayant droit* (claimant), with the authority to decide the new patronymic. This person served like the patriarchal father in the French civil code who wielded extensive powers over his family. The ayant droit choose his family's new patronymic name, and he reported its individual members by first name, age, and relationship to the French registrar. In other words, he alone controlled this part of the family's formation in the état civil, a considerable authority. However, he could not invite relatives at will to join him under his family name. Rather, his position in the kinship ranks of the extended family decided what relations joined him, a calculation that occurred automatically. As will be explained shortly, this produced a smaller family than the extended relations that Algerians preferred, even if many families successfully requested an exception to the rules. In the end, a group of people who knew themselves bound by blood might not share the same name. If the family can be thought of as a tree, made up of branches, the état civil essentially took a ripsaw to it, felling its limbs from the main trunk. At the same time, the état civil cut the family tree from its roots, felling it as quickly as any axe-wielding forester. The nasab or genealogical name disappeared in the French records, appearing only on the backside of a new identity card.[10] While the first master registers allowed for recording the isms of a dead father and paternal grandfather, in the generations ahead these were left off. Poor record keeping compounded this loss over time, along with lapses in registrations. These meant that patronyms changed from one generation to the next or among individual family members.[11] Only a family's own archives might maintain its continuity.

Unofficial names and testimonial records had shrinking legal relevance in an era moving rapidly towards documentary forms of proof monopolized by the state. Going forward from the 1882 law, Algerians had to use their patronym and état civil-based documents in nearly every administrative, legal, and police encounter.[12] Patronyms structured tax roll and titles for individuated property, including lands slated for expropriation or sequestering. Military and civil pensions required a patronym, as did nearly any form of state benefits.[13] The system of police also depended on the new family name: The records of anyone arrested, detained, deported, or accused of a crime had to include the patronym, as did requests for internal travel permits or passports to go abroad. Even volunteers for military service had to enlist under their patronym, which in this case served both as an identification device to screen people seeking to enlist under different names to collect enlistment bonuses and as a legal subjectivity for volunteers swearing an oath of service.[14] (Conscription, introduced in 1912 for Muslim Algerians, used a much looser system wherein even age could be established by "public knowledge" rather than an état civil or documentary forms of proof.[15]) Moreover, every act and judgment made in Islamic courts had to contain the *nom patronymique* of the concerned individuals, supplanting long-standing practices that decided identity through sworn testimony. Finally, everyone who occupied a position in public life had to identify themselves by their patronym, including schoolteachers, Muslim clerics, and people working within Islamic courts, along with civil servants, rural officials such as the caïds, and those working as secretaries, translators, and forest guards. While many managed to live off of this legal and administrative grid, including masses of landless peasants and pastoralists who avoided contact with the state as best they could, the patronym dominated life. Indeed, those who did not have a patronym were dubbed "SNP" or "Without Patronymic Name" (*sans nom patronymique*) as a workaround solution to process paperwork.

Generally speaking, the état civil produces continuity within a lineage over time—a documentary record of the family line conserved in the archive for posterity. However, the "état civil of the natives" produced ruptures. If by some miracle an intrepid genealogist today follows an Algerian family back to the first French records issued in the 1890s, they will not be able to go any further nor connect this branch with the rest of what once stood as the original family. In short, Algerians came into the modern era of civil records constituted as subjects in cesuras, rather than connections.

This final chapter divides into two parts. The first examines the legal stakes of including Algerian Muslims in the état civil and its potential impact on a legal system that ensured white supremacy. Although most French officials pushed for the civil registry so that they could better know and control Algerians, it risked shaking up a system of legal exclusions, something that they did not wish or fully anticipate. The second part explores how the registration of Algerians occurred, and how Algerians managed the process. Rather than breaking out in revolt, as fearmongers in the colonial administration predicted, Algerians cooperated with registrars. This provided them with some measure of agency, including a choice of name, even if they did not get their first choice as the popular names in a village went quickly. Algerians could not always control the process, nor prevent the arbitrary break up of their extended family. But in some cases, they availed themselves of a relaxing of the rules to request the regrouping of family branches that would have otherwise been severed. While the whole project sought to cut the Algerian family down to size, French planers had to scale this back to make their new documentary system compatible with Islamic inheritance law, which required an expanded record of family relations. For their part, some Algerians also sought a smaller family, or simply to cut unwanted members out. Civil registration provided them an opportunity to remake their families, eliminating problematic members, particularly those who became rivals at times of inheritance and succession. The documents examined show cases where they used the état civil to exclude these relations from their official records.

Algerians before the law: The stakes of legal assimilation

Over the course of the nineteenth century, Algerians occupied a special status with regards to French law. Although they found themselves accountable to its punishments and power of command, the doors to nearly all the law's rights and protections closed to them.[16] Like the character in Franz Kafka's famous parable, they stood "Before the Law" but remained outsiders to it.[17] The gates to the inner reaches of the law, where the halls of citizenship and rights lay, remained firmly closed. The état civil appeared at a moment when Algeria's political and legal institutions entered a period of accelerated change. Up to 1870, Algeria had been essentially a military colony, administered through the Ministry of War and the office of the governor general in Algiers, with only a short two-year interruption when a separate ministry held the reins (1858–1860). The governor general came from high-ranking army officers, and he exercised nearly autocratic domination, ruling through decree rather than a regular system of laws enacted by the government according to the constitution.[18] The men who occupied this position exploited the prerogatives exercised by the military in war zones to decide policy as they saw fit.[19] These military institutions sustained authoritarianism in Algeria, even at moments when metropolitan France moved toward greater democracy, such as the Second Republic (1848–1852). The army's basic mission in life was to give orders and make war. It did not have the habit of governing by consent. While previous generations of historians have played up colonial officers acting as "enlightened despots" with regard to Algerians, as a rule the French army adopted a clear stance of enmity toward local people.[20]

White settlers certainly benefited from military rule, but it also negatively affected their lives. Among the diverse legal statuses and nationalities of the settlers, those with French citizenship saw themselves entitled to the same civil and political rights as citizens in the metropole. They campaigned to have Algeria's manner of government regularized, or "assimilated" to France. The process began as early as 1845 when civilian governance appeared in places with significant European populations, and three years later Frenchmen in Algeria started electing deputies to represent them in the National Assembly in Paris. At the same time, Algeria's administrative units were renamed from "provinces," an outdated term with strong links to the Old Regime, to "departments," a name change that symbolically cemented the transition toward civilian rule.[21] Decades later, as France entered a sustained period of parliamentary democracy under the Third Republic beginning in 1870, this shift accelerated. The new minister of justice, Adolph Crémieux, dismantled military rule across Algeria's three departments during his first months in office, and in a decree that bears his name he extended French citizenship to Algerian Jews, numbering some twenty to thirty thousand people.[22] Most often remembered as the new republic's gift to Algerian Jews, this decree facilitated the move toward civil administration, eliminating the troublesome irregularity of separate status for this significant minority. Another law (26 June 1889) furthered assimilation by automatically extending French citizenship to children born in Algeria to (non-Muslim) foreign parents. Citizenship came either at birth, for those whose parents had also been born on French territory, or at the age of majority, for the children of those born abroad. This gave clear legal definition to Algeria's white population, forming them into a single privileged bloc, despite their various class, ethnic, and political divides.[23] The Algerian Sahara alone was left in the army's hands for administrative purposes.

What did assimilation mean for more than two million Algerian Muslims? By the time assimilation moved into top gear under the Third Republic, Algerians were no longer foreigners to France.[24] The Sénatus-Consulte of 14 July 1865, promulgated by Napoleon III, naturalized Algerian Jews and Muslims en masse as French nationals. As mentioned in chapter 5, this was the second key law that came out of the Arab Kingdom era, following the Sénatus-Consulte of 1863 that recognized Algerian property rights. As it conferred French nationality, however, the 1865 law withheld citizenship. Algerians had no political rights and hardly any civil and civic rights, leaving them substantially diminished next to French citizens. Although French, Algerians' status fell lower than white foreigners. A slim path to citizenship opened to those who were willing to renounce their separate personal status (*statut personnel*). This form of legal pluralism allowed Muslims (and Jews up to 1870) to use confessional law or customary rules rather than the French civil code to decide family matters. French policymakers thereby argued that even if religious laws were valid, they were "irreconcilable" to French citizenship, which was based on specific social institutions, as well as legally sanctioned relations between men and women, fathers and children.[25] In this way, Islam stood as an unassimilable remainder, an "accursed share" to French citizenship.[26] That is to say, it exceeded citizenship's capacity for absorption, while simultaneously revealing citizenship's own incapacities and parochialism, undermining the universal rationales that sustained its privileges. People who had been newly made French in one part of their legal being were told that their faith blocked entry to the law's rights. From the government's perspective, the argument was a potent one. It made inequality appear an effect of religious difference and the believer's own intransigence (clinging to their separate personal status), not discrimination and racism on the lawmaker's part. If Muslims did not have the rights of citizenship, the cause lay in their own decision to opt for a communal identity enshrined in an "archaic" legal code.[27] Thus, when the government's reporter presented the nationality law of 1865 to parliament, he justified the exclusion of Algerians easily without debate, stating that "Muslim statute is irreconcilable with French law."[28]

French citizenship represented an impossible choice to Algerians. Whatever they gained in rights, they did not want the French civil code to apply to their families. Moreover, those who adopted it risked denunciation as apostates. When two progressive French deputies floated the idea of naturalizing Algerian Muslims en masse in 1887, as had happened to Algerian Jews in 1870, it provoked a hostile response from those whom it would supposedly benefit. In Constantine, Muslim leaders circulated a petition opposing the idea that gained some 1,700 signatures. These people feared the loss of their personal status and separate family law if they were automatically naturalized French citizens.[29] The importance of a Muslim's personal status grew to such an extent that subsequent Islamic reformers embraced it as the last refuge of the Algerian *nafs* (soul or self) where colonized Muslims became whole and authentic.[30] The matter came to a head in 1937–1938 when a fatwa, or legal opinion, condemned any Muslim who abandoned their personal status in favor of French citizenship. Authored by the leader of the Algerian Islamic reform movement, ʿAbd al-Ḥamīd ibn Bādīs (Ahmed Ben Badis, Fr.), this fatwa presented naturalization as apostasy (*irtidād*), resulting in a near permanent excommunication from the Muslim community. Ibn Bādīs wrote: "Naturalization in a non-Islamic nationality requires rejecting the judgments of the Shari'a. Whoever rejects these judgments is considered as having withdrawn from Islam."[31] Because opting for the French civil code produced permanent legal effects on the person and their family, Ibn Bādīs reasoned that the naturalized Algerian could only undo their apostasy by emigration to a country under Muslim law, abandoning their homeland. Otherwise, the excommunication passed to the apostate's children as soon as they reached the age of majority, and it likely radiated outward to the apostate's spouse, as did the French civil code itself. The fatwa gave no consideration to the Muslim wife of a husband who chose French citizenship, but Ibn Bādīs did write that a Muslim's marriage with a Frenchwoman also constituted apostasy because it automatically tied the couple to the French civil code. So too was settling an inheritance according to French law or forum shopping between French and Muslim courts to obtain a favorable judgment. In sum, in this colonial context, apostasy came not from one's inner belief, nor neglecting one of Islam's five pillars, nor a refusal of established dogma. Instead, *irtidād* or "withdrawal from Islam" depended on the regime of law to which one was bound. As long as French citizenship could not be had without the submission of the citizen to the civil code, as French lawmakers required, then by Ibn Bādīs's opinion one could not be a French citizen and a Muslim. It was almost as if the colonial context had revealed a sixth pillar of Islam, or at least that is how an ordinary person might have experienced this. The editors at *Baṣā'ir*, the reformist newspaper where the fatwa first appeared, took pains over the following months to explain the decision to the public.[32]

The misfired attempts to grant citizenship to Algerian Muslims in 1887 did not get far, even if Ibn Bādīs worried about it fifty years later. Had Algerians themselves not rejected the idea of naturalization, few in the government and fewer in the colonial administration and settler community in Algeria who implemented law on the ground would have accepted making French Muslims the legal equals of white citizens. Quite the contrary, the French Republic did nothing meaningful to improve the status of Algerians nor include them in its democracy and regime of rights. In 1881 lawmakers affirmed the most oppressive system imaginable when they inaugurated the *indigénat* or indigenous penal code (beginning with the law of 28 June 1881). This suspended due process for colonized subjects and held them to a list of crimes and punishments that did not apply to any other class of people, citizens and resident foreigners alike.[33] Expanded from Algeria to other parts of the French empire, the *indigénat* became a mainstay of the Republic's legal approach to colonized subjects. Essentially, when France turned the corner toward democracy in its European territories, it doubled down on racist authoritarian rule for its colonized subjects in the rest of the world. In the case of Algerians, this extended to people who were legally French. The *indigénat* transferred the military's exceptional legal and disciplinary powers, designed for war and occupation, to ordinary civil administrators who wielded them at their discretion in peacetime. Speaking for all of France's overseas territories, in a review of an important book on the subject, historian Isabelle Merle states that this amounted to an effective "extension of war in peace."[34] A few years before the *indigénat* became law, a voice of settler opinion in Algeria explained his hopes for the new order in the clearest terms. France had to "impose an unconditional tutelage on the Natives," he wrote. "For us, a complete civil regime, for them a special regime. To us, Freedom; to them, Obedience."[35] The "us" and the "them" of this statement were both French by nationality, even if only one side, white French men (women lost significant civil rights at marriage and never had access to political rights), enjoyed the full legal rights associated with this nationality.

The état civil: Unbalancing the colonial legal regime

Although the colonial divide evoked here stood self-evident and eternal to this man, the status quo was not impervious to change, including that coming from unexpected quarters. An état civil for Algerian Muslims, for example, carried with it potential risks that neither French lawmakers nor Algerians could see clearly in advance. Born of the emancipatory moment of the French Revolution, the état civil was inseparably bound to the civil code. While it sometimes served as a political technology of control, biopolitics, and the surveillance state, lawmakers lauded it as the key to emancipate the citizen.[36] Revolutionary lawmakers, like Louis-Jérôme Gohier, viewed the état civil through the lens of civic religion, with the procedures of registration conceived as quasi-religious rite. With regard to recording the birth of a child, he viewed it as a sort of civil baptism. When the newborn was brought into the city hall to be registered by his father, this child was "carried upon the altar of the fatherland." Gohier continued: "In this first act relating to human life is recorded the sacred principle that all men are born and die free and equal in rights. In registering the name of a newborn on the registers of the children of the fatherland, the magistrates of the people guarantee him in the name of the nation, freedom, justice, equality."[37]

What happened, then, when the names of Algerian Muslims appeared alongside other men and women in the registries, French citizens or white foreigners who enjoyed civil rights?[38] And what happened to the gatekeeping powers invested in the regime of separate personal status and the field of Islamic law? Did something as banal as recording vital acts in the secularized French registry threaten the seemingly impermeable borders between Islam and the Republic, or subject and citizen? Registration in the état civil never represented an automatic path to citizenship, nor were these volumes exclusive to citizens, as I have shown in the discussion of the état civil and questions of sovereignty. However, the civil registries and the civil code carried with them what might be called the expectation or presumption of rights, if not the equal exercise thereof. To grasp this, it is useful to remember that the état civil meant two things. On one hand, there were the registers themselves, the physical volumes recording the vital statistics for births, marriages, and deaths, and the relevant names, dates, family relations, localities, and professions that made up the legal subject. When policymakers discussed the état civil for Algerian Muslims, this is what they had in mind. On the other hand, the état civil was literally what its name said it was, i.e., one's "civil status" calculated from this information. In the most basic terms, having an état civil meant nothing less than "the ability to exercise rights," as the architects of the Civil Code originally put it in 1801.[39] Not having one amounted to the equivalent of civil death, banishment from the institutions of public life. In this sense, one can speak of "bestowing" (*accorder*) an état civil on French Muslims, as occurred previously for Protestants and Jews back in 1788, before the full inauguration of modern rights, when Louis XVI recognized their vital registers as a way of bringing them into the fold.[40] To put it in contemporary terms, one could say that an état civil represented the juridical precondition for rights, or the "right to have rights," as Hannah Arendt expressed it.[41]

Among vital events, the act of marriage posed the greatest threat to the line that separated Muslims' personal status from the French code. By appearance, putting a marriage into the état civil was no more difficult than recording births or deaths. The problem lay in the fact that setting a marriage in writing within the registry's pages did not passively *record* marriages but *constituted* their validity in French law. Eager to monopolize marriage, Revolutionary lawmakers in 1792 stripped the clergy of their ability to sanctify the couple. Marriages might be celebrated with a mass, but these had no weight by law, or, as one manual put it, "religious marriage exists only in the realm of conscience and sentiment."[42] What, then, to do with an état civil for Muslims who contracted their marriages according to religious law? The question remained a problem for authorities into the twentieth century.[43] Although the exact vernacular practices of Algerian marriage ceremonies varied according to social class and region, a marriage's legal validity rested not on written documents but rather on a publicly witnessed ceremony (*'aqd al-nikāḥ*) centered on the couple's verbal declarations of consent, with the wife's consent typically conveyed by her father.[44] A shared recitation of the Fatiha prayer solemnized the marriage, and it was completed by payment of the dowry (*ṣadāq* or *mahr*) and sexual consummation. While the terms of a marriage contract might be spelled out in writing, marriages did not require a documentary record, nor did they need a notable to officialize the event.

Up to this point, colonial officials had largely steered clear of Muslim marriage in their efforts to record vital statistics, asking only that Algerians report their births and deaths, not marriages and divorces.[45] The tropes of Muslim fanaticism justified colonial officials' conservative approach to marriage. For example, during the pilot registration drive undertaken in Constantine in the 1850s, the protests of a man forced to register his wife were framed as an example of Algerian misogyny. When the man objected that his wife entered the records as if she were livestock, the reporter interpreted this as illustrating the "indifference of Arabs for their wives."[46] This official's intentional construction of prejudice in this comment is clear. Rather than this man's indifference to the women and girls in his family, most likely his comment expressed his disgust with a government that counted people like animals.

By 1882 lawmakers wanted the état civil in Algeria to meet metropolitan standards including Muslims. This required registering their marriages. Doing this without upsetting the existing state of affairs required carefully designed procedures that joined the two systems without causing them to collapse into each other, thereby nullifying the separate spheres of personal status and its justification for the legal debasement of Muslims. However, few French officials debating the état civil understood Muslim marriage and divorce well, and they ignored those who did. On one hand, they hyped things like "child marriage" and polygamy to show up the incommensurability of the Algerian family with French institutions, as Judith Surkis has shown.[47] On the other hand, they acted on the assumption that Algerian marriage could be converted easily to existing concepts in French law through the use of analogs and rough equivalences, as historian Sarah Ghabrial's research reveals.[48] As they went forward with the état civil, however, officials had to reckon with difficult questions of method. For example, could the legal prerogatives held by an officer of the état civil be shared with a religious authority like a cadi, mufti, or imam, or did a "secular" analog need to be found, such as the local caïd (a French-invested Algerian administrator) or the *djemâa* (official village council)?[49] And even if the French state shared its authority with these figures, the types of rites and rituals used to constitute an état civil marriage would have to be decided. Would the Fatiha prayer typically recited in weddings be acceptable within a ceremony sanctioned by the French government? Could Muslims pronounce their French marriage "In the name of God," as the Fatiha begins, or would they have to substitute "In the name of the French People"?

Possible solutions to these questions existed in the reciprocity model of *locus regit actum* used to recognize vital events performed by foreign authorities for French citizens living abroad. Algeria was French territory, however, and invoking *locus regit actum* here raised thorny questions concerning sovereignty and legal pluralism that few wanted to visit. It would not be long before critically minded jurists like Émile Larcher bluntly pointed out the fundamental inconsistences in Algerian law, stating in his important assessment in 1923 that the law in Algeria had lapsed into feudalism with regard to the legal status of Muslims. "Citizens are the nobles or the lords, the natives are the commoners or the serfs," Larcher wrote.[50] Moreover, if personal status allowed the law to split and create separate classes of Frenchmen and women with colonized Muslims standing apart, the état civil invoked a single field of sovereignty that did not divide easily. Moreover, there were questions to consider from the perspective of Islam and Muslims. A valid Muslim marriage did not require an official to solemnize the union but only the partners' consent verified by two witnesses. Any arrangement in which a French-invested Muslim agent had to officiate risked violating the integrity of Islamic marriage and, thereby, the logic of separate spheres on which a Muslim's personal status depended.

These challenges revealed themselves when the governor general issued an order in 1875 requiring Muslims to record their marriages in a provisional civil registry as a step toward a regular état civil.[51] The order presented this as a simple recording of an act whose legal significance occurred elsewhere.[52] However, the governor general neglected to provide guidelines and procedures, and as a result Algerians raised many questions because they felt that registration compromised their marriages. The governor general was at pains to downplay the stakes:

> The goal of this circular is not, in fact, to affect in any way the personal status of the natives, nor to modify the traditional or local forms of Muslim marriage . . . [nor] is there any question of having the officer of the état civil or the representative of the *djemâa* officiate the marriage. These functionaries are in no way called upon to intervene in the celebration of the marriage, [and] their role will be limited to the registration of marriages already concluded.[53]

This model of maintaining existing practices seemed to settle the question of personal status when seen from the governor general's perspective, but administrators in the field still faced problems. One of the most difficult was deciding what constituted proof of marriage when few unions yielded written documents but only the oral testimonial proofs. In his effort to clarify the matter, the governor general revealed his ignorance, assuming that a cadi, a French salaried imam, or the village assembly would issue a document that the couple could take to French authorities for registration. In spite of efforts to strip the registration of Muslim marriages of its legal ramifications, it risked opening a Pandora's Box on the colonial system. How could the French and "Native" fields be merged into the état civil without compromising the integrity of Muslims' personal status and thereby the logic by which forced Algerians outside of rights?

Seven years later, the 1882 état civil law offered no solution to this problem. Even as it announced that the "état civil of natives" was distinct from that used for others and would not upset personal status, it could not say what this meant in actual procedures. On the thorny topic of marriage, it relied on silences to work around the issue. While the law mandated that Muslim marriages and divorces be registered in the civil registry, it passed over what type of marriage was admissible to the état civil (i.e., was a French official necessary?), and it left off enforcement mechanisms that might have brought the question to a head. The law simply turned a blind eye on these matters. When the question eventually came before the Appeals Court of Algiers in 1905, French judges doubled down on the governor general's early attempt, claiming that the registration of Muslim marriages was purely an "administrative affair" that had no impact on the marriage's legal validity.[54] This effectively downgraded the état civil for Muslims and bracketed its effects on the civil status of Algerian Muslims. For their part, most Algerians did not push the matter by getting into the finer points of the law, fearful that they might compromise their separate personal status. Instead, most declined to register their marriages or announce their divorces to the French after the initial registration drive. The administrators responsible for the état civil were content to let the matter lie. Almost as soon as the ink dried on the first master registers in the 1890s, commentators noted that the marriage registries were a "dead letter," and they would remain so well into the twentieth century.[55]

Breaking up the family, the ayant droit

Several years passed after passage of the 1882 law before workable procedures made it possible to begin registration. A first set of instructions went to the printers in 1885, followed by another in 1888. Together they numbered well over a hundred pages. To ensure that the average civil servant understood the rules, they received a small guidebook. It included examples of hand-drawn family trees and registry pages.[56] Registration fieldwork started with the posting of bilingual French and Arabic notices at the mayor's office of the main commune announcing the event, and these also went up at the cadi's court and the main square. Public criers made announcements on market day.[57] Heads of families were asked to bring any written records bearing names to the interview so that any previously used patronyms carried over, such as those conferred by the Warnier Law a decade earlier. Otherwise, unsworn testimony from the family head, the ayant droit, alone sufficed to establish the family's membership. This person also chose the family's new patronym. French teams did the actual registration work, composed of a French registrar (*commissaire*) assisted by an interpreter, and sometimes accompanied by the local Algerian secretary (*khodja*). It was expected that the registrar would be recruited from within the colonial administration, generally a municipal functionary, but he did not have to be an actual officer of the état civil, such as a mayor, nor vested with the same legal authority as this officer. The only requirement was French citizenship. Ideally, officials looked for commissioners who had some familiarity with Arabic, but they did not make it a requirement. Regardless of their civil status and skills, Jews were forbidden from working as registrars, with the governor general's office weighing in that their presence risked sparking Muslim hostility.[58] Overseeing the work at each prefecture was a committee composed of six individuals, including two notables recruited from outside the administration. One of these had to be a European with knowledge of Islamic law and Arabic, and the second was to be a Muslim notable from the Islamic court system or chosen from among municipal or departmental leaders.[59] A member of the Ibn Bādīs family of Constantine, Cherif ben Mekki Benbadis (Sharīf ibn Makkī ibn Bādīs, Ar.), the cadi of Constantine, served in this role for this eastern department.

Officials understood that when they had completed their work, people who considered themselves part of a common family would not share the same name.[60] As the instruction book acknowledged: "It will be the case that a group of relatives, having a common progenitor and living together, will as a result [of the registration procedures] form several families, each one having its own patronymic by law."[61] Fragmenting Algerian social institutions had long been part of colonial policy. Indeed, planners boasted how the état civil might break up the tribe and better individuate land tenure in the debates that preceded the 1882 law.[62] As it happened, the mechanism performing this break worked nearly imperceptibly, a function of the rules that decided whom to include on a family's genealogical tree and whom to leave off.

The role of the presumed family head merits special attention. Near the top of the family tree stood this person who was dubbed the ayant droit, literally the person "having the right" to lead the family, or in English the "claimant" to this position. This did not represent a family's actual head (or more likely heads), inasmuch as family leadership was a dynamic affair in real life. On the family tree drawn by the French registrar, the ayant droit's name appears underlined in red and marked by "AD." The ayant droit appeared in the genealogical tree as a patriarch, the oldest living man who stood as the family's point of departure.[63] To avoid difficulties deciding who occupied the real position of leadership, planners relied on a fixed formula to decide this position. Viewed from the perspective of the other family members, the ayant droit might be a grandfather, father, paternal uncle, or eldest brother. No one considered that a woman's leadership in affairs of marriage, health, and reproduction, among other spheres, might qualify her to be an ayant droit. French officials allowed for women to become a claimant only if she had outlived all the men in her father's family, leaving her theoretically isolated.

The ayant droit decided the family's boundaries and size. This was not an elective decision: the claimant did not get to choose which relatives would join them to share the family name (although no mechanism ensured they did not leave off unwanted people, as I will discuss). Rather, a calculation based on the claimant's place in the family structure determined the family's size. The law of 1882 spelled out the claimant in a particularly convoluted passage: "Each native having neither an ascendant male in the paternal line, nor a paternal uncle, nor an older brother, will be held to choose a patronymic name when the master register is established. If the native has an ascendant male in the paternal line, or a paternal uncle, or an older brother, the choice of the patronymic name belongs successively to the first, the second, to the third."[64] In other words, the ayant droit role was decided by age, hierarchy within agnatic kinship relations, and gender. Anticipating that the law's language would cause problems, the guidebook transformed it into a series of questions the registrar posed to determine if someone qualified as the claimant: Do you have a living uncle? Do your dead brothers have descendants?[65]

Left unmentioned in the instructions, but most important to the family's fate, was the fact that the ayant droit had to be alive on registration day. Male longevity determined the new family's size, sometimes outweighing other demographic factors, like fecundity or age at marriage. Those families that had a claimant aged in their sixties or seventies would automatically increase in size, grouping together up to three generations, while those whose male members had died earlier would necessarily be much smaller, including only one or two living generations. Demographic historians have estimated that the average life expectancy of an Algerian man in 1900 only stood at about thirty-four years old.[66] This astonishingly short life left the claimants few opportunities to regroup family branches across the generations. The état civil rules also favored families that counted more men in their ranks. While a woman appeared in the genealogical trees alongside her brothers and agnatic kin, her children never appeared on her family tree but were listed in that of their father. In sum, the 1882 law created a narrow Algerian family, which, while it was not parsed down to a nuclear couple, was considerably depleted. Had it not been for a relaxation of the rules in 1888, which allowed for combining several claimants into a single-family unit, Algerians would have faced extremely fragmented families.

A new name: The patronymic

The new family name served as the central organizing device of the état civil, and in theory this name became permanent. This crowning name is worth unpacking. There was no attempt at this point to impose a French-styled *nom de particule* as in the 1870s (although these names carried over into the état civil in cases where they had been conferred). Instead, registrars received instructions to "encourage the natives to conserve their name or that of their father when this name is sufficiently distinctive."[67] When Algerians had their choice of name, the reasoning went, they would embrace it. The ayant droit chose the patronym, except in cases where that person did not appear, refused to give a name, or insisted on a name already in use, in which case the French registrar could confer a name of his own choosing.[68] The archives fall silent on how often officials imposed names. Registrars had examples of suitable types of names in an updated list in the new *Vocabulaire*, and registrars made sure that the French spellings conformed to this reference. Left unclarified was whether Algerians could select a name that did not appear in the master list. They could not, however, adopt a name that someone else from the same district had already chosen. For identification purposes, different families were forbidden from sharing the same name in a single village.[69] This aimed to "avoid confusions that might result by the adoption of [same] patronymic in the same district."[70] As the popular names were crossed off, people registering later had to accept patronymics they might otherwise not have chosen. Also limiting the choices was the fact that planners tried to produce distinct classes of names from among existing names. Certain names were reserved for the given prénom, ruling out most of the popular isms for use as patronyms. Guidebooks reiterated this, warning registrars to heed the French-made distinctions between first and last names. Not valid as patronyms were names "well recognized as first names like Amar, Himane, Moussa, Kaddour, Larbi, Ahmed, Taïeb, etc."[71] This meant that although the nom was supposed to be a patronymic name, it was rarely the father's actual name, i.e., his ism as present in his children's nasab. There would have been too many families named "Benahmed" or "Benali." As a workaround, registrars made slight changes to the French spelling that made for technically distinct names. In the case of first names repeating within the same family, "Sehir" (Arabic, *ṣaghrīr*, "the younger") or "Kebir" (Arabic, *kabīr*, "the elder") could be added for siblings with the same first name.[72]

Although names had historically decided the boundaries of communities, there were no guidelines concerning ethnicity and race with regard to patronyms. Officials ignored the question of religion, assuming that the "état civil of natives" included only Muslims. But a handful of converts lived in Algeria, people who had either embraced Christianity freely or did so under duress, as occurred with Algerian children collected by missionaries in times of famine and crisis.[73] Converts typically bore names that clearly communicated their status as in-between communities, belonging to neither Europeans nor Algerians. They had a Christian first name conferred at baptism and an Algerian patronymic.[74] For example, in 1897 a man named Richard Mohammed Benkrerech came to the attention of the mayor of Attafs, a farming town in central Algeria, because he lacked parental records.[75] The mayor explained that he did not have any because he had been taken as a child by the White Fathers missionary society and raised as a Christian. The question likely came from someone who did not know Algeria well because the man's name clearly communicated his conversion and the sort of natal alienation experienced by converts, known in Algeria as "M'tourni," an Arabization of "turncoats" (Fr. *retourne sa veste*).[76] "Benkrerech" used what might have been a fictive nasab that clearly marked that he was not a European. On the other hand, his Christian first name, "Richard," showed that he was not Muslim either. His second prénom, "Mohammed," departed from long-standing understandings that reserved the Prophet's name for Muslims. He mostly likely had this name when he arrived in the missionaries' orphanage as a child. Historian Joseph Peterson has uncovered a case that speaks volumes to the politics of names among the converts. In 1882 Algerian students studying at a White Father's seminary located in the Aveyron region of France used name politics to protest the poor conditions they suffered compared to the privileges enjoyed by the other students. They refused to use their Christian names and reverted to their original Algerian names as part of their protest strategy.[77] The cultural codes of names are not always so clear-cut. There are instances of Muslim parents choosing French names as their child's prénom when recording births, as shown in chapter 5 by the example of the Algerian gendarme who named his daughter "Louise." In this case, there is no evidence to suggest that conferring a French name implied a religious conversion, unlike the case with the White Fathers' converts. Later, some Algerian men who went to work in metropolitan France married local women and gave typically French names to their children, while keeping their Algerian patronym. The état civil did not formally forbid Christian or French patronyms to Muslim Algerians.

When registrars recorded Algerians, they looked up a proposed name in a master list of Arabic names, an updated and expanded *Vocabulaire* published in 1885. Building on the 1865 volume, this alphabetically arranged list included more than 13,500 Arabo-Islamic names, written in Arabic script, with their equivalent in French letters.[78] The list simplified Algerian names to the maximum and streamlined them for French usages. Along with distinguishing between prénom and nom, the list parsed names by gender to ensure that unskilled registrars made appropriate choices. Editors of the new list abandoned efforts to find a system of transliteration that might work for both Arabic and Berber. Rather, they converted the latter to Arabic when equivalences existed and then gave spellings for these names as they sounded to the French ear. This erased the distinctive features that distinguished Arabic and Tamazight names. Names originating in Turkish or other languages received no special consideration. The system of conversion from the 1860s that privileged pronunciation over the written word carried over. Editors of the new *Vocabulaire* wrote that "you will find in the present collection certain names with a defective spelling according to the grammar, but we thought it good to maintain this because it corresponds best to the pronunciations used in the places where the names were recorded."[79] The rules disfigured written forms of names. The simplest example is the "ibn" or "bin" in the nasab that the *Vocabulaire* attached to the following name with a hyphen, or it was simply amalgamated as in "Bennini" (bin Nīnī), turning two separate Arabic words into one French name. The same liaison was used for kunyas, so that Bū Sh'ala became "Bouchala" in French.[80] In these cases, the supposed streamlining actually defeated administrative purposes. It bogged down alphabetized indexes with pages upon pages of names beginning with "ben-" and "bou-." The *Vocabulaire* of 1885 contains thirty-three pages of names starting with "bou-," making the search for names an onerous task.

Algerian reactions: Changing names

While Algerians had many reasons to oppose registration, they did not do so in significant numbers. The armed insurrections predicted by those who opposed the Muslim état civil never materialized, nor did widespread refusals to register. In some areas, registrars reported problems contacting people because of the difficulties of travel, but cases of outright refusals appear rarely.[81] The closest thing documented in the archive occurred in Staouëli, a commune just outside Algiers. Here a sizable portion of Muslim inhabitants never appeared in the civil registers. Why this happened is not clear. Staouëli's Muslims did not organize openly or make any formal protest, nor did any low grumbling make its way back to the Algiers Prefecture through informants. Indeed, the lacunae did not appear until officials started reviewing the draft documents. They explained the problem through the trope of Muslim intransigence to modernity.[82] However, the gaps in the records could have easily resulted from administrators themselves failing to properly do their work. In any case, only a few other incidents drew enough attention to become the object of inquiry.[83] Otherwise, registration went smoothly, and French officials repeatedly expressed their satisfaction with the cooperation of local people. Often they credited themselves with the success, by way of boasting their good relations with Algerians. One registrar reported to his superiors how well things went for him in 1893: "The natives always showed good will . . . and it must be added that there was reciprocity in this respect, and that I never sought to annoy or offend them in any way in my work."[84] In the case of a village near Batna at the Sahara's northern edge, the local people took extra efforts to ensure that their names went into French records properly, with the report stating that "the natives . . . pointed out on their own accord the unwitting omissions made in the field survey."[85] For this official, the cooperation demonstrated that transparency and choice were essential to the état civil's success. "This fortuitous attitude stems from the fact that the registrar took great pains to explain the purpose of the law to people and to recommend that they choose their own patronymic name from among their ancestor's names and to carefully avoid any farcical or abusive appellation."

Failing to register represented an infraction that could be punished, but the success of the état civil depended more on Algerian cooperation than compulsion and fear. The fact that so many Algerians registered their families at this time likely had less to do with their readiness to obey colonial commands than the fact that many thought they had a stake in the new order. Even if they feared taxation, conscription, and other as yet unknown burdens that might come in the wake of the état civil, they reckoned that having official French documents represented a prudent choice. Algerians had to deal more frequently with colonial institutions at this time, and having an état civil facilitated these encounters. These encounters included buying land, and by the end of the nineteenth century a handful of wealthy Algerian families successfully participated in the land markets as buyers, even if the net effect of land transfer overwhelmingly privileged Europeans.[86]

Some took the état civil very seriously. These attitudes reveal themselves most clearly in the petitions sent to colonial officials to fix errors in their records. Once the genealogical trees and master registers were officialized, following a one-month period when revisions and edits could be made freely, corrections required a decree issued by the governor general.

Algerians had to present a formal request that went through several layers of the administration, making it a time-consuming undertaking. Nevertheless, when they found mistakes, Algerians made the effort to get errors in their état civil rectified. Many requests of this sort are preserved in the archive, showing that people took an active role in ensuring that their état civil names and family relations were accurate or suited them.

These requests to correct names most often concerned a patronymic, which registrars had entered incorrectly or spelled wrong. Most of the requests contain only a few documents that give little indication of the circumstances. An exception is a comparatively robust file concerning a cobbler in Constantine who in 1893 addressed a letter to the prefecture to have his patronymic name corrected.[87] His family name had been erroneously recorded as "Bouhabik," whereas he already had established "Drici" as his patronymic elsewhere. The Drici name appeared on an official document in Amor's possession, and he had used it in his dealings in Muslim courts and his trade. He stated that the erroneous "Bouhabik" patronymic caused "a confusion that would cause him and his entire family the most serious prejudice." The meaning of the different names never made it into discussion. *Ḥabaq* means basil in Arabic, so Bouhabik literally meant the "man of the basil," although its actual meaning is open to interpretation. The Arabic spelling for the Drici name he preferred does not appear in the extant documents. It was almost certainly a variation on the name of the prophet Idris, generally written "Drīsī." Amor used this name in common with a cousin, a fifty-year-old ironsmith named Mohammed, and another cousin, a fifty-five-year-old woman named Safia. In all, this family numbered nine living people.

The average Algerian artisan did not have the skills or connections to handle this sort of request on their own. Amor engaged the services of a letter writer, likely a professional, who had a good grasp how the administration operated.[88] This person drafted the letter in French on neatly lined paper and included Drici's age (thirty-eight) and address (42 rue de Périgny). He clearly stated the grounds for the request and its justifications. The letter's header included the date (21 June 1893) and the addressee, and it concluded with a signature drawn in a separate hand. The cobbler's name appeared in a signature made of carefully shaped French letters, which may or may not have been written by Amor Drici. In any case, the signature spells out "Armar ben Rabah," whereas elsewhere in the file the first name was spelled "Amor," a discrepancy that administrators did not seem to notice or linger on. In all, the letter contained all the necessary information and responded to the formatting norms for this sort of request. It did its work. Within a few days, officials at Constantine's Prefecture office had pulled the relevant files from the archive and tracked down the source of the naming error. The prefect wrote to the governor general endorsing the request. In about two weeks, Amor had in hand a decree dated 3 July 1893 officializing his family's change of name to Drici.[89]

While this case went smoothly, one can ask why Amor Drici took the trouble in the first place. He had a patronym, but what did he care what the French called him? Drici appeared written in French letters, a language he probably did not use often in Constantine, a city where the Arabic language held great sway in public life. For that matter, he probably did not understand French all that well, even if he may have spoken some in his interactions with settlers. It is unknown if the Dricis held much property beyond their tools, and Amor did not seem to be involved in any legal cases that needed a correct name in the colonizer's language to go before courts or notaries. Indeed, the file contains no obvious motives. The only grounds for action that can be deduced from it is that Amor had an attachment to the Drici name itself. Indeed, writing on Amor's behalf, the letter writer justified the name change request "because it is a family name inherited from his ancestors . . . he is determined to keep it." The cobbler and his family understood that their social being depended on this name, which his family apparently had taken to using in common before the French reforms, as sometimes occurred. It embedded them in a larger web of social relations of kin, neighbors, and work. In other words, Drici was not an arbitrary, nominal sign, and the Dricis would not feel themselves to be the same under a different name.[90] Even if it appeared in foreign letters, their name merited preservation. Moreover, Amor appears to have recognized the symbolic power of the French-language records, meaning that he understood that if he wanted to keep his name in the future, in any language, it needed to correspond with what was in his état civil.

Even people who seemingly had less at stake went to great lengths to ensure that their official names appeared correctly. In 1892 a woman named Ḥuwa bint Muḥammad bin Slīman (Houa bent Mohamed ben Sliman, Fr.), also living in Constantine, found an erroneous patronymic in her new documents and set out to get it fixed. In her case, this led to a long and difficult process. The identity card she received at the finalization of her état civil gave her the patronymic "Ben Saïda" (Bin Saʿīda, Ar.), a name she had never used, whereas she was known already as "Hamedi" (Ḥamadī, Ar.).[91] Ḥuwa had no children or husband, and she counted only a younger sister on her genealogical tree. Like Amor Drici, nothing in her file suggests that she had a case coming before a colonial official that might need French documents. She simply wished to keep her name.

Rather than hiring a letter writer, Ḥuwa Ḥamadī started with the Muslim courts. She asked two men to present her case to the cadi's court (*mahakma*) of Constantine in person. One was a notable named Sī Ḥamū 'Abd al-Razāq, who had served in a colonial spahi unit, and the other was Sh'aban bin Qadūr, a merchant originally from Hammam Righa, many days travel away. The two men knew Ḥuwa but were not related to her. Sharīf ibn Badīs presided along with two other jurists. They heard the testimony given by Ḥuwa's intermediaries, who verified that they knew her to be named Ḥamadī. The court then drafted a letter in Arabic, detailing her case, and addressed it to the French state prosecutor in Constantine.[92] Although ibn Badīs sat on the local état civil central committee, he did not have the authority to initiate the change within the *mahakma* court, as Ḥamadī might have hoped. For his part, the French prosecutor read the letter in a translation made by the judicial interpreter, Isaac Darman. Deciding that it fell outside of his responsibilities, he forwarded the file to the prefecture.

At this point, Ḥuwa separately engaged a professional French-language letter writer and directly made her case to the prefect.[93] A letter dated 31 May 1892 stated:

> I have the honor of asking you to kindly rectify my surname, which is "Hamedi," as it appears in the notarized document I am sending you herewith, instead of "Ben Saïda," which was given to me by mistake on my identity card, which I am [also] sending you. Prior to this letter, I had already sent a request to the public prosecutor of Constantine, trying to obtain this rectification. He informed me that I should contact you.
>
> In the hope that you will give a favorable response to my request. I have the honor to be, Monsieur the Prefect, with the deepest respect, your most humble and most obedient servant.

At the letter's end, Ḥuwa Ḥamadī's name appears in French letters in the same hand as the rest of the letter, along with her address (rue de 26e de ligne, no. 4, Constantine).

Ḥuwa Ḥamadī showed considerable determination to get her name fixed, more so than Amor Drici. She no doubt expended capital asking the two men to represent her in the cadi's court, and these sorts of administrative and legal interventions required money. The letter writer certainly charged a fee for his services, and the *mahakma* might have required some sort of payment. For his part Darman, the government translator, noted the cost for his work, a price of 6 francs, added to which were the costs of official paper bond and document fees in governmental stamps, which added another 1 franc 20 centimes. In all, this represented a not completely insignificant sum in cash money at the time. Unlike Amor's case, Ḥuwa's request took a long time to get rectified. The prefect and the prosecutor wrangled over where responsibility for the case lay. The governor general's office wanted to know if the registrar had made a mistake, or if he had imposed the name on his own because Ḥuwa would not cooperate. If the latter were the case, her name would not be changed. Had she originally chosen a name and later had second thoughts?[94] The officials reviewing her case were reluctant to work from the facts as Ḥuwa Ḥamadī stated them. At one point they even summoned her to testify at the prefecture office, an imposing building that sat in a relatively upscale European neighborhood, an unfamiliar and intimidating experience for most any Algerian at this time.[95] Ultimately, it took nine months and a flurry of correspondence before her request was officialized with a decree (1 February 1893) legalizing the change to "Hamedi."

How to account for the different response given to Ḥuwa's request and the many questions officials put to it? The French documents spell out their own explanation in their stories of procedure told in the idioms bureaucratic rationality. In the minds of administrators in Constantine and Algiers, the correctness of their procedure decided the "correct" name. But there is reason to be skeptical that this alone decided their reaction to Ḥuwa's request. Officials took a fine-toothed comb to her file, and they were unwilling to overlook any errors on her part. For example, Ḥuwa's first letter, sent to the wrong office and in Arabic, delayed things and required a paid translation. Had her letter writer made an incorrect turn of phrase, missed a date or address, officials could have rejected her request outright or sent it back. By contrast, no one raised an alarm over the irregular signature in Drici's file. One suspects that gender prejudice played a role. The male-centered symbolic order of the French onomastic system assumed and reinforced a male-centered social order. Although Algerian society had its own patriarchal forms that might function as analogs to the French model in the civil code, the vagaries of actual life meant that individual cases departed from this model. Ḥuwa headed her own family, consisting of herself and a sister. They had no living male kin, and no children. To the officials' mind, these women had little at stake in a correct name. One hears skepticism and sighs of frustration in the administrator's response to her request. Why does she bother? When the original registrar weighed in, he thinly veiled his discontent that he had been called back: He had finalized Constantine's état civil three years ago, and how could he remember this case among the eight thousand families recorded?[96] Certainly, these administrators recognized that she needed an état civil and a name in the new order. For example, if the sisters had property to put to deed, they would need this new legal identity. But the "Ben Saïda" name could do this work perfectly well in their minds, and in any case, right or wrong, this name would one day die with them. Ḥuwa might have been known as a Ḥamadī to her friends and neighbors, an argument that the *mahakama* court made in its letter on her behalf. In the French officials' minds, however, the truth of this woman's name did not belong to her or Algerian society, but to themselves.

For their part, neither Ḥuwa nor Amor contested the principle of imposing a French-styled patronymic nom in the place of their nasab. Nor did they protest the stripping down of their original multipart name into a prénom + nom form or express reservations with their names appearing in French letters. (Those presiding in the cadi's court also did not protest the new onomastic norms when they intervened in Ḥamadī's case, even though as custodians of Islamic law they might have done so.) If they had any such misgivings, the letter writers most likely kept them out of the document, not wishing to compromise their clients' cases.

The genealogical trees of Takitount

Other sources expand our knowledge of Algerian reactions to the état civil, shifting from the name itself to how it affected the composition of actual families. Before French registrars recorded patronyms into the master volume, they first mapped out family relations in genealogical trees. The full records of the family trees for a village called Takitount provide sufficient materials for an expanded study of how civil registration affected these families. Takitount lies at the southern flanks of the Kabylia Mountains. The local dialect of Tamazight predominated here, although Arabic-speaking Algerians also lived in the area alongside their Berberophone neighbors. Most of the people in Takitount belonged to the 'Amushās (Amoucha, Fr.) tribe, which extended into the many adjacent settlements, numbering about thirty-five thousand people in all.[97] In the 1860s, French officials divided the 'Amushās into five separate units as part of the administrative redistricting that came with the Sénatus-Consulte of 1863.[98] Along with recognizing Algerian property rights, this law restructured rural administration. It replaced larger circumscriptions called *cheïkats, caïdats,* and *aghaliks*, many of which were carryovers of Ottoman-era administrative units, with a smaller subdivision dubbed *douars.*[99] Whereas previous units might encompass tens of thousands of people, a *douar* typically included only one thousand to three thousand people, living in one or several villages or hamlets. Putting people into smaller units better concentrated colonial authority, or they promised a "tighter control of indigenous leaders and a more penetrating political surveillance of native people," as one study reported.[100] For example, the formidable Awlād 'Abd al-Nūr confederation, which lived nearby, was slated for "disaggregation" in 1868 when administrators separated them into ten *douars* as part of an effort to fragment the political and military cohesion of this tribe, which numbered about twenty-five thousand people.[101] In some cases, officials renamed *douars* after geographic features, a nearby spring, mountain range, or river ford, rather than use existing tribal names based on a founding ancestor. In this way, they brought the symbolic power of group names to bear on the administrative breakup, as geographer Brahim Atoui has demonstrated.[102] For their part, the Amushās at Takitount did not lose their name when they were divided into *douars*. But the tribe's name was downgraded, applied only to a small hamlet in the district.

In 1890 a French registrar completed the état civil survey for families at Takitount.[103] He divided the village of 1,833 people into 187 named families, each with their own genealogical tree. All the family trees appear only in French letters. The largest family counted forty-three members, while most were considerably smaller. At the very bottom were twenty-five single individuals, each with their own patronym. Most of these were women, seventeen total, who had outlived their agnatic male kin. While some of these women likely lived in their children's households, they could not share a patronym with them by the terms of the 1882 law. Such women headed their own "family" as the ayant droit. Placed alongside robust, full families, they appear as solitary stragglers on the pages of the village registry. The registrars conferred their patronymic nom by carrying over their given ism name rather than taking the trouble to ascribe a separate name that might be needed for another family according to the rule that patronyms could not repeat themselves in a single district.[104] But registrars did not follow this rule religiously. The oldest of these women (and the oldest living person in the village as the French registrar figured it) was an eighty-year-old woman. She was named Fatima bent Mohammed ben Mihoub and had the patronymic "Brahmia."[105]

The average family size at Takitount calculates at about ten members, with the median family numbering near seven people. Typical of them was the Baouche family (figure 6.1), which had seven living members from a single generation, all siblings.[106]

The Baouche genealogical tree started with the grandfather Mohammed and the father Saou, both of whom had died and were marked with an "M" for *mort* (dead). This left the oldest son, twenty-five-year-old Saïd, as the claimant, with his name underlined. Below the new Baouche

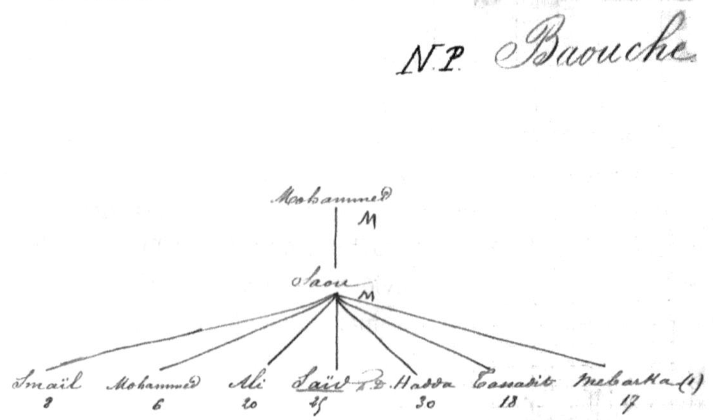

FIGURE 6.1 Baouche, "Arbres généalogiques." Source: FR ANOM Aix-en-Provence 9377//14-*Touts droits réservés*. Note: "M"=dead (*mort*). First name with age underneath. Ayant droit (underlined center) is Saïd, twenty-five years old.

patronymic, the registrar counted his three sisters (Hadda, thirty; Tassadit, eighteen; and Mebarka, seventeen) and three younger brothers (Ali, twenty; Mohammed, six; and Smaïl, eight). He entered a note for the youngest sister, Mebarka, saying she had married and moved to another nearby village. Otherwise, the Baouche all lived in Takitount, where they farmed.

Less typical was the largest family at Takitount, the Daoudis (figure 6.2), who numbered forty-three living members (forty-five total).[107] Their case illustrates well the procedural forces determining family size, and the particular way the ayant droit functioned to hold a family together or to break it apart. Sixty-year-old Mahammed stood as the family's claimant, and he had one sister (Halima, fifty-five) and three deceased brothers (Tahar, Kaci, and Daoud).[108] This was a modest-sized group of siblings, but the brothers all had had many children before they died (topped by Tahar, with seven children).

This generation of the Daoudis had in turn fathered another generation of children. In all, the family counted three living generations, which made for a dense genealogical tree. The registrar was at pains to fit it onto a single sheet of paper. The family's size had a great deal to do with Mahammed Daoudi's age. Among the ayants droit at Takitount, the average age was forty-eight. Mahammed had lived to sixty, outliving all his siblings except for his younger sister. The importance of male longevity to family size shows up clearly. Had Mahammed passed away even days before registration, the family would been broken up into four separate branches, one for each of the original brothers. Mahammed's own branch was the smallest: he only had three young children, none of whom had yet married. But because he was still alive, Mahammed could claim his dead brothers' lines, the largest of which belonged to Tahar and numbered twenty-two living members.

There are no signs that people at Takitount protested their new patronymical name, one way that their agency might be assessed. However, many succeeded in attenuating the état civil's fragmenting effects more subtly and more effectively. They requested to combine family branches by placing two or more claimants on the same tree. The Hammadi family, for example, combined two paternal cousins, named Abdallah and Saïd. Their fathers had passed away, making each of them an ayant droit. Normally they should have been in separate family trees, but they asked the

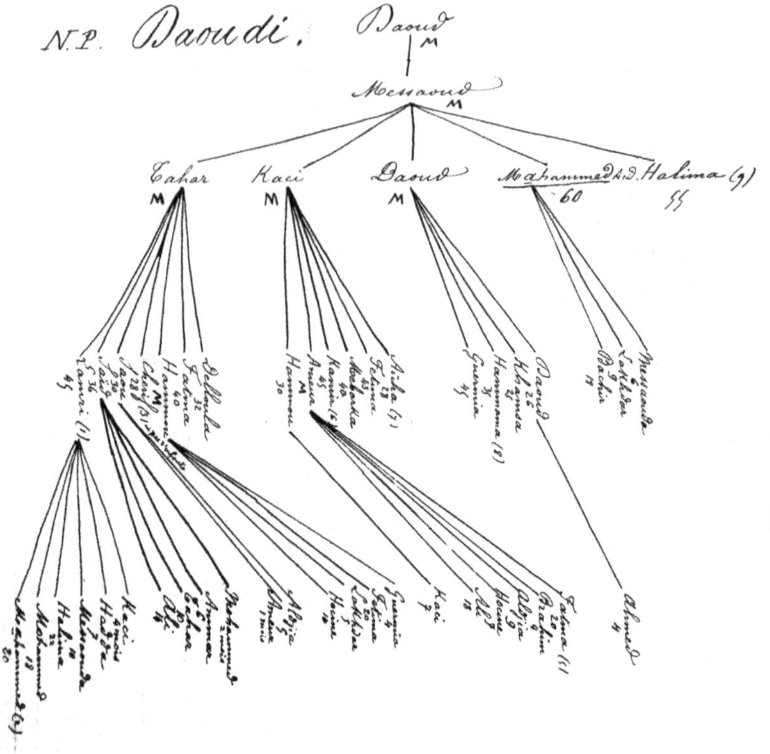

FIGURE 6.2 Daoudi, "Arbres généalogiques." Source: FR ANOM Aix-en-Provence 9377//14-*Touts droits réservés*. Note: ayant droit (underlined) is Mahammed, sixty years old.

registrar to place them together.[109] This doubled the size of the Hammadi family, which now numbered twelve people, instead of two separate families of five and seven people each. In another example, the Sahnoun family combined two paternal cousins, each one a claimant, who normally would have gone into the books under separate patronymics.[110] This did not yield a large group, only six people, but it saved this already small family from being divided in half. The Azzoug family (figure 6.3) presents the most dramatic example. It consisted of four separate claimants, all paternal first cousins. These men's children and the children of their male siblings totaled forty-two living people (forty-nine total), spread across three living generations.[111] Had they not requested the change, the largest

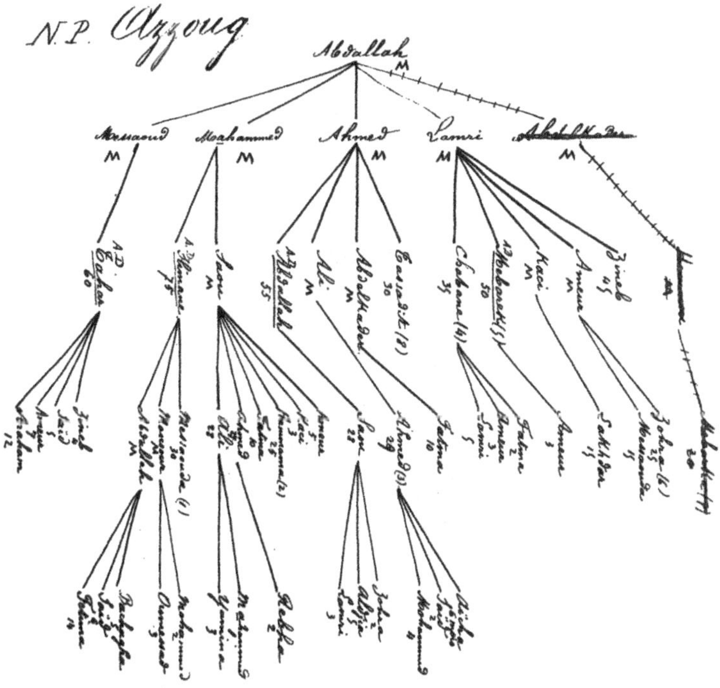

FIGURE 6.3 Azzoug, "Arbres généalogiques." Source: FR ANOM Aix-en-Provence 9377//14-*Touts droits réservés*. Note: ayants droit (underlined) are Tahar (sixty years old), Slimane (seventy-five years old), Abdallah (fifty-five years old), and Mebarek (fifty years old).

of the separately named branches would have had no more than sixteen living members, and the smallest only five.

In all, 30 families among the 187 at Takitount combined multiple ayants droit. Twenty-four of these had two claimants, like the Hammadis and the Sahnouns. There were four families with three claimants; one family counting four claimants; and one family made up of five claimants. In each of these cases, families that would have been considerably smaller joined branches to enlarge their size.

People at Takitount who combined multiple ayants droit used a relaxing of the rules announced in 1888.[112] "Occasionally the heads of closely related groups have asked to take the same patronymic when they are first cousins. It was decided that their request should be granted. At such a close degree of kinship, the family bond is strong; inheritance often remains in common; and family members may have an interest in confirming, through a shared name, their status as *'aceb'* heirs, which Muslim law recognizes up to the sixth degree in the male line."[113] The concern here was to accommodate Islamic inheritance law, and the *aceb* heirs within the état civil parameters. Broadly speaking, Islamic law splits heirs into two classes.[114] One is called the *ahl al-farā'iḍ*, which consist of daughters, parents, spouses, and in some cases siblings. The new état civil records could accommodate these. However, they could not deal with the *'asaba* ("aceb" Fr.), a second class of heirs that extends much further into agnatic kin. While centering on sons and grandsons, the *'asaba* can reach into the outer layers of paternal kin, which would have been lost in the état civil's family trees. The relaxing of the rules allowed families to extend the legal relations of their family to at least the fourth degree of consanguinity and thereby include their agnatic first cousins. There was little overt discussion of the rationale for the change. It did not express French readiness to accommodate Algerian wishes for larger families. Policymakers up to this point consistently sought to fragment social relations, with *douars* just one example of a much larger effort. Nearly every aspect of name reform responded to the goal of individuating property and bringing farms up for sale. However, this ran up against the need to keep separate personal status viable, which depended in large part on the functioning of Islamic law with regard to the family. The relaxing of the ayant droit rules likely expressed an attempt to make the état civil compatible with Islamic law, thereby extending its reach into other fields and its potential power.

How large a family?

While the registrar in Takitount who accommodated requests to extend families did not have any problems when his records arrived for review by his superiors, in other cases, reprimands fell on registrars who recorded very large families. Higher officials considered the cases selectively. In some cases, having large families served colonial interests, while others did not. For example, the registrar working in the settlements near Collo, on the eastern coast, received an admonition from the governor general's office in 1891 for allowing too many local families to register under the same patronym. Having received the first drafts of records for some twenty-two thousand people in the region, officials in the capital found that the registrar, a man named Jean Louis Maurice Boët, had recorded as many as two hundred people under the same family name, with several other families numbering around one hundred people.[115] In a terse letter, officials in Algiers impressed on Boët the need to find what they called a *juste milieu* between imposing excessively small family sizes according to the original ayant droit rules while not allowing families to expand excessively based on the 1888 exception. For his part, Boët made no apologies for large families.[116] He argued that combining claimants guarded the interests of widowed or divorced women, in particular, preventing their separation in name from other relatives. Moreover, acceding to people's wishes sped up his work. If "I was to split the family," he wrote, registration would be impossible.[117]

Ceding to Algerian demands for larger families not only made registration more efficient for registrars like Boët, it also meant getting paid. And this put people in the field in conflict with their superiors. A registrar and his interpreter received a fixed sum for each person recorded. This was set at between 34 and 35 centimes a head for a civil servant already collecting a salary, a rate that doubled for freelancers. In both cases, the registrar and the interpreter split the money on a 60/40 basis. This meant that registrars had to work quickly to enroll as many people as possible to earn much money. Large families yielded the greatest return.[118] For example, the registrar who recorded the forty-two-person Azzoug family at Takitount received 8.82 francs for this record, having interviewed four claimants, while the pay for drafting the record of the solitary elderly woman, Fatima Brahmia, fell to 0.21 francs. The two hundred people that Boët recorded in a single family in Collo netted him 116.66 francs, a tidy sum for a civil servant at the time.[119]

Higher-ranking French officials occasionally had an incentive to protect the integrity of a large Algerian family when that family's interests coincided with their own. This happened with the Benbouzid (bin Bū Zīd Ar.) family, which lived in and around Aïn Beida, a commune in the department of Constantine. By the 1890s this family had a reputation for good relations with France. Its sons served in the military and worked in the administration.[120] One of the Benbouzids, Ali ben Larbi ben Mohammed, served as a highly decorated caïd. Rural administration depended on families like this, the so-called *grandes familles*, even as the general effect of French rule was to downgrade their status. So, when the registrar conducting fieldwork initially broke up the Benbouzids into seven separate genealogical trees, using four variations of the family name (Benbouzid, Zidi, Bouzidi, Bouzid), higher-ups protested. When the files were reviewed in Algiers, an official wrote in the margin, "Attention. This is the case of an important family which has a name in political affairs. See that the leader, Ali ben Larbi, has been recorded under the name of Benbouzid in the 1st and 3rd category families."[121] In this case, officials saw to it that this powerful family remained intact.

Pruning one's own family tree: Civil registration and exclusion

In general, the greater a family's size, the more resources it could pool and the stronger it stood overall. In its ideal, or idealized, form, the Muslim family serves as a source of succor, support, and identity, even if this model did not always realize itself in practice.[122] Thus, the primary response of Algerians to civil registration was to combine multiple ayants droit and keep their family intact. In some cases, however, people petitioned to *exclude* members, essentially directing the French registrars toward the branches that they wanted cut from the main trunk. If the family served as an institution of strength in colonial-era Algeria, it was not free of internal conflict. Inheritance and other material interests significantly raised the stakes and drove these efforts to exclude. État civil registration provided an opportunity for a family's strongest members, or those best able to use the colonial system, to redo their families according to their own interests. An 1890 example concerning the family of a man named Hadj Benmounah illustrates this approach at work and sheds light on the links that tied civil registration to complex questions of race and the legacies of slavery. The Benmounah family lived in small hamlet (Fedj-M'zala) midway between Algiers and Constantine.[123] A wealthy man, the eponymous patriarch, Hadj Benmounah, had fathered children with multiple women. They included at least one wife, as well as an enslaved African woman he owned, whom he took as his sexual concubine as allowed by Islamic law. The children of this woman grew alongside those born of his free wife(s), where, as the registrar put it, "they took part and place in the family and took root," a way of saying that their father had treated them equally.

By the time état civil registration took place, Hadj Benmounah had died. Normally, the registrar placed all children on an equal status in their father's genealogical trees, making no matrilineal distinctions. While these records provided the child's name and age, they took no account of their mother, which might be different for each child in cases of divorce or death of a wife and remarriage, as well as polygamy or concubinage. However, the children born to Hadj Benmounah's free wife(s) approached the French registrar seeking an exception. Rather than asking to expand their family tree, they tried to bar their siblings born to the concubine of their dead father. The case was a tricky one, and the registrar wrote for guidance to the central commission in Constantine. "Hadj Benmounah's legitimate children wonder whether they should accept their mixed race (*mulâtres*) brothers as part of the same family tree as themselves, and they fear that by accepting them, they are giving them rights to which they have no claim." The rights go unspecified in the documents but are almost certainly related to their share of their father's inheritance and other property the family controlled together.

The registrar tipped his hand on his opinions when he used "legitimate" to describe the petitioning Benmounah offspring. Here he used French concepts rather than those of Islamic law, which ordinarily decided family and inheritance cases. In general, Islamic law held that the children born of a union between a master and his enslaved concubine followed their father's status, meaning they were born free and legally equal to any other consanguineous children. Moreover, the enslaved concubine who bore the children of her master ascended to the status of *umm al-walad* (mother of the child), which forbade her sale and granted her manumission when her master died.[124] Therefore, their mother's status at the time she gave birth should not have affected the inheritance rights of her children, although an *umm al-walad* manumission made for extremely complicated cases.[125] Violence surrounded the institution of slavery at every angle, even if Islamic law offered ways to mitigate it.[126] People ignored the law, and slaves routinely suffered illegal acts. Race affected the matter. While Islamic law stated that religion rather than skin color was the basis for enslavement (with free-born Muslims excluded from enslavement), Africans of color faced long-standing beliefs that their skin color was prima facie grounds for their enslavement, a prejudice that extended to other people of color regardless of their origin or legal status, as if they all had the taint of slavery in their lineage.[127] The language used in the French documents makes it clear that Hadj Benmounah's concubine was a woman of color.

Hadj Benmounah's children hoped to use overlapping legal regimes and the gray areas that emerged around slavery under the French to exclude their siblings. Islamic law did not accord the same status to a free mistress as an enslaved concubine, with the former occupying a place closer to an "illegitimate" relationship in the French civil code. If it could be shown that the rival siblings had been born to a freewoman who shared their father's bed outside of wedlock, rather than an enslaved woman owned by the father, they could be denied a place within his family. French law appeared at this point. In 1848 the National Assembly abolished slavery in French territories, and in Algeria the 1848 law superseded Islamic law with regard to slavery and its impact on the family. Evidence suggests that abolition had a negligible immediate impact on many slaves, especially for enslaved women deeply imbedded in their master's family. For their part, French officials showed lassitude and declined to enforce the law out of indifference or for fear of upsetting their dealings with influential Algerians.[128] But regardless of the practical impact or lack thereof of abolition, all enslaved people in Algeria were legally free beginning in 1848. This fact informed the argument made by Hadj Benmounah's offspring to the French registrar. They used abolition to suggest that their rivals had been born to an unmarried free woman. In other words, because French law had abolished slavery in 1848, and their father had not married his concubine (a scenario suggested rather than asserted in the documents), the mother of their rival half-siblings had passed from the status of *umm al-walad* to adulteress.

Officials sitting at the central commission of the état civil in Constantine decided the case. They were led by Antoine Bozzo, a judicial interpreter in Constantine, and Jean de Dieu Laurent Larrera de Morel, a Cuban-born, French judge. They first considered Islamic family law. Although the case merited careful consideration before a full Muslim court, the French jurists did not consult with their counterparts. Even Sharīf ibn Bādīs, who sat on Constantine's cadi court as well as the état civil commission, was not consulted, being absent when the case appeared. Rather, Bozzo and Larrera de Morel looked up their answers in the annals of *droit musulman*, a codified version of Islamic law adapted for colonial use and translated into French.[129] Based on their readings, they sided with Hadj Benmounah's children who wished to expel their half-siblings from the family's état civil. In Bozzo's and Larrera de Morel's opinion, if the latter "came into the world prior to the French occupation, at the time when slavery was not abolished, they must carry the name of the father and can have the same rights as the legitimate children." However, those born later were illegitimate.[130] The "child born of the cohabitation of a man and a woman with whom he is not linked by marriage and upon which he has no claim to as his property has no filiation with his father and cannot inherit from him," they decided. The governor general's office agreed, adding that the ages of the expelled siblings confirmed that they had been born after abolition.[131] These authorities never invited the children born to Hadj Benmounah's concubine to present their case, nor do these people even seem to have been aware that their link to their father was at risk as they did not write to French authorities regarding their case. Their opinions do not figure in the file, even indirectly.

Women offer a final case of branches eyed to be pruned through the état civil. As with Hadj Benmounah, property served as the driving force in these exclusions. Islamic law guaranteed daughters a portion of their father's estate (generally half that of their brothers). When a woman married into another family, perhaps moving to join her spouse in another village, her share of inheritance risked passing to her husband's family through the couple's children or by other means. Keeping estates intact and viable long concerned Maghrebi families. Lucette Valensi summed up the problem in her study of rural Tunisia, writing that "death divides what life assembles."[132] Various strategies have appeared over time to keep a family's patrimony intact, most all of them focused on curtailing a woman's right to inheritance. For example, religious endowments (*ḥubūs* or *waqf*) neutralized a woman's inheritance by preemptively dedicating a property to charitable purposes and making it untransferable. In particular, landowners could exclude a woman from her share of a field or orchard by placing it in a private endowment (*waqf al-ahlī*), which allowed the rest of the family to benefit from it.[133] Another tactic was to have a woman make a "donation" (*hiba*) of her share to her agnatic kin.[134] Allan Christelow, who has done some of the most thorough work in the colonial-era Islamic court archives in Algeria, concludes that "though women could in theory inherit land, they seldom did."[135] In some regions, customary law served to disinherit women. Finally, consanguineous marriages (parallel cousin marriage) commonly contained women's inheritance in Algeria at this time. The marriage of a woman to a patrilineal cousin ensured that her property remained within her father's extended family.[136]

How did the état civil figure in these strategies aimed at disinheriting women? The most clearly drawn evidence comes from women writing to authorities to have their civil records changed, citing or alluding to inheritance concerns. In 1896 a woman from Aïn el Ksar, a *douar* near Batna, wrote directly to the governor general to complain that she had been left off the état civil rolls and wanted to be included in her family's genealogical tree. "Although I am one of the direct heirs, I see that I am outside of the family."[137] Her name appears in the request in French letters, although it gives its full Arabic form, with a three-generational nasab, "Hezîa bent Haida ben Braham ben Ahmed Khodja ben Ferhat." Hezîa wished to belong to the final level of relations, the Ferhat family, formed out of her great-great-grandfather's kin. It consisted of nineteen people (along with six women who had married into it, two of them from the city of Constantine) living in Aïn el Ksar.[138]

After a short investigation, administrators decided that, indeed, they had made an error in leaving Hezîa off the état civil, but she could not join the Ferhats.[139] Headed by her second cousins, once removed, this family was too distant in relation to her. Instead, Hezîa had to join the Ahmed Khodja family, led by her aunt. The fact that a woman was the ayant droit meant that all the ascendant agnatic male members had died. Although Hezîa and her aunt might have actually lived among other related people, including the Ferhats, officially they belonged to the smallest of families with a sterile name. Most important, if Hezîa was an heir to the Ferhat branch, as her letter put it, the administrator's decision to legally exclude her from it fell as a major disappointment. The état civil's way of calculating family relations and attributing names placed her material interests in jeopardy, symbolically erasing Hezîa's ties to her extended kin and property.

The data from the genealogical trees in Takitount reveals even a more significant impact on women's inheritance rights. Overall, the population data for colonial Algeria shows a slight underrepresentation of women and girls in all records combined. Kamel Kateb calculates a "normal" gender ratio for this era to be slightly imbalanced at 105 boy births to 100 girls, based on reported births, meaning that some baby girls went undeclared.[140] The data for Takitount echoes this pattern. Here the overall numbers split between 44 percent female and 56 percent male. However, these numbers shift considerably when age segments are isolated. The people of Takitount showed little reluctance to register girls, and even female babies a few months old appear commonly in the family trees. This suggests that the men who reported their families to the French registrar included most of their young female kin, their daughters and nieces, naming and registering these girls along with everyone else. These girls had beautiful names, with the most common being "Fatma" (and variants "Fetima," "Fatnia"), "Tassadit," "Merbarka," and "Oumessad." If gender prejudice was to be a part of these girls' lives going forward, they came into the world with beautiful names, with their elders proudly recoding them in the état civil. However, at the age of adulthood, when the stakes for women's membership in the family changed, women's numbers fall off considerably relative to men. Most important, the Takitount records show a pronounced imbalance between women and men at the level of the ayant droit generation. This was the most consequential level in the family tree with regard to property, when the father had died and families faced the question of inheritance.[141] Making a count of those who stood at the same generational level as the claimant, i.e., the ayant droit, his siblings, and first cousins, shows only 29 percent women for 71 percent men in Takitount.[142] This dramatic figure merits consideration in light of the themes emerging at the end of this chapter. It will be recalled that women who had married and moved away, like anyone absent from the village on registration day, had to be included in their father's family tree.[143] Thus, while women at Takitount might have joined a spouse to live elsewhere, when they returned home, they should have been able to find themselves in the village's état civil alongside their brothers, uncles, and male cousins. Instead, hundreds of them simply disappeared in name at that moment when they had rights to a share of the family's patrimony.

French authorities said nothing about these disappearing women, which they hardly noticed. They bore responsibility, however, for having invested the ayant droit with such extensive and unchecked powers to decide the family. Unlike regular état civil records—births, marriages, and deaths—the first master registers of the "état civil of the natives" did not require witnesses. The ayant droit alone reported, and the registrar accepted his information at his word. The claimant did not have to swear an oath, nor did he need to present corroborating testimony or documents. Although the records yielded in this first round of civil registration bore the full force of French law, it was more like a census than an état civil. Thus, it contained none of the security devices designed to thwart forgery or fraud that protected the integrity of a regular état civil record.[144] For example, Hezîa's problems would have been easily solved had one of her distant cousins who served as the Ferhats' ayant droit elected to include her, claiming her as a sister or an aunt. No one in the colonial administration would have been the wiser. But Hezîa's cousins had no incentive to do so, and the rules privileged their word outright. Undoubtedly, many people, women and men, were left off by mistake rather than malice. The fact that people frequently moved increased the likelihood of omissions. A claimant might easily forget a lone cousin—man or woman—who had moved away, so too someone who was in the military, in prison, or exiled from Algeria. But as the records at Takitount show, women at the age of inheritance suffered the most.

The "état civil of the natives" promised colonial officials a way to know, command, and shape the Algerian family, making it assimilable to French-dominated institutions. Written into the état civil, the newly conferred names mapped out social relations like branches of a tree, some of which might be cut back or left to grow, depending on the circumstances. But this project could only go so far. Maintaining the inequalities of French Algeria depended on playing up the perceived alterity of Algerian society; erasing this alterity on the pages of a civil registry compromised an essential alibi for a racist and untenable system of governance. Moreover, Algerians had something to say about their names and their families, even if the French registrars controlled the books. People like the Constantine cobbler recognized how the new names affected actual social relations, as well as one's sense of self and belonging. Likewise, Ḥuwa Ḥamadī' and Hezîa Ferhat understood that their new names decided fundamental ontological questions like who one was and whom one could be with, as well as material ones, such as what one had. All these people corrected their new names, even if they could not read the French letters in which they were written. In other cases, Algerians turned civil registration into an occasion to control the distribution of wealth and power in their favor, including or excluding certain members in the registry. It solidified existing hierarchies to the detriment of people of color or married women, some of whom completely disappeared.

Conclusion

Remember Their Names

Upon the completion of their work in the 1890s, officials in Algeria lauded the état civil as one of the crowning pieces of colonial law and administration. And France soon extended it to other parts of its North African empire. The état civil came to Tunisia in a decree in 1886, only five years after the French protectorate began; and a subsequent decree in 1919 made it obligatory to register births and deaths for everyone living in the country. In Morocco a series of decrees beginning in 1915 sketched the foundations for civil registry, but it remained optional for Muslims and Moroccan Jews until after the Second World War.[1] In both places, actual registration lagged well behind the law, and the main work of completing the civil registry started after independence, when a more robust apparatus of regulations and implementation appeared.[2]

In Algeria, almost as soon as they had finished the master registers, administrators started complaining that Algerians were not keeping up their records, reporting the births and deaths in their family as required. They might have easily anticipated this eventuality. Reporting every vital act was difficult for Algerians, who probably saw the risks of not doing so fade in comparison with the burdens it took to do so. For every birth or death in the family, someone had to report it to the nearest état civil registrar. In rural areas, where the French presence was sparse, this easily meant several days travel. By law a birth had to be reported within three days or risk a minimum of six days in jail and a sixteen-franc fine; for a death, the deadline was twenty-four hours, and the declaration had to be made before burial.[3] Many people found it easier to simply stay away from the registrar, once the first registration drive was completed and the family had some ID cards they could use if necessary with a new patronym. In 1896 one official estimated that Algerians reported only about half of new births and deaths and almost no marriages or divorces.[4] Moreover, the French registrars themselves had done shoddy work in some of the original master registers, leaving thousands of people off the rolls. Many had genealogical trees that were "defective and lacked uniformity."[5] In the years leading up to World War I, officials discovered that some communities had been left entirely off. In the town of Tablat, for example, which lay only about 70 kilometers by road from the capital, local officials wrote in 1891 that they had failed to register many people and asked the prefecture with embarrassment what to do.[6] In other cases, Algerians who lived abroad or who were absent during the registration drive found themselves without vital records.[7] Indeed, the archives are full of internal correspondence in which officials sorted out how to handle unregistered people.[8] In 1913 a report focused on military-age men estimated that at least 100,000 did not have état civil records.[9] French officials later concluded that only about six births out of ten had been recorded in the years between 1901 and 1930.[10] Military service proved to be the first major test of the civil registry when conscripts and volunteers reported to the barracks. While the paper documents some carried purported to be the documentary equivalent of the real person, the medical examination of real bodies revealed soldiers who were much older or younger than their état civil records indicated. Many recruits did not have their own documents and used the records of a dead brother or cousin because their families had never reported their births, nor that of the dead relative.[11]

The Colonization of Names has shown how names figured in colonial strategies to accumulate and monopolize symbolic power. The book surveyed the Algerian name prior to its assimilation to French onomastic norms and the French language, and then it followed the impact of these changes and the purposes they served. I have argued that prior to their colonization, Algerians did not fully possess their names in the sense of autonomous individuals exercising control over their identity. Names belonged to others. Certainly, some people struggled under this onomastic regime, saddled with nicknames calling out their bad looks and personality ticks. But rather than excluding such people from society, these names bound them to it. The interpersonal relations that embedded individuals within society and produced them as a social subject were made possible in open and ever evolving names. Moreover, names connected people across time, joining them to past generations, as well as across shared cultural heritages like language and religion. During a person's lifetime, their names changed and meanings shifted based on the context or the intentions of others. For their part, French colonial officials found existing names confusing and at cross-purposes to their goals. Therefore, they fixed personal names according to modern rules established in France. If Algerian names historically gave symbolic expression to lived social relations, this book has shown how a new French naming system fixed identities from the outside with an official name that privileged transparency and uniformity above all.

The fact that the "état civil of the natives" struggled to achieve its goals in the twentieth century might be read as yet another failure in the colonial annals, like so many other aborted European efforts that historians have found in the archive and thrown onto the junk pile of colonial hubris. But the historiographical trend of highlighting colonial failures and the resiliency of colonized societies provides insufficient closure to this story. How to come to terms with the past? History shows that no golden age of names existed before the colonial era that might somehow be reclaimed to fulfill a longing for an era of symbolic wholeness or to provide an onomastic foundation for national identities and individual subjectivities today.[12]

As this book reaches its end, it is useful to briefly reconsider the historical materials from other perspectives. In his canonical novel *Nedjma* in 1956, Kateb Yacine addressed the état civil's impact on Algerian social institutions like the family and the tribe. "The tribe's ruin was completed in the état civil; the four registers in which the survivors were counted and divided," he wrote. Kateb made this comment while telling the story of the Beni Keblout, a fictionalized tribe in eastern Algeria, which the French targeted for decimation. In the novel, this decimation is recounted generations later by an aged character who tells the account to a younger relative. The old man's story merits citing at length:

> The new authorities completed their work of destruction by separating the Sons of Keblout into four branches, "for administrative convenience"; the men in the first register were allotted lands at the other end of the province which were immediately expropriated; to this branch belonged your father and Sidi Ahmed. The men in the second register received jobs in the magistracy and were sent to the different centers [across the country]; my father belonged to this branch. The men of the third branch, although listed in a separate register, received almost the same treatment, but moved still farther away by contracting too many marriages with other less stricken families. As for those of the fourth branch, they kept the destroyed mosque, the mausoleum, the little bit of land, [and] the ancestral standard.[13]

The reader might see in this account an example of resistance to colonialism: Although beaten, a tribal elder transmits the memory of the ancestors across the generations. However, Kateb's primary interest lies elsewhere. His exemplum tells a story of falling apart, rather than coming together. The ties that bound tribes like the Beni Keblout were complex, but for the sake of unpacking Kateb's account, one can say that this social bond made itself concrete less in blood than in the tribe's name. When the Beni Keblout lost their common name, they lost one another and the memory of themselves.

Names join people to people, as well as people to place. They do so in a way that announces social relationships so that people can organize and know themselves. This symbolic organization lies at the foundation of norms and the law. Perhaps the most famous theorization of names and this type of symbolic power is psychoanalyst Jacques Lacan's concept the "Name-of-the-Father," a sign that provided the psychological coherence of the subject. Although I arrive at this concept late in the book, it has informed the way I have approached the historical materials throughout, even as I have avoided using it as a theoretical grid that might be superimposed on the archives. Without the "Name-of-the-Father," Lacan argued, the subject risked tipping into psychosis.[14] It was not without reason, then, that commentators saw in the patronymic a way to discuss the law writ large, with this name standing as the fundamental signifier, or anchoring point, for a whole symbolic system of normative rules, prohibitions, and structures of power.[15] In many ways, Lacan's model follows how the patronymic purportedly functioned in France, providing social order and law to chaos, roughly speaking.[16] Colonial officials saw themselves doing this work in Algeria, ending the "anarchy" of Algerian family with the imposition of the patronymic. From the historical perspectives offered in this book, however, one can ask: What if the modern name did not counter disorder but did its bidding?

Kateb Yacine's novel helps to interrogate this question. Appearing in the second year of the Algerian Revolution (1954–1962), *Nedjma* is widely recognized as the origin story of the modern Algerian nation, but it hardly resembles the uplifting ones offered in official versions.[17] To be sure, Kateb wrote of a people forged in their collective struggle for freedom. He devoted himself to this struggle and remained loyal to it his whole life. But like Lacan, Kateb was interested in discordant origin stories such as Oedipus and its terrifying themes of repressed family relationships, incest, and alienation. Self-consciously writing as a colonized Algerian using French, the Other's language, Kateb presented such themes naturally enough. Therefore, he draws deeply problematic heroes in his national coming-of-age drama. They bear the scars of a century of French occupation, people who lost their direction, vagabonding around Algeria as uprooted outsiders in their own country. Most fatefully, Kateb tells us, these Algerians did not keep the Prophet's advice concerning their family ties: they no longer knew their nasabs, or even their father's name. In other words, Kateb tells of an Algerian nation of orphans and bastards, children whose lineages were broken in lies and violence.

Kateb did not lay the responsibility for this tragedy solely at the colonizers' feet. The character who narrated the fate of the Beni Keblout in the passage cited had himself played an important role in destroying his own family. This man is named Si Mokhtar, a Beni Keblout patriarch. He had personally profited from the French-led breakup of the tribe, which converted its ancestral farmlands into cash. The old man pocketed this money and squandered it in a debaucherous life.[18] Among the many women in the old libertine's past is the titular character Nedjma's mother, a Frenchwoman whom he kidnapped and raped. Si Mokhtar's crime was not driven by some sort of primordial hatred of the colonizer, taking the white man's wife in revenge. Rather, Si Mokhtar attacked the Frenchwoman, a European Jewish woman originally married to a notary in Marseille, in an effort to humiliate a fellow Algerian Muslim, her lover who lived in Constantine. Although her exact parentage is undecided in the novel, the child born afterward, the girl called Nedjma, is taken by Si Mokhtar to be raised secretly in another family unaware of the circumstances of her conception. In this way, Si Mokhtar hopes to conceal his crime.

In Arabic, *nedjma* means "star" or "constellation" (*najm*), and as the novel's eponym it might appear as the Algerian star that was then rising in the world's sky of free and independent nations that had thrown off colonial rule. Nedjma grows into adulthood as a woman of stunning beauty and influence, exercising a powerful gravitational force on all those around her. She remains silent, however, and her star traces a troubled path. Nedjma's parentage concealed from her, she enters unknowingly into an incestuous marriage with a brother born to another of Si Mokhtar's secret adulterous relations. In this way Kateb's novel tells a story of multifaceted violence, the fire and blood of defeat in battle, on one hand, but also the violence unleashed by the confusion of family origins and signs, on the other. These two are clearly linked for Kateb, as the destruction of the Beni Keblout shows. As a metaphor for the nation, therefore, *Nedjma* leaves the Algerian people doubly wounded: The physical annihilation of more than a million people over the course of the nineteenth century was amplified by the rupture of their symbolic world.

How, then, to measure the impact of names in Kateb's novel and in Algeria's history? In the first major French-language study of colonial trauma in Algeria, published in 2018, the psychoanalyst Karima Lazali reads the novel from her field's understanding of the name, and its role in the symbolic constitution of the subject.[19] She writes, "Incest is the direct result of the wreckage of genealogies wrought by the colonial order. Incest and murder spring from confusion (*brouillage*), which establishes a sort of hole in the question of identity: once the name that establishes one's identity, recognizability, and affiliations disappears, one is left asking, 'Who is who?' "[20] Lazali's question perfectly captures the experience of any reader of *Nedjma* who struggles to resolve Kateb's difficultly laid-out family relationships among the characters, a confusion that his modernist prose and disjointed narrative, all written in brilliant French, amplify. But it also speaks to the experiences of Lazali's generation. She reads *Nedjma* to understand transgenerational trauma in Algeria after its independence. She is particularly concerned with the violence suffered at the end of the twentieth century, a civil war that has come to be named the "Black" or "Dark Decade" (*Décennie Noire*, ca. 1991–2002). (The shock of the violence ensured that these events went unnamed for a long time.) Lazali sees this violence as the return of the colonial repressed. The "who is who" question emerging from *Nedjma* anticipates, Lazali suggests, the frantic question of the 1990s: "Who is killing who?" (*qui tue qui?*). This call peaked in 1997 during a series of deplorable massacres that swept across the country, targeting its most vulnerable and innocent people. To this date, few perpetrators have been brought to justice or even properly identified to the public.[21]

For his part, Kateb Yacine does not suggest that the French-conferred names alone produced the symbolic hole that led to *Nedjma*'s incestuous crises. While the état civil created the family's composition in French law, the names it contained did not decide in themselves the boundaries of something like the incest taboo or the family, contrary to Lazali's arguments.[22] Muslims in Algeria were bound to many other normative regimes beyond what the French could level at them.[23] In other words, the état civil could not in itself make Algerians forget their family relations. Historians have come to similar conclusions in other colonial histories. Commenting on debates concerning the census in colonial India, for example, historian Sumit Guha nicely evokes the impact and limits of colonial power when he writes that rather than the "totalizing classificatory grid" that Benedict Anderson famously saw, colonial institutions and governmental technologies worked "as tree-roots grow into rock—along its extant fractures and potential flaws."[24]

Nevertheless, historians are well served by listening to Lazali the psychoanalyst and Kateb the novelist. The names in the état civil stood as a powerful tool of social inscription, one that worked hand-in-hand with other modalities by which colonial power invested itself in society, compromising and in some instances upending existing institutions. This is important as we reflect on the history of the Algerian name in the nineteenth century, as well as the complexities and subtleties of Nedjma's case, whose colonial logic Kateb presents expertly. Si Mokhtar's crime, the violence of the rape and the repression of its memory, was his own. However, he had a ready accomplice, namely, the French state, which enabled this man's transgressions of the constraints Algerian society placed on his desire. The Lacanian "no" of the name, its prohibitive force, slacked in the generalized anomie unleashed by the renaming and exile of the Beni Keblout clans, a fictionalized version of a story that repeated itself in more than a century of actual massacres, sequestrations, and banishments.

As I have argued in the previous chapters, the lawmakers and colonial officials who drafted the "état civil of the natives" and its documentary regime of filiation did not intend it to separate children from their parents, but the French records did not prevent it. Arguably it made it much easier to do so than in Islamic law, which traditionally depended on sworn, living testimony, a dynamic and dialogic environment in which to establish truth that differed considerably from a piece of paper that cannot speak back.[25] Indeed, as Kateb's novel progresses, the reader learns of other potential suitors/rapists of Nedjma's mother, each one of which could have been Nedjma's father. In fact, men like this could easily have been the father of any number of real children born in eastern Algeria in the early twentieth century whose birth records indicate that they were of an "an unknown father," i.e., born to an unwed mother whom French law barred from recording the name of her child's known father without his consent.[26] Moreover, while the French state did not immediately appropriate the full role of kinship authority for itself, it had given itself the means to assume this position in those instances where the état civil and French law was concerned.[27] Again, the état civil did not possess a complete monopoly of symbolic power to decide the Algerian family. However, its records served as the necessary documentary support of the modern legal subject. Those who did not have an état civil or a patronym were interpellated in official situations by "SNP" (*sans nom patronymique* [without a patronymical name]), written into the field for nom in the form, which could not be left blank. At the time, SNP symbolized backwardness and an erasure of identity: After independence, the Algerian Republic banned its use.[28] Algerians would have likely been able to preserve the memory of their extended family as they went forward into the twentieth century, but this memory had little validity by French law, which treated it as a sort of folklore. In such cases, as families fell from the main trunk in different branches, it became easy enough for them to lose track of one another over time. Willful forgetting within the family's own archive might contribute to this in some cases, as with Si Mokhtar and many real-life family dramas, but historically determined forces—famines, epidemics, urbanization, migration, and war—weakened the social frameworks of memory.[29] A person walking in the wake of such disasters "alone remembers what others do not [and] resembles someone who sees what others do not see," as sociologist Maurice Halbwachs wrote just before World War II. Ultimately, Halbwachs concluded, this "person suffering from hallucinations . . . forgets the names that are no longer used by those around him."[30]

From this observation, then, a call resonates: Remember their names.

Notes

Introduction

1. Loi n° 2006-396 du 31 mars 2006 pour l'égalité des chances, in *Journal officiel de la République française: lois et décrets*, no. 79 (2 April 2006), 4950, https://www.legifrance.gouv.fr/eli/loi/2006/3/31/SOCX0500298L/jo/texte; Luc Behaghel, Bruno Crépon, and Thomas Le Barbanchon, "Évaluation de l'impact du CV anonyme: rapport final," École d'Économie de Paris (2011), https://ec.europa.eu/migrant-integration/library-document/evaluation-de-limpact-du-cv-anonyme-rapport-final_en.
2. Alexis Jenni, *L'Art français de la guerre* (Paris: Gallimard, 2011), 192 (my translation). The English translator has rendered this differently as the "colour of a surname." Alexis Jenni, *The French Art of War*, trans. Frank Wynne (London: Atlantic Books, 2017), 180.
3. Michel Wieviorka et al., eds., *La France raciste* (Paris: Seuil, 1992).
4. Joan Wallach Scott, *The Politics of the Veil* (Princeton, NJ: Princeton University Press, 2007), 11–20.
5. Jean Quéméneur, "Une difficile question: la graphie française des noms arabes," *Documents Nord-Africains* 13, no. 467 (7 February 1962): 1–12, http://koha-opac.histoire-immigration.fr/cgi-bin/koha/opac-retrieve-file.pl?id=ab3de13a7140681eb346e5d02158e4e6.
6. Ernest Mercier, *La propriété foncière chez les musulmans d'Algérie: ses lois sous la domination française, constitution de l'état civil musulman* (Paris: Leroux, 1891), 44 (my reconstruction of Arabic from French transliteration).
7. Law of 23 March 1882 in *Journal officiel de la République française* 14, no. 82 (24 March 1882), https://gallica.bnf.fr/ark:/12148/bpt6k6225434z?rk=42918;4.

8. Jack Goody, *The Logic of Writing and the Organization of Society* (Cambridge: Cambridge University Press, 1986); Cornelia Vismann, *Files: Law and Media Technology*, trans. Geoffrey Winthrop-Young (Stanford, CA: Stanford University Press, 2008); Delphine Gardey, *Écrire, calculer, classer: comment une révolution de papier a transformé les sociétés contemporaines (1800–1940)* (Paris: Découverte, 2008); Ben Kafka, *The Demon of Writing: Powers and Failures of Paperwork* (New York: Zone, 2012); John C. Rule and Ben S. Trotter, *A World of Paper: Louis XIV, Colbert de Torcy, and the Rise of the Information State* (Montreal: McGill-Queens University Press, 2014). To consider these questions in Europe's overseas territories, see Sumit Guha, "The Politics of Identity and Enumeration in India c. 1600–1990," *Comparative Studies in Society and History* 45, no. 1 (January 2003), 148–67; C. A. Bayly, *Empire and Information: Intelligence Gathering and Social Communication in India, 1780–1870* (Cambridge: Cambridge University Press, 1996); Karl Ittmann, Dennis D. Cordell, and Gregory H. Maddox, eds., *The Demographics of Empire: The Colonial Order and the Creation of Knowledge* (Athens: Ohio University Press, 2010).
9. Édouard-Léon Scott, *Noms de baptême et les prénoms*, 2nd ed. (Paris: Houssiaux, 1858), i.
10. Jacques Marie Boileux, *Commentaire sur le Code civil: contentent l'explication de chaque article séparément*, vol. 1, 6th ed. (Paris: Videcoq, 1851), 19; Raymond Saleilles, *De la personnalité juridique: histoire et théories* (Paris: Rousseau, 1910).
11. My thinking here is informed by post-Freudian psychoanalytic theory and particularly the "Name-of-the-Father" and its related concepts. As developed by Jacques Lacan and his readers, the Name-of-the-Father is a key signifier that makes possible the symbolic construction of meaning and reality and dependent social institutions, such as language, law, and sexuality. In this way, one can understand how the name enables power, working through language, to invest itself in individual subjects. I take up this question in the conclusion of this book.
12. Farid Benramdane, "Qui es-tu? J'ai été dit: de la destruction de la filiation dans l'état civil d'Algérie ou éléments d'un onomacide sémantique," *Insaniyat* 10 (January–April 2000): 79–87. "Onomacide" appears in the title of this essay, but Benramdane leaves it unconceptualized in the pages that follow.
13. Achille Mbembe, *Critique of Black Reason*, trans. Laurent Dubois (Durham, NC: Duke University Press, 2017), 78.
14. Kamel Daoud, *The Meursault Investigation*, trans. John Cullen (New York: Other Press, 2014).
15. Mostefa Lacheraf, *Des noms et des lieux: mémoires d'une Algérie oubliée* (Algiers: Casbah, 1998); Hosni Kitouni, "L'état civil des indigènes et ses avatars," ms., https://www.academia.edu/11040218/LETAT_CIVIL_DES_INDIGENES_ALGERIENS.
16. Hassan Remaoun and Ahmed Yalaoui, "In memoriam, à notre collègue Abdelkader Djeghloul (1946–2010)," *Insaniyat*, nos. 51–52 (2011): 17–20.
17. Salem Chaker, "Onomastique Libyco-Berbère (Anthroponymie)," in *Encyclopédie berbère*, vol. 35: *Oasitae-Ortaïas*, ed. Salem Chaker (Paris: Peeters, 2013), 5762.

18. Decree of 18 September 1963, in *Journal officiel de la République algérienne démocratique et populaire* 2, vol. 69 (20 September 1963).
19. René Gallissot, "GUERROUDJ Jacqueline," *Le Maitron; dictionnaire biographique, movement ouvrier, mouvemenet social* (2013), https://maitron.fr/spip.php?article151483; René Gallissot, "GUERROUDJ Abdelkader," *Le Maitron; dictionnaire biographique, movement mouvrier, mouvemenet social* (2013), https://maitron.fr/spip.php?article151482; Djamila Amrane, *Des femmes dans la guerre d'Algérie* (Paris: Karthala, 1994).
20. Decree no. 71-157 of 3 June 1971, in the *Journal officiel de la République algérienne*, no. 615 (11 June 1971).
21. Mehdi Bsikri, "Entre 30 000 et 35 000 changements de nom de famille depuis l'indépendance," *El Watan* (8 September 2012), https://www.elwatan.com/archives/actualites/entre-30-000-et-35-000-changements-de-nom-de-famille-depuis-lindependance-08-09-2012; Émeline Wuilbercq, "Algérie: changer de nom pour tirer un trait sur le passé colonial?," *Jeune afrique* (31 January 2014), https://www.jeuneafrique.com/165948/societe/alg-rie-changer-de-nom-pour-tirer-un-trait-sur-le-pass-colonial/.
22. As recorded, respectively, in *Journal officiel de la République algérienne démocratique et populaire*, 12 May 1981, 429 (Arabic: 8 Raban 1401, 597); 17 August 1976, 806 (Arabic: 21 Sha'abān 1396, 1017); 5 September 1976, 850 (Arabic: 10 Ramḍān 1396).
23. Hosni Kitouni, "L'indigènisation de l'Algérien" ms., 2017, n.p.
24. Article 10, Constitution of 1963, http://www.conseil-constitutionnel.dz/index.php/fr/1963.
25. Preamble, Constitution of 1963; Mauricio Sierra and Germán Elías Berríos, "Depersonalization: A Conceptual History," *History of Psychiatry* 8 (1997): 213–29.
26. Albert Memmi, *The Pillar of Salt* (1957), in *The Albert Memmi Reader*, ed. Jonathan Judaken and Michael Lejman (Lincoln: University of Nebraska Press, 2021), 35–49; and Mohammed Harbi, *L'Algérie et son destin: croyants ou citoyens* (Paris: Arcantère, 1992). In his book reflecting on problems in the 1990s, Harbi characterized this alienation as a "cultural homelessness" (*clochardisation culturelle*), a colonial-inflicted anomie that wreaked havoc in postcolonial Algeria (p. 15). See also Yoav Di-Capua, *No Exit: Arab Existentialism, Jean-Paul Sartre, and Decolonization* (Chicago: University of Chicago Press, 2018); Omnia El Shakry, *The Arabic Freud: Psychoanalysis and Islam in Modern Egypt* (Princeton, NJ: Princeton University Press, 2017); Stefania Pandolfo, *Knot of the Soul: Madness, Psychoanalysis, Islam* (Chicago: University of Chicago Press, 2018); and Daho Djerbal, "The Sweet 60s: Between the Liberation of Peoples and the Liberty of Individuals, or the Difficult Representation of the Self," *Red Thread* 2, https://red-thread.org/en/the-sweet-60s-between-the-liberation-of-peoples-and-the-liberty-of-individuals-or-the-difficult-representation-of-the-self/. Karima Lazali's points on this question are taken up in the conclusion.
27. Frantz Fanon, *Alienation and Freedom*, ed. Robert J. C. Young and Jean Khalfa, trans. Steven Corcoran (London: Bloomsbury, 2018), 434.

28. Frantz Fanon, *The Wretched of the Earth*, trans. Richard Philcox (New York: Grove Press, 2004), 182.
29. Gérard Mauger, "Violence" in *Abécédaire de Pierre Bourdieu*, ed. Jean-Philippe Cazier (Mons: Sils Maria, 2006), 206. Ouerdia Yermeche uses symbolic violence fruitfully in her publications.
30. Pierre Bourdieu, *Masculine Domination*, trans. Richard Nice (Stanford, CA: Stanford University Press, 2001), 35.
31. Pierre Bourdieu, *Language and Symbolic Power*, trans. Gino Raymond and Matthew Adamson (Cambridge, MA: Harvard University Press, 1991), 170.
32. Timothy Mitchell, *Rule of Experts: Egypt, Techno-Politics, Modernity* (Berkeley: University of California Press, 2002), 176.
33. Lahouari Addi, *Sociologie et anthropologie chez Pierre Bourdieu* (Paris: Découverte, 2002).
34. Pierre Bourdieu, *Pascalian Meditations*, trans. Richard Nice (Stanford, CA: Stanford University Press, 2000), 170.
35. Ranajit Guha, *Dominance Without Hegemony: History and Power in Colonial India* (Cambridge, MA: Harvard University Press, 1997), 65.
36. Bourdieu, *Language and Symbolic Power.*
37. Benramdane, "Qui es-tu?," 79–87.
38. George Steinmetz points to overlaps between Lacan and Bourdieu, as well as the latter's antipathy to psychoanalysis, in George Steinmetz, "Bourdieu's Disavowal of Lacan: Psychoanalytic Theory and the Concepts of 'Habitus' and 'Symbolic Capital,'" *Constellations* 13, no. 4 (2006): 445–64.
39. Brahim Atoui, "Toponymie et colonisation française en Algérie," *Bulletin des sciences géographiques* (Institut national de cartographie et de télédétection) 5 (2000): 36.
40. For example, the village of Sidi Amer received its first official road sign in the summer of 2010 (personal observation). See also Mansour Margouma, "La toponymie algérienne: lecture préliminaire de la dénomination de l'espace," *Esprit critique: Revue internationale de sociologie et de sciences sociales* 11, no. 1 (Winter 2008), http://194.214.232.113/publications/1101/esp1101article08.pdf; Farid Benramdane and Brahim Atoui, eds., *Nomination et dénomination: Des noms de lieux, de tribus et de personnes en Algérie* (Oran: CRASC, 2005); Farid Benramdane and Brahim Atoui, *Toponymie et anthroponymie de l'Algérie: Recueil bibliographique générale* (Oran: CRASC, 2005); Farid Benramdane, "Histoire(s) et enjeu(x) d'une (re)dé/dé/dénomination: la Place rouge de Tiaret," *Insaniyat* 17–18 (May–December 2002): 63–70; Atoui, "Toponymie et colonisation"; "Directives toponymiques à l'usage des éditeurs de cartes et autres éditeurs," Groupe d'experts des Nations unies sur les noms géographiques, Working Paper no. 78, 17–28 January 2000, https://unstats.un.org/unsd/geoinfo/UNGEGN/docs/20th-gegn-docs/20th_gegn_WP78.pdf; Brahim Atoui, "La toponymie et sa transcription cartographique," *Bulletin de l'INC des sciences géographiques* no. 1 (1998): 40–48; Brahim Atoui, "Toponymie et espace en Algérie" (PhD diss., Université d'Aix Marseille I, 1996); Foudil Cheriguen, *Toponymie*

algérienne des lieux habités (Algiers: Épigraphe, 1993). Colonial-era toponymic research includes Arthur Pellegrin, *Essai sur les noms de lieux d'Algérie et de Tunisie* (Tunis: Éditions SAPI, 1949); André Basset, "Sur la toponymie berbère et spécialement sur la toponymie chaouïa Aït Frah," *Onomastica* 2, no. 2 (1948): 123–26; Émile Laoust, *Contribution à une étude de la toponymie du haut Atlas* (Paris: Geuthner, 1942); Louis Massignon, *Le Maroc dans les premières années du XVIe siècle. Tableau géographique d'après Léon l'Africain* (Algiers: Jourdan, 1906); Gustave Mercier, *Étude sur la toponymie berbère de la région de l'Aurès* (s.l.: s.n, n.d.).

41. Mohand-Akli Haddadou, *Dictionnaire toponymique et historique de l'Algérie* (Tizi-Ouzou, Algeria: Achab, 2012).
42. Thucydides, *History of the Peloponnesian War*, trans. Rex Warner (New York: Penguin, 1976), 402.

1. What Is in a Name?

1. Toni Morrison, *Beloved* (New York: Penguin, 1987), 91.
2. Cynthia Lyles Scott, "A Slave by Any Other Name: Names and Identity in Toni Morrison's *Beloved*," in *Toni Morrison's Beloved*, ed. Harold Bloom (New York: Bloom's Literary Criticism, 2009), 197–98.
3. Roland Barthes, "Proust and Names," in *New Critical Essays*, trans. Richard Howard (Evanston, IL: Northwestern University Press, 2009), 60.
4. Marcel Proust, cited in Leo Bersani, *Marcel Proust: The Fictions of Art and Life*, 2nd ed. (Oxford: Oxford University Press, 2013), 202.
5. Orlando Patterson, *Slavery and Social Death: A Comparative Study* (Cambridge, MA: Harvard University Press, 1982), 55.
6. Martin Klein, *Slavery and Colonial Rule in French West Africa* (Cambridge: Cambridge University Press, 1998), 10.
7. Marcia Wright, *Strategies of Slaves and Women: Life-Stories from East/Central Africa* (New York: Lilian Barber Press, 1993), 191, 196; Klein, *Slavery and Colonial Rule*, 194; Yacine Daddi Addoun, "L'Abolition de l'esclavage en Algérie, 1816–1871" (PhD diss., York University, 2010), 96.
8. Scholarship in English includes Gabriele vom Bruck and Barbara Bodenhorn, eds., *The Anthropology of Names and Naming* (Cambridge: Cambridge University Press, 2006); Stephen Wilson, *The Means of Naming: A Social and Cultural History of Personal Naming in Western Europe* (London: University College London Press, 1998); Carole Hough, ed., *The Oxford Handbook of Names and Naming* (Oxford: Oxford University Press, 2016).
9. My thanks to historian Craig Harline for introducing me to Ginzburg in the undergraduate seminar he taught at the University of Idaho in the late 1980s.
10. Carlo Ginzburg, *The Cheese and the Worms: The Cosmos of a Sixteenth-Century Miller*, trans. John and Anne Tedeschi (Baltimore: Johns Hopkins University Press, 1980), xi.

11. Lucette Valensi, *Mardochée Naggiar: Enquête sur un inconnu* (Paris: Stock, 2008), 350. Emphasis added.
12. Fanny Colonna, *Le meunier, les moines et le bandit, des vies quotidiennes dans l'Aurès (Algérie) du XXe siècle* (Arles: Sinbad, 2010), 89. On the use of irony and multiple meanings in names that colonized people used for colonizers, see Osumaka Likaka, *Naming Colonialism: History and Collective Memory in the Congo, 1870–1960* (Madison: University of Wisconsin Press, 2009), chap. 3.
13. Alain Corbin, *The Life of an Unknown: The Rediscovered World of a Clog Maker in Nineteenth-Century France*, trans. Arthur Goldhammer (New York: Columbia University Press, 2001), ix.
14. On the phenomenon of literary pseudonyms, see Ralph W. Schoolcraft, *Romain Gary: The Man Who Sold His Shadow* (Philadelphia: University of Pennsylvania Press, 2002); and Stephanie Newell, *The Power to Name: A History of Anonymity in Colonial West Africa* (Athens: Ohio University Press, 2013).
15. Ferdinand de Saussure, *Course in General Linguistics*, trans. Roy Harris (London: Bloomsbury, 2013), 131.
16. James Raven, "The Oxford Dictionary of National Biography: Dictionary or Encyclopaedia?," *Historical Journal* 50, no. 4 (December 2007): 991–1006.
17. Walter Benjamin, "On Language as Such and on the Language of Man," in *Selected Writings*, vol. 1: *1913–1926*, ed. Marcus Bullock and Michael W. Jennings (Cambridge, MA: Harvard University Press, 1996), 65.
18. Pre-Christian commentators did not understand Adam as a prophet and thus did not see his names as emanating from God but from his own creativity. William F. McCants, *Founding Gods, Inventing Nations: Conquest and Culture Myths from Antiquity to Islam* (Princeton, NJ: Princeton University Press, 2012), 22.
19. Momme Brodersen, *Walter Benjamin: A Biography*, trans. Malcolm R. Green and Ingrida Ligers (London: Verso, 1996), 91. My understanding of Benjamin's theory of language is informed by Martin Jay, *The Dialectical Imagination: A History of the Frankfurt School and the Institute of Social Research, 1923–1950* (Berkeley: University of California Press, 1973), 261–63; Anson Rabinbach, "Between Enlightenment and Apocalypse: Benjamin, Bloch and Modern German Jewish Messianism," *New German Critique* 34 (Winter 1985): 78–124; Max Pensky, *Melancholy Dialectics: Walter Benjamin and the Play of Mourning* (Amherst: University of Massachusetts Press, 1993), 47–51; Beatrice Hanssen, "Language and Mimesis in Walter Benjamin's Work," in *The Cambridge Companion to Walter Benjamin*, ed. David S. Ferris (Cambridge: Cambridge University Press, 2004), 54–72; Samuel Weber, *Benjamin's—abilities* (Cambridge, MA: Harvard University Press, 2008), 45–48.
20. Walter Benjamin, "The Task of the Translator," in *Selected Writings*, 1:260.
21. Benjamin, "On Language," 65. Italics in the original.
22. Hanssen, "Language and Mimesis," 59.
23. Weber, *Benjamin's-abilities*, 46.
24. Weber, 48.

25. The links between Benjamin's thought on the name and Romantics like Novalis is made clear in Hans Blumenberg, *Work on Myth*, trans. Robert M. Wallace (Cambridge, MA: MIT Press, 1985), 48–49.
26. Pensky, *Melancholy Dialectics*, 49.
27. Rabinbach, "Between Enlightenment and Apocalypse," 105–6. Martin Jay tells this fall slightly differently: Man's "names and God's were not the same. As a result, there developed a chasm between name and thing, and the absolute adequacy of divine speech was lost. To Benjamin, formal logic was the barrier that separated the language of Paradise from its human counterpart. Man tended to overname things by abstractions and generalizations." Jay, *Dialectical Imagination*, 261–62. Tracie Matysik (personal communication, January 2023) points out that Benjamin's ideas on language, given in the *Origins of German Trauerspeil* (1928), depended not on a model of pure origins and a subsequent fall but on language's allegorical character, wherein meaning emerges relationally, not directly. The point has implications for understandings of colonization and language inasmuch as the transformation wrought by colonialism would not be understood as effacing an original pure language but represent one more variant of language, albeit a particularly melancholic and even traumatic one. This understanding of language informs chapter 2 of this book, dealing with precolonial Algerian onomastics. On the fascist manipulation of language, see Federico Finchelstein, *A Brief History of Fascist Lies* (Berkeley: University of California Press, 2020).
28. Cited in Jay, *Dialectical Imagination*, 233.
29. A translation popular among German readers at this time was that published in the "Universal-Bibliothek" by Max Henning, *Der Koran: aus dem Arabischen übertragen und mit einer Einleitung versehen* (Leipzig: Philipp Reclam, 1901).
30. Jacques Lacan, *On the Names-of-the-Father*, trans. Bruce Fink (Cambridge, UK: Polity, 2013), 78.
31. Q 2:30 in *The Qur'an*, trans. Alan Jones (Exeter, UK: Gibb Memorial Trust, 2007), 28.
32. Q 3:31–34 in *The Qur'an*, 28.
33. See Tabari, *The History of al-Ṭabarī: General Introduction, and, From the Creation to the Flood*, ed. and trans. Franz Rosenthal (Albany: State University of New York Press, 1989), 266–72.
34. Daniel Gimaret, *Les Noms divins en islam, exégèse lexicographique et théologique* (Paris: Cerf, 1988); Louis Gardet, "al-Asmā' al-Ḥusnā," *Encyclopaedia of Islam New Edition Online (EI-2 English)* (Brill).
35. Daniel Madigan explains, "The Qur'ân is concerned first of all with making clear that it is God who has all knowledge and that others, whether angels, jinn or human beings, know only as much as God chooses to reveal to them." Daniel A. Madigan, *The Qur'ân's Self-Image: Writing and Authority in Islam's Scripture* (Princeton, NJ: Princeton University Press, 2001), 103. See also Franz Rosenthal, *Knowledge Triumphant: The Concept of Knowledge in Medieval Islam* (Leiden: Brill, 1970).

36. Cornelia Schöck, "Adam and Eve," *Encyclopedia of the Qur'ān*, vol. 1: *A–D*, ed. Jane Dammen McAuliffe (Leiden: Brill, 2001), 22–26; Leigh N. B. Chipman, "Adam and the Angels: An Examination of Mythic Elements in Islamic Sources," *Arabica* 49, no. 4 (October 2002): 429–55; Cornelia Schöck, *Adam im Islam: ein Beitrag zur Ideengeschichte der Sunna* (Berlin: K. Schwarz, 1993).
37. Louis Massignon, *The Passion of al-Hallāj: Mystic and Martyr of Islam*, vol. 3: *The Teaching of al-Hallāj*, trans. Herbert Mason (Princeton, NJ: Princeton University Press, 1982), 171.
38. Pierre Bourdieu, *The Logic of Practice*, trans. Richard Nice (Stanford, CA: Stanford University Press, 1990), 91.
39. Pierre Bourdieu, *Language and Symbolic Power*, trans. Gino Raymond and Matthew Adamson (Cambridge, MA: Harvard University Press, 1991), 105.
40. Bourdieu, 105–6. Michel de Certeau expresses this slightly differently: "The proper name assigns to the subject a locus in language and therefore 'secures' an order of sociolinguistic practice." Michel de Certeau, *The Writing of History*, trans. Tom Conley (New York: Columbia University Press, 1988), 256.
41. Patricia Crone, *God's Rule: Government and Islam* (New York: Columbia University Press, 2004), 40.
42. Michael P. Fitzsimmons, *The Place of Words: The Académie Française and Its Dictionary During an Age of Revolution* (Oxford: Oxford University Press, 2017).
43. Pierre Bourdieu, *On the State: Lectures at the Collège de France, 1989–1992*, ed. Patrick Champagne et al., trans. David Fernbach (Cambridge, UK: Polity, 2014), 163–71.
44. I see a political community as analogous to other subjectivities that begin as "an inchoate collection of desires." Jacques Lacan, *The Seminar of Jacques Lacan*, Book 3: *The Psychoses, 1955–1956*, ed. Jacques-Alain Miller, trans. Russell Grigg (New York: Norton, 1993), 39. Or, as de Certeau wrote: "The name given to the child is the demonstration for his body to be constructed." Michel de Certeau, *Heterologies: Discourse of the Other* (Minneapolis: University of Minnesota Press, 1986), 112.
45. Sabine Hake, personal communication, January 2023.
46. Proclamation of the Assemblée Nationale Constituante, 25 September 1962, confirmed by a ministerial declaration of 26 October 1962. The texts were published in the government's *Journal official* 1, no. 1 (26 October 1962).
47. The 1963 constitution can be found at https://www-el—mouradia-dz.translate.goog/ar/algeria/texts/previous-constitutions.
48. Émeline Lecuit, Denis Maurel, and Duško Vitas, "La traduction des noms propres: une étude en corpus," *Corpus* 10 (2011): 202; Michel Ballard, *Le Nom propre en traduction* (Paris: Ophrys, 2001).
49. Bagehot, "Beijing or Peking?," *Economist* (11 November 2010), https://www.economist.com/johnson/2010/11/11/beijing-or-peking.
50. Jacques Derrida, "Des Tours de Babel," chapter 8 in *Psyche: Inventions of the Other*, vol. 1, ed. Peggy Kamuf and Elizabeth Rottenberg (Stanford, CA: Stanford University Press, 2007), 192, 198. See also Geoffrey Bennington and Jacques Derrida,

Derrida (Paris: Seuil, 2008), 143–48; Jacques Derrida, *On the Name*, ed. Thomas Dutoit, trans. David Wood, John P. Leavey, Jr., and Ian McLeod (Stanford, CA: Stanford University Press, 1995).

51. Aldo Frigerio, "Some Objections to the Metalinguistic Theory of Proper Names," in *Les théories du sens et de la référence: hommage à Georges Kleiber*, ed. René Daval et al. (Reims: Presses universitaires de Reims, 2014), 405–18, esp. 410–11; Emilia Higert, "Noms propres: prédicat de dénomination et traductibilité sont-ils inconciliables?," in *Sens, formes, langage: Contributions en l'honneur de Pierre Frath*, ed. René Daval et al. (Reims: ÉPURE, 2014), 201–21.
52. "Geographical Names Database," UNGEGN World Geographical Names, https://unstats.un.org/unsd/geoinfo/geonames/. Although the Algerian government has recognized Tamazight as an official language, the UN database does not give Algeria's name in Tamazight.
53. The United Nations Group of Experts on Geographical Names project is explained at http://unstats.un.org/unsd/geoinfo/UNGEGN/default.html. See also Henri Dorion and Jean Poirier, *Lexique des termes utiles à l'étude des noms des lieux* (Québec: Presses de l'Université de Laval, 1975), 48, 95–96.
54. Natural Resources Canada, "Resolutions Adopted at the Eleven United Nations Conferences on the Standardization of Geographical Names" (n.d., s.n.), 41, https://unstats.un.org/unsd/ungegn/documents/RES_UN_E_updated_1-11_CONF.pdf.
55. The Algerian government's most recent statement to UNGEGN is "Directives toponymiques à l'usage des éditeurs de cartes et autres éditeurs," Working Paper no. 78 from the 20th session of UNGEGN, 17–28 January 2000, https://unstats.un.org/unsd/geoinfo/UNGEGN/docs/20th-gegn-docs/20th_gegn_WP78.pdf.
56. Carole Hough, "Settlement Names," in *The Oxford Handbook of Names and Naming*, ed. Carole Hough (Oxford: Oxford University Press, 2016), 92.
57. On the ideological construction of toponyms like "Maghreb," see Abdelmajid Hannoum, *The Invention of the Maghreb: Between Africa and the Middle East* (Cambridge: Cambridge University Press, 2021). See also Ramzi Rouighi, *The Making of a Mediterranean Emirate: Ifrīqiyā and Its Andalusis, 1200–1400* (Philadelphia: University of Pennsylvania Press, 2011), 1–4.
58. Ministre de la Guerre to Lieutenant général Berthezène, 1 July 1831, Service Historique de la Défense (hereafter SHD) 1h8.
59. Hélène Blais, *Mirages de la carte: L'invention de l'Algérie coloniale XIXe–XXe siècle* (Paris: Fayard, 2014), 86, 179.
60. J. M. Darmet, *Carte de la colonie française d'Alger, de la régence de Tunis et de la partie nord de l'empire de Maroc* (Paris: s.n., 1836).
61. Blais, *Mirages de la carte*, 180. See also Benjamin Claude Brower, *A Desert Named Peace: The Violence of France's Empire in the Algerian Sahara, 1844–1902* (New York: Columbia University Press, 2009), 214.
62. Constantin-François Volney, *Travels Through Syria and Egypt*, vol. 1, 3rd ed. (London: Robinson, 1805), 80–81.

63. A. Pellegrin, *Essai sur les noms de lieux d'Algérie et de Tunisie, étymologie, signification* (Tunis: S.A.P.I., 1949), 212–16; Karima Dirèche, *Chrétiens de Kabylie, 1873–1954: Une action missionnaire dans l'Algérie coloniale* (s.l.: Bouchène, 2004).
64. Jennifer E. Sessions, *By Sword and Plow: France and the Conquest of Algeria* (Ithaca, NY: Cornell University Press, 2011).
65. Gouverneur général Valée to Ministère de la Guerre, 11 October 1838, SHD 1h58.
66. Ministère de la Guerre to Gouverneur général Valée, 31 October 1838, SHD 1h58.
67. Gouverneur général Bugeaud to Ministère de la Guerre, 10 March 1843. Archives Nationales d'Outre-Mer (hereafter ANOM) 2ee3.
68. Gouverneur général Bugeaud to Ministère de la Guerre, Bivouac de l'oued Bou Bara, 23 May 1843, SHD 1h90.
69. Gouverneur général Bugeaud to Ministère de la Guerre, "Orléansville, le 25 May 1843," SHD 1h90. See also the description in R. Pontier, *Souvenirs de l'Algérie, ou Notice sur Orléansville et Tenès* (Valenciennes: Giard, 1850), 4.
70. Jan C. Jansen, *Erobern und Erinnern: Symbolpolitik, öffentlicher Raum und französischer Kolonialismus in Algerien, 1830–1950* (Munich: Oldenbourg, 2013), 104.
71. Brahim Atoui, "L'Odonymie d'Alger: passé et présent, quels enseignements?," in *Nomination et dénomination des noms de lieux, de tribus et de personnes en Algérie*, ed. Farid Benramdane and Brahim Atoui (Oran: Centre de recherché en anthropologie sociale et culturelle, 2005), 27–28; Blais, *Mirages de la carte*, 91; and Jean-Jacques-Germain Pelet, *Plan d'Alger et des environs* (Paris: Dépôt général de la guerre, 1832).
72. Jansen, *Erobern und Erinnern*, 243–49.
73. Paul Révoil, *Tableau général des communes de l'Algérie* (Algiers: Giralt, 1902).
74. Stephanie V. Love, "The Poetics of Grievance: Taxi Drivers, Vernacular Placenames, and the Paradoxes of Post-Coloniality in Oran, Algeria," *City and Society* 33, no. 3 (2021): 422–43.
75. See, for example, http://popodoran.canalblog.com/archives/2011/11/07/13663851.html; http://www.piedsnoirs-aujourdhui.com/histoir2.html; and http://www.algerie-dz.com/forums/archive/index.php/t-20870.html, consulted 18 Febuary 2017; Jean-Marc Lopez, "Naissance de l'Algérie," *Pieds-Noirs d'hier et d'aujourd'hui*, no. 94 (October 1998), 20–21.
76. Cited in Martin Evans, *Algeria: France's Undeclared War* (Oxford: Oxford University Press, 2012), 262.
77. Cited in Blais, *Mirages de la carte*, 15.
78. Andrew Fitzmaurice, *Sovereignty, Property and Empire, 1500–2000* (Cambridge: Cambridge University Press, 2014). For the French case, see Isabel Merle, "La construction d'un droit foncier colonial: De la propriété collective à la constitution des réserves en Nouvelle-Calédonie," *Enquête* 7 (1999): 1–21.
79. Lopez, "Naissance de l'Algérie," 21.
80. Frédéric Bobin and Olivier Faye, "Macron and Algeria: Five Years of a Troubled Relationship," *Le Monde* (English service) (25 August 2022), https://www.lemonde.fr/en/le-monde-africa/article/2022/08/25/macron-and-algeria-five-years-of-a

-troubled-relationship_5994733_124.html#:~:text=Macron%20evoked%20an%20 Algerian%20%22political,That's%20the%20question.%22.

81. Guy Pervillé, "Comment appeler les habitants de l'Algérie," *Cahiers de la Méditerranée* 54 (June 1997): 60.
82. Dominick LaCapra, *History and Criticism* (Ithaca, NY: Cornell University Press, 1985), 28. See also Ethan Kleinberg, "Just the Facts: The Fantasy of a Historical Science," *History of the Present* 6, no. 1 (Spring 2016): 87–103; and Ethan Kleinberg, Joan Wallach Scott, Gary Wilder, "Theses on Theory and History," *History of the Present* 10, no. 1 (2020): 157–65.
83. Seeking to buttress his nationalism with culturally French credentials, Max Régis changed his Italian patronym from "Milano" to "Régis" in 1890. His father had moved to Algeria from Milan in 1864. Acte de Naissance, Emile Maxime Régis Milano, Sétif, 18 June 1873, http://anom.archivesnationales.culture.gouv.fr /caomec2/osd.php?territoire=ALGERIE&acte=445312; Anonymous, *L'Œuvre des antijuifs d'Alger* (Algiers: Imprimerie Commerciale, 1899), 45.
84. Guy Turbet-Delof, *L'Afrique barbaresque dans la littérature française aux XVIe et XVIIe siècles* (Geneva: Droz, 1973), 24. On the word's ancient use, see Erich S. Gruen, *Rethinking the Other in Antiquity* (Princeton, NJ: Princeton University Press, 2011).
85. Rouighi, *Inventing the Berbers*, 15–20, 125–28; Maya Shatzmiller, *The Berbers and the Islamic State: The Marīnid Experience in Pre-Protectorate Morocco* (Princeton, NJ: Markus Wiener, 2000).
86. Miriam Hoexter and Tal Shuval, "Algiers," in *Encyclopaedia of Islam Three Online*, ed. K. Fleet et al. (Leiden: Brill, 2007). See also René Lespès, "L'origine du nom française 'd'Alger' traduisant 'El Djezaïr,'" *Revue africaine* 67 (1926): 80–84; and Guy Turbet-Delof, "Notes lexicologiques sur la désignation de certaines collectivités ethniques ou géographiques d'Afrique du Nord," *Le Français moderne* 2 (April 1970): 151–54.
87. Tal Shuval, *La ville d'Alger vers la fin du XVIIIe siècle: population et cadre urbain* (Paris: CNRS, 1998); Andrew C. Hess, *The Forgotten Frontier: A History of the Sixteenth-Century Ibero-African Frontier* (Chicago: University of Chicago Press, 1978), 253. On "doubling" of northwestern African toponyms, see Jocelyne Dakhlia, *Lingua franca: histoire d'une langue métisse en Méditerranée* (Arles: Actes Sud, 2008), 134–36.
88. François Foppens, *Le Dictionnaire géographique contenant les Roiaumes, les provinces, les villes, les fleuves, et les autres lieux les plus considérables du monde* (Brussels: Foppens, 1694), 13–14.
89. Michel Antoine Baudrand, *Dictionnaire géographique universel, contenant une description exacte des États, royaumes, villes, forteresses, montagnes, caps, iles, presqu'iles, lacs, mers, golfes, détroits etc. de l'Univers* (Amsterdam: Halma, 1701), 35–36.
90. Turbet-Delof, "Notes lexicologiques," 151.
91. Turbet-Delof, 152; Pierre Dan, *Histoire de Barbarie et de ses corsaires* (Paris: Rocolet, 1637), 134.
92. "Instructions rédigées par le Ministre des Affaires Étrangères pour M. le Commandant en chef de l'armée envoyée contre la Régence d'Alger," 18 April 1830, Centre

des Archives diplomatiques de La Courneuve (hereafter CADC) Mémoires et documents, Algérie, 5.

93. Claude Bontems points to two official usages of "Algérie" after 1830, in a royal ordinance of 1 December 1831 (arts. 1 and 2) and in another dated 12 May 1832 (art. 1). Claude Bontems, *L'Algérie, ses instituions et son droit à l'épreuve de la colonisation* (Paris: Bouchène, 2018), 14n10, 19. Bontems incorrectly calls "Algérie" a neologism.
94. Terms like "Maghreb" and "Afrique du Nord" replaced Barbarie as the scope of French territorial interests in the region took form. See Hannoum, *Invention of the Maghreb*.
95. Examples from the decree of 8 September 1830 and the decree of 14 February 1832. Ministère de la Guerre, *Collections des actes du gouvernement depuis l'occupation d'Alger jusqu'au 1e octobre 1834* (Paris: Imprimerie royale, 1843), 10, 163.
96. Sol, "Du système à suivre pour la colonisation d'Alger," *Le Spectateur militaire* 19 (15 April–15 September 1835): 481.
97. Émile Larcher, *Traité élémentaire de législation algérienne*, vol. 1, 3rd ed. (Paris: Rousseau, 1923), 172, 183–86.
98. Claude Bontems, *Le droit musulman algérien à l'époque colonial: de l'invention à la codification* (Geneva: Slatkine, 2014), 32. See also the differing opinions in the original sources in Robert Estoublon, *Bulletin judicaire de l'Algérie*, vol. 1: *1830–1848* (Algiers: Jourdan, 1890), 1–2.
99. Charles-André Julien, *Histoire de l'Algérie contemporaine*, vol. 1: *La conquête et les débuts de la colonisation (1827–1871)*, 3rd ed. (Paris: Presses universitaires de France, 1986), 114. The phrase has made a lasting impact on the field. John Ruedy took up Julien's language in his *Modern Algeria: The Origins and Development of a Nation* (Bloomington: Indiana University Press, 1992), a book that stood as the definitive English-language survey of Algeria for twenty-five years. In 2017 the work that supplanted it—James McDougall, *A History of Algeria* (Cambridge: Cambridge University Press, 2017), 58—used more guarded language.
100. The dividing line between common and proper nouns is a notoriously imprecise one in many languages, with the same word often going easily between different parts of speech. Like English, French uses an uppercase initial letter to mark names and set them apart from common nouns. Capitalized, "Tartuffe" is the name of Molière's famous character, while the lowercase *tartuffe* is a common noun meaning hypocrite. Beyond that, things can be complicated, and specialized guides are required to decide if a noun is common or proper. In the early nineteenth century, the rules governing the French language were in a period of considerable upheaval, leaving ambiguity between these parts of speech. This was doubly so for legal language, which Ferdinand Brunot lamented was "inutilement archaïque et parfois barbare" in his massive history of the French language, *Histoire de la langue française des origines à nos jours*, vol. 10: *La Langue classique dans la tourmente* (Paris: Colin, 1968), 884. For the differences between names and nouns in French, see Kristoffer Nyrop, *Grammaire historique de la langue française*, vol. 4: *Sémantique* (Copenhagen: Gyldendalske boghandel, Nordisk forlag, 1913), 353–62. Contemporary

rules are given in *Lexique des règles typographiques en usage à l'Imprimerie nationale*, 5th ed. (Paris: Imprimerie nationale, 2002).

101. "Ordonnance du 22 juillet 1834," *Le Moniteur universel*, no. 225 (13 August 1834), 1.
102. Colonial-era texts relied on obfuscation to transform the dey's 5 July 1830 surrender into a document transferring sovereignty to France. One of the most complete accounts of the legislation and administrative measures by which France asserted its sovereignty is given as a footnote in Aimé Poivre, *Les Indigènes algériens, leur état civil et condition juridique* (Algiers: Dubos, 1862), 16. Among contemporary historians, Claude Bontems has pointed up most clearly the legal ambiguity of France's position in *Le droit musulman algérien*, 32. See also his *Algérie, ses institutions*, 1–38; and *Manuel des institutions algériennes de la domination turque à l'indépendance*, vol. 1: *La domination turque et le régime militaire* (Paris: Cujas, 1976), 109–45.
103. Georg Friedrich von Martens, *Recueil des traités . . . depuis 1761*, 2nd ed., vol. 1 (Göttingen: Dieterich, 1817), 591–96; Pierre Antonetti, *Histoire de la Corse* (Paris: Laffont, 1973), 400–402. My thanks to Thierry Pastorello, librarian at the Bibliothèque nationale de France, for help in resolving this question.
104. Jean Meyer et al., *Histoire de la France colonial*, vol. 1: *Des origines à 1914* (Paris: Colin, 1991), 339.
105. "Instructions pour la Commission d'Afrique," in *Procès-verbaux et rapports de la commission nommée par le Roi, le 7 juillet 1833, pour aller recueillir en Afrique tous les faits propres à éclairer le gouvernement sur l'état du pays et sur les mesures que réclame son avenir* (Paris: L'imprimerie royale, 1834), 13.
106. *Procès-verbaux et rapports . . . 7 juillet 1833*; *Procès-verbaux et rapports de la Commission d'Afrique instituée par ordonnance du Roi du 12 décembre 1833* (Paris: L'imprimerie royale, 1834); *Supplément aux procès-verbaux de la commission d'Afrique, instituée par ordonnance royale du 12 décembre 1833* (Paris: L'imprimerie royale, 1834). Some of the commission's reports were published separately: See *Colonisation de l'Ex-Régence d'Alger, Documents officiels* (Paris: Michaud, 1834).
107. Xavier Yacono, "La Régence d'Alger en 1830 d'après des commissions de 1833–1834" (part 2), *Revue de l'Occident musulman et de la Méditerranée* 2 (1966): 247.
108. *Procès-verbaux et rapports . . . 7 juillet 1833*, 225; *Procès-verbaux et rapports . . . 12 décembre 1833*, 413, 455.
109. Blais, *Mirages de la carte*, 54.
110. A. Carpentier and G. Frèrejouan Du Saint, *Répertoire général alphabétique du droit français*, vol. 30: *Patentes-possessoire* (Paris: Sirey, 1902), 844–81.
111. The Planiol manual of civil law defined possession as "a state of affairs which consists in holding a thing in an exclusive way and in realizing with it the same material acts of use and enjoyment *as if* one were its owner." Marcel Planiol, *Traite élémentaire de droit civil*, vol. 1: *Principes généraux*, 11th ed. (Paris: Libraire générale, 1928), 746. Emphasis added.
112. Carpentier and Frèrejouan Du Saint, *Répertoire général*, 30:845.
113. Rafe Blaufarb, *The Great Demarcation: The French Revolution and the Invention of Modern Property* (Oxford: Oxford University Press, 2016), 218.

114. Lauren Benton and Benjamin Straumann, "Acquiring Empire by Law: From Roman Doctrine to Early Modern European Practice," *Law and History Review* 28, no. 1 (2010): 3. See also Bain Attwood, *Empire and the Making of Native Title: Sovereignty, Property and Indigenous People* (Cambridge: Cambridge University Press, 2020), 18–20.
115. Benton and Straumann, "Acquiring Empire by Law," 17, 30.
116. Ferdinand de Cussy, *Dictionnaire ou Manuel-lexique du diplomate et du consul* (Leipzig: Brockhaus, 1846), 140, 573.
117. Teresa Davis, "The Ricardian State: Carlos Calvo and Latin America's Ambivalent Origin Story for the Age of Decolonization," *Journal of the History of International Law* 20, no. 1 (2020): 32–51. See also Calvo's role in restricting the concept of military occupation in Eyal Benvenisti, "The Origins of the Concept of Belligerent Occupation," *Law and History Review* 26, no. 3 (Fall 2008): 621–48; and Peter M. R. Stirk, *The Politics of Military Occupation* (Edinburgh: Edinburgh University Press, 2009), 11, 33.
118. Charles Calvo, *Dictionnaire de droit international public et privé*, vol. 2 (Berlin: Puttkammer, 1885), 291; Antony Anghie, *Imperialism, Sovereignty and the Making of International Law* (Cambridge: Cambridge University Press, 2005), 82–84.
119. Calvo, *Dictionnaire de droit international*, 2:291.
120. Calvo, 1:174–76. For the history of the European doctrine of conquest, see Sharon Korman, *The Right of Conquest: The Acquisition of Territory by Force in International Law and Practice* (Oxford: Oxford University Press, 1996). More attentive to the increasing modern opposition to conquest as a mode of acquisition is Stirk, *Politics of Military Occupation*, 10–27.
121. *Archives parlementaires de 1787 à 1860*, vol. 90: *du 6 mai au 6 aout 1834* (Paris: Dupont, 1894), 558, 559. Italics in original.
122. *Archives parlementaires*, 90:559.
123. *Le Moniteur algérien* continued to use old terms into September 1834. See decree of 17 September 1834 in *Le Moniteur algérien* 3, no. 138 (19 September 1834): 1.
124. "Régence d'Alger" is used in Antoine-Remy Frémin, *Théâtre de la guerre en Afrique comprenant les régences d'Alger, de Tunis, Tripoli et de l'empire du Maroc* (Paris: Hocquart, 1837); Pierre Lapie et al., *Carte comparée des régences d'Alger et de Tunis* (Paris: Piquet, 1838); and Auguste-Henri Dufour et al., *Carte de la régence d'Alger et d'une partie du bassin de la Méditerranée: donnant le rapport qui existe entre la France et les États barbaresques*, new ed. (Paris: Picquet, 1840). "Algérie" appears in Jean-Jacques-Germain Pelet, *Carte de l'Algérie dressée au Dépôt général de la guerre* (Paris: Kaeppelin, 1838); and Auguste-Henri Dufour, *Algérie: dédiée au roi* (Paris: Simonneau, 1838).
125. A. Beaupré, *Carte générale de l'Algérie: ou des possessions françaises dans le nord de l'Afrique, pour servir à l'intelligence des opérations militaires ou commerciales* (Paris: [s.n.], 1836).
126. *Le Moniteur algérien* 4, no. 152 (2 January 1835): 1; and *Le Moniteur algérien* 3, no. 138 (19 September 1834): 1, respectively. Some instances of wavering between a common and proper noun for possessions might have been errata, which were frequent in the *Le Moniteur algérien*. For example, when publishing the 1834 text in which

the governor general first used the proper "possessions" denomination—a letter he addressed to his soldiers—editors misspelled the word "French" in his title as *faançaises*, or "Feench." Letter of Lieutenant général Comte d'Erlon to soldiers, 28 September 1834, *Le Moniteur algérien* 3, no. 140 (3 October 1834): 1.

127. Anonymous, "Note pour le Ministre sur les Affaires d'Algérie," 12 May 1835, ANOM F80 1671. Original case.
128. *Recueil général des lois et ordonnances*, vol. 6 (Paris: Bureaux de l'administration du journal des notaires et des avocats, 1836), 271; F. Benezet, *Le Tribunal supérieur et la Cour d'appel d'Alger: résumé chronologique des lois, ordonnances, décrets et arrêtés concernant ces hautes juridictions, de 1830 à 1896* (Algiers: Jourdan, 1896), 8–13; Casimir Frégier, *De la contrainte par corps ou De l'emprisonnement civil en Algérie* (Constantine: Alessi and Arnolet, 1863), 23; Casimir Frégier, *Pensées de Théophile Abdallah; ou De l'interprétation en Algérie* (Sétif: Veuve Vincent, 1863), 25; Victor Valette, *Un projet de loi sur la réorganisation de l'Algérie* (Algiers: Cheniaux-Franville, 1881), 27.
129. *Bulletin des lois du Royaume de France IXe série*, vol 17: *nos. 583 à 619* (Paris: Imprimerie royale, 1839).
130. Ministère de la Guerre, Direction des Affaires africaines to Gouverneur général Valée, 14 October 1839, no. 89, SHD 1h64, dossier 1. Italics and word case as in original.
131. Charles-Louis Pinson de Ménerville, *Dictionnaire de la législation algérienne: manuel raisonné des lois, ordonnances, décrets, décisions et arrêtés* (Algiers: Philippe, 1853), 300–315. As Pinson de Ménerville put it, "On this date appeared a new modification in the administrative regime of the colony. The official denomination *Algeria* replaced French possessions in the north of Africa" (297).
132. Daniel Defoe, *Robinson Crusoe*, ed. Michael Shinagel (New York: Norton, 1975), 56, 80.
133. Fruitful perspectives on the question of language, names, silence, and sovereignty emerge in J. M. Coetzee's novel *Foe* (New York: Penguin, 1986), a retelling of Daniel Defoe's original *Robinson Crusoe*; and the reading of Gayatri Chakravorty Spivak, *A Critique of Postcolonial Reason: Toward a History of the Vanishing Present* (Cambridge, MA: Harvard University Press, 1999), 186–90.

2. "Tell Me Your Name"

1. Abdelmajid Hannoum, *The Invention of the Maghreb: Between Africa and the Middle East* (Cambridge: Cambridge University Press, 2021), 24–29. For precolonial names in Congo, see Osumaka Likaka, *Naming Colonialism: History and Collective Memory in the Congo, 1870–1960* (Madison: University of Wisconsin Press, 2009), chap. 1.
2. For an early critique of "heritage and recovery" model of decolonization, see Abdallah Laroui, *A History of the Maghrib: An Interpretive Essay*, trans. Ralph Manheim (Princeton, NJ: Princeton University Press, 1977), 382–83. Also Ahmad Agbaria, *The Politics of Arab Authenticity: Challenges to Postcolonial Thought* (New York: Columbia University Press, 2022).

3. This section draws on the work of scholars in the field of classical Arabic onomastics, primarily Annemarie Schimmel, *Islamic Names* (Edinburgh: Edinburgh University Press, 1989); and Jacqueline Sublet, *Le Voile de nom: Essai sur le nom propre arabe* (Paris: Presses universitaires de France, 1991). Also helpful is Franz-Christoph Muth, "Proper Names," in *Encyclopedia of Arabic Language and Linguistics*, vol. 3, ed. Kees Versteegh (Leiden: Brill, 2006), 717–24. The comprehensive reference on Arabic names is El-Said M. Badawi et al., *Muʿjam asmāʾ al-ʿArab* [Dictionary of Arab names], 2 vols. (Muscat: Jāmiʿat al-Sulṭān Qābūs; and Beirut: Maktabat Lubnān, 1991). In English, see Salahuddin Ahmed, *A Dictionary of Muslim Names* (New York: New York University Press, 1999). At the center of this field is the *Onomasticon Arabicum* project, begun in the early twentieth century by Leone Caetani (d. 1935) and Giuseppe Gabrieli (d. 1942) and expanded and digitized by subsequent researchers in the 1970s. Tens of thousands of names are in this database, most drawn from the biographical dictionaries that flourished between the ninth and sixteenth centuries. See https://onomasticon.irht.cnrs.fr/.
4. Richard Bulliet, "A Quantitative Approach to Medieval Muslim Biographical Dictionaries," *Journal of the Economic and Social History of the Orient* 13, no. 2 (April 1970), 195–211; and John A. Nawas, "Biography and Biographical Works," in *Medieval Islamic Civilization: An Encyclopedia*, vol. 1, ed. Josef W. Meri (New York: Routledge, 2006), 110–12.
5. One example is the *Ḥilyat al-awliyā* of Abu Naim al-Isfahani (d. 1038), partially translated as Aḥmad ibn ʿAbd Allāh Abū Nuʿaym al-Iṣbahānī, *The Beauty of the Righteous and Ranks of the Elite*, trans. Muhammad Al-Akili (Philadelphia: Pearl Pub. House, 1995). The formalization of the classical name in the Mameluk era is discussed in Sublet, *Voile du nom*, 158–59.
6. The practice of forming a *nisba* that referenced place of education was prevalent among students in the Sous region of Morocco. Nico van den Boogert, *The Berber Literary Tradition of the Sous* (Leiden: Nederlands Instituut voor het Nabije Oosten, 1997), 24. For concise discussion of the *nasab* and *nisba*, see entries by Franz Rosenthal and Jacqueline Sublet, respectively, in the *Encyclopaedia of Islam New Edition Online (EI-2 English)* (Brill).
7. Élie Tabet, *Notes sur l'organisation des tribus et l'étymologie des nom propres* (Oran: Association ouvrière, 1882), 38.
8. Jacqueline Sublet, "Dans l'Islam médiéval, nom en expansion, nom à l'étroit: L'exemple d'Ibn Fuwaṭî," in *L'écriture du nom propre*, ed. Anne-Marie Christin (Paris: Harmattan, 1998), 123.
9. Richard W. Bulliet, review of *Voile de nom* by Jacqueline Sublet, in *Journal of the American Oriental Society* 113, no. 1 (January–March 1993): 125.
10. Jacqueline Sublet, "La prosopographie arabe," *Annales ESC* 25, no. 5 (1970): 1236–39; Richard W. Bulliet, *The Patricians of Nishapur: A Study in Medieval Islamic Social History* (Cambridge, MA: Harvard University Press, 1972), esp. part 2; Carl F. Petry, *The Civilian Elite of Cairo in the Later Middle Ages* (Princeton, NJ: Princeton University Press, 1981); Mohamed Meouak "Les méthodes biographique et prosopographique: leur

application pour l'histoire sociale d'al-Andalus (milieu IIe/VIIIe-fin IVe/Xe siècles)," *Mélanges de la Casa de Velázquez* 28, no. 1 (1992): 191–208; David Morray, *An Ayyubid Notable and His World: Ibn al-ʿAdīm and Aleppo as Portrayed in His Biographical Dictionary of People Associated with the City* (Leiden: Brill, 1994); Isabelle Grangaud, *La Ville imprenable: une histoire sociale de Constantine au 18e siècle* (Constantine, Algeria: Média Plus, 2004), 40–77; Majied Robinson, "Prosopographical Approaches to the *Nasab* Tradition: A Study of Marriage and Concubinage in the Tribe of Muḥammad, 500–750 CE" (PhD diss., University of Edinburgh, 2013). On general questions, see Giovanni Levi, "Les usages de la biographie," *Annales HSS* 44, no. 6 (1989): 1329–30.

11. Bulliet, *Patricians of Nishapur*, 100–104.
12. As told in Muḥammad ibn Muḥammad ibn Ṣaṣrā, *A Chronicle of Damascus, 1389-1397*, ed. and trans. William M. Brinner, vol. 1, (Berkeley: University of California Press, 1963), 183–84; Arabic text in Ṣaṣrā, *Chronicle of Damascus*, 2:138.
13. Silvestre de Sacy, *Chrestomathie arabe*, vol. 1 (Paris: Imprimerie Royale, 1826), 329–30; Ernest Carette, *Études sur la Kabilie proprement dite*, vol. 1 (Paris: Imprimerie Nationale, 1848), 78; Tabet, *Notes sur l'organisation des tribus*, 25–26.
14. Maternal nasabs generally stand either as testimony to powerful mothers or, conversely, as pejorative markers of their child's illegitimacy, with the mother's name marking the absent father. In the early Islamic period, maternal nasabs were fairly common, used to honor mothers and to help distinguish among siblings within complex families. Later, maternal nasabs appear among the elite of the Almoravid empire (eleventh–twelfth centuries), reflecting the prominence of women. Adeel Mohammadi, "The Ambiguity of Maternal Filiation (nasab) in Early and Medieval Islam," *Graduate Journal of Harvard Divinity School* 11 (Spring 2016): https://projects.iq.harvard.edu/hdsjournal/ambiguity-maternal-filiation-nasab-early-and-medieval-islam; Stefan Leder, "Nasab as Idiom and Discourse," *Journal of the Economic and Social History of the Orient* 58 (2015): 63; Christian Müller, Muriel Roiland, and Jacqueline Sublet, "Method of Arabic Onomastics," 11 (introduction to the online database *Onomasticon Arabicum*), http://onomasticon.irht.cnrs.fr. For women in Almoravid society, see Amira K. Bennison, *The Almoravid and Almohad Empires* (Edinburgh: Edinburgh University Press, 2016), 158–64; and Osire Glacier, "Zaynab al-Nafzawiyya," *Dictionary of African Biography* Online, 2011.
15. Abraham Marcus, *The Middle East on the Eve of Modernity: Aleppo in the Eighteenth Century* (New York: Columbia University Press, 1989), 63.
16. Franz Rosenthal, "Nasab," *Encyclopaedia of Islam New Edition Online (EI-2 English)* (Brill). For nasabs and their place in early understandings of historical causation, see Franz Rosenthal, *A History of Muslim Historiography* (Leiden: Brill, 1968); Chase F. Robinson, *Islamic Historiography* (Cambridge: Cambridge University Press, 2003), 66–74; ʿAbd al-ʿAziz Duri, *The Rise of Historical Writing Among the Arabs* (Princeton, NJ: Princeton University Press, 1983), esp. 50–54; and Tarif Khalidi, *Arabic Historical Thought in the Classical Period* (Cambridge: Cambridge University Press, 1994), 49–61. See also Ibn al-Kalbī, *Ǧamharat an-nasab: das genealogische Werk des Hišam Ibn Muḥammad al-Kalbī*, 2 vols., ed. and trans. Werner Caskel and G. Strenziok (Leiden:

Brill, 1966); M. J. Kister and M. Plessner, "Notes on *Caskel's Ǧamharat an-nasab*," *Oriens* 25/26 (1976): 48–68; S. D. Goitein, review of *Ǧamharat an-nasab* in *Journal of the American Oriental Society* 90, no. 4 (October–December 1970): 548–51.

17. Leder, "Nasab as Idiom and Discourse"; Pierre Bonte et al., eds., *Al-Ansâb, la quête des origines: Anthropologie historique de la société tribale arabe* (Paris: Maison des sciences de l'homme, 1991).
18. Ibn 'Abd Rabbih, *The Unique Necklace*, vol. 3, trans. Issa Boullata (Reading, UK: Garnet, 2011), 227.
19. The findings of Arabo-Islamic onomastic research can be usefully thought of in conjunction with Jacque Derrida when he deconstructs what is "proper" in the name: The name "has never been, as the unique appellation reserved for the presence of a unique being, anything but the original myth of transparent legibility present under the obliteration; it is because the proper name was never possible except through its functioning within a classification and therefore within a system of differences, within a writing retaining the traces of difference, that the interdict was possible, could come into play, and, when the time came, as we shall see, could be transgressed; transgressed, that is to say restored to the obliteration and the non-self-sameness [*non-propriété*] at the origin." Jacques Derrida, *Of Grammatology*, trans. Gayatri Chakravorty Spivak (Baltimore: John Hopkins University Press, 1976), 109.
20. Andrew Shryock, *Nationalism and the Genealogical Imagination: Oral History and Textual Authority in Tribal Jordan* (Berkeley: University of California Press, 1997), 274–76, 311–13.
21. Abdelahad Sebti, "Au Maroc sharifisme citadin, charisme et historiographie," *Annales HSS* 41, no. 2 (March–April 1986): 451; for a case of purportedly spurious genealogy, see David Hart, "An Awkward Chronology and a Questionable Genealogy: History and Legend in a Saintly Lineage in the Moroccan Central Atlas, 1397–1702," *Journal of North African Studies* 6, no. 2 (Summer 2001): 95–116.
22. Muḥammad ibn Ṣāliḥ Majdī, *Hilyat al-Zamān bi-Manāqib Khādim al-Waṭan* (Cairo: Maktabat Muṣṭafā al-Bābī al-Ḥalabī, 1958), 17–18.
23. Abraham Marcus discusses noble privileges and fraudulent genealogies in *Eve of Modernity*, 61–62. For the tax exemptions enjoyed by nobles, see Lucette Valensi, *Tunisian Peasants in the Eighteenth and Nineteenth Centuries*, trans. Beth Archer (Cambridge: Cambridge University Press, 1985), 230.
24. Muḥammad ibn Muḥammad Ibn Maryam, *Al-Bustān fī Dhikr al-Awliyā' wa-al-'Ulamā' bi-Tilimsān* (Algiers: al-Maṭba'ah al-Tha'ālibīyah, 1908), 8; French translation, *Jardin des biographies des saints et savants de Tlemcen par Ibn Maryem ech-Cherif el-Melity*, trans. F. Provenzali (Algiers: Fontana Frères, 1910), 5. See also Kisaichi Masatoshi, "Three Renowned 'Ulamā Families of Tlemcen: The Maqqarī, the Marzūqi and the 'Uqbānī," *Journal of Sophia Asian Studies* 22 (2004): 121–37; Osama Abi-Mershed, "The Transmission of Knowledge and the Education of the 'Ulama in the Late Sixteenth-Century Maghrib: A Study of the Biographical Dictionary of Muhammad Ibn

Maryam," in *Biography and the Construction of Identity and Community in the Middle East*, ed. Mary Ann Fay (New York: Palgrave, 2001), 19–36.

25. Sublet, *Voile du nom*, 8.
26. Shryock, *Nationalism and the Genealogical Imagination*, 319–21. See also Jonathan Glasser, *The Lost Paradise: Andalusi Music in Urban North Africa* (Chicago: University of Chicago Press, 2016); Brinkley Messick, *The Calligraphic State: Textual Domination and History in a Muslim Society* (Berkeley: University of California Press, 1992), 15–36.
27. Albert Socin (d. 1899), a Swiss-born linguist and specialist of dialectical Arabic, undertook the fullest colonial-era study of Algerian personal names. Albert Socin, "Die arabischen Eigennamen in Algier," *Zeitschrift der Deutschen Morgenländischen Gesellschaft* 52, no. 3 (1898): 471–500. See also Ouerdia Yermeche, "Le patronyme algérien: essai de catégorisation sémantique," in *Nomination et dénomination des noms de lieux, de tribus et de personnes en Algérie*, ed. Farid Benramdane and Brahim Atoui (Oran: Centre de recherché en anthropologie sociale et culturelle, 2005), 61–82.
28. On the importance of regional identities, see Allan Christelow, *Algerians Without Borders: The Making of a Global Frontier Society* (Gainesville: University Press of Florida, 2012), 11. Names specific to southwestern Algeria are in Amar Mahmoudi, "De l'usage des prénoms rares des hautes plaines de l'ouest algérien (Frenda, Ain Dheb, Medrissa, El Bayadh, Labiod Sidi Cheikh)," in *Des noms et des noms: état civil et anthroponymie en Algérie*, ed. Farid Benramdane (Oran: CRASC, 2005), 39–44.
29. Yermeche, "Le patronyme algérien."
30. Joseph Desparmet, *Coutumes institutions, croyances des Indigènes de l'Algérie*, vol. 1: *L'Enfance, le mariage et la famille*, 2nd ed. (Alger: Carbonel, 1948), 20–23; Eugène Daumas, *La Vie arabe et la société musulman* (Paris: Lévy, 1869), 122–23; Dale F. Eickelman, "Rites of Passage: Muslim Rites," in *Encyclopedia of Religion*, ed. Lindsay Jones, vol. 11, 2nd ed. (Detroit: Macmillan Reverence, 2005), 725–26.
31. Lila Abu-Lughod, *Veiled Sentiments: Honor and Poetry in a Bedouin Society* (Berkeley: University of California Press, 1986).
32. Mouloud Feraoun, *The Poor Man's Son: Menrad, Kabyle Schoolteacher*, trans. Lucy R. McNair (Charlottesville: University of Virginia Press, 2005), 32.
33. Saoud Azizi, "Le nom de personne dans l'oasis de Figuig: Un système de codification des relations sociales," in *La culture Amazighe: réalités et perceptions*, ed. Hammou Belghazi (Rabat: Institut royal de la culture amazighe, 2017), 41–62.
34. R. Y. Ebied and M. J. L. Young, "A Note on Muslim Name-Giving According to the Day of the Week," *Arabica* 24, fasc. 3 (September 1977). 326–28.
35. Arabic linguistics marks a distinction between the *ism murtajal*, a class of nouns that exist only as names, and the *ism manqūl*, names derived or "transferred" from common nouns. Aziz al-Azmeh, "Linguistic Observations on the Theonym Allāh," in *In the Shadow of Arabic, The Centrality of Language to Arabic Culture: Studies Presented to Ramzi Baalbaki on the Occasion of His Sixtieth Birthday*, ed. Bilal Orfali (Leiden: Brill, 2011), 272; Tabet, *Notes sur l'organisation des tribus*, 35.
36. Carette, *Études sur la Kabilie*, 90.

37. Annemarie Schimmel, *And Muhammad Is His Messenger: The Veneration of the Prophet in Islamic Piety* (Chapel Hill: University of North Carolina Press, 1985), n. 25.
38. Desparmet, *Coutumes institutions, croyances*, 23.
39. Daumas, *Vie arabe*, 122.
40. Louis-Jacques Bresnier, *Chrestomathie arabe: lettres, actes et pièces diverses avec la traduction française en regard* (Algiers: Bastide, 1857), 28.
41. Isabelle Grangaud, *Ville imprenable*; Socin, "Arabischen Eigennamen in Algier," 491–92.
42. Socin, "Arabischen Eigennamen in Algier," 484, 487, and 493; Mostefa Lacheraf, *Des noms et des lieux: mémoires d'une Algérie oubliée* (Algiers: Casbah, 1998), 149.
43. Socin, "Arabischen Eigennamen in Algier," 481, 484.
44. Marcelin Beaussier, *Dictionnaire pratique arabe-français* (Algiers: Jourdan, 1887), 139.
45. Karim Ould-Ennebia, "Histoire de l'état civil des Algériens: Patronymie et acculturation," *Revue maghrébine des études historiques et sociales*, no. 1 (September 2009): 11.
46. Henri Fleisch, *Traité de philologie arabe*, vol. 1: *Préliminaires, phonétique, morphologie nominale* (Beirut: Imprimerie Catholique, 1961), 271–73; Mohammed ben Dawoud el-Sanhadjy [Muḥammad ibn Muḥammad al-Ṣanhājī Ibn Ajurrūm (1273–1323)], *Djaroumiya, grammaire arabe élémentaire*, ed. and trans. Marcelin Beaussier (Algiers: Bastide, 1846), 54.
47. Bresnier, *Cours*, 281; Lacheraf, *Noms et des lieux*, 150; Fleisch, *Traité de philologie arabe*, 1:271–73.
48. Petition 15 Sha'bān 1246, ANOM 1H1. Orthographic irregularity noted by Estefanía Valenzuela Mochón, personal correspondence, 3 December 2020.
49. Sublet, *Voile du nom*, 160–62.
50. Bresnier, *Chrestomathie arabe*, 480; Socin, "Arabischen Eigennamen in Algier," 487.
51. Edmond Doutté, *Un texte arabe en dialecte oranais* (Paris: Imprimerie nationale, 1903), 62.
52. Bresnier, *Chrestomathie arabe*, 440.
53. Bresnier, 36, 66–67; Carette, *Études sur la Kabilie*, 79; Daumas, *Vie arabe*, 68–69.
54. Isabelle Grangaud, "Le titre de *Sayyid* ou *Sî* dans la documentation constantinoise d'époque moderne: un marqueur identitaire en évolution," *Revue des mondes musulmans et de la Méditerranée*, no. 127 (July 2010), https://doi.org/10.4000/remmm.6604; C. E. Bosworth, "Sayyid," in *Encyclopaedia of Islam New Edition Online (EI-2 English)*.
55. Mohammed Ben Cheneb, *Proverbes arabes de l'Algérie et du Maghreb*, vol. 2 (Paris: Leroux, 1906), 21–22.
56. Belkassem Ben Sedira, *Dictionnaire français-arabe de la langue parlée en Algérie*, 5th ed. (Algiers: Jourdan, 1910), 129; Carette, *Études sur la Kabilie*, 84–85; Edward Westermarck, *Marriage Ceremonies in Morocco* (London: Macmillan, 1914), 318.
57. Julia A. Clancy-Smith, *Rebel and Saint: Muslim Notables, Populist Protest, Colonial Encounters (Algeria and Tunisia, 1800–1904)* (Berkeley: University of California Press, 1997), 231–32.
58. Bresnier, *Chrestomathie arabe*, 67,
59. Sublet, *Voile du nom*, 9, 46, 47.

60. Bresnier, *Chrestomathie arabe*, 67; William Mac Guckin de Slane and Charles-Hippolyte Gabeau, *Vocabulaire destiné à fixer la transcription en français des noms de personnes et de lieux usités chez les indigènes de l'Algérie* (Paris: Imprimerie impériale, 1868), 11; Beaussier, *Dictionnaire pratique*, 52–53, 268. As Beaussier notes, often the letter *wāw* was dropped and an elision made between the *bā'* and the next letter, e.g., Bū Ghār = Bghār, or "Boghar," as the name of the Algerian town.
61. Muḥammad ibn Aḥmad al-Ibshīhī, *Al-Mostaṭraf: recueil de morceaux choisis çà et là dans toutes les branches de connaissance réputées attrayantes*, vol. 2, trans. Gustav Rat, (Paris: Leroux, 1902), 22.
62. Grangaud, "Le titre de *Sayyid*."
63. Fatima Zohra Guechi, "*Mahkama* records as a Source for Women's History: The Case of Constantine," in *Beyond the Exotic: Women's Histories in Islamic Societies*, ed. Amir El-Azhary Sonbol (Syracuse, NY: Syracuse University Press, 2005), 155. See also Fatima Zohra Guechi, "Du 'nasab' au 'laqab:' héritages controversés," in *Constantine: une ville, des héritages*, ed. Fatima Zohra Guechi (Constantine, Algeria: Média Plus, 2004), 31–75; Clifford Geertz, "'From the Native's Point of View': On the Nature of Anthropological Understanding," in *Meaning in Anthropology*, ed. Keith Basso and Henry A. Selby (Albuquerque: University of New Mexico Press, 1976), 233.
64. *The Qur'ān*, trans. Alan Jones (Exeter: Gibb Memorial Trust, 2007), 476.
65. Sublet, *Voile du nom*, 88–91.
66. Bresnier, *Chrestomathie arabe*, 60.
67. Al-Ibshīhī, *Al-Mostaṭraf*, 1:26.
68. Denise A. Spellberg, *Politics, Gender, and the Islamic Past: The Legacy of 'A'isha bint Abi Bakr* (New York: Columbia University Press, 1994), 85.
69. L. Veccia Vaglieri, "'Ali ibn Abī Ṭālib," in *Encyclopaedia of Islam New Edition Online (EI-2 English)*; and Al-Ibshīhī, *Al-Mostaṭraf*, 1:27.
70. Al-Ibshīhī, *Al-Mostaṭraf*, 23.
71. Shelomoh Dov Goitein, "Nicknames as Family Names," *Journal of the American Oriental Society* 90, no. 4 (October–December 1970): 520, 518. On poet Robert Browning's use of play in interpreting Arabic names, see Hédi A. Jaouad, *Browning Upon Arabia: A Movable East* (Cham: Springer, 2018), 46–48, 114–16.
72. Homi K. Bhabha, "How Newness Enters the World: Postmodern Space, Postcolonial Times and the Trials of Cultural Translation," chap. 11 in *The Location of Culture* (London: Routledge, 1994), 313–17; Likaka, *Naming Colonialism.*
73. Henri Bissuel, *Les Touareg de l'Ouest* (Algiers: Jourdan, 1888), 200.
74. Augustin Bernard, "Sahara," in *La Vie politique à l'étranger*, ed. Ernest Lavisse (Paris: Charpentier, 1891), 386; Pascal Blanchard et al., eds., *Human Zoos: Science and Spectacle in the Age of Colonial Empires*, trans. Teresa Bridgeman (Liverpool: Liverpool University Press, 2008).
75. For Algerian Mahdism, see Mouloud Haddad, "Les maitres de l'Heure: Soufisme et eschatologie en Algérie coloniale (1845–1901), *Revue d'histoire du XIX*[e] *siècle* 41 (2010): 49–61.

76. In some accounts, the animal was a gazelle and his actual kunya was "Bū Ghazāl." Edouard de Neveu, *Les Khouan: ordres religieux chez les Musulmans de l'Algérie*, 2nd ed. (Paris: Guyot, 1846), 53, 64.
77. Charles Richard, *Étude sur l'insurrection du Dhara* [*sic*] (Algiers: Bastide, 1846), 13–14; Charles Brosselard, *Les Khouan: de la constitution des ordres religieux musulmans en Algérie* (Algiers: Bourget, 1859), 6; Anonymous, *Les princes en Afrique, Le duc de Montpensier* (Paris: Amyot, 1846), 21.
78. Alexandre Dumas, *Le Véloce ou Tanger, Alger et Tunis*, vol. 4 (Brussels: Muquardt, 1851), 57. Although Victor Hugo did not himself make the link between Bū Mā'aza and Esmeralda, he wrote about the Algerian leader, whom he had met in 1847, in prejudicial terms. Franck Laurent, *Victor Hugo face à la conquête de l'Algérie* (Paris: Maisonneuve et Larose, 2001).
79. Ferdinand Hugonnet, *Souvenirs d'un chef de bureau arabe* (Paris: Lévy, 1858), 49.
80. Hans Wehr, *A Dictionary of Modern Written Arabic (Arabic-English)*, 4th ed., ed. J. Milton Cowan (Urbana, IL: Spoken Language Services, 1994), 1016.
81. Documents concerning French projects with Gaga are in ANOM, 4h24, 4h26, 22h28, 22h33, and 22h54.
82. F. Steingass, *Arabic-English Dictionary* (New Delhi: Asian Educational Services, 2005), 213; Wehr, *Dictionary of Modern Arabic*, 150.
83. Alain Rey, *Dictionnaire historique de la langue française*, vol. 2: *Fo-Pr*, new ed. (Paris: Le Robert, 2019), 1523.
84. Gouverneur général Cambon to Général de la Roque, 15 April 1894, no. 990, CAOM 22h54.
85. B. G. Martin, *Muslim Brotherhoods in Nineteenth-Century Africa* (Cambridge: Cambridge University Press, 1976), 210.
86. Anonymous, "Muséologiques 87 au musée de l'A.N.P, histoire vivante," *El Djeich: revue de l'armée national populaire*, no. 296 (March 1988): 7.
87. David Cohen, *Le Parler arabe des Juifs de Tunis*, vol. 1: *Textes et documents linguistiques et ethnographiques* (Paris: Mouton, 1964), 12–17; Moshe Bar-Asher, "Hebrew Components in Judeo-Arabic, North Africa," *Encyclopedia of Hebrew Language and Linguistics*, Brill Online; Geoffrey Khan, "Judaeo-Arabic" in *Encyclopedia of Arabic Language and Linguistics*, vol. 2, ed. Kees Versteegh (Leiden: Brill, 2006), 526–36. Analogous phenomena can found in the Judeo-Berber idioms. See Joseph Chetrit, "Le judéo-berbère et ses usages au Maroc," in *Diglossie, hybridation et diversité intra-linguistique: études socio-pragmatiques sur les langues juives, le judéo-arabe et le judéo-berbère*, ed. Joseph Chetrit (Paris: Peeters, 2007), 213–352.
88. Abraham L. Udovitch and Lucette Valensi, *The Last Arab Jews: The Communities of Jerba, Tunisia* (New York: Harwood Academic, 1984).
89. For the colonial-era version of this view, see Eugène Daumas, *Moeurs et coutumes de l'Algérie: Tell, Kabylie, Sahara* (Paris: Hachette, 1855): 131–32; and Venture de Paradis, "Alger au XVIIIe siècle," *Revue africaine* 39, no. 219 (1895): 278.
90. Mehdi Ghouirgate, "Le berbère au Moyen Âge: une culture linguistique en cours de reconstitution," *Annales HSS* 3 (July–September 2015): 592; Mohamed Meouak,

La langue berbère au Maghreb médiéval (Leiden: Brill, 2015); Ahmed Elmounadi and Hachem Jarmouni, "Le périple des manuscrits amazighes," *Études et documents berbères* 1, no. 33 (2014): 149–57; Harry Stroomer, "Three Tashelhiyt Berber Texts from the Arsène Roux Archives," *Studies in Slavic and General Linguistics* 33 (2008): 389–97; Mohand Tilmatine, "Du Berbère à l'Amazighe: de l'objet au sujet historique," *Al-Andalus-Maghreb* 14 (2007): 225–47; Mohamed Meouak, "Langue arabe et langue berbère dans le Maghreb médiéval: notes de philologie et d'histoire," *Al-Andalus-Maghreb* 13 (2006): 329–35; Abdellah Bounfour, "Notes sur l'histoire du berbère (Tachelhit): essai de bilan et perspectives," in *Trames de langues: Usages et métissages linguistiques dans l'histoire du Maghreb*, ed. Jocelyne Dakhlia (Paris: Maisonneuve and Larose, 2004), 169–81; Nico van den Boogert, "Medieval Berber Orthography," in *Études berbères et chamito-sémitiques: mélanges offerts à Karl-G. Prasse*, ed. Salem Chaker (Paris: Peeters, 2000), 358–59; Nico van den Boogert, "Some Notes on Maghribi Script," *Manuscripts of the Middle East* 4 (1989): 30–43; and Nico van den Boogert and Maarten Kossmann, "Les premiers emprunts arabes en berbère," *Arabica* 44, no. 2 (1997): 317–22.

91. Michael O'Conner, "The Berber Scripts," in *The World's Writing Systems*, ed. Peter T. Daniels and William Brights (Oxford: Oxford University Press, 1996), 112–19; Dris Soulaimani, "Writing and Rewriting Amazigh/Berber Identity: Orthographies and Language Ideologies," *Writing Systems Research* 8, no. 1 (2016), 1–16.
92. Meouak, *Langue berbère*, 150–51; Salem Chaker, "Écriture (graphie arabe)," *Encyclopédie berbère*, vol 17: *Douiret-Eropaei*, ed. Gabriel Camps (Aix-en-Provence: Édisud, 1996), 2580.
93. Djamil Aïssani and Djemel Mechehed, "Usages de l'écriture et production des savoirs dans la Kabylie du XIXe siècle," *Revue des mondes musulmans et de la Méditerranée* 121–22 (April 2008): 239–59; A. Bounfour and D. Merolla, "Conte," in *Encyclopédie berbère*, vol. 14: *Conseil-Danse*, ed. Gabriel Camps (Aix-en-Provence: Édisud, 1994), 2081–88.
94. Ghouirgate, "Le berbère au Moyen Âge," 592.
95. Maarten Kossmann, *The Arabic Influence on Northern Berber* (Leiden: Brill, 2013).
96. Ramzi Rouighi, *Inventing the Berbers: History and Ideology in the Maghrib* (Philadelphia: University of Pennsylvania Press, 2019), 80.
97. Tal Shuval, "The Ottoman Algerian Elite and Its Ideology," *International Journal of Middle East Studies* 32, no. 3 (August 2000): 323–44. On the mixing of Turkish and Arabic languages, see Mohammed Ben Cheneb, *Mots turks et persans conservés dans le parler algérien* (Algiers: Carbonel, 1922). For the historiographical importance of the "Ottomaness" of North Africa, see M'hamed Oualdi, *A Slave Between Empires: A Transimperial History of North Africa* (New York: Columbia University Press, 2019).
98. Ismael Musah Montana, "The *Bori* Colonies of Tunis," in *Slavery, Islam and Diaspora*, ed. Behnaz A. Mirzai et al. (Trenton, NJ: Africa World Press, 2009), 155–67; and Ismael Montana, personal correspondence, June 2018. See also Chouki El Hamel, *Black Morocco: A History of Slavery, Race, and Islam* (Cambridge: Cambridge University Press, 2013), 155–208; Fatiha Loualich, "Emancipated Female Slaves in Algiers,"

in *Subalterns and Social Protest: History from Below in the Middle East and North Africa*, ed. Stephanie Cronin (London: Routledge, 2008), 200–209.

99. Dakhlia, *Lingua franca*, 487. See also Shelomo Dov Goitein, *Jews and Arabs: A Concise History of Their Social and Cultural Relations* (Mineola, NY: Dover, 2005), 131–40.
100. Rouighi, *Inventing the Berbers*; Jane E. Goodman, "Writing Empire, Underwriting Nation: Discursive Histories of Kabyle Berber Oral Texts," *American Ethnologist* 29, no. 1 (February 2002): 86–122.
101. Salem Chaker, "Onomastique Libyco-Berbère (Anthroponymie)," in *Encyclopédie berbère*, vol. 35: *Oasitae-Ortaïas*, ed. Salem Chaker (Paris: Peeters, 2013), 5763. Unless otherwise noted, this section draws its primary material from this article as well as Salem Chaker, "La langue berbère à travers l'onomastique médiévale: El-Bekri," *Revue de l'Occident musulman et de la Méditerranée* 35 (1983): 127–44.
102. Kamal Naït-Zerrad, *L'officiel des prénoms berbères* (Paris: Harmattan, 2003); Gabriel Camps, "Liste onomastique libyque, nouvelle édition," *Antiquités africaines*, nos. 38–39 (2002): 211–57; Gabriel Camps, "Liste onomastique libyque d'après les sources latines," *Revue des Études phéniciennes, puniques et des antiquités libyques* 7–8 (1992–1993): 39–73.
103. Mohand-Akli Haddadou, "Les couches diachroniques du vocabulaire berbère," in *Trames de langues: Usages et métissages linguistiques dans l'histoire du Maghreb*, ed. Jocelyne Dakhlia, 353–67 (Paris: Maisonneuve and Larose, 2004).
104. Examples from Chaker, "Onomastique Libyco-Berbère," 5767; and Ghouirgate, "Le berbère au Moyen Âge," 601.
105. Chaker, "Onomastique Libyco-Berbère," 5767.
106. Abdelaziz Allati, "Les noms de parenté en berbère," *Études et documents berbères* 41 (2019): 97–112.
107. Desparmet, *Coutumes institutions*, 22.
108. Mohand-Akli Haddadou, *Recueil de prénoms amazighs* (Algiers: Haut-Commissariat à l'Amazighité, 2003), 14.
109. Ghouirgate, "Le berbère au Moyen Âge," 601.
110. Van den Boogert, "Medieval Berber Orthography"; Meouak, *Langue berbère au Maghreb médiéval*, 183–84. See also Maarten Kossmann and Ramada Elghamis, "Preliminary Notes on Tuareg in Arabic Script from Niger," in *The Arabic Script in Africa Studies in the Use of a Writing System*, ed. Meikal Mumin and Kees Versteegh (Leiden: Brill, 2014), 79–90.
111. Rachid Ridouane, "Tashlhiyt Berber," *Journal of the International Phonetic Association* 44, no. 2 (2014): 216.
112. Kamel Chachoua, *L'islam kabyle (XVIIIe–XXe siècles): religion, État et société en Algérie* (Paris: Maisonneuve et Larose, 2002).
113. Rouighi, *Inventing the Berbers*, 133–91.
114. Kamel Chachoua, "Le piège: Kabyle de langue, Arabe de religion," *Revue des mondes musulmans et de la Méditerranée*, no. 124 (November 2008): 203–18.
115. Chachoua, *L'islam kabyle*, 155.
116. Chachoua, 157–62.

117. Marcelin Beaussier, *Dictionnaire pratique arabe-français*, ed. Mohamed Ben Cheneb, new ed. (Algiers: Maison des livres, 1958), 474.
118. Abū al-Qāsim Muḥammad Hafnāwī, *Kitāb Ta'rīf al-Khalaf bi-Rijāl al-Salaf*, vol. 1 (Algiers: Matba'at Bīyīr Fūntānah al-Sharqīyah, 1906), 41.
119. Ibnou Zakri's signature on the birth certificate can be found at http://anom.archivesnationales.culture.gouv.fr/caomec2/osd.php?territoire=ALGERIE&acte=941995.
120. Mahammed Hadj Sadok, "Ibn Zakrī," in *Encyclopaedia of Islam New Edition Online (EI-2 English)*. In his appraisal of Ibnou Zakri's claim in this entry, Hadj Sadok notes the skepticism of Hafnāwī, who discussed the reputed link and the problems of working between Berber and Arabic languages and family lines, concluding, "In matters of genealogy, people have to be taken at their word." Citing Hafnāwī, *Kitāb Ta'rīf*, 41.
121. Chachoua, *L'islam kabyle*, 162.
122. Joëlle Bahloul, "Noms et prénoms juifs nord-africains," *Terrain: Anthropologie et sciences humaines* 4 (March 1985): 62–69.
123. Karen B. Stern, *Inscribing Devotion and Death: Archeological Evidence for Jewish Populations of North Africa* (Leiden: Brill, 2008), 99–144. See also Haim Zeev Hirschberg, *A History of the Jews in North Africa*, vol. 1: *From Antiquity to the Sixteenth Century*, trans. M. W. Eichelberg, 2nd ed. (Leiden: Brill, 1974), 67–69; and Edwin D. Lawson, "Personal Naming Systems," in *The Oxford Handbook of Names and Naming*, ed. Carole Hough (Oxford: Oxford University Press, 2016), 180. In addition to specialists, lay scholars have written important studies. Along with sources cited specifically elsewhere in this chapter, see Maurice Eisenbeth, *Les juifs d'Afrique du Nord: démographie et onomastique* (Algiers: Imprimerie du Lycée, 1936); Sarah Leibovici, *Chronique des Juifs de Tétouan, 1860–1896* (Paris: Maisonneuve et Larose, 1984), 255–57; Joseph Tolédano, *Une histoire de familles: les noms de famille juifs d'Afrique du Nord des origines à nos jours* (Jerusalem: Ramtol, 1999); Paul Sebag, *Les noms des juifs de Tunisie: origines et significations* (Paris: Harmattan, 2002); and Jacques Taïeb, *Juifs du Maghreb: noms de famille et société* (Paris: Cercle de généalogie juive, 2004).
124. Robert Attal and Joseph Avivi, *Registres matrimoniaux de la communauté juive portugaise de Tunis aux XVIIIe et XIXe siècles* (Jerusalem: Ben-Zvi, 1989), 11–12.
125. David Corcos, "Réflexions sur l'onomastique judéo-nord-africaine," *Folklore Research Center Studies* 1 (1970): 2–3.
126. Eisenbeth, *Juifs de l'Afrique du Nord*, 69.
127. Goitein, *Jews and Arabs*, 131; Goitein, *Mediterranean Society*, vol. 1: *Economic Foundations* (Berkeley: University of California Press, 1967), 357–58; Abraham I. Laredo, *Les Noms des Juifs du Maroc: essai d'onomastique judéo-marocaine* (Madrid: Instituto B. Arias Montano, 1978), 93–96; Aaron Demsky, ed., *Pleasant Are Their Names: Jewish Names in the Sephardic Diaspora* (Bethesda: University Press of Maryland, 2010); Ben-zion C. Kaganoff, *A Dictionary of Jewish Names and Their History* (New York: Schocken, 1977).
128. Laredo, *Noms des Juifs du Maroc*, 93–94.

129. Hirschberg, *History of the Jews in North Africa*, 155–56. For Jews who spoke Berber, a similar process appears, as when the Arabic Yaqūb (Jacob) became 'Akān/'Aknīn, a Judeo-Berber form of the name. Corcos, "Réflexions sur l'onomastique," 4–5.
130. Laredo, *Noms des Juifs du Maroc*, 93. For biographical information on Laredo, see Mitchell Serels, "Laredo, Abraham Isaac," *Encyclopedia of Jews in the Islamic World* (2010).
131. Thus, in late medieval Egypt, S. D. Goitein, *Mediterranean Society*, 2:505, identified many names Jews used that sound quintessentially Muslim, such as Naṣr Allāh, 'Abd al-Karīm, Khaḍir, 'Abd al-'Aziz, and 'Abd al-Wāḥid.
132. Sebag, *Noms des juifs de Tunisie*, 30, 93, 138, 34, 76, and 33.
133. Harvey E. Goldberg, "The Social Context of North African Jewish Patronyms," *Folklore Research Center Studies* 3 (1972): 251.
134. Abraham L. Udovitch and Lucette Valensi, "Communautés juives en pays d'Islam: identité et communication à Djerba," *Annales HSS* 35, nos. 3–4 (May–August 1980): 765.
135. Joshua Schreier, *Arabs of the Jewish Faith: The Civilizing Mission in Colonial Algeria* (New Brunswick, NJ: Rutgers University Press, 2010).
136. Hirschberg, *History of the Jews in North Africa*, 156.
137. Udovitch and Valensi, *The Last Arab Jews*, 28.
138. Laredo, *Noms des Juifs du Maroc*, 96.
139. Bahloul, "Noms et prénoms juifs."
140. Laredo, *Noms des Juifs du Maroc*, 35.
141. Roland Barthes, *S/Z: An Essay*, trans. Richard Miller (New York: Hill and Wang, 1974), 10–11.

3. "Wherever the Flag Flies"

1. Jean-Étienne-Marie Portalis, meeting of 24 November 1801, quoted in *Archives parlementaires*, vol. 2: *du 29 frimaire an IX au 9 frimaire an X* (Paris: Dupont, 1863), 736.
2. Valentin Groebner, *Who Are You? Identification, Deception, and Surveillance in Early Modern Europe*, trans. Mark Kyburz and John Peck (New York: Zone Books, 2007).
3. Jan de Vries, "Population," in *Handbook of European History 1400–1600: Late Middle Ages, Renaissance and Reformation*, vol. 1: *Structures and Assertions*, ed. Thomas A. Brady, Jr., Heiko A. Oberman, and James D. Brady (Leiden: Brill, 1994), 4–9.
4. Gunnar Thorvaldsen, *Censuses and Census Takers: A Global History* (London: Routledge, 2018); Joshua Cole, *The Power of Large Numbers: Population, Politics, and Gender in Nineteenth-Century France* (Ithaca, NY: Cornell University Press, 2000), 49–54; Jacques and Michel Dupâquier, *Histoire de la démographie: la statistique de la population des origines à 1914* (Paris: Perrin, 1985); Nico Randeraad, *States and Statistics in the Nineteenth Century: Europe by Numbers*, trans. Debra Molnar (Manchester, UK: University of Manchester Press, 2010); Kemal H. Karpat, *Ottoman Population 1830–1914: Demographic and Social Characteristics* (Madison: University of Wisconsin Press, 1985); Karl

Ittmann et al., eds., *The Demographics of Empire: The Colonial Order and the Creation of Knowledge* (Athens: Ohio University Press, 2010); Sumit Guha, "The Politics of Identity and Enumeration in India c. 1600–1990," *Comparative Studies in Society and History* 45, no. 1 (2003): 148–67; Bernard S. Cohn, *Colonialism and Its Form of Knowledge: The British in India* (Princeton, NJ: Princeton University Press 1996). On statistics, see Ian Hacking, *The Taming of Chance* (Cambridge: Cambridge University Press, 1990); Stephen M. Stigler, *The History of Statistics: The Measurement of Uncertainty Before 1900* (Cambridge, MA: Harvard University Press, 1986); Theodore M. Porter, *The Rise of Statistical Thinking, 1820–1900* (Princeton, NJ: Princeton University Press, 1986); Tom Crook and Glen O'Hara, *Statistics and the Public Sphere: Numbers and the People in Modern Britain, c. 1800–2000* (London: Routledge, 2011).

5. Jean Bodin, *Six Books of the Commonwealth*, trans. M. J. Tooley (Oxford: Blackwell, 1967), 188; Vincent Denis, "Individual Identity and Identification in Eighteenth-Century France," in *Identification and Registration Practices in Transnational Perspective: People, Papers and Practices*, ed. Ilsen About, James Brown, and Gayle Lonergan (New York: Palgrave Macmillan, 2013), 17–30.
6. Benoît Laplante, "From France to the Church: The Generalization of Parish Registers in the Catholic Countries," *Journal of Family History* 44, no. 1 (2019): 24–51.
7. Previous to this, French kings had exerted increasing control over the parish registers kept by the church, beginning in 1539 when Francis I issued the ordinance of Villers-Cotterêts, which established rules for their registries, including the requirement that they no longer appear in Latin but French, the kingdom's new official language. Dupâquier and Dupâquier, *Histoire de la démographie*, chap. 2; Katie Chenoweth, *The Prosthetic Tongue: Print Technology and the Rise of the French Language* (Philadelphia: University of Pennsylvania Press, 2019), 229–60.
8. *Réimpression de l'ancien Moniteur, seule histoire authentique et inaltérée de la Révolution française*, vol. 12 (Paris: Plon, 1862), 93.
9. *État civil des citoyens, ou Analyse sommaire du décret du 20 septembre 1792, et de celui du 21 janvier dernier, avec des formules des différents actes de naissances, mariages et décès* (Paris: Knapen, 1793).
10. Suzanne Desan, *The Family on Trial in Revolutionary France* (Berkeley: University of California Press, 2004), 51. See also Jennifer Heuer, *The Family and the Nation: Gender and Citizenship in Revolutionary France, 1789–1830* (Ithaca, NY: Cornell University Press, 2005).
11. Gérard Noiriel, "The Identification of the Citizen: The Birth of Republican Civil Status in France," in *Documenting Individual Identity: The Development of State Practices in the Modern World*, ed. Jane Caplan and John Torpey (Princeton, NJ: Princeton University Press, 2001), 30.
12. Pierre Rosanvallon, *Le Sacré du citoyen: Historie du suffrage universel en France* (Paris: Gallimard, 1992). The état civil could also exclude voters, as happened during the 1848 revolution. See Michel Offerlé, "Les noms et le nombre: Individualisation et anonymisation de l'électeur," in *L'écriture du nom propre*, ed. Anne-Marie Christin (Paris: Harmattan, 1998), 253–66.

13. Cole, *Power of Large Numbers*, 49–54; Dupâquier and Dupâquier, *Histoire de la démographie*, 27; Michel Foucault, *Security, Territory, Population: Lectures at the Collège de France, 1977–78*, trans. Graham Burchell (New York: Palgrave, 2007), 12.
14. Cole, *Power of Large Numbers*, 39–40.
15. Louis-Jérôme Gohier, cited in *Réimpression de l'ancien Moniteur*, 12:708–9.
16. Although the Napoleonic Code purported to write the law from scratch, in fact it often meant working out existing legislation and putting right any inconsistencies or problems. Lawmakers carried over the état civil decree of 1792 into the new civil code's second article, promulgated in 1804. Jean-Louis Halpérin, *L'impossible code civil* (Paris: Presses universitaires de France, 1992); Jean-Michel Poughon, *Le code civil*, 2nd ed. (Paris: Presses universitaires de France, 1995).
17. Jacques Godechot, Beatrice F. Hyslop, and David L. Dowd, *The Napoleonic Era in Europe* (New York: Holt, Rinehart and Winston, 1971), 164–66.
18. Jacques Godechot, *La Grande nation: l'expansion révolutionnaire de la France dans le monde de 1789 à 1799*, vol. 1 (Paris: Aubier, 1956), 95.
19. Godechot, 2:422–28.
20. Clément de La Jonquière, *L'Expédition d'Égypt, 1798–1801*, vol. 2 (Paris: Charles-Lavauzelle, s.d.), 587–609; Joseph-Edmond Cattaui, *Histoire des rapports de l'Égypte avec la Sublime Porte (du XVIIIe siècle à 1841)* (Paris: Jouve, 1919), 64–66.
21. Lagét de Podio, *De la juridiction des consuls de France à l'étranger* (Paris: Trouvé, 1826), 185–200.
22. Antoine Pillet, *Recherches sur les droits fondamentaux des États* (Paris: Pedone, 1899), 36.
23. Louis Boullenois, *Traité de la personnalité et de la réalité des lois*, vol. 1 (Paris: Desprez, 1766), 493; Gabriel Baudry-Lacantinerie and Maurice Houques-Fourcade, *Traité théorique et pratique du droit civil: des personnes*, 2nd ed. (Paris: Larose, 1902), 172.
24. N. Gand, *Code des étrangers, ou État civil et politique en France des étrangers de tout rang et de toute condition, leurs droits et leurs devoirs* (Paris: chez l'auteur, 1853), 227. On the actual procedures followed by the diplomatic agents to "re-dress" foreign acts for use in France, see Baudry-Lacantinerie and Houques-Fourcade, *Traité théorique et pratique*, 727–35. An example of a transcribed marriage act from Prussia is given in Hippolyte Hallez d'Arros, *Nouveau manuel de l'officier de l'état civil et du secrétaire de mairie* (Metz: Alcan, 1854), 100.
25. Baudry-Lacantinerie and Houques-Fourcade, *Traité théorique et pratique*, 148, 149; Theodore Dwight Woolsey, *Introduction to the Study of International Law* (Boston: Munroe, 1860), 174.
26. Baudry-Lacantinerie and Houques-Fourcade, *Traité théorique et pratique*, 147.
27. Francis Taylor Piggott, *Exterritoriality: The Law Relating to Consular Jurisdiction and to Residence in Oriental Countries* (London: Clowes, 1892), 57. Also Baudry-Lacantinerie and Houques-Fourcade, *Traité théorique et pratique*, 144–48.
28. *Procès-verbaux du Conseil d'État: contentant la discussion du Code Napoléon*, vol. 1, 2nd ed. (Paris: Imprimerie impériale, 1808), 173.
29. Maia Pal, *Jurisdictional Accumulation: An Early Modern History of Law, Empires, and Capital* (Cambridge: Cambridge University Press, 2021), 41–43.

30. Edgar Lœning, "L'administration du Gouvernement-Général de l'Alsace durant la guerre de 1870–1871," *Revue de droit international* 5 (1873): 93.
31. Isabel V. Hull, *A Scrap of Paper: Breaking and Making International Law During the Great War* (Ithaca, NY: Cornell University Press, 2014), chap. 4, esp. 104–11.
32. Faustin Hélie, *Traité de l'instruction criminelle*, vol. 2; *De l'action publique et de l'action civile*, 2nd ed. (Paris; Plon, 1866), 84.
33. The concept of military occupation emerged as one way to deal with this situation. Generally speaking, it framed the occupation of a defeated state's territory as temporary. Having no right to make claims to sovereignty, the occupying force exercised only a state-like role in occupied territories, functioning as a trustee. This was eventually ratified in the Hague Regulations of 1907 (article 43) in terms of the occupier's duty to ensure public order, working within the framework of existing laws. Colonial protectorates drew from similar principles toward different ends. Mary Dewhurst Lewis, *Divided Rule: Sovereignty and Empire in French Tunisia, 1881–1938* (Berkeley: University of California Press, 2014). On the history of the concept of military occupation, see Eyal Benvenisti, *The International Law of Occupation*, 2nd ed. (Oxford: Oxford University Press, 2012), 20–42; Peter M. R. Stirk, *A History of Military Occupation from 1792 to 1914* (Edinburgh: Edinburgh University Press, 2016); and Peter M. R. Stirk, *The Politics of Military Occupation* (Edinburgh: Edinburgh University Press, 2009). Armed resistance to invaders is addressed in Karma Nabulsi, *The Traditions of War: Occupations, Resistance, and the Law* (Oxford: Oxford University Press, 1999), 177–240.
34. Honoré Perouse, *Napoléon Ier et les lois civiles du Consulat et de l'Empire* (Paris: Durand, 1866), 84. See also Jean-François Niort, *Homo civilis: contribution à l'histoire du Code civil français; 1804-1965*, vol. 1 (Aix-en-Provence: Presses universitaires d'Aix-Marseille, 2004), 209–340.
35. Gand, *Code des étrangers*, 238–49. See also the analytic annotations to arts. 47 and 48 of the civil code in Jean Baptiste Joseph Pailliet, *Manuel de droit française*, 6th ed. (Paris: Desoer, 1824), 21; Jean Anatole Garnier Dubourgneuf, *Nouveau manuel des officiers de l'état-civil* (Paris: Kleffer and Gambard, 1825), 55–56; Auguste François Teulet, *Dictionnaire des codes français* (Paris: Closel Frères and Rostaing, 1836), 500.
36. Article 48 states: "All acts of the état civil for French men and women living abroad will be valid if it was received, conforming to French laws, by diplomatic agents or consuls." The language here arguably left unresolved whether French diplomats are *performing* the acts themselves, an active intervention on local prerogatives, or passively *recording* acts that have taken place through local authorities, i.e., translating them and passing them on to the Ministry of Foreign Affairs in Paris. Commentators in the 1830s parsed the question of sovereignty by stressing that the diplomats had full rights as officers of the état civil only when all parties involved were French. Jacques Marie Boileux, *Commentaire sur le Code civil: contenant l'explication de chaque article séparément*, vol. 1, 6th ed. (Paris: Videcoq, 1851), 149. *Code civil des Français* (1803), art. 48, https://criminocorpus.org/fr/reperes/legislation/civil/premier/ii/i/1884-07-27/.

37. *Code civil des Français* (1803), art. 89, https://criminocorpus.org/fr/reperes/legislation/civil/premier/ii/v/1804-03-31/.
38. Hélie, *Traité de l'instruction criminelle*, 2:81–83; Joseph-Louis-Elzéar Ortolan, *Éléments de droit pénal, pénalité, juridictions, procédure* (Paris: Plon, 1855), 383–92.
39. Lœning, "Administration du Gouvernement-Général de l'Alsace," 93. To place this opinion in its context and debates about the military conquest of sovereignty, see Stirk, *History of Military Occupation*, 13.
40. François Piétri, *Étude critique sur la fiction d'exterritorialité* (Paris: Rousseau, 1895), 377–78.
41. François Laurent, *Principes de droit civil*, vol. 2 (Paris: A. Durand and Pedone-Lauriel, 1870), 22.
42. Adolf Arndt, "Strafgerichtsbarkeit im Kriege über Ausländer, insbesondere Kriegsgefangene," *Zeitschrift für Politik* no. 8 (1915): 514.
43. For the annexation of Belgium to France in 1795, see Edward James Kolla, *Sovereignty, International Law, and the French Revolution* (Cambridge: Cambridge University Press, 2017), 121–59. On Germany's annexation of French territory in 1871, see Sharon Korman, *The Right of Conquest: The Acquisition of Territory by Force in International Law and Practice* (Oxford: Oxford University Press, 1996), 91–93.
44. Quoted in David A. Bell, *The First Total War: Napoleon's Europe and the Birth of Warfare as We Know It* (Boston: Houghton Mifflin, 2007), 84. See also Sophie Wahnich, "Declaring Peace on Earth," in *France in the World: A New Global History*, ed. Patrick Boucheron, trans. Teresa Lavender Fagan et al. (New York: Other Press, 2019), 441–47; Martti Koskenniemi, *To the Uttermost Parts of the Earth: Legal Imagination and International Power, 1300–1870* (Cambridge: Cambridge University Press, 2021) 463–75.
45. Bell, *First Total War*, 84–119. See also Marc Belissa, "War and Diplomacy (1792–95)," in *The Oxford Handbook of the French Revolution*, ed. David Andress (Oxford: Oxford University Press, 2015), 418–35; Alan Forrest, *The Legacy of the French Revolutionary Wars: The Nation-in-Arms in French Republican Memory* (Cambridge: Cambridge University Press, 2009). Jacques Godechot sees the declaration in terms of short-term political maneuvering in *Grande nation*, 1:70–72. However, this moment should also be considered in relation to larger debates about war in the modern era, such as Immanuel Kant's notion of "perpetual peace" and his shift from an international order based on the balance of power to the order of law. For a postcolonial reading of the question, see Talal Asad, *On Suicide Bombing* (New York: Columbia University Press, 2007). The French invasion of Algeria and international law are addressed in Dzavid Dzanic, "The Civilizing Sea: The Ideological Origins of the French Mediterranean Empire, 1789–1870" (PhD diss., Harvard University, 2016). Contrasting understandings of the rupture between emancipatory principles and imperialism are given in Kolla, *Sovereignty*, 121–59; and Hervé Leuwers, "Révolution et guerre de conquête: Les origines d'une nouvelle raison d'État (1789–1795)," *Revue du Nord* 75, no. 299 (January–March, 1993): 21–40. On the emancipatory model in the conquest of Egypt, see Henry Laurens, *Les Origines intellectuelles de l'expédition d'Égypte: l'orientalisme islamisant en France, 1698–1798* (Istanbul: Isis, Institut français

d'études anatoliennes, 1987); Henry Laurens et al., *L'Expédition d'Égypte: 1798–1801* (Paris: Seuil, 1989); and Juan Cole, *Napoleon's Egypt: Invading the Middle East* (New York: St. Martin's Griffin, 2008).

46. Gillo Pontecorvo brilliantly plays up the sovereign powers imbedded in performing vital events in the FLN-officiated wedding scene in *The Battle of Algiers* (1966). See Matthew Evangelista, *Nationalism, and War: Conflict on the Movie Screen* (Cambridge: Cambridge University Press, 2011), 39–40.
47. Maxime du Camps, "L'état civil à Paris," *Revue des deux mondes* 10 (March–April 1874): 371; Garnier Dubourgneuf, *Nouveau manuel*, 16, 47–48; Ministre des Affaires Étrangères, "État civil consulaire," n.d., https://www.diplomatie.gouv.fr/fr/archives-diplomatiques/s-orienter-dans-les-fonds-et-collections/etat-civil-et-genealogie/article/actes-d-etat-civil-et-autres-archives-diplomatiques-et-consulaires.
48. Records found in ANOM 1aa70 and ANOM 1aa71 (both microfilmed in ANOM 45miom23).
49. ANOM 1aa70.
50. Joshua M. White, *Piracy and Law in the Ottoman Mediterranean* (Stanford, CA: Stanford University Press, 2017). See also Gillian Weiss, *Captives and Corsairs: France and Slavery in the Early Modern Mediterranean* (Stanford, CA: Stanford University Press, 2011); Daniel Panzac, *Barbary Corsairs: The End of a Legend 1800–1820*, trans. Victoria Hobson and John E. Hawkes (Leiden: Brill, 2005); Robert C. Davis, *Christian Slaves, Muslim Masters: White Slavery in the Mediterranean, the Barbary Coast, and Italy, 1500–1800* (New York: Palgrave Macmillan, 2003). The experiences of captivity are covered in Nabil Matar, *Mediterranean Captivity Through Arab Eyes, 1517–1798* (Leiden: Brill, 2021); Nabil Matar, *British Captives from the Mediterranean to the Atlantic, 1563–1760* (Leiden: Brill, 2014); Nabil Matar, *Turks, Moors, and Englishmen in the Age of Discovery* (New York: Columbia University Press, 1999); María Antonia Garcés, *Cervantes in Algiers: A Captive's Tale* (Nashville, TN: Vanderbilt University Press, 2002); and Bartolomé Bennassar and Lucile Bennassar, *Les Chrétiens d'Allah: l'histoire extraordinaire des renégats, XVIe et XVIIe siècles* (Paris: Perrin, 1989).
51. ANOM 1aa70.
52. Weiss, *Captives and Corsairs*, 110–16.
53. ANOM 1aa70.
54. Peter Sahlins, *Boundaries: The Making of France and Spain in the Pyrenees* (Berkeley: University of California Press, 1989); Charles Maier, *Once Within Borders: Territories of Power, Wealth, and Belonging Since 1500* (Cambridge, MA: Harvard University Press, 2016). Ottoman civil identification and legal subjectivity is covered in Vanessa Guéno, "S'identifier à l'aube de l'état civil (*nufûs*): les justiciables devant le tribunal civil de Homs (Syrie centrale) à la fin du XIXe siècle," *Revue des mondes musulmans et de la Méditerranée* 127 (July 2010): 193–211. For Egypt, see Khaled Fahmy, *In Quest of Justice: Islamic Law and Forensic Medicine in Modern Egypt* (Berkeley: University of California Press, 2018), 97–103.
55. Among the large field of studies on Ottoman law and the religious communities generally known as the *millet* system, see Heather J. Sharkey, *A History of Muslims,*

Christians, and Jews in the Middle East (Cambridge: Cambridge University Press, 2017), 81–88; and Karen Barkey, "Aspects of Legal Pluralism in the Ottoman Empire," in *Legal Pluralism and Empires, 1500–1850*, ed. Lauren Benton and Richard J. Ross (New York: New York University Press, 2013), 83–107. The territoriality of Islamic law is discussed in Khaled Abou El Fadl, "Islamic Law and Muslim Minorities: The Juristic Discourse on Muslim Minorities from the Second/Eighth to the Eleventh/Seventeenth Centuries," *Islamic Law and Society* 1, no. 2 (1994): 141–87. Samy Ayoub uses Hanafi sources to critically reevaluate Abou El Fadl's findings in "Territorial Jurisprudence, *Ikhtilaf al-Darayn*: Political Boundaries and Legal Jurisdiction," *Contemporary Islamic Studies* 2 (2012): 2012:2, http://dx.doi.org/10.5339/cis.2012.2. See also Samy A. Ayoub, *Law, Empire, and the Sultan: Ottoman Imperial Authority and Late Hanafi Jurisprudence* (Oxford: Oxford University Press, 2020).

56. Will Hanley suggests helpfully that the status accorded to Europeans in the capitulations themselves needs to be seen not in terms of their privileges but as a form of legal decentralization. Will Hanley, *Identifying with Nationality: Europeans, Ottomans and Egyptians in Alexandria* (New York: Columbia University Press, 2017), 11–12. On the Ottoman nationality law of 1869, see Will Hanley, "What Ottoman Nationality Was and Was Not," *Journal of the Ottoman and Turkish Studies Association* 3, no. 2 (2016): 277–98.
57. Jessica M. Marglin, *Across Legal Lines: Jews and Muslims in Modern Morocco* (New Haven, CT: Yale University Press, 2016), 48. See also Etty Terem's analysis of a Moroccan fatwa dealing with a Muslims seeking French protection (*ḥimāya* in Arabic). Etty Terem, *Old Texts, New Practices: Islamic Reform in Modern Morocco* (Stanford, CA: Stanford University Press, 2014), 76–85.
58. My understanding here is informed by Maurits H. Van den Boogert's work, which argues that viewed from the Ottoman perspective, the *ahdnames* ("capitulations," or commercial charters) and *beraths* (personal legal exemptions granted to foreign, non-Muslim residents) appear as integral to Ottoman law, not something imposed on it from the outside. Maurits H. van den Boogert, *The Capitulations and the Ottoman Legal System: Qadis, Consuls, and Beraths in the 18th Century* (Leiden: Brill, 2005), chap. 2. The capitulations and sovereignty problem later played itself out in the Hijaz and interimperial rivalries, or "legal imperialism," as studied by Michael Christopher Low, *Imperial Mecca: Ottoman Arabia and the Indian Ocean Hajj* (New York: Columbia University Press, 2020), 86–90.
59. For these crises in preprotectorate Tunisia, see Julia A. Clancy-Smith, *Mediterraneans: North Africa and Europe in an Age of Migration, c. 1800–1900* (Berkeley: University of California Press, 2011), 199–246; and in Egypt, Hanley, *Identifying with Nationality.*
60. Dzanic, "Civilizing Sea," 148–50.
61. Alexandre Deval went to Algiers as French consul in 1830. He was the nephew of Pierre Deval, the former consul, who had died in 1829.
62. On the complex history of treatymaking and imperialism, see Saliha Belmessous, "The Paradox of an Empire by Treaty," in *Empire by Treaty: Negotiating European*

Expansion, 1600–1900, ed. Saliha Belmessous (Oxford: Oxford University Press, 2015), 1–18.

63. David Todd, *A Velvet Empire: French Informal Imperialism in the Nineteenth Century* (Princeton, NJ: Princeton University Press, 2021), 95.
64. Erik De Lange, "The Congress System and the French Invasion of Algiers, 1827–1830," *Historical Journal* 64, no. 4 (2021): 953–55.
65. Edgard Le Marchand, *L'Europe et la conquête d'Alger* (Paris: Perrin, 1913), 183. The "extermination" in question here is that of the Algerian deylik, i.e., the liquidation of the existing Ottoman-Algerian state. Charles X responded to this opposition by mobilizing international law and its just war rhetoric. Benjamin Claude Brower, "Just War and Jihad in the French Conquest of Algeria," in *Just Wars, Holy Wars, and Jihads: Christian, Jewish, and Muslim Encounters and Exchanges*, ed. Sohail H. Hashmi (Oxford: Oxford University Press, 2012), 221–40.
66. Ozan Ozavci, *Dangerous Gifts: Imperialism, Security, and Civil Wars in the Levant, 1798-1864* (Oxford: Oxford University Press, 2021), 105–31; De Lange, "Congress System," 960.
67. Tal Shuval, "The Ottoman Algerian Elite and Its Ideology," *International Journal of Middle East Studies* 32, no. 3 (August 2000): 323–44.
68. Mustafa Reşid Bey, quoted in Ozavci, *Dangerous Gifts*, 189.
69. De Lange, "Congress System," 955–61, discusses a little-known, failed French effort to organize a European conference in May 1830 to decide the Algerian question.
70. Jennifer E. Sessions, *By Sword and Plow: France and the Conquest of Algeria* (Ithaca, NY: Cornell University Press, 2011).
71. Émile Larcher and Georges Rectenwald, *Traité élémentaire de législation algérienne*, vol. 2: *La justice, les personnes*, 3rd ed. (Paris: Rousseau, 1923), 626.
72. The power to inflict capital punishment was first reserved for the commander of the French army by a decree dated 15 October 1830. Ministère de la Guerre, *Collections des actes du gouvernement depuis l'occupation d'Alger jusqu'au 1e octobre 1834* (Paris: Imprimerie royale, 1843), 15. For the royal decree of 10 August 1834, arts. 44 and 45, see Charles-Louis Pinson de Ménerville, *Dictionnaire de la législation algérienne: manuel raisonné des lois, ordonnances, décrets, décisions et arrêtés* (Algiers: Philippe, 1853), 383.
73. Decree of 7 December 1830, in Pinson de Ménerville, *Dictionnaire de la législation algérienne*, 257–58. It took effect on 1 January 1831.
74. Publication of these acts fulfilled article 45 of the civil code, which stated the état civil must function as a public archive to assure transparency in legal relations between individuals. The openness of the état civil was modified by a subsequent law pertaining to birth records to protect from prejudice those born to fathers who refused to acknowledge their paternity. Ambroise Colin and Henri Capitant, *Cours élémentaire de droit civil français*, vol. 1 (Paris: Dalloz, 1914), 379–80, 388–89.
75. *Moniteur algérien*, 10 April 1832. In all, four marriages appeared in this issue. Several of them, including Grégoire and Perez, were reprinted in the next week's issue of the *Moniteur* in an apparent error.

76. Imperial Decree of 23 May–7 July 1853, in Pinson de Ménerville, *Dictionnaire de la législation algérienne*, 258.
77. Marriage and family practices of European settlers in this early era are analyzed in Guy Brunet and Kamel Kateb, *L'Algérie des Européens au XIXe: naissance d'une population et transformation d'une société* (Bern: Lang, 2018), 79–104.
78. Larcher and Rectenwald, *Traité élémentaire*, 626.
79. Henri Bénet, *L'État civil en Algérie: Traité théorique et pratique de la constitution de l'état civil des Indigènes Algériens* (Algiers: Minerva, 1937), 48–58.
80. No. 198, 10 October 1833, Commune d'Alger, 1833 Naissances, Tome 2, http://anom.archivesnationales.culture.gouv.fr/caomec2/osd.php?territoire=ALGERIE&registre=35291.
81. No. 188, 1 October 1833, Commune d'Alger, 1833 Naissances. Tome 2, http://anom.archivesnationales.culture.gouv.fr/caomec2/osd.php?territoire=ALGERIE&registre=35291
82. No. 20, 26 September 1835. Mariages (Européens) Alger, 1835, http://anom.archivesnationales.culture.gouv.fr/caomec2/osd.php?territoire=ALGERIE&registre=5. The text of the code civil concerning the rights and duties of marriage can be found at https://criminocorpus.org/fr/reperes/legislation/civil/premier/v/vi/1804-03-31/.
83. No. 4, 28 January 1835. Mariages (Européens) Alger, 1835, http://anom.archives-nationales.culture.gouv.fr/caomec2/osd.php?territoire=ALGERIE&registre=5.
84. The importance these French-drawn records for Muslims seeking divorce is stressed by Sarah Ghabrial, "The Traumas and Truths of the Body: Medical Evidence and Divorce in Colonial Algerian Courts, 1870–1930," *Journal of Middle East Women's Studies* 11, no. 3 (November 2015): 288.
85. Jessica Marglin proposes that historians seek a fluid and contextualized understanding of legal categories such as nationality in the Mediterranean at this time, arguing, for example, that a person can become more or less French depending on place, time, and context. This confirms recent studies, especially that of Noureddine Amara for Algeria, as well as Mary Lewis and M'hamed Oualdi, respectively, for colonial and precolonial Tunisia. This work is an important corrective to previous understandings, such as those of Rogers Brubaker and Patrick Weil, which rely on fixed understandings of nationality. I would add that the regime of civil rights itself, ensured in the French civil code, operated in a different modality. Unlike national belonging, which can be plotted on a spectrum, the civil code granted access to rights with a sort of on-off switch, or opening and closing doors, depending on how it calculated the exact status of the legal subject at a given moment in that person's life. The doors to some modalities of rights closed at certain moments (such as a woman's property rights upon her marriage), and others opened at different moments (such as the same woman's property rights when she was widowed). The effect, then, is not a fading in and out of the legal subject of national belonging, but rather a legal subject of civil rights who has to navigate a regime of rights that was effectively an internally divided funhouse equipped with

trapdoors, shifting floors, and distorting mirrors. Jessica M. Marglin, "Extraterritoriality and Legal Belonging in the Nineteenth-Century Mediterranean," *Law and History Review* 39, no. 4 (November 2021): 679–706, esp. 685–89; Noureddine Amara, "Faire la France en Algérie: émigration algérienne, mésusages du nom et conflits de nationalités dans le monde, de la chute d'Alger aux années 1930" (PhD diss., Université de Paris I, Sorbonne, 2019); Lewis, *Divided Rule*; M'hamed Oualdi, *A Slave Between Empires: A Transimperial History of North Africa* (New York: Columbia University Press, 2019); Rogers Brubaker, *Citizenship and Nationhood in France and Germany* (Cambridge, MA: Harvard University Press, 1992); Patrick Weil, *How to Be French: Nationality in the Making Since 1789*, trans. Catherine Porter (Durham, NC: Duke University Press, 2008).

86. Marie Françoise Nassero, born in Egypt, married Abdelmelir Abdelmicia in March 1820, in Archives municipales de Marseille (AMM) 1e403. "Laurent Abdela" born in Marseille to "Ahmet" on 22 December 1823, in AMM 3e35. For more on this community, see Ian Coller, *Arab France: Islam and the Making of Modern Europe, 1798–1831* (Berkeley: University of California Press, 2011), 130–31.
87. Alain Messaoudi, "Orientaux orientalistes: les Pharaon, interprètes du sud au service du nord," in *Sud-Nord; cultures coloniales en France (XIX-XX siècles)*, ed. Colette Zytnicki and Chantal Bordes-Benayoun (Toulouse: Privat, 2004), 243–55.
88. Alain Messaoudi, "Pharaon," in *Dictionnaire des orientalistes de langue française*, ed. François Pouillon (Paris: IISMM, Karthala, 2008), 758–60. The Algiers état civil gives a slightly different spelling of her name as "Théreze Mélassi Eyries."
89. No. 78, 18 April 1833, Commune d'Alger, 1833 Naissances. Tome 1, 1http://anom.archivesnationales.culture.gouv.fr/caomec2/osd.php?territoire=ALGERIE&registre=35291.
90. The Dauzat name dictionary originally speculated that "Chéhiré" is a likely alteration of French terms for ruffled hair, *chef huré* or *tête hérissée*. Albert Dauzat, *Dictionnaire étymologique des noms de famille et prénoms de France* (Paris: Larousse, 1951), 121, 334; Marie-Thérèse Morlet, *Dictionnaire étymologique des noms de famille* (Paris: Perrin, 1991), reviewed in *Nouvelle revue d'onomastique*, nos. 19–20 (1992): 236.
91. Jeanne Glennon LeComte, "The Pharaon Family," Levantine Heritage, http://www.levantineheritage.com/testi88.htm.
92. Qunsṭanṭīn Bāshā, *Tārīkh Usrat Al Fir'awn bi-Uṣūlihā wa-Furū'ihā* (Harissa, Lebanon: Maṭba'at al-Qiddīs Būlus, 1932), 120–23.
93. For the high proportion of Spanish-born women among marriages in Algeria in the 1830s, see Brunet and Kateb, *Algérie des Européens*, 218.
94. Thon, Louise Elisabeth Africa, born 27 November 1830, daughter of Joseph Thon and Maria Rosario Borgos. ANOM 1aa70 (45miom23).
95. Louise's father automatically conferred his nationality on the child by French law, overwriting that of the mother.
96. Thon, Louise Elisabeth, 1 February 1832, no. 17. Commune d'Alger, registres européens naissance, décès, mariages, http://anom.archivesnationales.culture.gouv.fr/caomec2/osd.php?territoire=ALGERIE&acte=1207316.

97. Article 11 of the Napoleonic Code stated: "The foreigner in France will enjoy the same civil rights that are accorded to the French by treaties of the state the foreigner belongs to." https://criminocorpus.org/fr/reperes/legislation/civil/premier/i/1804-03-31/.
98. Amara, "Faire la France en Algérie."
99. Historians are only beginning to fully calculate the impact of non-European law on colonial and international law. Preliminary research suggests the need to more fully account for the influence of Ottoman law and institutions on French colonial law in places like Algeria. See Saliha Belmessous's review of Jennifer Pitts, *Boundaries of the International* (2018) in the *American Historical Review* 125, no. 1 (February 2020): 195–96.
100. Filus, Isaac, 11 February 1834, no. 24. Commune d'Alger, registres européens naissance, http://anom.archivesnationales.culture.gouv.fr/caomec2/osd.php?territoire=ALGERIE&acte =1207757.
101. Alger, Naissances 1838, http://anom.archivesnationales.culture.gouv.fr/caomec2/osd.php?territoire=ALGERIE&registre=94.
102. Gouvernement Général de l'Algérie, *Tableau de la situation des établissements françaises dans l'Algérie* (Paris: Imprimerie Royale, 1838), 300. About 30,000 Jews lived in Algeria at the time, with about 80 percent of them in the major cities. Brunet and Kateb, *Algérie des Européens*, 34–37.
103. Isabelle Grangaud, "Prouver par l'écriture: propriétaires algérois, conquérants français et historiens ottomanistes," *Genèse* 1, no. 74 (2009): 25–45; François Dumasy, "À qui appartient Alger? Normes d'appartenance et conflits d'appropriation à Alger au début de la présence française," in *Appartenance locale et propriété au nord et au sud de la Méditerranée*, ed. Sami Bargaoui, Simona Cerutti, and Isabelle Grangaud (Aix-en-Provence: Institut de recherches et d'études sur les mondes arabes et musulmans, 2015), https://doi.org/10.4000/books.iremam.3396; François Dumasy, "Propriété foncière, libéralisme économique et gouvernement colonial: Alger, 1830–1840," *Revue d'histoire modern et contemporaine* 60, no. 2 (2016): 40–61. See also Robert Parks, "Local-National Relations and the Politics of Property Rights in Algeria and Tunisia" (PhD diss., University of Texas at Austin, 2011); Jean-Louis Autin, "La législation foncière en Algérie de 1830 à 1870, ou le triomphe de la raison juridique colonial," *Le procès* 18 (1987): 85–97; Jean-Philippe Bras, "L'imperfection de la propriété indigène, lieu commun de la doctrine juridique coloniale en Afrique du Nord," in *Appartenance locale et propriété*; Didier Guignard, "Les inventeurs de la tradition 'melk' et 'arch' en Algérie," in *Les acteurs des transformations foncières autour de la Méditerranée au XIXe siècle*, ed. Didier Guignard and Vanessa Guéno (Paris: Karthala, MMSH, IREMAM, 2013), 49–93.
104. Brenna Bhandar, *Colonial Lives of Property: Law, Land and Racial Regimes of Property* (Durham, NC: Duke University Press, 2018), 77–114.
105. Joshua Schreier, *Arabs of the Jewish Faith: The Civilizing Mission in Colonial Algeria* (New Brunswick, NJ: Rutgers University Press, 2010).

106. The marriage practices of Algerian Jews are analyzed in Brunet and Kateb, *Algérie des Européens*, 309–22.
107. No. 16 Registre des actes de mariages, ville de Alger, 1836, http://anom.archives-nationales.culture.gouv.fr/caomec2/osd.php?territoire=ALGERIE&acte=27389.
108. Decree of 10 August 1834, art. 43, in Ministère de la Guerre, *Bulletin official des actes du gouvernement*, vol. 1: *1er octobre 1834 jusqu'au 1er janvier 1839* (Paris: Imprimerie royale, 1843), 12.
109. Judith Surkis, *Sex, Law, and Sovereignty in French Algeria, 1830-1930* (Ithaca, NY: Cornell University Press, 2019), 75–82. See also Casimir Frégier, *Les Juifs algériens: leur passé, leur présent, leur avenir juridique* (Paris: Lévy, 1865), 123–74, divorce at 138; Bénet, *État civil en Algérie*, 59–71.
110. Schreier, *Arabs of the Jewish Faith*, 153–63; Sara Verskin, *Barren Women: Religion and Medicine in the Medieval Middle East* (Berlin: De Gruyter, 2020), 96–100.
111. At the time of my research (2019–2022), only the digitized état civil records were available to me, as travel to Algeria for foreigners became difficult and then near impossible because of the Hirak movement and Covid-19 closures. These records, scanned from microfilms copies made between 1967 and 1972 in Algeria, where the original registers remain, do not officially contain the records of Algerian Muslims. However, these acts were originally recorded in the same registers as Europeans, meaning that there was no practical way for the microfilming teams to exclude them. See note on the digitized database of état civil records consulted for this chapter on 20 August 2022 at http://anom.archivesnationales.culture.gouv.fr/caomec2/recherche.php?territoire=ALGERIE.
112. Jacques Budin, *La région de Annaba (Bône): colonisation et résistance, 1832-1914*, 2 vols. (Saint-Denis: Bouchène, 2020).
113. The birth records for this period are compiled in État Civil, Table annuelle des naissances, ville de Bône, 1832–1839, http://anom.archivesnationales.culture.gouv.fr/caomec2/resultats.php?territoire=ALGERIE&commune=BONE&nom=&prenom=&typeacte=TA_NA&annee=&debut=&fin=&vue=&x=30&y=16.
114. Fatma no. 27, État Civil, Registre des naissance de l'année 1836, Bône, http://anom.archivesnationales.culture.gouv.fr/caomec2/osd.php?territoire=ALGERIE&registre=5650.
115. Registre des actes de décès, ville de Bône, 1833, http://anom.archivesnationales.culture.gouv.fr/caomec2/osd.php?territoire=ALGERIE&registre=5810.
116. No. 17 and no. 182 in Registre des actes de décès, ville de Bône, 1834, http://anom.archivesnationales.culture.gouv.fr/caomec2/osd.php?territoire=ALGERIE&registre=5811.
117. Mabroka, no. 23, 6 March 1834, Registre des actes de décès, ville de Bône, 1834, http://anom.archivesnationales.culture.gouv.fr/caomec2/osd.php?territoire=ALGERIE&registre=5811
118. Yacine Daddi Addoun, "L'Abolition de l'esclavage en Algérie, 1816–1871" (PhD diss., York University, 2010); Benjamin Claude Brower *A Desert Named Peace: The Violence*

of France's Empire in the Algerian Sahara, 1844–1902 (New York: Columbia University Press, 2009), 141–96.

119. Bénet, *État civil en Algérie*, 74. See also the assessment in Larcher and Rectenwald, *Traité élémentaire*, 2:553.
120. Mary Lewis, *Divided Rule*, 73, reports on French plans in the 1880s to offer protection status to people living in the Touat oases in the Algerian Sahara as a means to shore up France's claims to these strategic sites vis-à-vis Morocco.
121. Among the many texts on biopolitics, one of the most useful for the purposes of this book remains Michel Foucault's lectures, especially his unpacking of non-juridical conceptualization of sovereignty, law, and freedom in Michel Foucault, *The Birth of Biopolitics: Lectures at the Collège de France, 1978–79*, ed. Michel Senellart, trans. Graham Burchell (New York: Palgrave Macmillan, 2008). However, historian Achille Mbembe's concept of "necropolitics" informs my thinking in this particular section. Mbembe rereads Foucault's biopolitics to account for colonialism, wherein death, not life, is the primary modality of power. Achille Mbembe, *Necropolitics*, trans. Steve Corcoran (Durham, NC: Duke University Press, 2019).
122. Charvillhac, *Guide de l'officier de l'état civil*, 14–16.
123. Jean-Christian-Marc Boudin, *Histoire statistique de la colonisation et de la population en Algérie* (Paris: Baillière, 1853), 29; Kamel Kateb, *Européens, "Indigènes" et Juifs en Algérie, 1830–1962: représentations et réalités des populations* (Paris: Institut national d'études démographiques, 2001), 29; Matthieu Loitron, "Quelle politique démographique pour l'Algérie coloniale?," in *L'Invention des populations: biologie, idéologie et politique*, ed. Hervé Le Bras and Sandrine Bertaux (Paris: Odile Jacob, 2000), 177–200.
124. Jacques Leonard, "Médecine et colonisation en Algérie au XIXe siècle," *Annales de Bretagne et des pays de l'Ouest* 84, no. 2 (1977): 487–88.
125. See the 1847 communication of Dr. Boudin to the French parlement in Léonard, "Médicine et colonisation," 487. The history of health in colonial Algeria is covered in William Gallois, *The Administration of Sickness: Medicine and Ethics in Nineteenth-Century Algeria* (Basingstoke, UK: Palgrave Macmillan, 2008); Claire Fredj, "L'hôpital militaire et l'accommodation à l'occupation en Algérie (années 1830–années 1850)," in *Le temps des hommes doubles*, ed. Jean-François Chanet, Annie Crépin, and Christian Windler (Rennes: Presses universitaires de Rennes, 2013), 177–94; and Claire Fredj, "Soigner une colonie naissante: les médecins de l'armée d'Afrique, les fièvres et la quinine, 1830–1870," *Mouvement social* 257, no. 1 (2017): 21–45. On the medical field's role in the development of racial thinking, see Patricia M. E. Lorcin, "Imperialism, Colonial Identity, and Race in Algeria, 1830–1870: The Role of the French Medical Corps," *Isis* 90, no. 4 (December 1999): 653–79; Charlotte Ann Chopin, "Embodying 'the New White Race': Colonial Doctors and Settler Society in Algeria, 1878–1911," *Social History of Medicine* 29, no. 1 (February 2016): 1–20.

126. Margaret Cook Anderson, *Regeneration Through Empire: French Pronatalists and Colonial Settlement in the Third Republic* (Lincoln: University of Nebraska Press, 2015).
127. General Duvivier cited in Jean-Joseph-Maximilien Lasnaveres, *De l'impossibilité de fonder des colonies européennes en Algérie* (Paris: Thunot, 1866), 15.
128. Boudin's work was cited in the United States and served as reference for Robert Knox's infamous racist ideas, indicating colonial Algeria's important role in the development of modern European racism. Robert Knox, *The Races of Men: A Fragment* (Philadelphia: Lea and Blanchard, 1850), 199–207.
129. Boudin, *Histoire statistique*, 17.
130. C. Kehl, "L'État civil des indigènes en Algérie," *Bulletin trimestriel de la Société de géographie et d'archéologie d'Oran* 52 (March 1931): 176.
131. Gouvernement Général de l'Algérie, *Tableau de la situation* (1838), 299. On the limits of the census in France, Dupâquier, *Histoire de la démographie*, 27; and Algeria Kamel Kateb, *Européens, "Indigènes" et Juifs*, 16–19, 97–103. On the use of état civil as a demographic tool in Algeria, see Sarah Ghabrial, "*Le 'fiqh francisé'*? Muslim Personal Status Law Reform and Women's Litigation in Colonial Algeria (1870–1930)" (PhD diss., McGill University, 2014), 97–103.
132. Boudin, *Histoire statistique*, 22.
133. A.-E. Victor Martin and L.-E. Foley, *Histoire statistique de la colonisation algérienne au point de vue du peuplement et de l'hygiène* (Paris: Germer-Baillière, 1851), 316.
134. Boudin, *Histoire statistique*, 21. On auto-genocide, see Patrick Brantlinger, *Dark Vanishings: Discourse on the Extinction of Primitive Races, 1800–1930* (Ithaca, NY: Cornell University Press, 1993).
135. Émile Bertherand, *Médecine et hygiène des Arabes: études sur l'exercice de la médecine et de la chirurgie chez les musulmans de l'Algérie* (Paris: Baillière, 1855), 217.
136. Eugène Bodichon, *Études sur l'Algérie et l'Afrique* (Algiers: self-pub., 1847), 128.
137. William Gallois, "The Genocidal French Conquest of Algeria, 1830–1847," in *The Cambridge World History of Genocide*. Vol. 2: *Genocide in the Indigenous, Early Modern and Imperial Worlds, from c.1535 to World War One*, ed. Ned Blackhawk et al. (Cambridge: Cambridge University Press, 2023), 3613–82; Benjamin Claude Brower, "Genealogies of Modern Violence: Arendt and Imperialism in Africa, 1830–1914," in *The Cambridge World History of Violence*, vol. 4: *1800 to the Present*, ed. Louise Edwards, Nigel Penn, and Jay Winter (Cambridge: Cambridge University Press, 2020), 246–62. The problem of measuring genocide based on intent (*dolus specialis*) is covered in Dirk Moses, *The Problems of Genocide: Permanent Security and the Language of Transgression* (Cambridge: Cambridge University Press, 2021), 22–24, 420–23.
138. Boudin, *Histoire statistique*, 21.
139. Knox, *Races of Men*, 206–7, 280.
140. Bénet, *État civil en Algérie*, 73.
141. Kateb, *Européens, "Indigènes" et Juifs*, 97–103.

142. It took nearly fifty years before colonial demographers solved the problem, a battle whose victory announced itself when European births first outnumbered deaths in 1865. René Ricoux, *La démographie figurée de l'Algérie; étude statistique des populations européennes qui habitent l'Algérie* (Paris: Masson, 1880), 216; Kateb, *Européens, "Indigènes" et Juifs*, 33; Loitron, "Quelle politique," 186–92.

4. "Am I That Name?"

1. Denise Riley, *"Am I That Name?": Feminism and the Category of "Women" in History* (Minneapolis: University of Minnesota Press, 1988); Denise Riley, *The Words of Selves: Identification, Solidarity, Irony* (Stanford, CA: Stanford University Press, 2000), 86.
2. *Le Moniteur algérien*, 17 April 1832.
3. James C. Scott, John Tehranian, and Jeremy Mathias, "The Production of Legal Identities Proper to States: The Case of the Permanent Family Surname," *Comparative Studies in Society and History* 44, no. 1 (January 2002): 4.
4. Ann Thomson, *Barbary and Enlightenment: European Attitudes Towards the Maghreb in the 18th Century* (Leiden: Brill, 1987), 2.
5. Daniel Panzac, *Barbary Corsairs: The End of a Legend 1800–1820*, trans. Victoria Hobson and John E. Hawkes (Leiden: Brill, 2005); Antonio de Sosa, *An Early Modern Dialogue with Islam: Antonio de Sosa's Topography of Algiers (1612)*, ed. María Antonia Garcés, trans. Diana de Armas Wilson (Notre Dame, IN: Notre Dame University Press, 2011). Gillian Weiss, *Captives and Corsairs: France and Slavery in the Early Modern Mediterranean* (Stanford, CA: Stanford University Press, 2011); Bartolomé Bennassar and Lucile Bennassar, *Les Chrétiens d'Allah: l'histoire extraordinaire des renégats, XVIe et XVIIe siècles* (Paris: Perrin, 1989); Moulay Belhamissi, *Les captifs algériens et l'Europe chrétienne (1518–1830)* (Algiers: ENL, 1988).
6. Vincent-Yves Boutin, "Reconnaissance des ville, forts et batteries d'Alger," 1808, Centre des Archives diplomatiques de La Courneuve (hereafter CADC), Mémoires et documents, Algérie, 10. Published as Vincent-Yves Boutin, *Aperçu historique, statistique et topographique sur l'état d'Alger* (Paris: Picquet, 1830).
7. Julia A. Clancy-Smith, *Mediterraneans: North Africa and Europe in an Age of Migration, c. 1800–1900* (Berkeley: University of California Press, 2011).
8. Dzavid Dzanic, "The Civilizing Sea: The Ideological Origins of the French Mediterranean Empire, 1789–1870" (PhD diss., Harvard University, 2016).
9. M. de Saint-Martin, "Précis des relations diplomatiques de la France avec Alger depuis la Restauration 1827," CADC, Mémoires et documents, Algérie, 11; Abdeljelil Temimi, *Le Beylik de Constantine et Ḥâdj 'Aḥmed Bey, 1830–1837* (Tunis: Revue d'histoire maghrébine, 1978), 52.
10. Anne Mézin, *Les consuls de France au siècle des Lumières (1715–1792)* (Paris: Ministère des Affaires Étrangères, 1997), 237–39.
11. Louis Lesbaupin, "Thierry de Fougeray, un condottière au XIXe siècle," in *Annales de la Société d'histoire et d'archéologie de l'arrondissement de Saint-Malo* (2008), 116.

12. L. Charles Féraud, *Histoire de La Calle* (Algiers: Jourdan, 1878), 588; René Bouyac, *Histoire de Bône* (Paris: Lecène, 1892), 122; Eugène Plantet, *Correspondance des Beys de Tunis*, vol. 3, *1770–1830* (Paris: Alcan, 1899), 457.
13. Alfred Nettement, *Histoire de la conquête d'Alger*, new ed. (Paris: Lecoffre, 1867), 143–44, 150.
14. Thierry, "Aperçu sur l'occupation d'Alger," 18 February 1830, CADC, Mémoires et documents, Algérie 11.
15. D'Aubignosc report, 30 April 1830; and Ministère de la Guerre to Ministère des Affaires Étrangères, 20 March 1830. Both in CADC, Mémoires et documents, Algérie 5; Nettement, *Histoire de la conquête*, 261–75.
16. Ministre de la Guerre to Ministre des Affaires Étrangères, 20 March 1830.
17. On the use of shifting terms between Arabic and French treaties, see the famous case of the Demsichels treaty, negotiated with 'Abd al-Qādīr in 1834. McDougall, *History of Algeria*, 63–64.
18. Général Bourmont, Ministre de la Guerre to Ministre des Affaires Étrangères, 20 March 1830, CADC, Mémoires et documents, Algérie, 5.
19. Gérardin to Bourmont, 28 April 1830; and d'Aubignosc, "Rapport sur la mission de Tunis 30 avril 1830," both in CADC, Mémoires et documents, Algérie, 5.
20. Hussayn Dey is described in detail in the following early sources: M. de Saint-Martin, "Précis des relations diplomatiques" (1827), CADC, Mémoires et documents, Algérie, 11; William Shaler, *Sketches of Algiers, Political, Historical, and Civil* (Boston: Cummings, 1826), 158–66 (French translation: *Esquisse de l'État d'Alger*, trans. Thomas-Xavier Bianchi [Paris: Ladvocat, 1830], 194–202); Thomas-Xavier Bianchi, *Relation de l'arrivée dans la rade d'Alger du vaisseau de S. M. "La Provence"* (Paris: self-pub., 1830), 24–26; Charles Préaux, "Notice sur le Dey d'Alger," *Journal des Sciences militaires des armées de terre et de mer* 22 (January–March 1831): 332–42; A. Chais, "Hussein-Pacha," in *Biographie universelle ancienne et moderne*, vol. 67: *Supplément, He-Iz* (Paris: Michaud, 1840), 502–7.
21. See, for example, the undated list of nineteen names, which are given along with the ethnicity of each person, ANOM 1h1.
22. See examples from 1832 in ANOM 1h2. On the problem of organizing colonial "facts," see George R. Trumbull IV, *An Empire of Facts: Colonial Power, Cultural Knowledge, and Islam in Algeria, 1870–1914* (Cambridge: Cambridge University Press, 2009), 48.
23. Among the many examples of the biographical reports in ANOM's 5h series, see "Notices biographiques sur les principales familles indigènes de la Divison," August 1859, ANOM 5h4. See also the files on Ben Abdesselam and Ben Yahya ben Aïssa, ANOM 5h28; and "Note sur la famille des Mahi Eddine," n.d., ANOM 5h29.
24. Guy Turbet-Delof, *L'Afrique barbaresque dans la littérature française aux XVIe et XVIIe siècles* (Genève: Droz, 1973), 3–41. See also Ramzi Rouighi, *Inventing the Berbers: History and Ideology in the Maghrib* (Philadelphia: University of Pennsylvania Press, 2019), 105–32.
25. Examples of the use of "Algérien" as a proper noun in official documents in "Mémoire sur les affaires d'Alger, les griefs de la France et la nécessité d'une

expédition contre cette place," December 1753, CADC, Mémoires et documents, Algérie, 10; "Mémorie," 23 August 1725, CADC, Mémoires et documents, Algérie, 13; and "Relation circonstanciée des opérations de la flotte espagnole depuis le 30 juin jusqu'au 15 juillet 18 July 1775," CADC, Mémoires et documents, Algérie, 10.

26. Proclamation of General Bourmont, Arabic language, with interlinear French translation, n.d [1830], CADC, Mémoires et documents, Algérie, 5. The names used in the Arabic draft in the Ministry of Foreign Affairs archives differ considerably from those that appear in the published French translation, which addresses itself in ethnonyms: *Aux Couloglis, fils de Trucs et Arabes habitant le territoire d'Alger.* In *Courrier français,* no. 159 (8 June 1830): 1.
27. Jean-Robert Henry, "L'identité imaginée par le droit: de l'Algérie coloniale à la construction européenne," in *Cartes d'identité: comment dit-on "nous" en politique?,* ed. Denis-Constant Martin (Paris: Presses de la Fondation nationale des sciences politiques, 1994), 41–63.
28. Michel de Certeau, *Heterologies: Discourse of the Other,* trans. Brian Massumi (Minneapolis: University of Minnesota Press, 1986), 112.
29. M. de Rémuzat (aka Henri Rémusat), "Petit aperçu sur la Régence d'Alger, ou Exposé d'un plan à suivre pour soumettre les Arabes," n.d., p. 10, ANOM F80 1671. Italics added.
30. Abbé Dopigez, *Souvenirs de l'Algérie et de la France méridionale* (Douai: Adam, 1840), 190. Italics added.
31. Jacques Cognat, "Colonisation d'Alger," report addressed to the Ministre de la Marine et des Colonies, 20 June 1837, ANOM F80 1672. Italics added.
32. J. Sabbatier, *Lettre sur la colonie d'Alger* (Paris: Delaunay, 1836), 10. Italics added.
33. Jocelyne Dakhlia, "1830, une rencontre?," in *Historie de l'Algérie à la période coloniale, 1830–1962,* ed. Abderrahmane Bouchène et al. (Paris: Découverte, 2014), 142–48.
34. Benjamin Claude Brower, *A Desert Named Peace: The Violence of France's Empire in the Algerian Sahara, 1844–1902* (New York: Columbia University Press, 2009), 14–26. See also Achille Mbembe, *On the Postcolony* (Berkeley: University of California Press, 2001), 5–6, 173–96.
35. A largely unknown figure, biographical details on Jacques Cognat, aka Cogniat, a doctor and occasional poet, can be found in Peter Gradenwitz, "Félicien David (1810–1876) and French Romantic Orientalism," *Musical Quarterly* 62, no. 4 (October 1976): 471–506.
36. Anonymous, "Colonie d'Alger," *Sémaphore de Marseille* 4, no. 1421 (22 August 1832): 1.
37. My thanks to M. Brady Brower for his clarifications in this section. The remaining errors are my own. Personal correspondence, August 2022.
38. Louis Althusser, "Ideology and Ideological State Apparatuses (Notes Towards an Investigation)," in Louis Althusser, *Lenin and Philosophy and Other Essays,* trans. Ben Brewster (New York: Monthly Review Press, 1971), 174–77. See also Judith Butler, *Psychic Life of Power: Theories in Subjection* (Stanford, CA: Stanford University Press, 1997), 95–105.

39. François Matheron, "Althusser," in *Le Maitron: dictionnaire biographique, mouvement ouvrier, mouvement social* (2008), https://maitron.fr/spip.php?article9962; No. 279, 3 February 1888, Commune d'Alger, 1833 Naissances, http://anom.archivesnationales.culture.gouv.fr/caomec2/osd.php?territoire=ALGERIE&acte=954277.
40. Had Louis Althusser consulted his father's birth certificate, the legacy of his father's name would have appeared even more complicated and confused. In these records, the father's full name is given as "ALTHUSSER, Charles François" in the header, while the longhand birth record itself has "Charles Joseph" as his given name. While this might have been a clerical error, Charles's own father used both the François and Joseph names at different points in his life.
41. Louis Althusser, *The Future Lasts Forever: A Memoir*, ed. Olivier Corpet and Yann Moulier Boutang, trans. Richard Veasey (New York: New Press, 1993), 54. Original italics.
42. Althusser, 55. Althusser rehearses the incest taboo and the name's role in establishing the subject of desire, even as it appears to my eye that he reworks Lacan's model.
43. Althusser, 79.
44. My thinking here is informed by the psychoanalytic concept of "symbolic identification." As explained by Slavoj Žižek, "The subject is always fastened, pinned, to a signifier which represents him for the other, and through this pinning he is loaded with a symbolic mandate, he is given a place in the intersubjective network of symbolic relations." Slavoj Žižek, *The Sublime Object of Ideology* (London: Verso, 1989), 125–26.
45. Yann Moulier Boutang, *Louis Althusser: Une biographie*, vol. 1: *La formation du mythe (1918–1956)* (Paris: Grasset, 1992), 57. See also René Gallissot, *Le Maghreb de traverse* (Saint-Denis: Bouchène, 2000), 263–89.
46. Abdelkader Djeghloul, *Éléments d'histoire culturelle algérienne* (Algiers: ENAL, 1984), 51–60, 165–69. See also Jennifer Pitts, "Liberalism and Empire in a Nineteenth-Century Algerian Mirror," *Modern Intellectual History* 6, no. 2 (2009): 287–313; Benjamin Claude Brower, "Just War and Jihad in the French Conquest of Algeria," in *Just Wars, Holy Wars, and Jihads: Christian, Jewish, and Muslim Encounters and Exchanges*, ed. Sohail H. Hashmi (Oxford: Oxford University Press, 2012), 232–36; Abla Gheziel, "Trois réactions 'algériennes' sur l'avenir de l'Algérie, 1830–1834," *Insaniyat*, nos. 65–66 (2014): 187–210; James McDougall, "A World No Longer Shared: Losing the *Droit de Cité* in Nineteenth-Century Algiers," *Journal of the Economic and Social History of the Orient* 60 (2017): 18–49.
47. See, for example, documents in ANOM 1e15 (microfilmed in 18miom14 and 18miom15). Arbitrary arrests were the subject of a letter in 1832 by the caid of the Beni Moussa, ANOM 1h2. The letter of welcome was addressed by the Malikite mufti of Algiers to General Berthezène, who served in Algiers from February to December 1831 and enjoyed a generally favorable reputation there. ANOM 18miom15. On Berthezène, see Charles-Robert Ageron, *Le gouvernement du général Berthezène à Alger en 1831* (Paris: Bouchène, 2005).

48. Fatiha Sifou, "La protestation algérienne contre la domination française: plaintes et pétitions (1830–1914)" (PhD diss., Université de Provence, 2004); Fatiha Sifou, "Les premières réactions politiques algériennes face à la conquête française (1830–1834)," *Majala al-'Ulūm al-Insāniya* 6, no. 1 (2017): 35–51.
49. Béatrice Fraenkel, *La signature, genèse d'un signe* (Paris: Gallimard, 1992); Geoffrey Khan, "An Arabic Legal Document from the Umayyad Period," *Journal of the Royal Asiatic Society* 4, no. 3 (November 1994): 365–66; Adam Gacek, *Arabic Manuscripts: A Vademecum for Readers* (Leiden: Brill, 2009), 14–16. On the signature fashioned into a seal, see C. E. Bosworth, J. Deny, and Muhammad Yusuf Siddiq, "Tughra," in *Encyclopaedia of Islam New Edition Online (EI-2 English)* (Brill). For colonial South Asia, see Bhavani Raman, *Document Raj: Writing and Scribes in Early Colonial South India* (Chicago: University of Chicago Press, 2012), 142–51.
50. Brinkley Messick, *Shari'a Scripts: A Historical Anthropology* (New York: Columbia University Press, 2018), 277.
51. Marcelin Beaussier, *Dictionnaire pratique arabe-français* (Algiers: Jourdan, 1887), 171.
52. Philippe-Antoine Merlin, *Répertoire universel et raisonné de jurisprudence*, vol. 31: *Sép.-Sub*, 5th ed. (Paris: Tarlier, 1828), 156–222; *Nouveau dictionnaire des notaires*, vol. 3: *L-V* (Paris: Conseil des notaires, 1838), 606–9.
53. This example comes from one of the many lesson books that taught Arabic language and North African epistolary practices to administrators. Belkacem Ben Sedira, *Cours pratique de langue arabe* (Algiers: Jourdan, 1875), 302–3. For other Arabic examples, some analytically annotated, see Belkassem Ben Sedira, *Manuel épistolaire de langue arabe* (Algiers: Jourdan, 1893); and Belkassem Ben Sedira, *Cours gradué de lettres arabes manuscrites* (Algiers: Jourdan, 1893). On these guidebooks and others, see Sylvette Larzul, "Les manuels de langue arabe des débuts de l'Algérie coloniale (1830–1871)," in *Manuels d'arabe d'hier et d'aujourd'hui: France et Maghreb, XIXe–XXIe siècle*, ed. Sylvette Larzul and Alain Messaoudi (Paris: Bibliothèque nationale de France, 2013), 57–78.
54. Louis Machuel, *Manuel de l'arabisant, ou recueil d'actes judiciaires*, vol. 2 (Algiers: Jourdan, 1881), i. For notaries in Constantine, see Fāṭima al-Zahra Qashī, "Shahūd al-'Adala fī Qusnṭīnīyat al-Qran al-Tāsa'a 'Ashr," *Insaniyat*, nos. 35–36 (2007): 57–76. Jessica Marglin discusses how notary signatures played a role in displacing oral testimony in favor of written testimonies in Moroccan courts during the nineteenth century. Jessica M. Marglin, *Across Legal Lines: Jews and Muslims in Modern Morocco* (New Haven, CT: Yale University Press, 2016), 38–39; and Jessica M. Marglin, "Written and Oral in Islamic Law: Documentary Evidence and Non-Muslims in Moroccan Shari'a Courts," *Comparative Studies in Society and History* 59, no. 4 (2017): 907.
55. Letter of the 'ulama, shayūkh, ashrāf, and a'yān of Algiers to the Ministre de la Guerre, 15 Sha'bān 1246 (28 January 1831), partial French translation and Arabic original, ANOM 1h1. The goals of the petitioners are discussed in Ageron, *Government du général Berthezène*, 33–35, 133.
56. My thanks to Estefanía Valenzuela Mochón, postdoctoral researcher at the Escuela de Estudios Árabes, Granada, for her painstaking transcription and paleographic

analysis of the names in this document. The text of the petition itself deserves a full reading, a task beyond my skills.

57. Isabelle Grangaud, "Le titre de *Sayyid* ou *Sî* dans la documentation constantinoise d'époque moderne: un marqueur identitaire en évolution," *Revue des mondes musulmans et de la Méditerranée*, no. 127 (July 2010), https://doi.org/10.4000/remmm.6604; Colette Establet, *Être caïd dans l'Algérie coloniale* (Paris: Éditions du Centre national de la recherche scientifique, 1991), 247–48.
58. Alain Messaoudi, *Les arabisants et la France coloniale: savants, conseillers, médiateurs, 1780–1930* (Lyons: ENS éditions, 2015).
59. On changing epistolary norms in the Arabic-language letters of French-invested *caïds*, see Establet, *Être caïd*, 250–51. The genre of official translation known as the *traduction analytique* is discussed in Augustin Jomier, *Islam, réforme et colonisation: une histoire de l'ibadisme en Algérie, 1882–1962* (Paris: Éditions de la Sorbonne, 2020), 133.
60. "*Contre-voie*" in the heading is the French title of Edward Said's memoir, originally published in English as *Out of Place*. It translates as "on the wrong track," but the homophonic *contre-voix* means "contrasting voices." The tension between these two meanings frames my reading of Aḥmad Abū Ḍarba/Ahmed Bouderba, a person whom I read in light of Said's own life. Edward W. Said, *À contre-voie: mémoires*, trans. Brigitte Caland and Isabelle Genet (Paris: Serpent à plumes, 2002).
61. Sifou, "Protestation algérienne," 17.
62. Some words are in order on the sources used in my fixing his name in this form, and how I will use it in my own voice. "Aḥmad Abū Ḍarba" is the form he used in his Arabic signature, and the nasab "bin Ismāʿīl" was recorded by his son when he entered his father's name (Ahmed Ismaël Bouderba) as part of the registration of his own marriage in the French vital registry. (This marriage act also gives the date and place of Aḥmad Abū Ḍarba's death as Tangier, June 1865.) In his publication of orientalist varia in 1902, Paul Eudel states that Mustapha is Ahmed Bouderba's father. However, the French archives from the pre-1830 period (see next note) state that he is Ahmed's uncle. With this man having essentially two names, one in French and one in Arabic, I faced difficult choices. I have chosen to use the Arabic "Abū Ḍarba" in those instances when the context suggests an Arabophone language environment and "Bouderba" when he writes in French or is part of a French-language conversation. This is an imperfect solution, and the reader should understand that in most cases the name should be read across languages as "Abū Ḍarba/Bouderba," such that his subject position remains unfixed. Ismaël Bouderba marriage act in the état civil is found at http://anom.archivesnationales.culture.gouv.fr/caomec2/osd.php?territoire=ALGERIE&acte=348476. Paul Eudel, *L'Orfèvrerie algérienne et tunisienne* (Algiers: Jourdan, 1902), 329.
63. Bouderba family details from "Procuration pour retirer les valeurs laissées en France," 13 August 1791, ANOM 1a100 (microfilm in 45miom7); "Déclaration de remise de fonds," 19 April 1820, ANOM 1a129 (microfilm in 45miom10); "Copie du jugement arbitral et répartiteur suite au naufrage de la bombarde française la

Confiance," 23 December 1821, ANOM 1a130 (microfilm in 45miom10); "Documents intéressant une partie du chargement de la bombarde l'*Aurore*," 4 January–1 February 1822, ANOM 1a131 (microfilm in 45miom10). On the precolonial merchant class of Algiers, see Mohamed Amine, "Les commerçants à Alger à la veille de 1830," *Revue d'histoire maghrébine* 22, nos. 77–78 (May 1995): 11–112. Further biographical details on Abū Ḍarba's son Ismaël/Ismā'īl (d. 1878), the interpreter and explorer, can be found in Alain Messaoudi, *Les arabisants et la France coloniale: Annexes* (Lyon: ENS Éditions, 2015), http://books.openedition.org/enseditions/3730; and my entry in *Dictionnaire des orientalistes de langue française*, ed. François Pouillon (Paris: IISMM and Karthala, 2008), 132–33. The reference to European tenants living in the Abū Ḍarba family properties concerns a Swiss family, the Amerens. See death certificate of Savier Ameren, 20 September 1830, in ANOM 1aa71 (microfilm in 45miom23).

64. Amine, "Les commerçants à Alger," 26.
65. Date of Bouderba's first arrival in France is given in Bouderba to Ministre de la Guerre, Marseille, 14 March 1837, ANOM 1h1.
66. Eusèbe de Salle, *Ali le renard, ou la conquête d'Alger (1830)*, vol. 2, 2nd ed. (Paris: Gosselin, 1832), 148–50. There is no record of the birth of any "Célestine Durand" in the état civil registers of Avignon for the 1792–1812 period. Archives Municipales d'Avignon 1e449, Table décennale des naissances (1793–1802), and 1e450 Table décennale des naissances (1802–1813). For Eusèbe de Salle, see the biographical notice by Lucette Valensi in *Dictionnaire des orientalistes*, 859–60.
67. Records show that in 1831 Durand was in Aix-en-Provence, convalescing from illness and presumably staying with relatives. People named Durand lived in five different households in Aix at the time. They ranged in occupation from a ropemaker, a tin worker, and a butcher's wife to a wealthy land surveyor and the wife of a legal solicitor. Draft of letter (Minister of War?), dated Paris, 21 March 1831, ANOM 1h1. "Recensement, liste nominative des habitants," 1831, Archives Municipales d'Aix-en-Provence, F1art.9.
68. Pierre Guiral, *Marseille et l'Algérie, 1830–1841* (Gap: Éditions Ophrys, 1957).
69. M. de Sartine to M. de La Tour, Versailles, 24 April 1775. Archives Départementales des Bouches-du-Rhône (hereafter ADBR) C3825.
70. Sequestrations of the property of Algerians in France were ordered in early 1799 and again in 1811 (see the 1811 case of Jacob Goslan, an Algerian man, who claimed French citizenship during the Revolution). ADBR 1q130 and 1q559. The expansive conception of Revolutionary citizenship is covered in Ian Coller, *Muslims and Citizens: Islam, Politics, and the French Revolution* (New Haven, CT: Yale University Press, 2020), 61–81.
71. Ian Coller, *Arab France: Islam and the Making of Modern Europe, 1798–1831* (Berkeley: University of California Press, 2011), 121–39; Pierre Triomphe, *1815: La Terreur blanche* (Toulouse: Privat, 2017).
72. Letter of 7 May 1830, Archives de la Chambre de Commerce de Marseille (ACCM) MQ5.5/03. This letter clarifies the financial dealings of Abū Ḍarba in Marseille,

which his enemies used against him, claiming essentially that he was a crooked businessman who defaulted on his debts. Instead, he respected the order of his government not to pay them.

73. État civil records consulted: Archives municipales de Marseille (AMM), 1e503, 1e504, 4e16, 4e17, 4e18, 3e30, 3e31, 3e32, 3e35, 3e38, 1e490, 1e491.
74. Domingo Gian Trapani, *Alger tel qu'il est*, 2nd ed. (Paris: Fayolle, 1830), 194–95.
75. The original French copy of the Convention with its signatures from 5 July 1830 appears to have been lost, as has, to my knowledge, the original Arabic version. The French text was republished widely in secondary sources throughout the nineteenth century, with some important variations in language. Claude Bontems includes an annotated copy in his *Manuel des institutions algériennes de la domination turque à l'indépendance*, vol. 1: *La domination turque et le régime militaire 1518–1870* (Paris: Cujas, 1976), 104–5.
76. Nacereddine Saidouni, *Le waqf en Algérie à l'époque Ottomane: XIe–XIIIe siècles de Hégire, XVIIe–XIXe siècles*, 2nd ed. (Kuwait City: Awaqf Public Fondation, 2009), 148–91.
77. Letter of Général Pelet to Général Berthezène, 26 May 1831, reproduced in Ageron, *Government du général Berthezène*, 134.
78. My approach in this section is informed by the following sources: for sovereignty and language, Jacques Lacan, "The Function and Field of Speech and Language in Psychoanalysis," in *Écrits: A Selection*, trans. Bruce Fink (New York: Norton, 2002), 79–80, 84–85; on language and subjectivity in northwestern Africa, Anne-Emmanuelle Berger, ed., *Algeria in Others' Languages* (Ithaca, NY: Cornell University Press, 2002), along with Jacques Derrida, *Monolingualism of the Other; or, The Prosthesis of Origin*, trans. Patrick Mensah (Stanford, CA: Stanford University Press, 1998); Abdelkebir Khatibi, *Le blessure du nom propre* (Paris: Denoël, 1974); Abdelkebir Khatibi, *Maghreb pluriel* (Paris: Denoël, 1983); Abdelkebir Khatibi, *Love in Two Languages*, trans. Richard Howard (Minneapolis: University of Minnesota Press, 1990). Also Abdelfattah Kilito, *The Tongue of Adam*, trans. Robyn Creswell (New York: New Directions, 2016); Abdelfattah Kilito, *Thou Shalt Not Speak My Language*, trans. Waïl S. Hassan (Syracuse, NY: Syracuse University Press, 2008); and Hoda El-Shakry, "Heteroglossia and the Poetics of the *Roman Maghrébin*," *Contemporary French and Francophone Studies* 20, no. 1 (2016): 8–17. Although the field is dominated by literary theory, historians have made crucial contributions. See especially Jocelyne Dakhlia, *Lingua franca: histoire d'une langue métisse en Méditerranée* (Arles, France: Actes Sud, 2008); M'hamed Oualdi, *A Slave Between Empires: A Transimperial History of North Africa* (New York: Columbia University Press, 2019); Lucette Valensi, *Mardochée Naggiar: Enquête sur un inconnu* (Paris: Stock, 2008); Natalie Zemon Davis, *Trickster Travels: A Sixteenth-Century Muslim Between Worlds* (New York: Hill and Wang, 2006); and Mercedes García-Arenal and Gerard Wiegers, *A Man of Three Worlds: Samuel Pallache, A Moroccan Jew in Catholic and Protestant Europe*, trans. Martin Beagles (Baltimore: Johns Hopkins University Press, 2003).
79. Antoine de Juchereau de Saint-Denis, *Considérations statistiques, historiques, militaires et politiques sur la régence d'Alger* (Paris: Delaunay, 1831), 194–95. On language

prejudices, see R. Anthony Lodge, *French: From Dialect to Standard* (London: Routledge, 1993), 153–87.

80. Ahmed Bouderba, "Mémoire de Bouderbah," ed. Georges Yver, *Revue africaine* 57 (1913): 220. The original French text reads: "Je commence par demander mille pardons au lecteur sur mon style en raison de mon peu de savoir de la langue française, ce qui fait qu'on ne pourra trouver ni découvrir de belle phrases."
81. The original passage in French reads: "Il faut que l'autorité tâche de faire tout son possible, de ne changer rien, ni dans leurs mœurs, ni dans leurs usages ou habitudes, surtout pour la religion, qui est la première base qu'il faut établir solidement avec le Musulman, sans jamais penser à la violer dans le moindre cas; il faut au contraire que les Français y prennent une bonne conduite, en donnant de bons exemples, en agissant avec justice et loyauté et modération, sans blesser personne ni dans sa croyance, ni dans ses usages. Cette manière d'agir introduira la véritable civilisation: en voyant votre conduite sage et juste, alors les indigènes, de leur propre volonté, chercheront peu à peu à changer leurs mœurs et leurs habitudes. Je peux dire sans blesser personne que, jusqu'à présent, les indigènes qui n'ont connu les Français qu'à Alger, ont une très mauvaise opinion de cette nation magnanime, à cause que la grande majorité des Français qui sont allés dans ce pays, y sont sans morale et sans aucune croyance, même d'existence de Dieu, ce qui fait un très mauvais effet dans l'esprit publique, surtout quand un Arabe, un bédouin ou un habitant de ville, quand il va porter sa plainte devant une autorité, s'ils ont le malheur de prononcer le nom de Dieu, pour solliciter, ils sont de suite apostrophés de la manière la plus révoltante; il y en a qui ont abandonné leurs réclamations pour ne pas entendre leurs outrages envers l'Être suprême." Bouderba, "Mémoire," 238–39.
82. The edited transcript of Bouderba's testimony was published in *Procès-verbaux et rapports de la Commission d'Afrique instituée par ordonnance du Roi du 12 décembre 1833* (Paris: L'imprimerie royale, 1834), 39–43. The original transcript of his deposition is located in ANOM F80 9.
83. Many historians have cast doubt on the authorship of some of the other French-language texts written by Algerians of this era, suggesting that they must have been written or overwritten by French authors. Charles-André Julien began this historiographical trend in his *Histoire de l'Algérie* of 1964 when he wrote that Ḥamdān bin 'Uthmān Khūja's language in the *Mirror* was derivative, "having been suggested by the liberals of Paris whose terminology it echoes." In the case of Bouderba's 1834 text, Julien's student, Charles-Robert Ageron, continued casting doubts about authorship in Bouderba's case by pointing out differences between the transcript of his address and the subsequently published text. To a lesser extent, the work of Alain Messaoudi, a scrupulous reader of this archive, slips into this trope when he points up differences between the handwriting in the main text of Bouderba's letters and the signature itself, suspecting that Bouderba's wife was the author of his letters and he only signed them. This may be true (the handwriting in Bouderba's signature itself changes over time); however, such a division of labor within the couple does not mean that Bouderba's ideas are not his own, nor should his

wife's collaboration make them any less authentic. Rather it should refocus attention on the intellectual production of the Bouderba-Durand couple. Charles-André Julien, *Histoire de l'Algérie contemporaine*, vol. 1: *La conquête et les débuts de la colonisation (1827–1871)*, 3rd ed. (Paris: Presses universitaires de France, 1986), 95; Ageron, *Gouvernement du général Berthezène*, 39, 137–40; Messaoudi, *Arabisants et la France coloniale*, annexe 4n24.

84. The impact of this thinking on the scientific study of psychology is discussed in M. Brady Brower, *Unruly Spirits: The Science of Psychic Phenomena in Modern France* (Urbana: University of Illinois Press, 2010), 29–30.
85. Saba Mahmood, *Politics of Piety: The Islamic Revival and the Feminist Subject* (Princeton, NJ: Princeton University Press, 2005), 1–39; Louis Althusser, *For Marx*, trans. Ben Brewster (London: Verso, 1996), 233–36.
86. Henry Laurens, *Orientales I: Autour de l'expédition d'Égypte* (Paris: CNRS Éditions, 2004), 147–64; John Tolan, Henry Laurens, and Gilles Veinstein, *Europe and the Islamic World: A History* (Princeton, NJ: Princeton University Press, 2012), chap. 10.
87. "Notea sur le contenu des demandes du Sr. Abourdarbach," n.a., n.d. (ca. March 1831), ANOM 1h1.
88. Beaussier, *Dictionnaire pratique*, 383–84.
89. Ismaël Bouderba's application for French nationality became official on 23 March 1855. Dossier no. 3126x6, BB/11/650. Ségolène de Dainville-Barbiche et al., *Dossiers de demandes: naturalisations, admissions à domicile, réintégrations dans la qualité de français, autorisations de servir ou de se faire naturaliser à l'étranger, changements de nom, dispenses pour mariage, majorats, dotations, armoiries (1851–1858)* (Pierrefitte-sur-Seine: Archives nationales de France, 2017), 414.
90. Eudel, *Orfévrerie algérienne*, 330.
91. Bouderba to Maréchal Soult, 17 May 1831; Bouderba to Maréchal Soult, 15 May 1833; Bouderba to Maréchal Soult, 3 June 1833; Bouderba to Gouverneur général, par intérim, 15 June 1836; Bouderba to Gouverneur général, par intérim, 1 July 1836; Bouderba to commander of Bône, 1 July 1836; Bouderba to Gouverneur général, 30 July 1836; Bouderba to Gouverneur général, 3 October 1836; Bouderba to Ministère de la Guerre, 14 March 1837; and Bouderba to unspecified French minister, 15 November 1837. All in ANOM 1h1.
92. "Demandes d'Aboudarbah pour ses compatriotes," 12 March 1831; Bouderba to Maréchal Soult, 7 March 1840; Bouderba to unspecified prefect, 6 May 1840; Bouderba to Ministre de l'Intérieur, 4 April 1846. All in ANOM 1h1.
93. The exception to this is "Demandes d'Aboudarbah pour ses compatriotes," where he writes his Arabic name in full (ism + kunya), placing it underneath the French but outside of the two loops.
94. Davis, *Trickster Travels*, 84.
95. Oualdi, *Slave Between Empires*, 29; Valensi, *Mardochée Naggiar*, 351.
96. Davis, *Trickster Travels*, 65.
97. The collapse of the lingua franca around 1830 speaks to this change. As Jocelyne Dakhlia argues, this "no man's language" did not make identity claims, and using

it did not imply that anyone's culture was superior. Pidgin French took its place, resulting in the nefarious racialized language hierarchies of colonial societies. See Dakhlia, *Lingua franca*.

98. Mikhail Bakhtin, *Problems of Dostoevsky's Poetics*, trans. Caryl Emerson (Minneapolis: University of Minnesota Press, 1984), 232–36. See also Mikhail Bakhtin, *The Dialogic Imagination: Four Essays*, ed. Michael Holquist, trans. Caryl Emerson and Michael Holquist (Austin: University of Texas Press, 1981), 259–422.
99. Bakhtin, *Problems*, 233.
100. Bakhtin, 234. My italics.
101. General Clauzel, then leading French forces in Algeria, imprisoned Bouderba and other Algerian notables in 1836 as part of a plan to silence them. He collaborated with the deputy mayor of Algiers, a man named Germont, known to Algerians as the "Yellow Snake." Anonymous, unaddressed, n.d. resumé of the "Partie Maure affair," ANOM 1h1.
102. Bouderba to Ministère de l'Intérieur, 4 April 1846, ANOM 1h1. The Bouderba family address in Marseille is given in a dossier prepared in May 1840 on his behalf by a French notary (Barthelemy Louis Raynaud), attesting to his close governmental connections, including several invitations to dine with King Louis-Philippe. ANOM 1h1.
103. Ageron, *Gouvernement du général Berthezène*, 37.
104. Brower, *Desert Named Peace*, 14–19; details of the 'Ūfiyya killings in Louis-André Pichon, *Alger sous la domination française* (Paris: Barrois et Duprat, 1833), 131–37.
105. Ageron, *Gouvernement du général Berthezène*, 37.
106. Pichon, *Alger sous la domination*, 430. On the Katshāwa mosque seizure, see Florian Pharaon, *Épisodes de la Conquête: cathédrale et mosquée* (Paris: Lahure, 1880).
107. Thierry Lentz, *Savary: le séide de Napoléon* (Paris: Fayard, 2001), 7–11.
108. Georges de Beauchamp, *Traité de graphologie, théorique et pratique* (Paris: Blériot, 1895), 300–301. See also Léo Lespès, *Le Livre des 400 auteurs: nouvelles, contes, voyages, légendes critique, histoire, théâtres* (Paris: Magasin des familles, 1850), 48–59. For nineteenth-century graphology, see Fraenkel, *Signature*, 211–20.
109. Annette Poizner, *Clinical Graphology: An Interpretive Manual for Mental Health Practitioners* (Springfield, IL: Thomas, 2012), 110. See also Stanislaw Lem, *Solaris*, trans. Joanna Kilmartin and Steve Cox (San Diego: Harvest Harcourt, 1987), 72.
110. "Note sur le contenu des demandes du Sr. Abourdarbach," n.a., n.d. (ca. March 1831), ANOM 1h1.
111. Bouderba did keep up a steady correspondence with his contacts in the French government into the 1840s. In some of these he used his doubled signature again. These efforts led to nothing beneficial for Algerians in the short term, but they traced a path for his son, Ismaël, who made a career as a translator and explorer in Algeria. Ismaël transitioned the family into government service, business, and the liberal professions, some of the same fields they had occupied before 1830. Eventually some rose to prominence within the Young Algerian movement, an important chapter in the anticolonial nationalist movement of the 1900s.

5. In Others' Names

1. The influence of this model on later onomastic norms, otherwise decided by custom, is discussed in Anne Lefebvre-Teillard, *Le nom, droit et histoire* (Paris: Presses universitaires de France, 1990), 56.
2. Stephen Wilson, *The Means of Naming: A Social and Cultural History of Personal Naming in Western Europe* (London: University College London Press, 1998), 5–15; Katharina Leibring, "Given Names in European Naming Systems," in *The Oxford Handbook of Names and Naming*, ed. Carole Hough (Oxford: Oxford University Press, 2016), 203; Lefebvre-Teillard, *Nom, droit et histoire*, chaps. 1–2, baptism names at 38–39, 50–53; Nicole Lapierre, *Changer de nom* (Paris: Stock, 1995); Monique Bourin, "L'écriture du nom propre et l'apparition d'une anthroponymie à plusieurs éléments en Europe occidentale (XIe–XIIe siècles)," in *L'écriture du nom propre*, ed. Anne-Marie Christin (Paris: Harmattan, 1997), 193–213.
3. This is the problem faced by Umberto Eco's character in *The Name of the Rose*, the sleuth-hound monk William. As a careful reader of signs, he first approached the murders in the abbey thinking that the perpetrator was acting out a system or plan. By the end he realizes, as Eco writes, that "I behaved stubbornly, pursuing a semblance of order, when I should have known well that there is no order in the universe." Umberto Eco, *The Name of the Rose*, trans. William Weaver (New York: Harcourt Brace Javanovich, 1984), 599.
4. Lefebvre-Teillard, *Nom, droit et histoire*, 29–35, 56–57.
5. Lefebvre-Teillard, 49–110; Delsalle, *Histoires de familles*, 137–39.
6. Law of 19–23 June 1790; see Lefebvre-Teillard, 114–17.
7. Lefebvre-Teillard, 122.
8. Eusèbe Salverte, *Essai historique et philosophique sur les noms d'hommes, de peuples et de lieux*, vol. 1 (Paris: Bossange, 1824), 1. See also Léonce Hallez-Claparède, *Des Noms propres* (Paris: Douniol, 1868); Adolphe de Coston, *Origine, étymologie et signification des noms propres et des armoiries* (Paris: Aubry, 1867); Justin Sabatier, *Encyclopédie des noms propres* (Paris: Petit Journal, 1865); Édouard-Léon Scott, *Les noms de baptême et les prénoms: nomenclature, signification, tradition, légende, histoire, art de nommer*, 2nd ed. (Paris: Houssiaux, 1858); Albert de Rochetal, *Le caractère par le prénom: suivi de la liste des prénoms usuels avec l'explication des qualités et défauts que chacun d'eux impose à celui qui le porte* (Paris: Bischoff, 1908).
9. The Law of 11 Germinal year XI (1 April 1803) establishing official standards for first names was not eased until 1993. Lefebvre-Teillard, *Nom, droit et histoire*, 129.
10. Lefebvre-Teillard, 119.
11. Coston, *Origine, étymologie et signification*, 38–39.
12. Coston, 42.
13. On procedures for name changes, see Anonymous, "Nom (et Prénom)," in *Répertoire général alphabétique du droit français*, vol. 28: *Ministère Public-Numéraire*, ed. Édouard Fuzier-Herman, Adrien Carpentier, and Georges Frèrejouan Du Saint (Paris: Sirey, 1901), 549.

14. Law of 11 Germinal XI in Lefebvre-Teillard, *Nom, droit et histoire*, 129.
15. In the absence of a master list of acceptable names, local registrars decided what names met the criteria. They had a reputation of wielding these powers arbitrarily or not at all. See Édouard Lévy, *La Question des prénoms* (Paris: Libraire judicaire, 1913).
16. Decret of 20 July 1808, *Bulletin des lois de la République française*, 4th series, vol. 9: *1808* (Paris: Imprimerie impérial, 1809), 27–28. Esther Benbassa, *The Jews of France: A History from Antiquity to the Present*, trans. M. B. DeBevoise (Princeton, NJ: Princeton University Press, 1999), 90. The law targeted primarily Alsatian Jews who had followed onomastic practices distinct from communities in other parts of France.
17. Coston, *Origine, étymologie et signification*, 32.
18. Buffin, *Dictionnaire des familles qui ont fait modifier leurs noms, depuis 1803 jusqu'en 1865* (Paris: Delaroque, 1877), 11, 75, 77. By contrast, decrees in 1808 and 1813 decided that Jews could use biblical names as given *prénoms*, with the rationale that the Bible figured within ancient history. Anonymous, "Nom (et Prénom)," 556.
19. Gérard Noiriel, "The Identification of the Citizen: The Birth of Republican Civil Status in France," in *Documenting Individual Identity: The Development of State Practices in the Modern World*, ed. Jane Caplan and John Torpey (Princeton, NJ: Princeton University Press, 2001), 47.
20. Gabriel Baudry-Lacantinerie, *Précis de droit civil*, vol. 1, 11th ed. (Paris: Sirey, 1911), 91.
21. Lefebvre-Teillard, *Nom, droit et histoire*, 162.
22. Alfred Nizard, "Droit et statistiques de filiation en France: Le droit de la filiation depuis 1804," *Population* 32, no. 1 (1977): 91–122.
23. Joseph-Armand Lallier, *De la Propriété des noms et des titres: origine des noms et des titres, procédure des changements de noms, protection de la propriété des noms et des titres, du nom commercial* (Paris: Giard, 1890), 1–10, 361–70.
24. Ordinary people lived differently from how the scenario depicted in the all-powerful patronym makes out. See Rachel G. Fuchs, *Contested Paternity: Constructing Families in Modern France* (Baltimore: Johns Hopkins University Press, 2008), 51–53; and Carolyn J. Eichner, "In the Name of the Mother: Feminist Opposition to the Patronym in Nineteenth-Century France," *Signs* 39, no. 3 (Spring 2014): 659–83. See also Mari Ruti, *The Singularity of Being: Lacan and the Immortal Within* (New York: Fordham University Press, 2012), 105–26.
25. Gabriele vom Bruck and Barbara Bodenhorn, " 'Entangled in Histories': An Introduction to the Anthropology of Names and Naming," in *The Anthropology of Names and Naming*, ed. Gabriele vom Bruck and Barbara Bodenhorn (Cambridge: Cambridge University Press 2006), 3–4, 26. See also James C. Scott, *Seeing Like a State: How Certain Schemes to Improve the Human Condition Have Failed* (New Haven, CT: Yale University Press, 1998), 64–71.
26. Order of 11 May 1848 and Imperial Decree of 8 August 1854. Charles-Louis Pinson de Ménerville, *Dictionnaire de la législation algérienne, premier supplément: manuel des lois, ordonnances, décrets, décisions et arrêtés publiés au "Bulletin officiel des actes du gouvernement" pendant les années 1853, 1854, 1855* (Algiers: Philippe and Cosse, 1856), 4.

27. Noureddine Amara, "Faire la France en Algérie: émigration algérienne, mésusages du nom et conflits de nationalités dans le monde, de la chute d'Alger aux années 1930" (PhD diss., Université de Paris I, Sorbonne, 2019).
28. Bureau Arabe du Département de Constantine to Ministère de la Guerre, 2 July 1856, no. 340, ANOM 12h51.
29. Bureau Arabe, 2 July 1856, no. 340, ANOM 12h51.
30. Osama W. Abi-Mershed, *Apostles of Modernity: Saint-Simonians and the Civilizing Mission in Algeria* (Stanford, CA: Stanford University Press, 2010), 159–200, quote at 174. See also Annie Rey-Goldzeiguer, *Le Royaume arabe: la politique algérienne de Napoléon III, 1861–1870* (Algiers: Société Nationale d'Edition et de Diffusion, 1977), 209–23; Charles-Robert Ageron, *Les Algériens musulmans et la France (1871–1919)*, vol. 1 (Paris: Presses universitaires de France, 1968), 343–66. On the eighteenth-century *régnicoles*, see Peter Sahlins, *Unnaturally French: Foreign Citizens in the Old Regime and After* (Ithaca, NY: Cornell University Press, 2004), 29–31.
31. "Lettre de l'Empereur au Gouverneur de l'Algérie" in *Constitution de la propriété en Algérie* (Algiers: Bouyer, 1863), 4.
32. The law of 1863 closed the door on an option that had fascinated settlers, speculators, and colonial jurists alike: nationalizing Algerian farmlands without compensation. This proposed using a combination of controversial European notions of *terra nullius* and the rights of conquest, along with a narrowly instrumental reading of Islamic law, so that the French state might claim all Algerian territory as within its domain and then distribute coveted farmlands to settlers. Abi-Mershed, *Apostles of Modernity*, 154–58; Claude Bontems, *Le droit musulman algérien à l'époque colonial: de l'invention à la codification* (Geneva: Slatkine, 2014), 82–88. See also Jean-Philippe Bras, "L'imperfection de la propriété indigène, lieu commun de la doctrine juridique coloniale en Afrique du Nord," in *Appartenance locale et propriété au nord et au sud de la Méditerranée*, ed. Sami Bargaoui, Simona Cerutti, and Isabelle Grangaud (Aix-en-Provence: Institut de recherches et d'études sur les mondes arabes et musulmans, 2015), https://books.openedition.org/iremam/3441?lang=en; James McDougall, *A History of Algeria* (Cambridge: Cambridge University Press, 2017), 94–99. On the use of the legal concept of *res/terra nullius* in European imperialism, see Andrew Fitzmaurice, *Sovereignty, Property and Empire, 1500–2000* (Cambridge: Cambridge University Press, 2014).
33. Abi-Mershed, *Apostles of Modernity*, 175–77; Michael Brett, "Legislating for Inequality in Algeria: The Senatus-Consulte of 14 July 1865," *Bulletin of the School of Oriental and African Studies, University of London* 51, no. 3. (1988): 440–61.
34. François Dumasy "Propriété et société coloniale. La Commission de colonisation et la Mitidja en 1842–1843," in *Propriété et société en Algérie contemporaine: Quelles approches?*, ed. Didier Guignard (Aix-en-Provence: Institut de recherches et d'études sur le monde arabe et musulman, 2017), 44–58, http://books.openedition.org/iremam/3614.
35. Rapport au Gouverneur Général, "Analyse: naturalisation des Indigènes, question des noms patronymiques," July 1866, ANOM 12h53.

36. Cited in William MacGuckin de Slane and Charles Gabeau, *Vocabulaire destine à fixer la transcription en français des noms de personnes et de lieux usités chez les indigènes de l'Algérie* (Paris: Imprimerie impériale, 1868), i.
37. The work of the first commission is collected in the file "Orthographe des noms arabes. Réf décision du GGA, 16 juillet 1855," ANOM 1i27.
38. "Dictionnaire destiné à fixer la transcription en français des mots géographique et ethnographiques de l'Algérie," ANOM 1i27.
39. Beaussier put this knowledge into his French-Arabic dictionary, which first appeared in 1871. It became the definitive reference for Maghribi Arabic in the colonial era. It has gone through multiple editions, including substantial revisions made by Mohammed Ben Cheneb in the 1958 edition, and the supplement published in 1959 by Jérôme Lentin. Marcelin Beaussier, Mohammed Ben Cheneb, and Jérôme Lentin, *Dictionnaire pratique arabe-français: arabe maghrébin* (Paris: Ibis Press, 2006). See also the discussion of the *Dictionnaire* in Alain Messaoudi, "Renseigner, enseigner: Les interprètes militaires et la constitution d'un premier corpus savant 'algérien' (1830–1870)," *Revue d'histoire du XIXᵉ siècle* 41 (2010): 97–112.
40. The first studies of the Berber language appear in print in the mid-nineteenth century. They focused on the main points of grammar and bilingual dictionaries. A transcription system for Berber in French letters first appeared in 1858. However, none of these works gives more than passing attention to onomastics. Jean-Michel Venture de Paradis, *Grammaire et dictionnaire abrégés de la langue berbère* (Paris: Imprimerie royale, 1844); *Dictionnaire français-berbère* (Paris: Imprimerie Royale, 1844); Adolphe Hanoteau, *Essai de grammaire Kabyle* (Algiers: Bastide, 1858).
41. Salem Chaker, *Berbères d'aujourd'hui* (Paris Harmattan, 1989), 116; Mohand-Akli Haddadou, *Recueil de prénoms amazighs* (Algiers: Haut-Commissariat à l'Amazighité, 2003), 14. Separate studies for Berber names were slow to appear. See Charles de Foucauld, *Dictionnaire abrégé Touareg-Français de noms propres (dialecte de l'Ăhaggar)* (Paris: Larose, 1940).
42. Salem Chaker, "Onomastique Libyco-Berbère (Anthroponymie)," in *Encyclopédie berbère*, vol. 35: *Oasitae-Ortaïas*, ed. Salem Chaker (Paris: Peeters, 2013), 5762.
43. Report from the meeting of 30 July 1890, Préfecture d'Algiers, Commission Centrale de l'état civil des indigènes, ANOM 12h52.
44. Mac Guckin de Slane and Gabeau, *Vocabulaire.*
45. Secrétariat général du Gouvernement Général de l'Algérie to préfets, 15 April 1869, no. 595, ANOM 1i27. In 1875 a new commission of French Arabists began work on revisions to Mac Guckin de Slane and Gabeau's *Vocabulaire* to correct its many errors and fill in its lacunae. Gouvernement Général Civil de l'Algérie et Affaires Financières to Chef d'État-Major Général, September 1875, ANOM 12h53; Rapport sur le mode de transcription en français des noms de personnes et de lieux arabes, Gouvernement Général de l'Algérie, application de la loi du 26 juillet 1873, ANOM 12h53.

46. Essafia Amorouayach, "Adaptation d'anthroponymes algériens à l'orthographe française," *Synergies Algérie*, no. 24 (2017): 228–29; Ouerdia Yermeche, "L'état civil algérien: genèse d'un processus redénominatif," *Publications PNR du CRASC* (2005): 25–27.
47. Richard Lepsius, *Standard Alphabet for Reducing Unwritten Languages and Foreign Graphic Systems to a Uniform Orthography in European Letters*, 2nd ed. (London: Williams and Norgate; Berlin: Hertz, 1863), 25. See also Floris Solleveld, "Lepsius as a Linguist: Fieldwork, Philology, Phonetics, and 'the Hamitic Hypothesis,'" *Language and History* 63, no. 3 (2020): 193–213.
48. For these questions in the period before European hegemony, see Ronit Ricci, *Islam Translated: Literature, Conversion, and the Arabic Cosmopolis of South and Southeast Asia* (Chicago: University of Chicago Press, 2011).
49. Alain Messaoudi, *Les arabisants et la France coloniale, 1780–1930: savants, conseillers, médiateurs* (Lyon: ENS Éditions, 2015), 306–21.
50. Katie Chenoweth, *The Prosthetic Tongue: Print Technology and the Rise of the French Language* (Philadelphia: University of Pennsylvania Press, 2019), 149–63.
51. Mac Guckin de Slane and Gabeau, *Vocabulaire*, vi.
52. Mac Guckin de Slane and Gabeau, iii.
53. Esther-Miriam Wagner, *Linguistic Variety of Judaeo-Arabic in Letters from the Cairo Genizah* (Leiden: Brill, 2010), 25–68.
54. Wagner, *Linguistic Variety of Judaeo-Arabic*, 29.
55. Messaoudi, *Arabisants et la France coloniale*, 33, 88–91.
56. Abi-Mershed, *Apostles of Modernity*, 188–200.
57. Ouahmi Ould-Braham, "À propos de l'ouvrage pédagogique de Belkassem ben Sedira: le *Cours de langue kabyle* (1887)," *Études et documents berbères* 2, no. 42 (2019): 7–44. The most recent edition of Ben Sedira's venerable series of Arabic-French dictionaries appeared in 2001. Belkacem Ben Sedira, *Dictionnaire français-arabe* (Geneva: Slatkine, 2001).
58. Messaoudi, *Arabisants et la France coloniale*, 326.
59. Louis-Jacques Bresnier, *Cours pratique et théorique de langue arabe* (Algiers: Bastide, 1855), 21.
60. Mac Guckin de Slane and Gabeau, *Vocabulaire*, iv–ix.
61. Technical problems with Lepsius's Standard Alphabet are addressed in Judith T. Irvine, "Subjected Words: African Linguistics and the Colonial Encounter," *Language and Communication* 28 (2008): 335.
62. Jacques Lacan, "The Symbolic, The Imaginary, and the Real," in *On the Names-of-the-Father*, trans. Bruce Fink (Cambridge, UK: Polity, 2013), 18.
63. "Project de décret relatif à l'état civil des indignes musulmans," Préfecture d'Oran, Bureau des Affaires Indigènes, 30 November 1875, ANOM 12h51. This call for specialists to implement the project was echoed in Council of Ministers in Paris. See Bellemare, "Rapport au conseil," n.d., no. 1247, debated in the council, 6 April 1876, ANOM 12h51.
64. Mac Guckin de Slane and Gabeau, *Vocabulaire*, vi.

65. Joseph Errington, *Linguistics in a Colonial World: A Story of Language, Meaning and Power* (Malden: Blackwell, 2008); Jean Comaroff and John Comaroff, *Of Revelation and Revolution: Christianity, Colonialism and Consciousness in South Africa*, vol. 1 (Chicago: University of Chicago Press, 1991), 213–30; Johannes Fabian, *Language and Colonial Power: The Appropriation of Swahili in the Former Belgian Congo, 1880–1938* (Cambridge: Cambridge University Press, 1986). On the history of the French language in colonial French West Africa, see Cécile Van Den Avenne, *De la bouche même des indigènes: échanges linguistiques en Afrique colonial* (Paris: Vendémiaire, 2017); and Laurent Dubreuil, *Empire of Language: Towards a Critique of (Post)colonial Expression*, trans. David Fieni (Ithaca, NY: Cornell University Press, 2013), esp. chaps. 5 and 6.
66. Julie Candler Hayes, "Translation and the Transparency of French," *Translation Studies* 5, no. 2 (2012): 214.
67. Irvine, "Subjected Words," 331.
68. Katherine E. Hoffman, "Purity and Contamination: Language Ideologies in French Colonial Native Policy in Morocco," *Comparative Studies in Society and History* 50, no. 3 (2008): 724–52.
69. Bresnier, *Cours pratique*, 519. Conceptualizing Arabic as diglossic remains controversial today. See Kristen Brustad, "Diglossia as Ideology," in *The Politics of Written Language and the Arab World*, ed. Jacob Høigilt and Gunvor Mejdell (Leiden: Brill, 2017): 41–67.
70. Messaoudi, *Arabisants et la France coloniale*, 295–96.
71. Auguste Cherbonneau, *Éléments de la phraséologie française avec une traduction en arabe vulgaire (idiôme africain) à l'usage des indigènes* (Paris: Hachette, 1851).
72. Messaoudi, *Arabisants et la France coloniale*, 316.
73. Joan Leopold, ed., *Prix Volney Essay Series*, vols. 1A and 1B: *The Prix Volney: Its History and Significance for the Development of Linguistic Research* (Dordrecht: Kluwer Academic, 1999).
74. Messaoudi, *Arabisants et la France coloniale*, 320; Jacques Rancière, *The Ignorant Schoolmaster: Five Lessons in Intellectual Emancipation*, trans. Kristin Ross (Stanford, CA: Stanford University Press, 1991).
75. For the colonial chapter in the long debate about the relationship of speech to writing, see Errington, *Linguistics in a Colonial World.*
76. Bresnier, *Cours pratique*, 19.
77. Anthony Lodge, "Molière's Peasants and the Norms of Spoken French," *Neuphilologische Mitteilungen* 92, no. 4 (1991), 485–99. On the patronizing treatment of popular classes and their language in the *poissard* genre, see Robin Howells, "The Eighteenth-Century *Conte*," in *The Cambridge History of French Literature*, ed. W. Burgwinkle, N. Hammond, and E. Wilson, (Cambridge: Cambridge University Press, 2011), 374–75.
78. Quote from the *Encyclopédie* in R. Anthony Lodge, *French: From Dialect to Standard* (London: Routledge, 1993), 193.
79. Bresnier, *Cours pratique*, 518.
80. Edmond Combarel, cited in Messaoudi, *Arabisants et la France coloniale*, 194.

81. Julie Candler Hayes, *Translation, Subjectivity, and Culture in France and England, 1600–1800* (Stanford, CA: Stanford University Press, 2009); Ricci, *Islam Translated*, 32–65.
82. Paul de Man, *The Resistance to Theory* (Minneapolis: University of Minnesota, 1986), 73–105; Gayatri Chakravorty Spivak, *Outside in the Teaching Machine* (New York: Routledge, 1993), 179–200.
83. Dipesh Chakrabarty, *Provincializing Europe: Postcolonial Thought and Historical Difference* (Princeton, NJ: Princeton University Press, 2008), 72–96.
84. Alain Messaoudi, "Renseigner, enseigner," 110–11.
85. Jacques Derrida, "Des Tours de Babel," in *Psyche: Inventions of the Other*, vol. 1, ed. Peggy Kamuf and Elizabeth Rottenberg (Stanford, CA: Stanford University Press, 2007), 199.
86. Didier Guignard, "Le diptyque *propriété et société* en Algérie et ses retouches successives (XIXe–XXIe siècles)," in *Propriété et société en Algérie*, 10.
87. Although historians have made enormous progress untangling the complexity of the land regime, the importance of personal names to it remains underemphasized. Judith Surkis is among the few who have highlighted their role. Judith Surkis, *Sex, Law, and Sovereignty in French Algeria, 1830–1930* (Ithaca, NY: Cornell University Press, 2019), 129–31.
88. Warnier Law (26 July 1873), art. 17 in Henry Hugues and Paul Labrat, *Le Code algérien, recueil annoté suivant l'ordre alphabétique des matières des lois, décrets, décisions, arrêtés et circulaires formant la législation de l'Algérie publiés de 1872 à 1878* (Paris: Challamel, 1878), 363.
89. Algerians proved to be adept in using their own land tenure practices, such as indivision (*sharika*), and the courts to block land sales. Prior to 1873, when they still retained parts of Islamic law governing property, they successfully used the legal principle of *shafāʿa* to prevent sales of land outside of the family. They also contracted a mortgage known as *rahniyya*, which created layers of overlapping interests and multiple claims on property. Finally, lands placed in religious endowments (*habūs*) also served to block sales. Allan Christelow, *Muslim Law Courts and the French Colonial State in Algeria* (Princeton, NJ: Princeton University Press, 1985), 72–78; Bras, "L'imperfection de la propriété indigène."
90. Decree of 9 June 1831, in *Recueil des actes du Gouvernement de l'Algérie, 1830–1854* (Algiers: Imprimerie du Gouvernement, 1856), 9; Alain Sainte-Marie, "Législation foncière et société rurale l'application de la loi du 26 juillet 1873 dans les douars de l'Algérois," *Études rurales* 57 (January–March 1975): 61–87.
91. Charles Picot, *Éléments du Code Napoléon: exposé par demandes et par réponses: ouvrage destiné à vulgariser les lois françaises* (Paris: Coupé, 1868), 14.
92. Karen Offen, *The Woman Question in France, 1400–1870* (Cambridge: Cambridge University Press, 2017), 48–54.
93. M. F. P. Herchenroder, "The Capacity of Married Women in French Law," *Journal of Comparative Legislation and International Law* 20, no. 4 (1938): 196.
94. Muriam Haleh Davis, *Markets of Civilization: Islam and Racial Capitalism in Algeria* (Durham, NC: Duke University Press, 2022).

95. Tiphaine Barthelemy, "Patronymic Names and *Noms de Terre* in the French Nobility in the Eighteenth and the Nineteenth Centuries," *History of the Family* 5, no. 2 (2000): 181–97. For fraud associated with noble names, see Reynald Abad, "La falsification d'identité en France, du règne personnel de Louis XIV à la veille de la Révolution," *French Historical Studies* 39, no. 3 (August 2016): 482–84.
96. Anonymous, "Nom (et Prénom)," *Répertoire général alphabétique*, 543–44.
97. Barthelemy, "Patronymic Names and *Noms de Terre*," 182, 185.
98. Gérard Chouquer, *Dictionnaire des questions foncières pendant la colonisation de l'Algérie au XIXe siècle* (Paris: Publi-Topex, 2020), 28; Arthur Pellegrin, "Noms de toponymie africaine: les noms de lieux empruntés au règne animal," *IBLA, Revue de l'Institut des belles lettres arabes* 12 (1949): 77–80.
99. Alexandre Bellemare, *Grammaire arabe (idiome d'Algérie), à l'usage de l'armée et des employés civils de l'Algérie* (Paris: Hachette, 1854), 188–89; Élisée Reclus, *Nouvelle géographie universelle*, vol. 11: *L'Afrique septentrionale* (Paris: Hachette, 1886), 887; Auguste Cherbonneau, *Dictionnaire français-arabe pour la conversation en Algérie* (Paris: Imprimerie Nationale, 1884), 47; Louis-Jacques Bresnier, *Chrestomathie arabe: lettres, actes et pièces diverses avec la traduction française en regard* (Algiers: Bastide, 1857), 70.
100. Affaires indigènes to Gouverner Général, 28 March 1875, no. 12, ANOM 12h51.
101. "Note: noms patronymiques (loi du 26 Juillet 1873)," signed: Devauly. n.d. (ca. 1874–75), ANOM 12h53. Devauly failed to note that the Arabic word *kabsh* for sheep had a double entendre meaning cuckold (*kabsh faḥl*), making it a doubly problematic choice for a family name. See Marcelin Beaussier, *Dictionnaire pratique arabe-français* (Algiers: Jourdan, 1887), 578.
102. "Note: noms patronymiques," Devauly, ANOM 12h53.
103. Stéphane Gsell, *Enquête administrative sur les travaux hydrauliques anciens en Algérie* (Paris: Imprimerie nationale, 1902), 53–54; Auguste Cherbonneau, "Explorations et missions," *Revue de géographie* 10 (January–June 1882): 154.
104. Devauly's competency in Arabic is unknown. He may have been fooled by the relatively ubiquity of "Idols" as a toponym—referencing the many ancient ruins that punctuated the Algerian landscape—into thinking it was considered benign, translating *al-aṣnām* for his French readers as "the statues."
105. "Note: noms patronymiques," Devauly, ANOM 12h53.
106. Anonymous, "Nom (et Prénom)," in *Répertoire général alphabétique du droit*, 545. For names in slave society, see Susan Benson, "Injurious Names: Naming, Disavowal, and Recuperation in Contexts of Slavery and Emancipation," in *The Anthropology of Names and Naming*, ed. Gabriele vom Bruck and Barbara Bodenhorn (Cambridge: Cambridge University Press 2006), 177–99.
107. "Ces noms de famille durs à porter," Moi je, A2, 20 March 1985, https://www.youtube.com/watch?v=LGT0dnejgpM.
108. Lallier, *Propriété des noms*, 205–8.
109. See the case studies in Jean-Pierre Bardet and Guy Brunet, eds., *Noms et destins des sans famille* (Paris: Presses de l'Université Paris-Sorbonne, 2007).

110. Hosni Kitouni, "L'indigénisation de l'Algérien" (ms., 2017), not paginated.
111. The examples from Norès were cited in Henri Bénet's *L'État civil en Algérie: Traité théorique et pratique de la constitution de l'état civil des Indigènes Algériens* (Algiers: Minerva, 1937), 117. They then appeared (with additional examples) in Charles-Robert Ageron, *Algériens musulmans et la France*, 1:181. Through Ageron, Norès's examples then reappear in contemporary studies, including Karim Ould-Ennebia, "Histoire de l'état civil des Algériens: Patronymie et acculturation," *Revue maghrébine des études historiques et sociales*, no. 1 (September 2009): 24; and Farīd bin Ramḍān (Farid Benramdane), "Tadmīr al-Nasab fī al-Ḥāla al-Madanīya bil-Jaza'ir," *Insāniyāt* 2 (2010): 91.
112. Edmond Norès, *Essai de codification du droit musulman algérien (statut personnel)* (Algiers: Jourdan, 1909), 76.
113. I have worked from the digitized database of état civil records compiled at ANOM. It includes scanned registers for the period 1830–1921 and a separate nominative index that covers the period up to 1904. For a discussion of this archive's construction with regard to marriage registers, see Guy Brunet and Kamel Kateb, *L'Algérie des Européens au XIXe: naissance d'une population et transformation d'une société (Bern: Lang, 2018)*, 343–46. See also Formihttp://anom.archivesnationales.culture.gouv.fr/caomec2/recherche.php?territoire=ALGERIE, consulted 20 August 2022.
114. Mohamed ben Mohamed ben Djeriou, no. 87, 9 March 1858, Registre des actes de naissance, ville de Médéa 1858, http://anom.archivesnationales.culture.gouv.fr/caomec2/osd.php?territoire=ALGERIE&acte=346007; Zakia Seddik Djeriou, no. 8, 12 October 1900, Registre des actes de naissance, ville de Villars, 1903, http://anom.archivesnationales.culture.gouv.fr/caomec2/osd.php?territoire=ALGERIE&acte=487088; Louise Djeriou, no. 10, 2 October 1903, Registre des actes de naissance, ville de Villars, 1903, http://anom.archivesnationales.culture.gouv.fr/caomec2/osd.php?territoire=ALGERIE&acte=487131.
115. The records show that Cheikh Bou Rouis routinely accompanied Muslims declaring births to the French administration in Médéah, serving as their witness. See Registre des actes de naissance, ville de Médéa 1858, http://anom.archivesnationales.culture.gouv.fr/caomec2/osd.php?territoire=ALGERIE&registre=16934.
116. Registre des actes de naissance, ville de Villars, 1900 and 1903, http://anom.archivesnationales.culture.gouv.fr/caomec2/osd.php?territoire=ALGERIE&acte=487088; http://anom.archivesnationales.culture.gouv.fr/caomec2/osd.php?territoire=ALGERIE&acte=487131.
117. Some anecdotal evidence supports my argument with regard to this name. "Bū Shādi" is the name of a well-known Egyptian poet who lived at the same time (Ahmed Zaki Abu Shadi, d. 1919), and "Bū Jarw" has appeared with some frequency as a name used by Arabs over time, including many in Algeria today. Moreover "Jarw" appears through translation. In the 1980s it appeared as the first name of the Bobby Ewing character in the Arabic language translation of the US television series *Dallas*. Translators reportedly played upon the homophony between "Bobby" and "puppy" and gave the Arabic equivalent of the latter, *jarw*, as his name. Andrew

Hammond, *Popular Culture in the Arab World: Arts, Politics, and the Media* (Cairo: American University in Cairo Press, 2007), 60–61.

118. Ernest Mercier, *La propriété foncière chez les musulmans d'Algérie: ses lois sous la domination française, constitution de l'état civil musulman* (Paris: Leroux, 1891), 41.
119. Jacqueline Sublet, *Le Voile de nom: Essai sur le nom propre arabe* (Paris: Presses universitaires de France, 1991), 187–94.
120. Chaker, "Onomastique libyco-berbère," 5768.
121. Kamal Naït-Zerrad, *L'officiel des prénoms berbères* (Paris: Harmattan, 2003), 12; personal correspondence, Ramdane Touati, 7 November 2017.
122. The scholarship is vast and uneven, ranging from recent anthropological and medical histories to many colonial-era studies, analytically dubious but with empirical value. Ellen Amster, *Medicine and the Saints: Science, Islam, and the Colonial Encounter in Morocco, 1877–1956* (Austin: University of Texas Press, 2013); Edmond Doutté, *Magie et religion dans l'Afrique du Nord* (Algiers: Jourdan, 1909), 317–30; Louis Lataillade, *Coutumes et superstitions obstétricales en Afrique du Nord* (Algiers: Charry, 1936); Eusèbe Vassel, "La Littérature populaire des Israélites tunisiens," *Revue tunisienne* 13 (1906): 217–32; J. Herber, "La main de Fatma," *Hespéris* (1927): 209–19; Eugène Lefébure, "La main de Fatma," *Bulletin de la Société de Géographie d'Alger* 12 (1907): 411–17.
123. Jean Desparmet, *Le mal magique: ethnographie traditionnelle de la Mettidja* (Paris: Geuthner, 1932), 83.
124. C. Kehl, "L'État civil des indigènes en Algérie," *Bulletin trimestriel de la Société de géographie et d'archéologie d'Oran* 52 (March 1931): 181–82.
125. Benam, "Expressions à l'algérienne IX," Forum Algérie, http://www.algerie-dz.com/forums/archive/index.php/t-223718.html; A. Giménez Reíllo, "Uso de alcuñas," Anís del moro, https://anisdelmoro.blogspot.com/2014/04/uso-de-alcunas.html (both accessed 14 June 2019).
126. Beaussier, *Dictionnaire pratique*, 689; Hans Wehr, *A Dictionary of Modern Written Arabic (Arabic-English)*, 4th ed., edited by J. Milton Cowan (Urbana, IL: Spoken Language Services, 1994), 1168.
127. Frantz Fanon, *Black Skins, White Masks*, trans. Charles Lam Markmann (New York: Grove Press, 1967), 30–40. See also Dubreuil, *Empire of Language*, 110–14.
128. Van Den Avenne, *De la bouche même*, chap. 6.
129. Fanon, *Black Skins*, 32.
130. Dominic LaCapra, *History in Transit: Experience, Identity, Critical Theory* (Ithaca, NY: Cornell University Press, 2004), 58–59. On analogous questions with regard to riddles and creole, see Megan Vaughan, *Creating the Creole Island: Slavery in Eighteenth-Century Mauritius* (Durham, NC: Duke University Press, 2005), 212–20.
131. For an example of looking down on the colonizer for their failures to master Arabic, see 'Abd al-Raḥman al-Jabartī, *Al-Jabartī's Chronicle of the First Seven Months of the French Occupation of Egypt*, ed. and trans. S. Moreh (Leiden: Brill, 1975), 42–47. See also Rifā'a Rāfi' Ibn Badawī al-Ṭahṭāwī, *An Imam in Paris*, trans. Daniel Newman (London: Saqi, 2004), 186–88.

132. See at https://www.youtube.com/watch?v=JkIZlGeRoR0, 55:00. See also Elizabeth M. Perego, *Humor and Power in Algeria, 1920 to 2021* (Bloomington: Indiana University Press, 2023).

6. A Colonial État Civil

1. Jean-Pierre Laporte et al., "Olivier (La culture de l'olivier, de l'Antiquité à la Kabylie Contemporaine)," *Encyclopédie berbère*, vol. 35: *Oasitae-Ortaïas*, ed. Salem Chaker (2013), http://journals.openedition.org/encyclopedieberbere/2812.
2. Al-Tirmidhi, https://sunnah.com/tirmidhi:1979.
3. The most important directives included the decree of 8 August 1854, which called for the état civil (births and deaths) of Muslims in civil territories, and the administrative order of 20 May 1868, which extended this requirement to some military and mixed jurisdictions. Henri Bénet, *L'État civil en Algérie: Traité théorique et pratique de la constitution de l'état civil des Indigènes Algériens* (Algiers: Minerva, 1937), 73–83. Apart from the registration drive in Constantine in 1854, neither produced significant results.
4. Robert Estoublon and Adolphe Lefébure, *Code de l'Algérie annoté* (Algiers: Jourdan, 1896), 568–75; Émile Larcher and Georges Rectenwald, *Traité élémentaire de législation algérienne*, vol. 2, 3rd ed. (Paris: Rousseau, 1923), 563.
5. État civil registration began first in the Constantine region in 1887. In some places, locust infestations or major administrative projects like the quinquennial census interrupted the work. Rapport à M. Le Président de la Commission Centrale de l'État Civil des Indigènes, Alger, 17 June 1893, ANOM 12h85.
6. C. Kehl, "L'État civil des indigènes en Algérie," *Bulletin trimestriel de la Société de géographie et d'archéologie d'Oran* 52 (March 1931): 200.
7. Kehl, 200.
8. The état civil registration consumed half of proposed state expenses in the budget for Muslim law in 1890. "Projet du budget de 1890, services du Gouvernement Général de l'Algérie," in *Journal officiel de la République française, Documents parlementaires, Chambre des députés: annexes aux procès-verbaux des* séances (Paris: Imprimerie du Journal officiel, 1889), 136. The first nominative census, rather than a headcount, was accomplished in 1881. Kamel Kateb, *Européens, "Indigènes" et Juifs en Algérie, 1830–1962: représentations et réalités des populations* (Paris: Institut national d'études démographiques, 2001), 20, 103.
9. Hosni Kitouni, *La Kabylie orientale dans l'histoire: pays des Kutama et guerre colonial* (Algiers: Casbah, 2013), 251.
10. See examples in ANOM 12h85.
11. On the stakes of these records for Algerian citizenship today, especially for Algerians born and living abroad, see Kamel Saïdi, *La nationalité algérienne: décryptage d'une identité confisquée* (Paris: Publisud, 2015), 56–60, 88–95, 152; Delphine Perrin,

"Identité et transmission du lien national au Maghreb: étude comparée des codes de la nationalité," *L'Année du Maghreb* 3 (2007): 479–97.

12. Article 14 of the law of 23 March 1882 requiring the use of the patronymic, and subsequent decrees and administrative orders, as explained in Estoublon and Lefébure *Code de l'Algérie*, 573. Gouvernement Général de l'Algérie, Affaires Indigènes, Personnelle Militaire to Préfet de Constantine, 21 March 1917, no. 1334 and Procureur de la République to Préfet de Constantine, 3 May 1924, no. 5, both in ANOM FRANOM9377 14.
13. Dónal Hassett, *Mobilizing Memory: The Great War and the Language of Politics in Colonial Algeria, 1918–39* (Oxford: Oxford University Press, 2019), 179, 181–85. See also Gabriel Koehler-Derrick and Melissa M. Lee, "War and Welfare in Colonial Algeria" *International Organization* 77 (Spring 2023): 263–93.
14. Larcher and Rectenwald, *Traité élémentaire de législation algérienne*, 2:417–18.
15. Decree of 3 February 1912, Art. 9. In *Journal officiel de la République française*, no. 37 (7 Febuary 1912), 1209.
16. On nineteenth-century understandings of state sovereignty as the right of command, see Louis Le Fur, *État fédéral et confédération d'états* (Paris: Marchal and Billard, 1896), 395, 417.
17. On the problem of Algerians as outsiders to a law they are bound to, or "*hors la loi sous la loi*," see Noureddine Amara, "Faire la France en Algérie: émigration algérienne, mésusages du nom et conflits de nationalités dans le monde, de la chute d'Alger aux années 1930" (PhD diss., Université de Paris I, Sorbonne, 2019), 164–65. See also Farid Lekéal, "Justice et pacification: de la Régence d'Alger à l'Algérie: 1830–1839," *Histoire de la justice* 1, no. 16 (2005): 13–30. On Kafka's parable, see Hélène Cixous, *Readings: The Poetics of Blanchot, Joyce, Kafka, Kleist, Lispector, and Tsvetayeva*, trans. Verena Andermatt Conley (Minneapolis: University of Minneapolis Press, 1991), 1–27; Jacques Derrida, "Before the Law," in *Acts of Literature*, ed. Derek Attridge (New York: Routledge, 1992), 181–220; Giorgio Agamben, *Homo Sacer: Sovereign Power and Bare Life*, trans. Daniel Hellen-Roazen (Stanford, CA: Stanford University Press, 1998), 49–62; Roberto Buonamano "Kafka and Legal Critique," *Griffith Law Review* 25, no. 4 (2016): 581–99. Kafka frames the historical work of Adam M. McKeown study of sovereignty, law, and identity in *Melancholy Order: Asian Migration and the Globalization of Borders* (New York: Columbia University Press, 2008), esp. 349–68.
18. Charles-Louis Pinson de Ménerville, *Dictionnaire de la législation algérienne: manuel raisonné des lois, ordonnances, décrets, décisions et arrêtés* (Algiers: Philippe, 1853), 297–339. See also Claude Bontems, *Manuel des institutions algériennes de la domination turque à l'indépendance*, vol. 1: *la domination turque et le régime militaire* (Paris: Cujas, 1976), 173–207; Claude Collot, *Les Institutions de l'Algérie durant la période colonial (1830–1962)* (Paris: Éditions du CNRS; Algiers: Office des publications universitaires, 1987), 31–34.
19. Alfred Franque, *Lois de l'Algérie, du 5 juillet 1830 (occupation d'Alger) au 1ère janvier 1841* (Paris: Corréard, 1844), 167–68.

20. Jacques Frémeaux, *Les bureaux arabes dans l'Algérie de la conquête* (Paris: Denoël, 1993), 266.
21. Bontems, *Manuel des institutions algériennes*, 1:191, 196. Elsewhere Bontems notes that the concept of the metropolitan department itself is incompatible with a colonial administration. Claude Bontems, *L'Algérie, ses instituions et son droit à l'épreuve de la colonisation* (Paris: Bouchène, 2018), 91.
22. Sophie B. Roberts, *Citizenship and Antisemitism in French Colonial Algeria, 1870–1962* (Cambridge: Cambridge University Press, 2017), 5–13; Pinson de Ménerville, *Dictionnaire de la législation*, 3:228.
23. Patrick Weil, *How to Be French: Nationality in the Making Since 1789*, trans. Catherine Porter (Durham, NC: Duke University Press, 2008), 214; Laure Blévis "La citoyenneté française au miroir de la colonisation: étude des demandes de naturalisation des 'sujets français' en Algérie colonial," *Genèses*, no. 53 (2003): 25–47; Andrea L. Smith, "Citizenship in the Colony: Naturalization Law and Legal Assimilation in 19th Century Algeria," *Political and Legal Anthropology Review* 19, no. 1 (May 1996): 33–49.
24. Jessica M. Marglin, "Citizenship and Nationality in the French Colonial Maghreb," *Routledge Handbook of Citizenship in the Middle East and North Africa*, ed. Roel Meijer, James Sater, and Zahra Baba (New York: Routledge, 2020), 45–60; Saliha Belmessous, *Assimilation and Empire: Uniformity in French and British Colonies, 1541–1954* (Oxford: Oxford University Press, 2013), 117–204.
25. Louis Flandin, cited in Pinson de Ménerville, *Dictionnaire de la législation*, 2:152. The clearest and most concise discussion of French personal law in colonial Algeria is Judith Surkis, *Sex, Law, and Sovereignty in French Algeria, 1830–1930* (Ithaca, NY: Cornell University Press, 2019), 96–100.
26. George Bataille, *The Accursed Share: An Essay on General Economy*, trans. Robert Hurley, 3 vols. (New York: Zone Books, 1991–1993).
27. Joan Wallach Scott, *The Politics of the Veil* (Princeton, NJ: Princeton University Press, 2007); Surkis, *Sex, Law, and Sovereignty.*
28. Flandin, cited in Pinson de Ménerville, *Dictionnaire de la législation*, 2:152.
29. Ouanassa Siari Tengour, "Constantine, 1887: des notables contre la 'naturalisation,'" in *Historie de l'Algérie coloniale*, ed. Abderrahmane Bouchène et al. (Paris: Découverte, 2014), 235–38.
30. James McDougall, *History and the Culture of Nationalism in Algeria* (Cambridge: Cambridge University Press, 2006), 94, citing Ibn Bādīs.
31. *Baṣā'ir* (14 January 1938), 2.
32. The fatwa appeared inauspiciously in *Baṣā'ir* in August 1937 (fatwa dated 2 Jumuda al-Thani 1356). The editors republished it five months later in a special issue accompanied by an explicative preface by Al-'Arbī al-Tabassī, *Baṣā'ir*, 14 January 1938. Although she does not deal with the fatwa, for context see Charlotte Courreye, *L'Algérie des Oulémas: Une histoire de l'Algérie contemporaine (1931–1991)* (Paris: Éditions de la Sorbonne, 2020), 23–65. See also McDougall, *History and the Culture of Nationalism.*

33. Sylvie Thénault, "Le 'code de l'indigénat,'" in *Historie de l'Algérie coloniale*, ed. Abderrahmane Bouchène et al., 200–206; Didier Guignard, *L'Abus de pouvoir dans l'Algérie colonial: Visibilité et singularité* (s.l.: Presses universitaires de Paris Ouest, 2010), 43–104; Emmanuelle Saada, "La loi, le droit et l'indigène," *Droits* 43, no. 1 (2006): 165–90; Isabelle Merle, "Retour sur le régime de l'indigénat: genèse et contradictions des principes répressifs dans l'empire français," *French Politics, Culture and Society* 20, no. 2 (2002): 77–97.
34. Isabelle Merle review of *De l'indigénat*, by Olivier Le Cour Grandmaison, *Genèses*, no. 86 (March 2012): 151. See also Gregory Mann, "What Was the 'Indigénat'? The 'Empire of Law' in French West Africa," *Journal of African History* 50, no. 3 (2009): 331–53; Isabelle Merle, "De la 'légalisation' de la violence en contexte colonial: le régime de l'indigénat en question." *Politix* 17, no. 66 (2004): 137–62.
35. Charles Marchal cited in Charles-Robert Ageron, *Les Algériens musulmans et la France (1871-1919)*, vol. 1 (Paris: Presses universitaires de France, 1968), 343. The original reads: "*Pour nous la Liberté, pour eux l'Autorité.*" For context, see Ageron, *Les Algériens musulmans*, 1:343–66.
36. Joshua Cole, *The Power of Large Numbers: Population, Politics, and Gender in Nineteenth-Century France* (Ithaca, NY: Cornell University Press, 2000), 39–54; Suzanne Desan, *The Family on Trial in Revolutionary France* (Berkeley: University of California Press, 2004), 47–92; Gérard Noiriel, "The Identification of the Citizen: The Birth of Republican Civil Status in France," in *Documenting Individual Identity: The Development of State Practices in the Modern World*, ed. Jane Caplan and John Torpey (Princeton, NJ: Princeton University Press, 2001), 28–48.
37. Louis-Jérôme Gohier, cited in *Réimpression de l'ancien Moniteur, seule histoire authentique et inaltérée de la Révolution française*, vol. 12 (Paris: Plon, 1862), 708; Noiriel, "Identification of the Citizen."
38. Apart from the early cases mentioned, Muslim Algerians appeared in the same état civil registries as Europeans. This was not the case later in Morocco, nor to the same extent Tunisia, where the protectorate government recognized separately drawn baptismal documents for Christians. Paul Decroux, "L'État civil dans les milieux indigènes de l'Afrique du Nord," Centres de hautes études d'administration musulmane, 2 November 1945, ANOM 10APOM960.
39. Jean-Étienne-Marie Portalis, meeting of 24 November 1801, cited in *Archives parlementaires*, vol. 2: *du 29 frimaire an IX au 9 frimaire an X* (Paris: Dupont, 1863), 736.
40. Reynald Abad, "La falsification d'identité en France, du règne personnel de Louis XIV à la veille de la Révolution," *French Historical Studies* 39, no. 3 (August 2016): 471–508; Benjamin Faucher, "Les registres de l'état civil protestant en France depuis le XVIe siècle jusqu'à nos jours," *Bibliothèque de l'École des Chartes* 84 (1923): 328–32; Roger Chastanier, *Un aspect des lois relatives aux minorités religieuses: L'état civil des protestants, 1550-1792* (Nîmes: Chastanier, 1922); Charles Dardier, "Les registres de l'état civil des protestants de Nîmes, de 1571–1792," *Bulletin historique et littéraire (Société de l'Histoire du Protestantisme Français)* 23, no. 3 (1874): 141–43. For the vital

records of Jews in France, see Esther Benbassa, *The Jews of France: A History from Antiquity to the Present*, trans. M. B. DeBevoise (Princeton, NJ: Princeton University Press, 1999), 78–79; Zosa Szajkowski, "The Reform of the *État-Civil* of the French Jews During the Revolution of 1789," *Jewish Quarterly Review* 49 no. 1 (July 1958): 63–83.

41. Hannah Arendt, *The Origins of Totalitarianism*, new ed. (New York: Harcourt, 1973), 298.
42. Adolphe Franck, *Philosophie du droit civil* (Paris: Alcan, 1886), 61.
43. Naomi Davidson, *Only Muslim: Embodying Islam in Twentieth-Century France* (Ithaca, NY: Cornell University Press, 2012), 149–58.
44. Maurice Gaudefroy-Demombynes, *Les cérémonies du mariage chez les indigènes de l'Algérie* (Paris: Maisonneuve, 1901), 1–23.
45. Bénet, *État civil en Algérie*, 77; Kehl, "État civil des indigènes," 174–80.
46. Bureau Arabe de Département de Constantine to Ministère de la Guerre, 2 July 1856, no. 340, ANOM 12h51.
47. Surkis, *Sex, Law, and Sovereignty.*
48. Sarah Ghabrial, "*Le 'fiqh francisé'*? Muslim Personal Status Law Reform and Women's Litigation in Colonial Algeria (1870–1930)" (PhD diss., McGill University, 2014), 71–77, 89–97.
49. Edmond Norès, *Essai de codification du droit musulman algérien (statut personnel)* (Algiers: Jourdan, 1909), 156–68.
50. Larcher and Rectenwald, *Traité élémentaire de législation algérienne*, 2:362.
51. Estoublon and Lefébure *Code de l'Algérie*, 640n1; Bénet, *État civil en Algérie*, 77–79.
52. Estoublon and Lefébure, *Code de l'Algérie*, 640n1.
53. Circular of 26 July 1875, cited in Bénet, *État civil en Algérie*, 77–78.
54. Judgement of 31 May 1905, cited in Kehl, "État civil des indigènes," 206.
55. Bénet, *État civil en Algérie*, 200.
56. Gouvernement Général de l'Algérie, *Instructions pour l'exécution de la loi du 23 mars 1882 et du règlement d'administration publique du 13 mars 1883 sur l'état civil des indigènes musulmans de l'Algérie* (Algiers: Fojosso, 1885); Gouvernement Général de l'Algérie, *Instruction: état civil des indigènes, 20 avril 1888* (Algiers: Fojosso, 1888); E. Cornu, *Guide pratique pour la constitution de l'état civil des indigènes* (Algiers: Jourdan, 1889).
57. Gouvernement Général de l'Algérie, *Instructions pour l'exécution de la loi* 1885, 10.
58. Gouvernement Général de l'Algérie, 13.
59. Gouvernement Général de l'Algérie, 17.
60. Gouvernement Général de l'Algérie, 29.
61. Gouvernement Général de l'Algérie, 30.
62. *Constitution de la propriété en Algérie* (Algiers: Bouyer, 1863), 31, 57–58, ANOM F80 1806.
63. *Procès-verbaux des délibérations: session de décembre 1879: Conseil supérieur de gouvernement (Algiers)* (Algiers: Duclaox, 1880), 412.
64. *Journal official de la République française: Lois et décrets* 14, no. 82 (24 March 1882), 1.
65. Cornu, *Guide pratique*, 12–13.

66. Mohammed Kouidri, "Colonisation, indépendance et développement humain en Algérie: quel bilan?," *Insaniyat*: 65–66 (2014): fig. 1, https://journals.openedition.org/insaniyat/14852; and Kateb, *Européens, "Indigènes" et Juifs*, 296.
67. Cornu, *Guide pratique*, 34.
68. Cornu, 43.
69. Gouvernement Général de l'Algérie, *Instructions* 1885, 65, 56.
70. Cornu, *Guide pratique*, 22.
71. Cornu, 38.
72. Gouvernement Général de l'Algérie, *Instructions* 1885, 68; "Procès-Verbal de la séance de 12 juin 1888," ANOM 12h52.
73. Joseph W. Peterson, *Sacred Rivals: Catholic Missions and the Making of Islam in Nineteenth-Century France and Algeria* (Oxford: Oxford University Press, 2022); Bertrand Taithe, "Missionary Hubris in Colonial Algeria? Founding and Governing Christian Arab Villages 1868–1930," in *Christian Missions and Humanitarianism in the Middle East, 1850–1950: Ideologies, Rhetoric, and Practices*, ed. Inger Marie Okkenhaug and Karène Sanchez Summerer (Leiden: Brill 2020), 133–54; Bertrand Taithe, "Algerian Orphans and Colonial Christianity in Algeria 1866–1939," *French History* 20, no. 3 (2006), 240–59.
74. Peterson, *Sacred Rivals*, 71.
75. Maire de la Commune des Attafs, to Sous-Préfet de Miliana, 2 April 1897, ANOM 12h85.
76. Karima Dirèche, *Chrétiens de Kabylie, 1873-1954: Une action missionnaire dans l'Algérie coloniale* (s.l.: Bouchène, 2004).
77. Peterson, *Sacred Rivals*, 189.
78. Gouvernement Général de l'Algérie, *Vocabulaire destiné à fixer la transcription en français des noms des indigènes* (Algiers: Jourdan, 1885).
79. Gouvernement Général de l'Algérie, viii.
80. Gouvernement Général de l'Algérie, 45.
81. Note pour M. le chef du 7e bureau, Gouvernement Général de l'Algérie, 2e bureau, 9 November 1887, no. 4185, ANOM 12h53.
82. Préfect d'Alger to Gouvernement Général de l'Algérie, 8 November 1897, no. 11951, ANOM 12h85.
83. Note, 9 November 1887, no. 4185; and Département de Constantine, Arrondissement de Sétif, Commune Mixte de Maâdid, to Sous-Préfet Arrondissement de Sétif, 10 February 1896, no. 321. Both in ANOM 12h53.
84. Rapport à M. le Président de la Commission Centrale de l'État Civil des Indigènes, Alger, 17 June 1893, ANOM 12h85.
85. "Rapport du Commissaire de l'État Civil sur l'ensemble de ses opérations," 15 December 1890, ANOM 12h54.
86. Mohammed Harbi, *Une vie debout*, vol. 1: *Mémoires politiques, 1945–1962* (Paris: Découverte, 2001), 7–31; McDougall, *History of Algeria*, 98–100.
87. Letter of Amor ben Rabah to Préfet de Constantine, 21 June 1893, ANOM 12h65.
88. The rules for requesting a name correction appear in Gouvernement Général de l'Algérie, *Instructions* 1885, 76.

89. Préfecture de Constantine, État civil des Indigènes to Gouvernement Général de l'Algérie, 23 June 1893, no. 100; Decree 3 July 1893, ANOM 12h65.
90. Reading this question from Shakespeare, Catherine Belsey explains: "The signifier, however arbitrary, is not at the disposal of the subject. Romeo's name precedes him, makes him a subject, locates him in the community of Verona. It is not optional." Catherine Belsey, "The Name of the Rose in '*Romeo and Juliet*,'" *Yearbook of English Studies* 23 (1993): 133. See also Jacques Derrida, "Aphorism Countertime," in *Psyche: Inventions of the Other*, vol. 2, ed. Peggy Kamuf and Elizabeth Rottenberg (Stanford, CA: Stanford University Press, 2008), 127–42.
91. Arabic spellings as they appear in the Arabic letter, dated 14 Shuwwal 1309; French spellings as they appear in the translation, dated 12 May 1892, ANOM 12h65.
92. Arabic letter dated 14 Shawwal 1309 and French translation dated 12 May 1892, ANOM 12h65.
93. Letter to Préfet de Constantine, 31 May 1892, ANOM 12h65.
94. Préfecture de Constantine, État civil des Indigènes to Gouvernement Général de l'Algérie, 18 July 1892, no. 1260; Minute de la lettre écrite, Gouvernement Général de l'Algérie, 6e bureau to Préfet de Constantine, 26 July 1892, no. 3800. Both in ANOM 12h65.
95. Préfecture de Constantine, État civil des Indigènes to Gouvernement Général de l'Algérie, 5 August 1892, no. 1413, ANOM 12h65.
96. Letter of Boët to Préfet, 7 January 1893, ANOM 12h65.
97. The 'Amushās were linguistically diverse. Some spoke Arabic, others Berber. Generally speaking, tribes formed according to the principle of kinship, but not every tribe was made up of people who thought themselves related to each other. For their part, the 'Amushās traced their origins to an Ottoman decision that placed several groups under the same caïd, an administrative approach the French carried over. While the 'Amushās had developed a sense of community over the years, they remembered their separate origins. In the 1860s the 'Amushās living in Takitount reported that they consisted of two groups, one calling themselves the Awlād Mirḥūm, who originated in the steppes of Algeria (the al-Ḥuḍna region), and the Awlād Manṣūr bin Sa'īd, which had migrated from around Miliana, two distinct and far separated places. "Tribu des Amoucha," ANOM 44kk55; F. Accordo, *Tableau général des communes de l'Algérie* (Algiers: Fontana, 1892), 150; Ernest Carette and Auguste Warnier, *Carte de l'Algérie divisée par tribus* (s.l.: s.n., 1846). See also Hugh Roberts, *Berber Government: The Kabyle Polity in Pre-Colonial Algeria* (London: Tauris, 2014), 43–49.
98. Paul Révoil, *Tableau général des communes de l'Algérie* (Algiers: Giralt, 1902), 192; F. Accardo, *Répertoire alphabétique des tribus et douars de l'Algérie* (Algiers: Jourdan, 1879), 76–77.
99. Colette Establet, *Être caïd dans l'Algérie coloniale* (Paris: Éditions du Centre national de la recherche scientifique, 1991), 209–26; Abderrazak Djellali, "Le caïdat en Algérie au XIXe siècle," *Cahiers de la Méditerranée* 45, no. 1 (1992): 37–49; Henri Brenot, *Le Douar, cellule administrative de l'Algérie du nord* (Algiers: Heintz, 1938); Élie Tabet, *Notes sur l'organisation des tribus et l'étymologie des nom propres* (Oran: Association ouvrière,

1882), 15; Philippe Marçais, *Textes arabes de Djidjelli* (Paris: Presses universitaires de France, 1954), 11.

100. Brenot, *Douar, cellule*, 21.
101. Rapport à l'Empereur, 20 May 1868, ANOM F80 1808.
102. Brahim Atoui, "Toponymie et espace en Algérie" (PhD diss., Université de Provence Aix Marseille I, 1996), 188–91.
103. At the time of registration, the administration Takitount had recently passed to what was known as a *commune mixte*, a type of community, which, although predominately Algerian, came under the authority of a locally seated French civilian administrator.
104. This was the case for a woman originally named Aïcha bent Mohammed ben Dergam, who was reportedly seventy-five years old, or Cherifa bent Cherif ben Ahmed, recorded as seventy years old, whose patronymics were listed as Aïcha and Cherifa, respectively. No. 5 Aïcha and no. 52 Cherifa in M. Feutray, "État civil des indigènes, Commune mixte des Amouchas, Arbres généalogiques," May 1890, ANOM 9377//14.
105. No. 47, Brahmia, "Amouchas Arbres généalogiques," 1890.
106. No. 23, Baouch, "Amouchas Arbres généalogiques," 1890.
107. No. 58, Daoudi, "Amouchas Arbres généalogiques," 1890.
108. No. 1, Abbache, "Amouchas Arbres généalogiques," 1890.
109. No. 81, Hammadi, "Amouchas Arbres généalogiques," 1890.
110. No. 162, Sahnoun, "Amouchas Arbres généalogiques," 1890.
111. No. 20, Azzoug, "Amouchas Arbres généalogiques," 1890.
112. Gouvernement Général de l'Algérie, *Instruction 20 avril 1888*, 12–13; Cornu, *Guide pratique*, 22–23.
113. Gouvernement Général de l'Algérie, *Instruction 20 avril 1888*, 13.
114. Basic principles of Sunni inheritance law and secondary sources can be found in David S. Powers, "Inheritance," in *Oxford Bibliographies in Islamic Studies*, ed. Andrew Rippin (Oxford: Oxford University Press, 2015), https://www.oxfordbibliographies.com. The application of these rules, however, varied considerably based on context. See the two important essays by David S. Powers, "The Islamic Inheritance System: A Socio-Historical Approach" (1990) and "Orientalism, Colonialism, and Legal History: The Attack on Muslim Family Endowments in Algeria and India" (1989), both republished in David S. Powers, *The Development of Islamic Law and Society in the Maghrib:* Qāḍīs, Muftīs *and Family Law* (New York: Routledge, 2016).
115. Minute de la note écrite, Gouvernement Général de l'Algérie, 6e bureau, 4 March 1891, no. 1511, ANOM 12h54.
116. Boët spoke frankly in part because he enjoyed considerable security in his position, having married the daughter of an important official in the Department of Constantine's administration. ANOM no. 112. Boët and Lesbros marriage, 1 September 1887, http://anom.archivesnationales.culture.gouv.fr/caomec2/osd.php?territoire=ALGERIE&acte=1380703

117. Department of Constantine, État Civil des Indigènes, Boët to Préfet, 30 April 1891, ANOM 12h54.
118. Gouvernement Général de l'Algérie, *Instruction 20 avril 1888*, 4; Cornu, *Guide pratique*, 118–19.
119. Jean Le Bihan, *Au service de l'État: Les fonctionnaires intermédiaires au XIXe siècle* (Rennes: Presses universitaires de Rennes, 2008), 61–98.
120. Gilbert Meynier, *L'Algérie révélée, la guerre de 1914–1918 et le premier quart du XXe siècle*, new ed. (Saint-Denis: Bouchène, 2015), 202.
121. Préfet de Constantine, État civil des Indigènes to Gouvernement Général de l'Algérie, 18 August 1894, no. 2471, ANOM 12h68.
122. Rachid Boudjedra, *The Repudiation*, trans. Golda Lambrova (Colorado Springs: Three Continents Press, 1995).
123. Procès-Verbal de la séance de 26 septembre 1890, Préfecture de Constantine, Commission Centrale de l'État Civil des Indigènes, ANOM 12h52.
124. Yacine Daddi Addoun, "'So That God Frees the Former Masters from Hell Fire': Salvation Through Manumission in Nineteenth Century Ottoman Algeria," in *Crossing Memories: Slavery and African Diaspora*, ed. Ana Lucia Araujo, Mariana P. Candido, and Paul E. Lovejoy (Trenton, NJ: Africa World Press, 2011), 237–60.
125. Marion H. Katz, "Concubinage, in Islamic law," in *Encyclopaedia of Islam Three Online*, ed. K. Fleet et al. (Brill, 2007).
126. Sexual violence, rape, and forced abortions suffered by enslaved women with *umm al-walad* status are discussed in Ehud R. Toledano, *As If Silent and Absent: Bonds of Enslavement in the Islamic Middle East* (New Haven, CT: Yale University Press, 2007), 83–87.
127. Chouki El Hamel, *Black Morocco: A History of Slavery, Race, and Islam* (Cambridge: Cambridge University Press, 2013); Bruce S. Hall, *A History of Race in Muslim West Africa, 1600–1960* (Cambridge: Cambridge University Press, 2011); Ismael Montana, *The Abolition of Slavery in Ottoman Tunisia* (Gainesville: University Press of Florida, 2013); Mohammed Ennaji, *Serving the Master: Slavery and Society in Nineteenth-Century Morocco*, trans. Seth Graebner (New York: St. Martin's Press, 1999); Ehud R. Toledano, *Slavery and Abolition in the Ottoman Middle East* (Seattle: University of Washington Press, 1998); Martin Klein, *Slavery and Colonial Rule in French West Africa* (Cambridge: Cambridge University Press, 1998).
128. Benjamin Claude Brower *A Desert Named Peace: The Violence of France's Empire in the Algerian Sahara, 1844–1902* (New York: Columbia University Press, 2009), 141–96. See also Benjamin Claude Brower, "Rethinking Abolition in Algeria: Slavery and the 'Indigenous Question,'" *Cahiers d'études africaines* 49, no. 195 (2009), 805–27; Yacine Daddi Addoun, "L'Abolition de l'esclavage en Algérie, 1816–1871" (PhD diss., York University, 2010); Raëd Bader, "L'esclavage dans l'Algérie colonial, 1830–1870," *Revue d'historie maghrébine* 26, nos. 93–94 (1999): 57–69.
129. Claude Bontems, *Le droit musulman algérien à l'époque colonial: de l'invention à la codification* (Geneva: Slatkine, 2014); Bontems, *Algérie, ses instituions*. The civil status of

enslaved and formerly enslaved people is discussed in Édouard Sautayra and Eugène Cherbonneau, *Droit musulman*, vol. 2: *Des successions* (Paris: Maisonneuve, 1873–1874), 114.

130. The wording reveals confusion as to when France had actually abolished slavery, which was not in 1830 with the French occupation as this document implies, but eighteen years later. A subsequent reader of the report added parentheses around "before the French occupation" in the document, pointing out the error.
131. Gouvernement Général de l'Algérie to Préfet de Constantine, 28 October 1890, no. 6324, ANOM 12h54.
132. Lucette Valensi, *Tunisian Peasants in the Eighteenth and Nineteenth Centuries*, trans. Beth Archer (Cambridge: Cambridge University Press, 1985), 78.
133. David S. Powers, "Law and Custom in the Maghrib, 1475–1400; "On the Disinheritance of Women" (2006); and "The Maliki Family Endowment Legal Norms and Social Practices" (1993), all republished in Powers, *Development of Islamic Law*. See also Fouad Soufi, "Famille, femmes, histoire: notes pour une recherche," *Insaniyat* 4 (1998): 109–18.
134. Allan Christelow, *Muslim Law Courts and the French Colonial State in Algeria* (Princeton, NJ: Princeton University Press, 1985), 72.
135. Christelow, *Muslim Law Courts*, 154.
136. Germaine Tillion, *My Cousin, My Husband: Clans and Kinship in Mediterranean Societies*, trans. Quintin Hoare (London: Saqi, 2007).
137. Hezîa bent Haida ben Braham ben Ahmed Khodja ben Ferhat to Gouverneur Général, Ain El Ksar, 25 September 1896, ANOM 12h68.
138. Ferhat, no. 120, Commune Mixte d'Aïn El Ksar, copy made October 1896, ANOM 12h68.
139. Préfecture de Constantine to Gouvernement Général, 9 November 1896, no. 2998, ANOM 12h68.
140. Kateb, *Européens, "Indigènes" et Juifs*, 281–84.
141. The registrars did not tally numbers by sex. Figures provided here are based on my count of names parsed by their gender codes. "Amouchas Arbres généalogiques," 1890, ANOM 9377//14.
142. Figure based on the 127 family trees at Takitount in which the ayant droit has siblings. "Arbres généalogiques," 1890, ANOM 9377//14.
143. Cornu, *Guide pratique*, 63–64.
144. Jean Anatole Garnier Dubourgneuf, *Nouveau manuel des officiers de l'état-civil 1825* (Paris: Kleffer and Gambard, 1825), 17–41; Armand Blanche, *Code-Formulaire des actes de l'état civil* (Paris: Dupont, 1884), 9–18.

Conclusion

1. Paul Decroux, "L'État civil dans les milieux indigènes de l'Afrique du Nord," Centres de hautes études d'administration musulmane, 2 November 1945, ANOM 10APOM960; Paul Decroux, "L'état-civil au Maroc," *Hesperis* 37 (1950): 237–88.

2. Ali El Youbi and Said Warit, "Rapport sur le système d'État Civil Marocain," working paper, African Workshop on Strategies of Accelerating the Improvement of Civil Registration and Vital Statistics Systems, United Nations Economic and Social Council, Rabat, Morocco, 1995, https://unstats.un.org/unsd/demographic/meetings/wshops/1995_Rabat_CRVS/Docs/Marocain.pdf.
3. Henri Bénet, *L'État civil en Algérie: Traité théorique et pratique de la constitution de l'état civil des Indigènes Algériens* (Algiers: Minerva, 1937), 195–96.
4. Decroux, "État civil dans les milieux indigènes."
5. Justice Musulman Mahakma de Mascara to Procureur de la République, 3 June 1914. 12h54. In Barika a registrar who fell ill turned his task over to underlings who lacked training. Préfet de Constantine, Affaires Indigènes, to Gouvernement Général de l'Algérie, Affaires Indigènes, 10 March 1915, no. 5417, ANOM 12h52.
6. Commune Mixte de Tablat to Préfet d'Alger, 4 April 1891 no. 292, and 7 October 1891 no. 1171. Both in ANOM 12h52.
7. See cases in ANOM 12h54.
8. These are found in ANOM 12h92.
9. Parquet du Procureur Général to Gouvement Général de l'Algérie, 10 July 1920, no. 1656X19GG, ANOM 12h54.
10. Kamel Kateb, *Européens, "Indigènes" et Juifs en Algérie, 1830–1962: représentations et réalités des populations* (Paris: Institut national d'études démographiques, 2001), 126–28.
11. C. Kehl, "L'État civil des indigènes en Algérie," *Bulletin trimestriel de la Société de géographie et d'archéologie d'Oran* 52 (March 1931): 211.
12. Dominick LaCapra, "Trauma, Absence, Loss," *Critical Inquiry* 25, no. 4 (Summer 1999): 696–727.
13. Kateb Yacine, *Nedjma*, trans. Richard Howard (Charlottesville: University of Virginia Press, 1991), 169–70. Kateb Yacine's own name is tricky. "Kateb" is his surname (nom), and "Yacine" is his given name (prénom). He reversed their order deliberately as a pen name.
14. Samuel M. Weber, "Introduction to the 1988 Edition," in Daniel Paul Schreber, *Memoirs of My Nervous Illness*, ed. and trans. Ida MacAlpine and Richard A. Hunter (Cambridge, MA: Harvard University Press, 1988), xliv. There is a vast literature on Lacan's "Name-of-the-Father," a concept he developed in multiple texts. Russel Grigg unpacks it nicely in a discussion of its role in psychosis, a pathology that Lacan came to understand as stemming from the foreclosure of this sign, which otherwise anchored symbolic relations. Russell Grigg, *Lacan, Language, and Philosophy* (Albany: State University of New York Press, 2008), 8–19. Lacan's own introduction to the concept is his 1963 lesson, "Introduction to the Names-of-the-Father," in Jacques Lacan, *On the Names-of-the-Father*, trans. Bruce Fink (Cambridge, UK: Polity, 2013), 53–91. For a discussion of the concept's development in its historical context, see Elisabeth Roudinesco, *Jacques Lacan: An Outline of a Life and History of a System of Thought*, trans. Barbara Bray (New York: Columbia University Press, 1997), 260–90.

15. Jeanne Lorraine Schroeder, *The Four Lacanian Discourses or Turning Law Inside-Out* (London: Birkbeck Law Press, 2008).
16. The état civil as (re)connection is the theme of Patrick Modiano's collection of short stories in 1977, *Family Record*. Modiano's characters—orphans, exiles, abandoned children—struggle with the riddles of identity in the wake of war, revolution, and the violent dissolution of family ties. They have the feeling "of being the last survivor[s] of a vanished world." However, the "family record" (état civil) of the book's title offsets this by verifying identities and anchoring them within a genealogy. Patrick Modiano, *Family Record*, trans. Mark Polizzotti (New Haven, CT: Yale University Press, 2019).
17. Laurie A. Brand, *Official Stories: Politics and National Narratives in Egypt and Algeria* (Stanford, CA: Stanford University Press, 2014); Emmanuel Alcaraz, *Les lieux de mémoire de la guerre d'indépendance algérienne* (Paris: Karthala, 2017); Jill Jarvis, *Decolonizing Memory: Algeria and the Politics of Testimony* (Durham, NC: Duke University Press, 2021); Susan Slyomovics, *Monuments Decolonized: Algeria's French Colonial Heritage* (Stanford, CA: Stanford University Press, 2024).
18. Kateb, *Nedjma*, 135–36.
19. Karima Lazali, *Le trauma colonial: une enquête sur les effets psychiques et politiques contemporains de l'oppression coloniale en Algérie* (Paris: La Découverte, 2018), translated as *Colonial Trauma: A Study of the Psychic and Political Consequences of Colonial Oppression in Algeria*, trans. Matthew B. Smith (Medford, MA: Polity, 2021). Prior to Lazali's book was Ranjana Khanna, *Algeria Cuts: Women and Representation, 1830 to the Present* (Stanford, CA: Stanford University Press, 2008). See also Christiane Chaulet Achour and Faïka Medjahed, *Viols et filiations: Incursions psychanalytiques et littéraires en Algérie* (Algiers: Koukou, 2020).
20. Lazali, *Colonial Trauma*, 47. Translation modified. See also Patrick Crowley, "The Etat Civil: Post/colonial Identities and Genre," *French Forum* 29, no. 3 (Fall 2004): 79–94.
21. On the importance of the public trail to closure, see Richard J. Golsan, *Justice in Lyon: Klaus Barbie and France's First Trial for Crimes Against Humanity* (Toronto: University of Toronto Press, 2022).
22. Compare with Lazali, *Colonial Trauma*, 50: "This new French naming practices entirely abolishes the system that binds together the living and the dead. . . . The destruction of the name signals the death of a whole symbolic order wiped out by colonial law. And so individuals were renamed, or, rather, unnamed, on a massive scale by the colonial administration and therefore cut off from their respective genealogies. The risk, then, was that descendants from the same family may be given different patronymic, effectively making them strangers at birth and therefore subject to incest through marriage."
23. These are well summarized in Judith Surkis, *Sex, Law, and Sovereignty in French Algeria, 1830–1930* (Ithaca, NY: Cornell University Press, 2019), 8.
24. Sumit Guha, "The Politics of Identity and Enumeration in India c. 1600–1990," *Comparative Studies in Society and History* 45, no. 1 (2003): 155. The first quote is from

Benedict Anderson, *Imagined Communities: Reflections on the Origin and Spread of Nationalism* (London: Verso, 1991), 184.

25. David S. Powers, *Law, Society, and Culture in the Maghrib, 1300–1500* (Cambridge: Cambridge University Press, 2002), 45–46; Brinkley Messick, *The Calligraphic State: Textual Domination and History in a Muslim Society* (Berkeley: University of California Press, 1992).
26. See, for example, Cour de Constantine, Naissances, 1904, no. 48, 12 January 1904. http://anom.archivesnationales.culture.gouv.fr/caomec2/osd.php?territoire=ALGERIE&registre=38196.
27. Camille Robcis, *The Law of Kinship: Anthropology, Psychoanalysis, and the Family in France* (Ithaca, NY: Cornell University Press, 2013).
28. Jacqueline Sublet, "Noms de guerre, Algérie 1954–1962," in *Actas del XII Congreso de la U.E.A.I. (Málaga, 1984)* (Madrid: Huertas, 1986), 687–96. A decree in 1975 forbade the acronym "SNP" from appearing in Algeria's état civil. Karim Ould-Ennebia, "Histoire de l'état civil des Algériens: Patronymie et acculturation," *Revue maghrébine des études historiques et sociales*, no. 1 (September 2009): 5.
29. Adila Bennedjaï-Zou, host, "Mes années Boum, une enquête algérienne," podcast, produced by Marie Plaçais, *Les Pieds sur terre*, France Culture, 3 November–15 December 2016, 7 February–15 February 2018, https://www.radiofrance.fr/franceculture/podcasts/serie-mes-annees-boum-une-enquete-algerienne#concept-about.
30. Maurice Halbwachs, *On Collective Memory*, trans. Lewis A. Coser (Chicago: University of Chicago Press, 1992), 74.

Bibliography

Primary Sources

Abū Nuʻaym al-Iṣbahānī, Aḥmad ibn ʻAbd Allāh (d. 1038). *The Beauty of the Righteous and Ranks of the Elite*, translated by Muhammad Al-Akili. Philadelphia: Pearl Pub. House, 1995.

Accardo, F. *Répertoire alphabétique des tribus et douars de l'Algérie*. Algiers: Jourdan, 1879.

Arndt, Adolf. "Strafgerichtsbarkeit im Kriege über Ausländer, insbesondere Kriegsgefangene." *Zeitschrift für Politik* 8 (1915): 513–31.

Aubry, Charles, and Charles-Frédéric Rau. *Cours de droit civil français: d'après la méthode de Zachariae*. 5th ed., 12 vols. Paris: Marchal and Billard, 1897–1922.

Balzac, Honoré de. *Colonel Chabert*, translated by Carol Cosman. New York: New Directions, 1997.

Basset, André. "Sur la toponymie berbère et spécialement sur la toponymie chaouïa Aït Frah." *Onomastica* 2, no. 2 (1948): 123–26.

Baudrand, Michel Antoine. *Dictionnaire géographique universel, contenant une description exacte des Etats, royaumes, villes, forteresses, montagnes, caps, iles, presqu'iles, lacs, mers, golfes, détroits etc. de l'Univers*. Amsterdam: Halma, 1701.

Baudry-Lacantinerie, Gabriel. *Précis de droit civil*. 11th ed., 3 vols. Paris: Sirey, 1911–1914.

Baudry-Lacantinerie, Gabriel, and Maurice Houques-Fourcade, *Traité théorique et pratique du droit civil: des personnes*. 2nd ed. Paris: Larose, 1902.

Bazeille. "Étude sur les registres paroissiaux antérieur à l'établissement des registres de l'état civil." *Bulletin historique et philologique du Comité des travaux historiques et scientifiques* (1909): 327–59.

Beauchamp, Georges de. *Traité de graphologie, théorique et pratique*. Paris: Blériot, 1895.

Beaupré, A. *Carte générale de l'Algérie: ou des possessions françaises dans le nord de l'Afrique, pour servir à l'intelligence des opérations militaires ou commerciales.* Paris: [s.n.], 1836.

Beaussier, Marcelin. *Dictionnaire pratique arabe-français.* Algiers: Jourdan, 1887.

——. *Dictionnaire pratique arabe-français,* edited by Mohamed Ben Cheneb. New ed. Algiers: Maison des livres, 1958.

Beaussier, Marcelin, Mohammed Ben Cheneb, and Jérôme Lentin. *Dictionnaire pratique arabe-français: arabe maghrébin.* Paris: Ibis Press, 2006.

Bellemare, Alexandre. *Grammaire arabe (idiome d'Algérie), à l'usage de l'armée et des employés civils de l'Algérie.* Paris: Hachette, 1854.

Ben Cheneb, Mohammed. *Mots turcs et persans conservés dans le parler algérien.* Algiers: Carbonel, 1922.

——. *Proverbes arabes de l'Algérie et du Maghreb.* 3 vols. Paris: Leroux, 1904–1907.

Bénet, Henri. *L'État civil en Algérie: Traité théorique et pratique de la constitution de l'état civil des Indigènes Algériens.* Algiers: Minerva, 1937.

Benezet, F. *Le Tribunal supérieur et la Cour d'appel d'Alger: résumé chronologique des lois, ordonnances, décrets et arrêtés concernant ces hautes juridictions, de 1830 à 1896.* Algiers: Jourdan, 1896.

Bernard, Augustin. "Sahara." In *La Vie politique à l'étranger,* edited by Ernest Lavisse, 383–88. Paris: Charpentier, 1891.

Berthelot, Marcellin, Hartwig Derenbourg, and Camille Dreyfus. *La grande encyclopédie: inventaire raisonné des sciences, des lettres et des arts.* 31 vols. Paris: Lamirault and Société anonyme de la Grande Encyclopédie, 1885–1902.

Bertherand, Émile. *Médecine et hygiène des Arabes: études sur l'exercice de la médecine et de la chirurgie chez les musulmans de l'Algérie.* Paris: Baillière, 1855.

Bianchi, Thomas-Xavier. *Relation de l'arrivée dans la rade d'Alger du vaisseau de S. M. "La Provence."* Paris, 1830.

Bissuel, Henri. *Les Touareg de l'Ouest.* Algiers: Jourdan, 1888.

Blanche, Armand. *Code-Formulaire des actes de l'état civil.* Paris: Dupont, 1884.

Bodichon, Eugène. *Études sur l'Algérie et l'Afrique.* Algiers, 1847.

Bodin, Jean. *Six Books of the Commonwealth,* translated by M. J. Tooley. Oxford: Blackwell, 1967.

Boileux, Jacques Marie. *Commentaire sur le Code civil: contenant l'explication de chaque article séparément.* 6th ed., 7 vols. Paris: Videcoq, 1851–1860.

Bouderba, Ahmed. "Mémoire de Bouderbah," edited by Georges Yver. *Revue africaine* 57 (1913): 218–44.

Boudin, Jean-Christian-Marc. *Histoire statistique de la colonisation et de la population en Algérie.* Paris: Baillière, 1853.

Boullenois, Louis. *Traité de la personnalité et de la réalité des lois.* 2 vols. Paris: Desprez, 1766.

Boutin, Vincent-Yves. *Aperçu historique, statistique et topographique sur l'état d'Alger.* Paris: Picquet, 1830.

Bouyac, René. *Histoire de Bône.* Paris: Lecène, 1892.

Brenot, Henri. *Le Douar, cellule administrative de l'Algérie du nord.* Algiers: Heintz, 1938.

Bresnier, Louis-Jacques. *Chrestomathie arabe: lettres, actes et pièces diverses avec la traduction française en regard*. Algiers: Bastide, 1857.

——. *Cours pratique et théorique de langue arabe*. Algiers: Bastide, 1855.

Brosselard, Charles. *Les Khouan: de la constitution des ordres religieux musulmans en Algérie*. Algiers: Bourget, 1859.

Buffin. *Dictionnaire des familles qui ont fait modifier leurs noms, depuis 1803 jusqu'en 1865*. Paris: Delaroque, 1877.

Bulletin des lois de l'Empire français. Paris: Imprimerie impérial, 1804–1814.

Bulletin des lois du Royaume de France. Paris: Imprimerie royale, 1814–1848.

Bulletin official du Gouvernement Général de l'Algérie. Vol. 6: *1866*. Algiers: Bouyer, 1867.

Calvo, Charles. *Dictionnaire de droit international public et privé*. 2 vols. Berlin: Puttkammer, 1885.

Camps, Maxime du. "L'état civil à Paris." *Revue des deux mondes* 10 (March–April 1874): 341–71.

Capitant, Henri. *Introduction à l'étude du droit civil: notions générales*. 5th ed. Paris: Pedone, 1929.

Carette, Ernest. *Exploration scientifique de l'Algérie*. Vol. 3: *Recherches sur l'origine et les migrations des principales tribus de l'Afrique septentrionale et particulièrement de l'Algérie*. Paris: Imprimerie impérial, 1853.

——. *Exploration scientifique de l'Algérie: études sur la Kabilie proprement dite*. Paris: Cosse and Dumaine, 1849.

——. *Recherches sur la géographie et le commerce de l'Algérie méridionale*. Paris: Imprimerie royale, 1844.

Carpentier, Adrien, and Georges Frèrejouan Du Saint, eds. *Répertoire général alphabétique du droit français*. 37 vols. Paris: Larose, Forcel, 1886–1924.

Chais, A. "Hussein-Pacha." In *Biographie universelle ancienne et moderne*. Vol. 67: *Supplément, He-Iz*, edited by Louis-Gabriel Michaud, 502–7. Paris: Michaud, 1840.

Charvillhac, M. *Le guide de l'officier de l'état civil*. Paris: Rondonneau, 1806.

Cherbonneau, Auguste. *Dictionnaire français-arabe pour la conversation en Algérie*. Paris: Imprimerie Nationale, 1884.

——. *Éléments de la phraséologie française avec une traduction en arabe vulgaire (idiôme africain) à l'usage des indigènes*. Paris: Hachette, 1851.

——. "Explorations et missions." *Revue de géographie* 10 (January–June 1882): 153–55.

Colin, Ambroise, and Henri Capitant. *Cours élémentaire de droit civil français*. 3 vols. Paris: Dalloz, 1914–1916.

Colonisation de l'Ex-Régence d'Alger, Documents officiels. Paris: Michaud, 1834.

Les Colons d'Alger à la France: Domination générale, colonisation progressive. Marseille: Olive, 1840.

Constitution de la propriété en Algérie. Algiers: Bouyer, 1863.

Cornu, E. *Guide pratique pour la constitution de l'état civil des indigènes*. Algiers: Jourdan, 1889.

Coston, Adolphe de. *Origine, étymologie et signification des noms propres et des armoiries*. Paris: Aubry, 1867.

Cussy, Ferdinand de. *Dictionnaire ou Manuel-lexique du diplomate et du consul.* Leipzig: Brockhaus, 1846.

Dan, Pierre. *Histoire de Barbarie et de ses corsaires.* Paris: Rocolet, 1637.

Darmet, J. M. *Carte de la colonie française d'Alger, de la régence de Tunis et de la partie nord de l'empire de Maroc.* Paris: s.n., 1836.

Daumas, Eugène. *Mœurs et coutumes de l'Algérie: Tell, Kabylie, Sahara.* Paris: Hachette, 1855.

——. *La Vie arabe et la société musulman.* Paris: Lévy, 1869.

Desparmet, Joseph. *Coutumes institutions, croyances des Indigènes de l'Algérie.* 2nd ed. Algiers: Carbonel, 1948.

——. *Le mal magique: ethnographie traditionnelle de la Mettidja.* Paris: Geuthner, 1932.

Dictionnaire français-berbère. Paris: Imprimerie Royale, 1844.

Dopigez, Abbé. *Souvenirs de l'Algérie et de la France méridionale.* Douai: Adam, 1840.

Doutté, Edmond. *Magie et religion dans l'Afrique du Nord.* Algiers: Jourdan, 1909.

Dufour, Auguste-Henri. *Algérie: dédiée au roi.* Paris: Simonneau, 1838.

Dufour, Auguste-Henri, and Charles Picquet. *Carte de la régence d'Alger et d'une partie du bassin de la Méditerranée: donnant le rapport qui existe entre la France et les États barbaresques.* New ed. Paris: Picquet, 1840.

Dumas, Alexandre. *Le Véloce ou Tanger, Alger et Tunis.* Vol. 4. Brussels: Muquardt, 1851.

Estoublon, Robert. *Bulletin judicaire de l'Algérie: Jurisprudence algérienne de 1830 à 1876.* 4 vols. Algiers: Jourdan, 1890–1891.

Estoublon, Robert, and Adolphe Lefébure. *Code de l'Algérie annoté.* Algiers: Jourdan, 1896.

État civil des citoyens, ou Analyse sommaire du décret du 20 septembre 1792, et de celui du 21 janvier dernier, avec des formules des différents actes de naissances, mariages et décès. Paris: Knapen, 1793.

Eudel, Paul. *L'Orfèvrerie algérienne et tunisienne.* Algiers: Jourdan, 1902.

Favard de Langlade, Guillaume-Jean. *Répertoire de la nouvelle législation civile.* 5 vols. Paris: Didot, 1823–1824.

Féraud, Charles. *Histoire de La Calle.* Algiers: Jourdan, 1878.

Foppens, François. *Le Dictionnaire géographique contenant les Roiaumes, les provinces, les villes, les fleuves, et les autres lieux les plus considérables du monde.* Brussels: Foppens, 1694.

Foucauld, Charles de. *Dictionnaire abrégé Touareg-Français de noms propres (dialecte de l'Ăhaggar).* Paris: Larose, 1940.

Franck, Adolphe. *Philosophie du droit civil.* Paris: Alcan, 1886.

Franque, Alfred. *Lois de l'Algérie, du 5 juillet 1830 (occupation d'Alger) au 1ère janvier 1841.* Paris: Corréard, 1844.

Frégier, Casimir. *De la contrainte par corps ou De l'emprisonnement civil en Algérie.* Constantine: Alessi and Arnolet, 1863.

——. *Les Juifs algériens: leur passé, leur présent, leur avenir juridique.* Paris: Lévy, 1865.

——. *Pensées de Théophile Abdallah; ou De l'interprétation en Algérie.* Sétif: Veuve Vincent, 1863.

Frémin, Antoine-Remy. *Théâtre de la guerre en Afrique comprenant les régences d'Alger, de Tunis, Tripoli et de l'empire du Maroc.* Paris: Hocquart, 1837.

Gand, N. *Code des étrangers, ou État civil et politique en France des étrangers de tout rang et de toute condition, leurs droits et leurs devoirs.* Paris, 1853.

Garnier Dubourgneuf, Jean Anatole. *Nouveau manuel des officiers de l'état-civil.* Paris: Kleffer and Gambard, 1825.

Gaschon, Jean-Baptiste. *Code diplomatique des aubains.* Paris: Foucault, 1818.

Gaudefroy-Demombynes, Maurice. *Les cérémonies du mariage chez les indigènes de l'Algérie.* Paris: Maisonneuve, 1901.

Giroud, A. *Instruction sur la tenue des registres de l'état-civil.* 3rd ed. Paris: Tètu, 1842.

Gouvernement Général de l'Algérie, *Instruction: état civil des indigènes, 20 avril 1888.* Algiers: Fojosso, 1888.

——. *Instructions pour l'exécution de la loi du 23 mars 1882 et du règlement d'administration publique du 13 mars 1883 sur l'état civil des indigènes musulmans de l'Algérie.* Algiers: Fojosso, 1885.

——. *Tableau de la situation des établissements françaises dans l'Algérie.* Paris: Imprimerie Royale, 1838.

——. *Vocabulaire destiné à fixer la transcription en français des noms des indigènes.* Algiers: Jourdan, 1885.

Hafnāwī, Abū al-Qāsim Muḥammad. *Kitāb Ta'rīf al-Khalaf bi-Rijāl al-Salaf.* 2 vols. Algiers: Matba'at Bīyīr Fūntānah al-Sharqīyah, 1906.

Hallez-Claparède, Léonce. *Des Noms propres.* Paris: Douniol, 1868.

Hallez d'Arros, Hippolyte. *Nouveau manuel de l'officier de l'état civil et du secrétaire de mairie.* Metz: Alcan, 1854.

Hanoteau, Adolphe. *Essai de grammaire Kabyle.* Algiers: Bastide, 1858.

Hélie, Faustin. *Traité de l'instruction criminelle.* 2nd ed., 8 vols. Paris: Plon, 1866–1867.

Herber, J. "La main de Fatma." *Hespéris* (1927): 209–19.

Herchenroder, M.F.P. "The Capacity of Married Women in French Law." *Journal of Comparative Legislation and International Law* 20, no. 4 (1938): 196–203.

Hugonnet, Ferdinand. *Souvenirs d'un chef de bureau arabe.* Paris: Lévy, 1858.

Hugues, Henry, and Paul Labrat. *Le Code algérien, recueil annoté suivant l'ordre alphabétique des matières des lois, décrets, décisions, arrêtés et circulaires formant la législation de l'Algérie publiés de 1872 à 1878.* Paris: Challamel, 1878.

Ibn Ājurrūm, Muḥammad ibn Muḥammad (Mohammed ben Dawoud el-Sanhadjy, 1273–1323). *Djaroumiya, grammaire arabe élémentaire*, edited and translated by Marcelin Beaussier. Algiers: Bastide, 1846.

Ibn al-Kalbī, *Ǧamharat an-nasab: das genealogische Werk des Hišam Ibn Muḥammad al-Kalbī*, edited and translated by Werner Caskel and Ger Strenziok. 2 vols. Leiden: Brill, 1966.

Ibn Maryam, Muḥammad ibn Muḥammad. *Al-Bustān fī Dhikr al-Awliyā' wa-al-'Alamā' bi-Tilimsān.* Algiers: al-Maṭba'ah al-Tha'ālibīyah, 1908.

——. *Jardin des biographies des saints et savants de Tlemcen* (translation of *Al-Bustān fī Dhikr al-Awliyā'*), translated by F. Provenzali. Algiers: Fontana Frères, 1910.

Ibn Ṣaṣrā, Muḥammad ibn Muḥammad. *A Chronicle of Damascus, 1389-1397*, edited and translated by William M. Brinner. 2 vols. Berkeley: University of California Press, 1963.

Ibshīhī, Muḥammad ibn Aḥmad. *Al-Mostaṭraf: recueil de morceaux choisis çà et là dans toutes les branches de connaissance réputées attrayantes*, translated by Gustav Rat. 2 vols. Paris: Leroux, 1899–1902.

Ionescu, Octavian. *La notion de droit subjectif dans le droit privé.* Paris: Sirey, 1931.

Jabartī, ʻAbd al-Raḥman. *Al-Jabartī's Chronicle of the First Seven Months of the French Occupation of Egypt*, edited and translated by S. Moreh. Leiden: Brill, 1975.

Journal officiel de la République algérienne démocratique et populaire. Algiers: Imprimerie Officielle, 1962–.

Journal officiel de la République française: Lois et décrets. Paris: Journaux officiels, 1881–2015.

Juchereau de Saint-Denys, Antoine de. *Considérations statistiques, historiques, militaires et politiques sur la régence d'Alger.* Paris: Delaunay, 1831.

Kehl, C. "L'État civil des indigènes en Algérie." *Bulletin trimestriel de la Société de géographie et d'archéologie d'Oran* 52 (March 1931): 173–212.

Knox, Robert. *The Races of Men: A Fragment.* Philadelphia: Lea and Blanchard, 1850.

Lallier, Joseph-Armand. *De la Propriété des noms et des titres: origine des noms et des titres, procédure des changements de noms, protection de la propriété des noms et des titres, du nom commercial.* Paris: Giard, 1890.

Laoust, Émile. *Contribution à une étude de la toponymie du haut Atlas.* Paris: Geuthner, 1942.

Lapie, Pierre, Charles-Benoît Hase, Amédée Jaubert, Flahaut, Lallemand, and Charles Picquet. *Carte comparée des régences d'Alger et de Tunis.* Paris: Piquet, 1838.

Larcher, Émile, and Georges Rectenwald. *Traité élémentaire de législation algérienne.* 3rd ed., 3 vols. Paris: Rousseau, 1923.

Lataillade, Louis. *Coutumes et superstitions obstétricales en Afrique du Nord.* Algiers: Charry, 1936.

Laurent, François. *Principes de droit civil.* 33 vols. Brussels: Bruylant-Christophe; Paris: Durand and Pedone-Lauriel, 1869–1878.

Le Fur, Louis. *État fédéral et confédération d'états.* Paris: Marchal and Billard, 1896.

Le Marchand, Edgard. *L'Europe et la conquête d'Alger.* Paris: Perrin, 1913.

Lefébure, Eugène. "La main de Fatma." *Bulletin de la Société de Géographie d'Alger* 12 (1907): 411–17.

Lepsius, C. R. *Standard Alphabet for Reducing Unwritten Languages and Foreign Graphic Systems to a Uniform Orthography in European Letters.* 2nd ed. London: Williams and Norgate; Berlin: Hertz, 1863.

Lespès, Léo. *Le Livre des 400 auteurs: nouvelles, contes, voyages, légendes critique, histoire, théâtres.* Paris: Magasin des familles, 1850.

Lévy, Édouard. *La Question des prénoms.* Paris: Libraire judicaire, 1913.

Lœning, Edgar. "L'administration du Gouvernement-Général de l'Alsace durant la guerre de 1870–1871." *Revue de droit international* 5 (1873): 69–136.

Loir, J.-N. *De l'état civil des nouveau-nés, au point de vue de l'histoire, de l'hygiène et de la loi.* Paris: Durand and Asselin, 1865.

Mac Guckin de Slane, William, and Charles-Hippolyte Gabeau. *Vocabulaire destiné à fixer la transcription en français des noms de personnes et de lieux usités chez les indigènes de l'Algérie.* Paris: Imprimerie impériale, 1868.

Machuel, Louis. *Manuel de l'arabisant, ou recueil d'actes judiciaires.* 2 vols. Algiers: Jourdan, 1877–1881.

Majdī, Muḥammad ibn Ṣāliḥ. *Hilyat al-Zamān bi-Manāqib Khādim al-Waṭan.* Cairo: Maktabat Muṣṭafā al-Bābī al-Ḥalabī, 1958.

Marsier, Émile. *Traité théorique et pratique des actes de l'état civil.* Paris: Dupont, 1873.

Martens, Georg Friedrich von. *Recueil des traités d'alliance, de paix, de trêve, de neutralité, de commerce, de limites, d'échange . . . depuis 1761.* 2nd ed., 8 vols. Göttingen: Dieterich, 1817–1835.

Martin, A.-E. Victor, and L.-E. Foley. *Histoire statistique de la colonisation algérienne au point de vue du peuplement et de l'hygiène.* Paris: Germer-Baillière, 1851.

Massignon, Louis. *Le Maroc dans les premières années du XVIe siècle. Tableau géographique d'après Léon l'Africain.* Algiers: Jourdan, 1906.

Mercier, Ernest. *La propriété foncière chez les musulmans d'Algérie: ses lois sous la domination française, constitution de l'état civil musulman.* Paris: Leroux, 1891.

——. *L'élévation de la famille El-Feggoun.* Constantine: Arnolet, 1879.

Mercier, Gustave. *Étude sur la toponymie berbère de la région de l'Aurès.* s.l.: s.n., n.d.

Merlin, Philippe-Antoine. *Répertoire universel et raisonné de jurisprudence.* 5th ed., 15 vols. Brussels: Tarlier, 1827–1828.

Mersier, Émile. *Traité théorique et pratique des actes de l'état civil.* Paris: Dupont and Marescq, 1873.

Ministère de la Guerre (France). *Bulletin official des actes du gouvernement.* Vol. 1: *1e octobre 1834 jusqu'au 1er janvier 1839.* Paris: Imprimerie royale, 1843.

——. *Collections des actes du gouvernement depuis l'occupation d'Alger jusqu'au 1e octobre 1834.* Paris: Imprimerie royale, 1843.

——. *Procès-verbaux et rapports de la Commission d'Afrique instituée par ordonnance du Roi du 12 décembre 1833.* Paris: L'imprimerie royale, 1834.

——. *Procès-verbaux et rapports de la commission nommée par le Roi, le 7 juillet 1833, pour aller recueillir en Afrique tous les faits propres à éclairer le gouvernement sur l'état du pays et sur les mesures que réclame son avenir.* Paris: L'imprimerie royale, 1834.

——. *Supplément aux procès-verbaux de la commission d'Afrique, instituée par ordonnance royale du 12 décembre 1833.* Paris: L'imprimerie royale, 1834.

Nettement, Alfred. *Histoire de la conquête d'Alger.* New ed. Paris: Lecoffre, 1867.

Neveu, Edouard de. *Les Khouan: ordres religieux chez les Musulmans de l'Algérie.* 2nd ed. Paris: Guyot, 1846.

"Nom (et Prénom)." In *Répertoire général alphabétique du droit français.* Vol. 28: *Ministère Public-Numéraire*, edited by Édouard Fuzier-Herman, Adrien Carpentier, and Georges Frèrejouan Du Saint, 541–60. Paris: Sirey, 1901.

Norès, Edmond. *Essai de codification du droit musulman algérien (statut personnel).* Algiers: Jourdan, 1909.

Nouveau dictionnaire des Notaires. 5 vols. Paris: Conseil des notaires, 1836–1838.

Pailliet, Jean Baptiste Joseph. *Manuel de droit française.* 6th ed. Paris: Desoer, 1824.

Pelet, Jean-Jacques-Germain. *Carte de l'Algérie dressée au Dépôt général de la guerre.* Paris: Kaeppelin, 1838.

——. *Plan d'Alger et des environs.* Paris: Dépôt général de la guerre, 1832.
Pellegrin, Arthur. *Essai sur les noms de lieux d'Algérie et de Tunisie.* Tunis: Éditions SAPI, 1949.
Perouse, Honoré. *Napoléon Ier et les lois civiles du Consulat et de l'Empire.* Paris: Durand, 1866.
Pharaon, Florian. *Épisodes de la Conquête: cathédrale et mosquée.* Paris: Lahure, 1880.
Pichon, Louis-André. *Alger sous la domination française.* Paris: Barrois et Duprat, 1833.
Picot, Charles. *Éléments du Code Napoléon: exposé par demandes et par réponses: ouvrage destiné à vulgariser les lois françaises.* Paris: Coupé, 1868.
Piétri, François. *Étude critique sur la fiction d'exterritorialité.* Paris: Rousseau, 1895.
Piggott, Francis Taylor. *Exterritoriality: The Law Relating to Consular Jurisdiction and to Residence in Oriental Countries.* London: Clowes, 1892.
Pillet, Antoine. *Recherches sur les droits fondamentaux des États.* Paris: Pedone, 1899.
Pinson de Ménerville, Charles-Louis. *Dictionnaire de la législation algérienne: manuel raisonné des lois, ordonnances, décrets, décisions et arrêtés.* Algiers: Philippe, 1853.
——. *Dictionnaire de la législation algérienne, code annoté et manuel raisonné des lois, ordonnances, décrets, décisions et arrêtés.* 3 vols. Algiers: Bastide and Jourdan, 1867–1877.
——. *Dictionnaire de la législation algérienne, premier supplément: manuel des lois, ordonnances, décrets, décisions et arrêtés publiés au "Bulletin officiel des actes du gouvernement" pendant les années 1853, 1854, 1855.* Algiers: Philippe and Cosse, 1856.
Planiol, Marcel. *Traite élémentaire de droit civil.* 11th ed., 3 vols. Paris: Libraire générale, 1928–1932.
Plantet, Eugène. *Correspondance des Beys de Tunis.* 3 vols. Paris: Alcan, 1893–1899.
Podio, Lagét de. *De la juridiction des consuls de France à l'étranger.* Paris: Trouvé, 1826.
Poivre, Aimé. *Les Indigènes algériens, leur état civil et condition juridique.* Algiers: Dubos, 1862.
Pontier, R. *Souvenirs de l'Algérie, ou Notice sur Orléansville et Tenès.* Valenciennes: Giard, 1850.
Préaux, Charles. "Notice sur le Dey d'Alger." *Journal des Sciences militaires des armées de terre et de mer* 22 (January–March 1831): 332–42.
Les princes en Afrique, Le duc de Montpensier. Paris: Amyot, 1846.
Procès-verbaux des délibérations: session de décembre 1879: Conseil supérieur de gouvernement. Algiers: Duclaox, 1880.
Procès-verbaux du Conseil d'État, contentant la discussion du Code Napoléon. 2nd ed., 4 vols. Paris: Imprimerie impériale, 1808.
Quéméneur, Jean. "Une difficile question: la graphie française des noms arabes." *Documents Nord-Africains* 13, no. 467 (7 February 1962): 1–12.
The Qur'ān, translated by Alan Jones. Exeter: Gibb Memorial Trust, 2007.
Reclus, Élisée. *Nouvelle géographie universelle.* 19 vols. Paris: Hachette, 1879–1894.
Recueil des actes du Gouvernement de l'Algérie, 1830–1854. Algiers: Imprimerie du Gouvernement, 1856.
Recueil général des lois et ordonnances. 17 vols. Paris: Bureaux de l'administration du journal des notaires et des avocats, 1830–1847.
Réimpression de l'ancien Moniteur, seule histoire authentique et inaltérée de la Révolution française. 32 vols. Paris: Plon, 1858–1870.
Révoil, Paul. *Tableau général des communes de l'Algérie.* Algiers: Giralt, 1902.
Richard, Charles. *Étude sur l'insurrection du Dhara* [*sic*]. Algiers: Bastide, 1846.

Ricoux, René. *La démographie figurée de l'Algérie; étude statistique des populations européennes qui habitent l'Algérie*. Paris: Masson, 1880.

Rochetal, Albert de. *Le Caractère par le prénom: suivi de la liste des prénoms usuels avec l'explication des qualités et défauts que chacun d'eux impose à celui qui le porte*. Paris: Bischoff, 1908.

Sabatier, Justin. *Encyclopédie des noms propres*. Paris: Petit Journal, 1865.

Sabbatier, J. *Lettre sur la colonie d'Alger*. Paris: Delaunay, 1836.

Saleilles, Raymond. *De la personnalité juridique: histoire et théories*. Paris: Rousseau, 1910.

Salle, Eusèbe de. *Ali le renard, ou la conquête d'Alger (1830)*. 2nd ed., 2 vols. Paris: Gosselin, 1832.

Salverte, Eusèbe. *Essai historique et philosophique sur les noms d'hommes, de peuples et de lieux*. 2 vols. Paris: Bossange, 1824.

Sautayra, Édouard, and Eugène Cherbonneau. *Du statut personnel et des successions*. 2 vols. Paris: Maisonneuve, 1873–1874.

Scott, Édouard-Léon. *Les Noms de baptême et les prénoms: nomenclature, signification, tradition, légende, histoire, art de nommer*. 2nd ed. Paris: Houssiaux, 1858.

Sedira, Belkassem Ben [Muḥammad ben Qāsim ben Ṣadīra]. *Cours gradué de lettres arabes manuscrites*. Algiers: Jourdan, 1893.

——. *Cours pratique de langue arabe*. Algiers: Jourdan, 1875.

——. *Dictionnaire français-arabe*. Geneva: Slatkine, 2001.

——. *Dictionnaire français-arabe de la langue parlée en Algérie*. 5th ed. Algiers: Jourdan, 1910.

——. *Manuel épistolaire de langue arabe*. Algiers: Jourdan, 1893.

Shaler, William. *Esquisse de l'État d'Alger* [translation of *Sketches of Algiers*], translated by X. Bianchi. Paris: Ladvocat, 1830.

——. *Sketches of Algiers, Political, Historical, and Civil*. Boston: Cummings, 1826.

Silvestre de Sacy, Antoine-Isaac. *Chrestomathie arabe*. 3 vols. Paris: Imprimerie Royale, 1826–1827.

Socin, Albert. "Die arabischen Eigennamen in Algier." *Zeitschrift der Deutschen Morgenländischen Gesellschaft* 52, no. 3 (1898): 471–500.

Sol. "Du système à suivre pour la colonisation d'Alger." *Le Spectateur militaire* 19 (15 April–15 September 1835): 481–510.

Tabari. *The History of al-Ṭabarī: General Introduction, and, From the Creation to the Flood*, edited and translated by Franz Rosenthal. Albany: State University of New York Press, 1989.

Tabet, Élie. *Notes sur l'organisation des tribus et l'étymologie des nom propres*. Oran: Association ouvrière, 1882.

Ṭahṭāwī, Rifāʿa Rāfīʿ Ibn Badawī. *An Imam in Paris*, translated by Daniel Newman. London: Saqi, 2004.

Teulet, Auguste François. *Dictionnaire des codes français*. Paris: Closel Frères and Rostaing, 1836.

Thucydides. *History of the Peloponnesian War*, translated by Rex Warner. New York: Penguin, 1976.

Tournade, Paul. *De l'Adoption, en droit romain: du Nom de famille et des titres de noblesse, en droit français*. Paris: Cotillon, 1882.

Trapani, Domingo Gian. *Alger tel qu'il est.* 2nd ed. Paris: Fayolle, 1830.
Valette, Victor. *Un projet de loi sur la réorganisation de l'Algérie.* Algiers: Cheniaux-Franville, 1881.
Vassel, Eusèbe. "La Littérature populaire des Israélites tunisiens." *Revue tunisienne* 13 (1906): 217–32.
Vayssettes, Eugène. *Histoire de Constantine sous la domination turque 1514–1837.* New ed. Saint-Denis: Bouchène, 2002.
Venture de Paradis, Jean-Michel. "Alger au XVIIIe siècle." *Revue africaine* 39, no. 219 (1895): 265–314.
——. *Grammaire et dictionnaire abrégés de la langue berbère.* Paris: Imprimerie royale, 1844.
Volney, Constantin-François. *Travels Through Syria and Egypt.* 3rd ed., 2 vols. London: Robinson, 1805.
Westermarck, Edward. *Marriage Ceremonies in Morocco.* London: Macmillan, 1914.
Woolsey, Theodore Dwight. *Introduction to the Study of International Law.* Boston: Munroe, 1860.

Secondary Sources

Abad, Reynald. "La falsification d'identité en France, du règne personnel de Louis XIV à la veille de la Révolution." *French Historical Studies* 39, no. 3 (August 2016): 471–508.
Abi-Mershed, Osama W. *Apostles of Modernity: Saint-Simonians and the Civilizing Mission in Algeria.* Stanford, CA: Stanford University Press, 2010.
——. "The Transmission of Knowledge and the Education of the 'Ulama in the Late Sixteenth-Century Maghrib: A Study of the Biographical Dictionary of Muhammad Ibn Maryam." In *Biography and the Construction of Identity and Community in the Middle East*, edited by Mary Ann Fay, 19–36. New York: Palgrave, 2001.
Abou El Fadl, Khaled. "Islamic Law and Muslim Minorities: The Juristic Discourse on Muslim Minorities from the Second/Eighth to the Eleventh/Seventeenth Centuries." *Islamic Law and Society* 1, no. 2 (1994): 141–87.
About, Ilsen. "Identités indigènes et police coloniale: L'introduction de l'anthropométrie judiciaire en Algérie, 1890–1910." In *Aux origines de la police scientifique: Alphonse Bertillon précurseur de la science du crime*, edited by Pierre Piazza, 280–301. Paris: Karthala, 2011.
About, Ilsen, and Vincent Denis. *Histoire de l'identification des personnes.* Paris: Découverte, 2010.
Abu-Lughod, Lila. *Veiled Sentiments: Honor and Poetry in a Bedouin Society.* Berkeley: University of California Press, 1986.
Addi, Lahouari. *Sociologie et anthropologie chez Pierre Bourdieu.* Paris: Découverte, 2002.
Addoun, Yacine Daddi. "L'Abolition de l'esclavage en Algérie, 1816–1871." PhD diss., York University, 2010.
——. " 'So That God Frees the Former Masters from Hell Fire': Salvation Through Manumission in Nineteenth Century Ottoman Algeria." In *Crossing Memories: Slavery and*

African Diaspora, edited by Ana Lucia Araujo, Mariana P. Candido, and Paul E. Lovejoy, 237–60. Trenton, NJ: Africa World Press, 2011.

Agamben, Giorgio. *Homo Sacer: Sovereign Power and Bare Life*, translated by Daniel Heller-Roazen. Stanford, CA: Stanford University Press, 1998.

Agbaria, Ahmad. *The Politics of Arab Authenticity: Challenges to Postcolonial Thought*. New York: Columbia University Press, 2022.

Ageron, Charles-Robert. *Le gouvernement du général Berthezène à Alger en 1831*. Paris: Bouchène, 2005.

——. *Les Algériens musulmans et la France (1871–1919)*. 2 vols. Paris: Presses universitaires de France, 1968.

Ahmed, Salahuddin. *A Dictionary of Muslim Names*. New York: New York University Press, 1999.

Aïssani, Djamil, and Djamel Mechehed. "Usages de l'écriture et production des savoirs dans la Kabylie du XIXe siècle." *Revue des mondes musulmans et de la Méditerranée* 121–22 (April 2008): 239–59.

Alcaraz, Emmanuel. *Les lieux de mémoire de la guerre d'indépendance algérienne*. Paris: Karthala, 2017.

Allati, Abdelaziz. "Les noms de parenté en berbère." *Études et documents berbères* 41 (2019): 97–112.

Althusser, Louis. *For Marx*, translated by Ben Brewster. London: Verso, 1996.

——. *The Future Lasts Forever: A Memoir*, edited by Olivier Corpet and Yann Moulier Boutang, translated by Richard Veasey. New York: New Press, 1993.

——. "Ideology and Ideological State Apparatuses (Notes Towards an Investigation)." In Louis Althusser, *Lenin and Philosophy and Other Essays*, translated by Ben Brewster, 127–86. New York: Monthly Review Press, 1971.

Amara, Noureddine. "Faire la France en Algérie: émigration algérienne, mésusages du nom et conflits de nationalités dans le monde, de la chute d'Alger aux années 1930." PhD diss., Université de Paris I Sorbonne, 2019.

Amine, Mohamed. "Les commerçants à Alger à la veille de 1830." *Revue d'histoire maghrébine* 22, nos. 77–78 (May 1995): 11–112.

Amorouayach, Essafia. "Adaptation d'anthroponymes algériens à l'orthographe française." *Synergies Algérie* 24 (2017): 225–34.

Amrane-Minne, Danièle Djamila. *Des femmes dans la guerre d'Algérie*. Paris: Karthala, 1994.

Amster, Ellen. *Medicine and the Saints: Science, Islam, and the Colonial Encounter in Morocco, 1877–1956*. Austin: University of Texas Press, 2013.

Anderson, Benedict. *Imagined Communities: Reflections on the Origin and Spread of Nationalism*. London: Verso, 1991.

Anderson, Clare. *Legible Bodies: Race, Criminality and Colonialism in South Asia*. Oxford: Berg, 2004.

Anghie, Antony. *Imperialism, Sovereignty and the Making of International Law*. Cambridge: Cambridge University Press, 2005.

Anonymous. "Muséologiques 87 au musée de l'A.N.P, histoire vivante." *El Djeich: revue de l'armée national populaire* 296 (March, 1988): 7.

Arendt, Hannah. *The Origins of Totalitarianism*. New ed. New York: Harcourt, 1973.

Arnaud, André-Jean. *Les origines doctrinales du code civil français*. Paris: Librairie générale de droit et de jurisprudence, 1969.

Asad, Talal. *On Suicide Bombing*. New York: Columbia University Press, 2007.

Atoui, Brahim. "La toponymie et sa transcription cartographique." *Bulletin de l'INC des sciences géographiques* 1 (1998): 40–48.

——. "L'Odonymie d'Alger: passé et présent, quels enseignements?" In *Nomination et dénomination des noms de lieux, de tribus et de personnes en Algérie*, edited by Farid Benramdane and Brahim Atoui, 23–51. Oran: Centre de recherché en anthropologie sociale et culturelle, 2005.

——. "Toponymie et colonisation française en Algérie." *Bulletin des sciences géographiques* (Institut national de cartographie et de télédétection) 5 (2000): 34–42.

——. "Toponymie et espace en Algérie." PhD diss., Université de Provence Aix Marseille I, 1996.

Attal, Robert, and Joseph Avivi. *Registres matrimoniaux de la communauté juive portugaise de Tunis aux XVIIIe et XIXe siècles*. Jerusalem: Ben-Zvi, 1989.

Attwood, Bain. *Empire and the Making of Native Title: Sovereignty, Property and Indigenous People*. Cambridge: Cambridge University Press, 2020.

Autin, Jean-Louis. "La législation foncière en Algérie de 1830 à 1870, ou le triomphe de la raison juridique colonial." *Le procès* 18 (1987): 85–97.

Ayoub, Samy A. *Law, Empire, and the Sultan: Ottoman Imperial Authority and Late Hanafi Jurisprudence*. Oxford: Oxford University Press, 2020.

——. "Territorial Jurisprudence, *Ikhtilaf al-Darayn*: Political Boundaries and Legal Jurisdiction." *Contemporary Islamic Studies* 1, no. 2 (2012). http://dx.doi.org/10.5339/cis.2012.2.

Azizi, Saoud. "Le nom de personne dans l'oasis de Figuig: Un système de codification des relations sociales." In *La culture Amazighe: réalités et perceptions*, edited by Hammou Belghazi, 41–62. Rabat: Institut royal de la culture amazighe, 2017.

Azmeh, Aziz al-. "Linguistic Observations on the Theonym Allāh." In *In the Shadow of Arabic, the Centrality of Language to Arabic Culture: Studies Presented to Ramzi Baalbaki on the Occasion of His Sixtieth Birthday*, edited by Bilal Orfali, 265–81. Leiden: Brill, 2011.

Badawi, El-Said M., and Muḥammad Ibn al-Zubayr. *Muʿjam Asmāʾ al-ʿArab* (*Dictionary of Arab Names*). 2 vols. Muscat: Jāmiʿat al-Sulṭān Qābūs; and Beirut: Maktabat Lubnān, 1991.

Bader, Raëd. "L'esclavage dans l'Algérie colonial, 1830–1870." *Revue d'historie maghrébine* 26, nos. 93–94 (1999): 57–69.

Bahloul, Joëlle. "Noms et prénoms juifs nord-africains." *Terrain: Anthropologie et sciences humaines* 4 (March 1985): 62–69.

Bakhtin, Mikhail. *The Dialogic Imagination: Four Essays*, edited by Michael Holquist, translated by Caryl Emerson and Michael Holquist. Austin: University of Texas Press, 1981.

——. *Problems of Dostoevsky's Poetics*, translated by Caryl Emerson. Minneapolis: University of Minnesota Press, 1984.

Balibar, Étienne. "Citizen Subject." In *Who Comes After the* Subject, edited by Eduardo Cadava, Peter Conner, and Jean-Luc Nancy, 33–57. New York: Routledge, 1991.

Ballard, Michel. *Le Nom propre en traduction.* Paris: Ophrys, 2001.

Bardet, Jean-Pierre, and Guy Brunet, eds. *Noms et destins des sans famille.* Paris: Presses de l'Université Paris-Sorbonne, 2007.

Barkey, Karen. "Aspects of Legal Pluralism in the Ottoman Empire." In *Legal Pluralism and Empires, 1500–1850*, edited by Lauren Benton and Richard J. Ross, 83–107. New York: New York University Press, 2013.

Barthelemy, Tiphaine. "Patronymic Names and *Noms de Terre* in the French Nobility in the Eighteenth and the Nineteenth Centuries." *History of the Family* 5, no. 2 (2000): 181–97.

Barthes, Roland. "Proust and Names." In *New Critical Essays*, translated by Richard Howard, 55–68. Evanston, IL: Northwestern University Press, 2009.

——. *S/Z: An Essay*, translated by Richard Miller. New York: Hill and Wang, 1974.

Bāshā, Qunsṭanṭīn. *Tārīkh Usrat Firʿawn bi-Uṣūlihā wa-Furūʿihā.* Harissa, Lebanon: Maṭbaʿat al-Qiddīs Būlus, 1932.

Bataille, George. *The Accursed Share: An Essay on General Economy*, translated by Robert Hurley. 3 vols. New York: Zone Books, 1991–1993.

Bayly, C. A. *Empire and Information: Intelligence Gathering and Social Communication in India, 1780–1870.* Cambridge: Cambridge University Press, 1996.

Beckett, Greg. "The Ontology of Freedom: The Unthinkable Miracle of Haiti." *Journal of Haitian Studies* 19, no. 2 (Fall 2013): 54–74.

Belhamissi, Moulay. *Les captifs algériens et l'Europe chrétienne (1518–1830).* Algiers: ENL, 1988.

Belissa, Marc. "War and Diplomacy (1792–95)." In *The Oxford Handbook of the French Revolution*, edited by David Andress, 418–35. Oxford: Oxford University Press, 2015.

Bell, David A. *The First Total War: Napoleon's Europe and the Birth of Warfare as We Know It.* Boston: Houghton Mifflin, 2007.

Belmessous, Saliha. *Assimilation and Empire: Uniformity in French and British Colonies, 1541–1954.* Oxford: Oxford University Press, 2013.

——. "The Paradox of an Empire by Treaty." In *Empire by Treaty: Negotiating European Expansion, 1600–1900*, edited by Saliha Belmessous, 1–18. Oxford: Oxford University Press, 2015.

Belsey, Catherine. "The Name of the Rose in '*Romeo and Juliet*.'" *Yearbook of English Studies* 23 (1993): 126–42.

Ben Hounet, Y. "Des tribus en Algérie? À propos de la déstructuration tribale durant la période coloniale." *Cahiers de la Méditerranée* 75 (2007): 150–71.

Benbassa, Esther. *The Jews of France: A History from Antiquity to the Present*, translated by M. B. DeBevoise. Princeton, NJ: Princeton University Press, 1999.

Benjamin, Walter. "On Language as Such and on the Language of Man." *Selected Writings.* Vol. 1: *1913–1926*, edited by Marcus Bullock and Michael W. Jennings, 62–74. Cambridge, MA: Harvard University Press, 1996.

Bennassar, Bartolomé, and Lucile Bennassar. *Les Chrétiens d'Allah: l'histoire extraordinaire des renégats, XVIe et XVIIe siècles.* Paris: Perrin, 1989.

Bennedjaï-Zou, Adila, host. "Mes années Boum, une enquête algérienne," podcast. Produced by Marie Plaçais. *Les Pieds sur terre.* France Culture. 3 November–15

December 2016, 7–15 February 2018. https://www.radiofrance.fr/franceculture/podcasts/serie-mes-annees-boum-une-enquete-algerienne#concept-about.

Bennington, Geoffrey, and Jacques Derrida. *Derrida*. Paris: Seuil, 2008.

Bennison, Amira K. *The Almoravid and Almohad Empires*. Edinburgh: Edinburgh University Press, 2016.

——. *Jihad and Its Interpretations in Pre-Colonial Morocco: State-Society Relations During the French Conquest of Algeria*. London: Routledge Curzon, 2002.

Benramdane, Farid [Farīd bin Ramḍān]. "Histoire(s) et enjeu(x) d'une (re)dé/dé/dénomination: la Place rouge de Tiaret." *Insaniyat* 17–18 (May–December, 2002): 63–70.

——. "Qui es-tu? J'ai été dit: de la destruction de la filiation dans l'état civil d'Algérie ou éléments d'un onomacide sémantique." *Insaniyat* 10 (January–April, 2000): 79–87.

——. "Tadmīr al-Nasab fī al-Ḥāla al-Madanīya bil-Jaza'ir." *Insāniyāt* 2 (2010): 85–93.

Benramdane, Farid, and Brahim Atoui, eds. *Nomination et dénomination: Des noms de lieux, de tribus et de personnes en Algérie*. Oran: CRASC, 2005.

——. *Toponymie et anthroponymie de l'Algérie: Recueil bibliographique générale*. Oran: CRASC, 2005.

Benson, Susan. "Injurious Names: Naming, Disavowal, and Recuperation in Contexts of Slavery and Emancipation." In *The Anthropology of Names and* Naming, edited by Gabriele vom Bruck and Barbara Bodenhorn, 177–99. Cambridge: Cambridge University Press, 2006.

Benton, Lauren. *Law and Colonial Cultures: Legal Regimes in World History, 1400-1900*. Cambridge: Cambridge University Press, 2002.

Benton, Lauren, and Benjamin Straumann. "Acquiring Empire by Law: From Roman Doctrine to Early Modern European Practice." *Law and History Review* 28, no. 1 (2010): 1–38.

Benvenisti, Eyal. *The International Law of Occupation*. 2nd ed. Oxford: Oxford University Press, 2012.

——. "The Origins of the Concept of Belligerent Occupation." *Law and History Review* 26, no. 3 (Fall 2008): 621–48.

Berger, Anne-Emmanuelle, ed. *Algeria in Others' Languages*. Ithaca, NY: Cornell University Press, 2002.

Bersani, Leo. *Marcel Proust: The Fictions of Art and Life*. 2nd ed. Oxford: Oxford University Press, 2013.

Bertrand, Régis. "Les cimetières des 'esclaves turcs' des arsenaux de Marseille et de Toulon au XVIIIe siècle." *Revue des mondes musulmans et de la Méditerranée* 99–100 (November 2002): 205–17.

Bhabha, Homi K. *The Location of Culture*. London: Routledge, 1994.

Bhandar, Brenna. *Colonial Lives of Property: Law, Land and Racial Regimes of Property*. Durham, NC: Duke University Press, 2018.

Blais, Hélène. *Mirages de la carte: L'invention de l'Algérie coloniale XIXe–XXe siècle*. Paris: Fayard, 2014.

Blanchard, Pascal, Nicolas Bancel, Gilles Boetsch, Éric Deroo, Sandrine Lemaire, Charles Forsdick, eds. *Human Zoos: Science and Spectacle in the Age of Colonial Empires*, translated by Teresa Bridgeman. Liverpool: Liverpool University Press, 2008.

Blaufarb, Rafe. *The Great Demarcation: The French Revolution and the Invention of Modern Property*. Oxford: Oxford University Press, 2016.

Blévis, Laure. "La citoyenneté française au miroir de la colonisation: étude des demandes de naturalisation des 'sujets français' en Algérie colonial." *Genèses* 53 (2003): 25–47.

Blumenberg, Hans. *Work on Myth*, translated by Robert M. Wallace. Cambridge, MA: MIT Press, 1985.

Bonte, Pierre, Édouard Conte, Constant Hamès, and Abdel Wedoud Ould Cheikh, eds. *Al-Ansâb, la quête des origines: Anthropologie historique de la société tribale arabe*. Paris: Maison des sciences de l'homme, 1991.

Bontems, Claude. *L'Algérie, ses instituions et son droit à l'épreuve de la colonisation*. Paris: Bouchène, 2018.

——. *Le droit musulman algérien à l'époque colonial: de l'invention à la codification*. Geneva: Slatkine, 2014.

——. *Manuel des institutions algériennes de la domination turque à l'indépendance*. Vol. 1: *La domination turque et le régime militaire*. Paris: Cujas, 1976.

Boogert, Maurits H. van den. *The Capitulations and the Ottoman Legal System: Qadis, Consuls, and Beratlıs in the 18th Century*. Leiden: Brill, 2005.

Boogert, Nico van den. *The Berber Literary Tradition of the Sous*. Leiden: Nederlands Instituut voor het Nabije Oosten, 1997.

——. "Medieval Berber Orthography." In *Études berbères et chamito-sémitiques: mélanges offerts à Karl-G. Prasse*, edited by Salem Chaker, 358–59. Paris: Peeters, 2000.

——. "Some Notes on Maghribi Script." *Manuscripts of the Middle East* 4 (1989): 30–43.

Boogert, Nico van den, and Maarten Kossmann. "Les premiers emprunts arabes en berbère." *Arabica* 44, no. 2 (1997): 317–22.

Borges, Jorge Luis. *Collected Fictions*, translated by Andrew Hurley. New York: Penguin, 1998.

Boudjedra, Rachid. *The Repudiation*, translated by Golda Lambrova. Colorado Springs: Three Continents Press, 1995.

Bounfour, Abdellah. "Notes sur l'histoire du berbère (Tachelhit): essai de bilan et perspectives." In *Trames de langues: Usages et métissages linguistiques dans l'histoire du Maghreb*, edited by Jocelyne Dakhlia, 169–81. Paris: Maisonneuve and Larose, 2004.

Bounfour, Abdellah, and D. Merolla. "Conte." *Encyclopédie berbère*. Vol. 14: *Conseil-Danse*, edited by Gabriel Camps, 2081–88. Aix-en-Provence: Édisud, 1994.

Bourdieu, Pierre. "The Force of Law: Toward a Sociology of the Juridical Field." *Hastings Law Journal* 38, no. 5 (July 1987): 814–54.

——. *Language and Symbolic Power*, translated by Gino Raymond and Matthew Adamson. Cambridge, MA: Harvard University Press, 1991.

——. *The Logic of Practice*, translated by Richard Nice. Stanford, CA: Stanford University Press, 1990.

——. *Masculine Domination*, translated by Richard Nice. Stanford, CA: Stanford University Press, 2001.

——. *On the State: Lectures at the Collège de France, 1989-1992*, edited by Patrick Champagne, Remi Lenoir, Franck Poupeau, and Marie-Christine Rivière, translated by David Fernbach. Cambridge, UK: Polity, 2014.

——. *Pascalian Meditations*, translated by Richard Nice. Stanford, CA: Stanford University Press, 2000).

Bourin, Monique. "L'écriture du nom propre et l'apparition d'une anthroponymie à plusieurs éléments en Europe occidentale (XIe–XIIe siècles)." In *L'écriture du nom propre*, edited by Anne-Marie Christin, 193–213. Paris: Harmattan, 1997.

Boutang, Yann Moulier. *Louis Althusser: Une biographie*. Paris: Grasset, 1992.

Brand, Laurie A. *Official Stories: Politics and National Narratives in Egypt and Algeria*. Stanford, CA: Stanford University Press, 2014.

Brantlinger, Patrick. *Dark Vanishings: Discourse on the Extinction of Primitive Races, 1800–1930*. Ithaca, NY: Cornell University Press, 1993.

Bras, Jean-Philippe. "L'imperfection de la propriété indigène, lieu commun de la doctrine juridique coloniale en Afrique du Nord." In *Appartenance locale et propriété au nord et au sud de la Méditerranée*, edited by Sami Bargaoui, Simona Cerutti, and Isabelle Grangaud. Aix-en-Provence: Institut de recherches et d'études sur les mondes arabes et musulmans, 2015). https://books.openedition.org/iremam/3441?lang=en.

Brett, Michael. "Legislating for Inequality in Algeria: The Senatus-Consulte of 14 July 1865." *Bulletin of the School of Oriental and African Studies, University of London* 51, no. 3. (1988): 440–61.

Brodersen, Momme. *Walter Benjamin: A Biography*, translated by Malcolm R. Green and Ingrida Ligers. London: Verso, 1996.

Brower, Benjamin Claude. *A Desert Named Peace: The Violence of France's Empire in the Algerian Sahara, 1844–1902*. New York: Columbia University Press, 2009.

——. "Genealogies of Modern Violence: Arendt and Imperialism in Africa, 1830–1914." In *The Cambridge World History of Violence*. Vol. 4: *1800 to the Present*, edited by Louise Edwards, Nigel Penn, and Jay Winter, 246–62. Cambridge: Cambridge University Press, 2020.

——. "Just War and Jihad in the French Conquest of Algeria." In *Just Wars, Holy Wars, and Jihads: Christian, Jewish, and Muslim Encounters and Exchanges*, edited by Sohail H. Hashmi, 221–40. Oxford: Oxford University Press, 2012.

——. "Rethinking Abolition in Algeria: Slavery and the 'Indigenous Question.'" *Cahiers d'études africaines* 49, no. 195 (2009): 805–27.

Brower, M. Brady. *Unruly Spirits: The Science of Psychic Phenomena in Modern France*. Urbana: University of Illinois Press, 2010.

Brubaker, Rogers. *Citizenship and Nationhood in France and Germany*. Cambridge, MA: Harvard University Press, 1992.

Bruck, Gabriele vom, and Barbara Bodenhorn, eds. *The Anthropology of Names and Naming*. Cambridge: Cambridge University Press 2006.

Brunet, Guy, and Kamel Kateb. *L'Algérie des Européens au XIXe: naissance d'une population et transformation d'une société*. Bern: Lang, 2018.

Brunot, Ferdinand. *Histoire de la langue française des origines à nos jours*. 13 vols. Paris: Colin, 1966–1979.

Brustad, Kristen. "Diglossia as Ideology." In *The Politics of Written Language and the Arab World*, edited by Jacob Høigilt and Gunvor Mejdell, 41–67. Leiden: Brill, 2017.

Bsikri, Mehdi. "Entre 30 000 et 35 000 changements de nom de famille depuis l'indépendance." *El Watan* (8 September 2012). https://www.elwatan.com/archives/actualites/entre-30-000-et-35-000-changements-de-nom-de-famille-depuis-lindependance-08-09-2012.

Budin, Jacques. *La région de Annaba (Bône): colonisation et résistance: 1832–1914.* 2 vols. Saint-Denis: Bouchène, 2020.

Bulliet, Richard W. *The Patricians of Nishapur: A Study in Medieval Islamic Social History.* Cambridge, MA: Harvard University Press, 1972.

——. "A Quantitative Approach to Medieval Muslim Biographical Dictionaries." *Journal of the Economic and Social History of the Orient* 13, no. 2 (April 1970): 195–211.

——. Review of *Voile de nom*, by Jacqueline Sublet. *Journal of the American Oriental Society* 113, no. 1 (January–March 1993): 125.

Buonamano, Roberto. "Kafka and Legal Critique." *Griffith Law Review* 25, no. 4 (2016): 581–99.

Butler, Judith. *Psychic Life of Power: Theories in Subjection.* Stanford, CA: Stanford University Press, 1997.

Camps, Gabriel. "Liste onomastique libyque d'après les sources latines." *Revue des Études phéniciennes, puniques et des antiquités libyques* 7–8 (1992–1993): 39–73.

——. "Liste onomastique libyque, nouvelle édition." *Antiquités africaines*, 38–39 (2002): 211–57.

Caplan, Jane, and John Torpey, eds. *Documenting Individual Identity: The Development of State Practices in the Modern World.* Princeton, NJ: Princeton University Press, 2001.

Carlier, Omar. "Mercier, Ernest." In *Dictionnaire des orientalistes de langue française*, edited by François Pouillon. Paris: Karthala, 2008.

Cattaui, Joseph-Edmond. *Histoire des rapports de l'Égypte avec la Sublime Porte (du XVIIIe siècle à 1841).* Paris: Jouve, 1919.

Certeau, Michel de. *Heterologies: Discourse of the Other*, translated by Brian Massumi. Minneapolis: University of Minnesota Press, 1986.

——. *The Writing of History*, translated by Tom Conley. New York: Columbia University Press, 1988.

Chachoua, Kamel. *L'islam kabyle (XVIIIe–XXe siècles): religion, État et société en Algérie.* Paris: Maisonneuve et Larose, 2002.

——. "Le piège: Kabyle de langue, Arabe de religion." *Revue des mondes musulmans et de la Méditerranée* 124 (November 2008): 203–18.

Chaker, Salem. *Berbères d'aujourd'hui.* Paris: Harmattan, 1989.

——. "Écriture (graphie arabe)." In *Encyclopédie berbère.* Vol 17: *Douiret-Eropaei*, edited by Gabriel Camps, 2580–83. Aix-en-Provence: Édisud, 1996.

——. "La langue berbère à travers l'onomastique médiévale: El-Bekri." *Revue de l'Occident musulman et de la Méditerranée* 35 (1983): 127–44.

———. "Onomastique Libyco-Berbère (Anthroponymie)." In *Encyclopédie berbère.* Vol. 35: *Oasitae-Ortaïas*, edited by Salem Chaker, 5760–79. Paris: Peeters, 2013.

Chakrabarty, Dipesh. *Provincializing Europe: Postcolonial Thought and Historical Difference.* Princeton, NJ: Princeton University Press, 2008.

Charnay, Jean-Paul. *La vie musulmane en Algérie d'après la jurisprudence de la première moitié du XXe siècle*. Paris: Presses universitaires de France, 1965.

Chastanier, Roger. *Un aspect des lois relatives aux minorités religieuses: L'état civil des protestants, 1550–1792*. Nîmes: Chastanier, 1922.

Chaulet Achour, Christiane, and Faïka Medjahed. *Viols et filiations: Incursions psychanalytiques et littéraires en Algérie*. Algiers: Koukou, 2020.

Chenoweth, Katie. *The Prosthetic Tongue: Print Technology and the Rise of the French Language*. Philadelphia: University of Pennsylvania Press, 2019.

Cheriguen, Foudil. *Toponymie algérienne des lieux habités*. Algiers: Épigraphe, 1993.

Chetrit, Joseph. "Le judéo-berbère et ses usages au Maroc." In *Diglossie, hybridation et diversité intra-linguistique: études socio-pragmatiques sur les langues juives, le judéo-arabe et le judéo-berbère*, edited by Joseph Chetrit, 213–352. Paris: Peeters, 2007.

Chipman, Leigh N. B. "Adam and the Angels: An Examination of Mythic Elements in Islamic Sources." *Arabica* 49, no. 4 (October 2002): 429–55.

Chouquer, Gérard. *Dictionnaire des questions foncières pendant la colonisation de l'Algérie au XIXe siècle*. Paris: Publi-Topex, 2020.

Christelow, Allan. *Algerians without Borders: The Making of a Global Frontier Society*. Gainesville: University Press of Florida, 2012.

——. *Muslim Law Courts and the French Colonial State in Algeria*. Princeton, NJ: Princeton University Press, 1985.

Cixous, Hélène. *Readings: The Poetics of Blanchot, Joyce, Kafka, Kleist, Lispector, and Tsvetayeva*, translated by Verena Andermatt Conley. Minneapolis: University of Minneapolis Press, 1991.

Clancy-Smith, Julia A. *Mediterraneans: North Africa and Europe in an Age of Migration, c. 1800–1900*. Berkeley: University of California Press, 2011.

——. *Rebel and Saint: Muslim Notables, Populist Protest, Colonial Encounters (Algeria and Tunisia, 1800–1904)*. Berkeley: University of California Press, 1997.

Coetzee, J. M. *Foe*. New York: Penguin, 1986.

Cohen, David. *Le Parler arabe des Juifs de Tunis*. 2 vols. Paris: Mouton, 1964–1975.

Cohen, Paul. "L'Imaginaire d'une langue nationale: L'état, les langues et l'invention du mythe de l'Ordonnance de Villers-Cotterêts à l'époque moderne en France." *Histoire épistémologie langage* 25, no. 1 (2003): 19–69.

Cohn, Bernard S. *Colonialism and Its Form of Knowledge: The British in India*. Princeton, NJ: Princeton University Press 1996.

Cole, Joshua. *Lethal Provocation: The Constantine Murders and the Politics of French Algeria*. Ithaca, NY: Cornell University Press, 2019.

——. *The Power of Large Numbers: Population, Politics, and Gender in Nineteenth-Century France*. Ithaca, NY: Cornell University Press, 2000.

Cole, Juan. *Napoleon's Egypt: Invading the Middle East*. New York: St. Martin's Griffin, 2008.

Coller, Ian. *Arab France: Islam and the Making of Modern Europe, 1798–1831*. Berkeley: University of California Press, 2011.

——. *Muslims and Citizens: Islam, Politics, and the French Revolution*. New Haven, CT: Yale University Press, 2020.

Collomp, Alain. "Le Nom gardé: La dénomination personnelle en Haute-Provence aux XVIIe et XVIIIe siècles." *L'Homme* 20, no. 4 (October–December, 1980): 43–61.

Collot, Claude. *Les Institutions de l'Algérie durant la période colonial (1830–1962)*. Paris: Éditions du CNRS; Algiers: Office des publications universitaires, 1987.

Colonna, Fanny. *Le meunier, les moines et le bandit, des vies quotidiennes dans l'Aurès (Algérie) du XXe siècle*. Arles: Sinbad, 2010.

Comaroff, Jean, and John Comaroff. *Of Revelation and Revolution: Christianity, Colonialism and Consciousness in South Africa*. 2 vols. Chicago: University of Chicago Press, 1991.

Corbin, Alain. *The Life of an Unknown: The Rediscovered World of a Clog Maker in Nineteenth-Century France*, translated by Arthur Goldhammer. New York: Columbia University Press, 2001.

Corcos, David. "Réflexions sur l'onomastique judéo-nord-africaine." *Folklore Research Center Studies* 1 (1970): 1–27.

Courreye, Charlotte. *L'Algérie des Oulémas: Une histoire de l'Algérie contemporaine (1931–1991)*. Paris: Éditions de la Sorbonne, 2020.

Cousseau, Vincent. "Population et anthroponymie en Martinique du XVIIe siècle à la première moitié du XIXe siècle: Étude d'une société coloniale à travers son système de dénomination personnel." PhD diss., Université des Antilles et de la Guyane, 2009.

Crone, Patricia. *God's Rule: Government and Islam*. New York: Columbia University Press, 2004.

Crook, Tom, and Glen O'Hara. *Statistics and the Public Sphere: Numbers and the People in Modern Britain, c. 1800–2000*. London: Routledge, 2011.

Crowley, Patrick. "The Etat Civil: Post/colonial Identities and Genre." *French Forum* 29, no. 3 (Fall 2004): 79–94.

Dainville-Barbiche, Ségolène de, Yvette Isselin, Monique Mayeur, Annie Poinsot, and Pierre Bureau. *Dossiers de demandes: naturalisations, admissions à domicile, réintégrations dans la qualité de français, autorisations de servir ou de se faire naturaliser à l'étranger, changements de nom, dispenses pour mariage, majorats, dotations, armoiries (1851–1858)*. Pierrefitte-sur-Seine: Archives nationales de France, 2017. https://www.siv.archives-nationales.culture.gouv.fr/siv/rechercheconsultation/consultation/ir/pdfIR.action?irId=FRAN_IR_055986.

Dakhlia, Jocelyne. "1830, une rencontre?" In *Historie de l'Algérie à la période coloniale, 1830–1962*, edited by Abderrahmane Bouchène, Jean-Pierre Peyroulou, Ouanassa Siari Tengour, and Sylvie Thénault, 142–48. Paris: Découverte, 2014.

——. *Lingua franca: histoire d'une langue métisse en Méditerranée*. Arles: Actes Sud, 2008.

Daoud, Kamel. *The Meursault Investigation*, translated by John Cullen. New York: Other Press, 2014.

Dardier, Charles. "Les registres de l'état civil des protestants de Nîmes, de 1571–1792." *Bulletin historique et littéraire (Société de l'Histoire du Protestantisme Français)* 23, no. 3 (1874): 141–43.

Dauzat, Albert. *Dictionnaire étymologique des noms de famille et prénoms de France*. Paris: Larousse, 1951.

Davidson, Naomi. *Only Muslim: Embodying Islam in Twentieth-Century France*. Ithaca, NY: Cornell University Press, 2012.

Davis, Muriam Haleh. *Markets of Civilization: Islam and Racial Capitalism in Algeria.* Durham, NC: Duke University Press, 2022.

Davis, Natalie Zemon. *Trickster Travels: A Sixteenth-Century Muslim Between Worlds.* New York: Hill and Wang, 2006.

Davis, Robert C. *Christian Slaves, Muslim Masters: White Slavery in the Mediterranean, the Barbary Coast, and Italy, 1500–1800.* New York: Palgrave Macmillan, 2003.

Davis, Teresa. "The Ricardian State: Carlos Calvo and Latin America's Ambivalent Origin Story for the Age of Decolonization." *Journal of the History of International Law* 20, no. 1 (2020): 32–51.

de Lange, Erik. "The Congress System and the French Invasion of Algiers, 1827–1830." *Historical Journal* 64, no. 4 (2021): 940–62.

De Man, Paul. *The Resistance to Theory.* Minneapolis: University of Minnesota, 1986.

Decroux, Paul. "L'état-civil au Maroc." *Hesperis* 37 (1950): 237–89.

Delany, Samuel R. *Babel-17.* New York: Vintage, 1966.

Delsalle, Paul. *Histoires de familles: les registres paroissiaux et d'état civil, du Moyen âge à nos jours.* Besançon: Presses universitaires de Franche-Comté, 2009.

Denis, Vincent. "Individual Identity and Identification in Eighteenth-Century France." In *Identification and Registration Practices in Transnational Perspective: People, Papers and Practices*, edited by Ilsen About, James Brown and Gayle Lonergan, 17–30. New York: Palgrave Macmillan, 2013.

——. *Une histoire de l'identité, 1715–1815.* Paris: Champ Vallon, 2008.

Derrida, Jacques. *The Beast and the Sovereign*, translated by Geoffrey Bennington. 2 vols. Chicago: University of Chicago Press, 2009–2011.

——. "Before the Law." In *Acts of Literature*, edited by Derek Attridge, 181–220. New York: Routledge, 1992.

——. *Monolingualism of the Other; or, The Prosthesis of Origin*, translated by Patrick Mensah. Stanford, CA: Stanford University Press, 1998.

——. *Of Grammatology*, translated by Gayatri Chakravorty Spivak. Baltimore: John Hopkins University Press, 1976.

——. *On the Name*, edited by Thomas Dutoit; translated by David Wood, John P. Leavey, Jr., and Ian McLeod. Stanford, CA: Stanford University Press, 1995.

—— *Psyche: Inventions of the Other*, edited by Peggy Kamuf and Elizabeth Rottenberg. 2 vols. Stanford, CA: Stanford University Press, 2007 and 2008.

Desan, Suzanne. *The Family on Trial in Revolutionary France.* Berkeley: University of California Press, 2004.

Di-Capua, Yoav. "*Nahda:* The Arab Project of Enlightenment." In *The Cambridge Companion to Modern Arab Culture*, edited by Dwight F. Reynolds, 54–74. Cambridge: Cambridge University Press, 2015.

——. *No Exit: Arab Existentialism, Jean-Paul Sartre, and Decolonization.* Chicago: University of Chicago Press, 2018.

Dirèche, Karima. *Chrétiens de Kabylie, 1873–1954: Une action missionnaire dans l'Algérie coloniale.* S.l.: Bouchène, 2004.

"Directives toponymiques à l'usage des éditeurs de cartes et autres éditeurs." Groupe d'experts des Nations unies sur les noms géographiques, Working Paper no. 78, 17–28. January 2000. https://unstats.un.org/unsd/geoinfo/UNGEGN/docs/20th-gegn-docs/20th_gegn_WP78.pdf.
Djeghloul, Abdelkader. *Éléments d'histoire culturelle algérienne.* Algiers: ENAL, 1984.
Djellali, Abderrazak. "Le caïdat en Algérie au XIXe siècle." *Cahiers de la Méditerranée* 45, no. 1 (1992): 37–49.
Djerbal, Daho. "Sans nom patronymique (SNP): De la dépossession du nom à l'expropriation de la terre par la carte." In *Made in Algeria: généalogie d'un territoire*, edited by Zahia Rahmani and Jean-Yves Sarazin, 183–86. Marseille: MUCEM, 2016.
——. "The Sweet 60s: Between the Liberation of Peoples and the Liberty of Individuals, or the Difficult Representation of the Self." *Red Thread 2.* https://red-thread.org/en/the-sweet-60s-between-the-liberation-of-peoples-and-the-liberty-of-individuals-or-the-difficult-representation-of-the-self/.
Dorion, Henri, and Jean Poirier. *Lexique des termes utiles à l'étude des noms des lieux.* Québec: Presses de l'Université de Laval, 1975.
Drouhard, Myriam. *Voyage au pays des aïeux: histoire et sources de la généalogie.* Rouen: Archives départementales de la Seine-Maritime, 1992.
Dubois, Laurent. *Avengers of the New World: The Story of the Haitian Revolution.* Cambridge, MA: Harvard University Press, 2004.
——. *A Colony of Citizens: Revolution and Slave Emancipation in the French Caribbean, 1787–1804.* Chapel Hill: University of North Carolina Press, 2004.
Dubreuil, Laurent. *Empire of Language: Towards a Critique of (Post)colonial Expression,* translated by David Fieni. Ithaca, NY: Cornell University Press, 2013.
Dugas de la Boissony, Christian. *L'état civil.* Paris: Presses universitaires de France, 1987.
Dumasy, François. "À qui appartient Alger? Normes d'appartenance et conflits d'appropriation à Alger au début de la présence française." In *Appartenance locale et propriété au nord et au sud de la Méditerranée*, edited by Sami Bargaoui, Simona Cerutti, and Isabelle Grangaud. Aix-en-Provence: Institut de recherches et d'études sur les mondes arabes et musulmans, 2015. https://doi.org/10.4000/books.iremam.3396.
——. "Propriété et société coloniale. La Commission de colonisation et la Mitidja en 1842–1843." In *Propriété et société en Algérie contemporaine: Quelles approches?*, edited by Didier Guignard, 44–58. Aix-en-Provence: Institut de recherches et d'études sur le monde arabe et musulman, 2017.
——. "Propriété foncière, libéralisme économique et gouvernement colonial: Alger, 1830–1840." *Revue d'histoire modern et contemporaine* 60, no. 2 (2016): 40–61.
Dupâquier, Jacques, and Michel Dupâquier. *Histoire de la démographie: la statistique de la population des origines à 1914.* Paris: Perrin, 1985.
Duri, ʿAbd al-ʿAziz. *The Rise of Historical Writing among the Arabs.* Princeton, NJ: Princeton University Press, 1983.
Dzanic, Dzavid. "The Civilizing Sea: The Ideological Origins of the French Mediterranean Empire, 1789–1870." PhD diss., Harvard University, 2016.

Ebied, R. Y., and M. J. L. Young. "A Note on Muslim Name-Giving According to the Day of the Week." *Arabica* 24, fasc. 3 (September 1977): 326–28.

Eco, Umberto. *The Name of the Rose*, translated by William Weaver. New York: Harcourt Brace Jovanovich, 1984.

Eichner, Carolyn J. "In the Name of the Mother: Feminist Opposition to the Patronym in Nineteenth-Century France." *Signs* 39, no. 3 (Spring 2014): 659–83.

Eisenbeth, Maurice. *Les juifs d'Afrique du Nord: démographie et onomastique.* Algiers: Imprimerie du Lycée, 1936.

El Hamel, Chouki. *Black Morocco: A History of Slavery, Race, and Islam.* Cambridge: Cambridge University Press, 2013.

El-Shakry, Hoda. "Heteroglossia and the Poetics of the *Roman Maghrébin*." *Contemporary French and Francophone Studies* 20, no. 1 (2016): 8–17.

El Shakry, Omnia. *The Arabic Freud: Psychoanalysis and Islam in Modern Egypt.* Princeton, NJ: Princeton University Press, 2017.

El Youbi, Ali, and Said Warit. "Rapport sur le système d'État Civil Marocain." Working paper, African Workshop on Strategies of Accelerating the Improvement of Civil Registration and Vital Statistics Systems, United Nations Economic and Social Council, Rabat, Morocco, 1995. https://unstats.un.org/unsd/demographic/meetings/wshops/1995_Rabat_CRVS/Docs/Marocain.pdf.

Elmounadi, Ahmed, and Hachem Jarmouni. "Le périple des manuscrits amazighes." *Études et documents berbères* 1, no. 33 (2014): 149–57.

Emerit, Marcel. "Les tribus privilégiées en Algérie dans la première moitié du XIXe siècle." *Annales: économies, sociétés, civilisations* 21, no. 1 (1966): 44–58.

Ennaji, Mohammed. *Serving the Master: Slavery and Society in Nineteenth-Century Morocco*, translated by Seth Graebner. New York: St. Martin's Press, 1999.

Errington, Joseph. *Linguistics in a Colonial World: A Story of Language, Meaning and Power.* Malden, MA: Blackwell, 2008.

Establet, Colette. *Être caïd dans l'Algérie coloniale.* Paris: Éditions du Centre national de la recherche scientifique, 1991.

Evangelista, Matthew. *Gender, Nationalism, and War: Conflict on the Movie Screen.* Cambridge: Cambridge University Press, 2011.

Fabian, Johannes. *Language and Colonial Power: The Appropriation of Swahili in the Former Belgian Congo, 1880–1938.* Cambridge: Cambridge University Press, 1986.

Fahmy, Khaled. *In Quest of Justice: Islamic Law and Forensic Medicine in Modern Egypt.* Berkeley: University of California Press, 2018.

Fanon, Frantz. *Alienation and Freedom*, edited by Robert J. C. Young and Jean Khalfa; translated by Steven Corcoran. London: Bloomsbury, 2018.

——. *Black Skins, White Masks*, translated by Charles Lam Markmann. New York: Grove Press, 1967.

——. *The Wretched of the Earth*, translated by Richard Philcox. New York: Grove Press, 2004.

Faucher, Benjamin. "Les registres de l'état civil protestant en France depuis le XVIe siècle jusqu'à nos jours." *Bibliothèque de l'École des Chartes* 84 (1923): 306–46.

Feraoun, Mouloud. *The Poor Man's Son: Menrad, Kabyle Schoolteacher*, translated by Lucy R. McNair. Charlottesville: University of Virginia Press, 2005.

Ferhati, Barkahoum. "Ouled Naïl, mythe et réalités (1830–1962)." In *L'Algérie et la France: dictionnaire*, edited by Jeannine Verdès-Leroux, 656–58. Paris: Laffont, 2009.

Finchelstein, Federico. *A Brief History of Fascist Lies*. Berkeley: University of California Press, 2020.

Fitzmaurice, Andrew. *Sovereignty, Property and Empire, 1500–2000*. Cambridge: Cambridge University Press, 2014.

Fitzsimmons, Michael P. *The Place of Words: The Académie Française and Its Dictionary During an Age of Revolution*. Oxford: Oxford University Press, 2017.

Fleisch, Henri. *Traité de philologie arabe*. Vol. 1: *Préliminaires, phonétique, morphologie nominale*. Beirut: Imprimerie Catholique, 1961.

Forrest, Alan. *The Legacy of the French Revolutionary Wars: The Nation-in-Arms in French Republican Memory*. Cambridge: Cambridge University Press, 2009.

Foucault, Michel. *The Birth of Biopolitics: Lectures at the Collège de France, 1978–79*, translated by Graham Burchell. New York: Palgrave Macmillan, 2008.

——. *Security, Territory, Population: Lectures at the Collège de France, 1977–78*, translated by Graham Burchell. New York: Palgrave, 2007.

——. *Society Must Be Defended: Lectures at the Collège de France, 1975–76*, translated by David Macey. New York: Picador, 2003.

Fraenkel, Béatrice. *La signature, genèse d'un signe*. Paris: Gallimard, 1992.

Fredj, Claire. "L'hôpital militaire et l'accommodation à l'occupation en Algérie (années 1830–années 1850)." In *Le temps des hommes doubles*, edited by Jean-François Chanet, Annie Crépin, and Christian Windler, 177–94. Rennes: Presses universitaires de Rennes, 2013.

——. "Soigner une colonie naissante: les médecins de l'armée d'Afrique, les fièvres et la quinine, 1830–1870." *Mouvement social* 257, no. 1 (2017): 21–45.

Frémeaux, Jacques. *Les bureaux arabes dans l'Algérie de la conquête*. Paris: Denoël, 1993.

Frigerio, Aldo. "Some Objections to the Metalinguistic Theory of Proper Names." In *Les théories du sens et de la référence: hommage à Georges Kleiber*, edited by Emilia Hilgert, Silvia Palma, Pierre Frath, and René Daval, 405–18. Reims: Presses universitaires de Reims, 2014.

Fuchs, Rachel G. *Contested Paternity: Constructing Families in Modern France*. Baltimore: Johns Hopkins University Press, 2008.

Gacek, Adam. *Arabic Manuscripts: A Vademecum for Readers*. Leiden: Brill, 2009.

Gallissot, René. *Le Maghreb de traverse*. Saint-Denis: Bouchène, 2000.

Gallois, William. *The Administration of Sickness: Medicine and Ethics in Nineteenth-Century Algeria*. Basingstoke, UK: Palgrave Macmillan, 2008.

——. "The Genocidal French Conquest of Algeria, 1830–1847." In *The Cambridge World History of Genocide*. Vol. 2: *Genocide in the Indigenous, Early Modern and Imperial Worlds, from c.1535 to World War One*, edited by Ned Blackhawk, Ben Kiernan, Benjamin Madley, and Rebe Taylor; general editor, Ben Kiernan, 3613–82. Cambridge: Cambridge University Press, 2023.

——. "Genocide in Nineteenth-Century Algeria." *Journal of Genocide Research* 15, no. 1 (2013): 69–88.

Garcés, María Antonia. *Cervantes in Algiers: A Captive's Tale*. Nashville, TN: Vanderbilt University Press, 2002.

García-Arenal, Mercedes, and Gerard Wiegers. *A Man of Three Worlds: Samuel Pallache, A Moroccan Jew in Catholic and Protestant Europe*, translated by Martin Beagles. Baltimore: Johns Hopkins University Press, 2003.

Gardey, Delphine. *Écrire, calculer, classer: comment une révolution de papier a transformé les sociétés contemporaines (1800–1940)*. Paris: Découverte, 2008.

Garval, Michael D. *A Dream of Stone: Fame, Vision, and Monumentality in Nineteenth-Century French Literary Culture*. Newark: University of Delaware Press, 2004.

Geertz, Clifford. "'From the Native's Point of View': On the Nature of Anthropological Understanding." In *Meaning in Anthropology*, edited by Keith Basso and Henry A. Selby, 221–37. Albuquerque: University of New Mexico Press, 1976.

Ghabrial, Sarah. "*Le 'fiqh francisé'*? Muslim Personal Status Law Reform and Women's Litigation in Colonial Algeria (1870–1930)." PhD diss., McGill University, 2014.

——. "The Traumas and Truths of the Body: Medical Evidence and Divorce in Colonial Algerian Courts, 1870–1930." *Journal of Middle East Women's Studies* 11, no. 3 (November 2015): 283–305.

Gheziel, Abla. "Trois réactions 'algériennes' sur l'avenir de l'Algérie, 1830–1834." *Insaniyat*, nos. 65–66 (2014): 187–210.

Ghouirgate, Mehdi. "Le berbère au Moyen Âge: une culture linguistique en cours de reconstitution." *Annales: histoire, sciences, sociales* 70, no. 3 (July–September 2015): 577–605.

Gimaret, Daniel. *Les Noms divins en islam, exégèse lexicographique et théologique*. Paris: Cerf, 1988.

Ginzburg, Carlo. *The Cheese and the Worms: The Cosmos of a Sixteenth-Century Miller*, translated by John and Anne Tedeschi. Baltimore: Johns Hopkins University Press, 1980.

Glasser, Jonathan. *The Lost Paradise: Andalusi Music in Urban North Africa*. Chicago: University of Chicago Press, 2016.

Godechot, Jacques. *La Grande nation: l'expansion révolutionnaire de la France dans le monde de 1789 à 1799*. 2 vols. Paris: Aubier, 1956.

Godechot, Jacques, Beatrice F. Hyslop, and David L. Dowd. *The Napoleonic Era in Europe*. New York: Holt, Rinehart and Winston, 1971.

Goitein, Shelomo Dov. *Jews and Arabs: A Concise History of their Social and Cultural Relations*. Mineola, NY: Dover, 2005.

——. *Mediterranean Society*. 6 vols. Berkeley: University of California Press, 1967–1999.

——. "Nicknames as Family Names." *Journal of the American Oriental Society* 90, no. 4 (October–December 1970): 517–24.

——. Review of *Čamharat an-nasab* in *Journal of the American Oriental Society* 90, no. 4 (October–December 1970): 548–51.

Goldberg, Harvey E. "The Social Context of North African Jewish Patronyms." *Folklore Research Center Studies* 3 (1972): 245–57.

Golsan, Richard J. *Justice in Lyon: Klaus Barbie and France's First Trial for Crimes Against Humanity*. Toronto: University of Toronto Press, 2022.

Goodman, Jane E. "Writing Empire, Underwriting Nation: Discursive Histories of Kabyle Berber Oral Texts." *American Ethnologist* 29, no. 1 (February 2002): 86–122.

Goody, Jack. *The Logic of Writing and the Organization of Society*. Cambridge: Cambridge University Press, 1986.

Gradenwitz, Peter. "Félicien David (1810–1876) and French Romantic Orientalism." *Musical Quarterly* 62, no. 4 (October 1976): 471–506.

Grangaud, Isabelle. *La Ville imprenable: une histoire sociale de Constantine au 18e siècle*. Constantine, Algeria: Média Plus, 2004.

——. "Le titre de *Sayyid* ou *Sî* dans la documentation constantinoise d'époque moderne: un marqueur identitaire en évolution." *Revue des mondes musulmans et de la Méditerranée* [online], 127 (July 2010). http://journals.openedition.org/remmm/6604; https://doi.org/10.4000/remmm.6604.

——. "Prouver par l'écriture: propriétaires algérois, conquérants français et historiens ottomanistes." *Genèse* 1, no. 74 (2009): 25–45.

Grangaud, Michelle. *État civil: inventaires*. Paris: P.O.L., 1998.

Grigg, Russell. *Lacan, Language, and Philosophy*. Albany: State University of New York Press, 2008.

Groebner, Valentin. *Who Are You? Identification, Deception, and Surveillance in Early Modern Europe*, translated by Mark Kyburz and John Peck. New York: Zone Books, 2007.

Gruen, Erich S. *Rethinking the Other in Antiquity*. Princeton, NJ: Princeton University Press, 2011.

Gsell, Stéphane. *Enquête administrative sur les travaux hydrauliques anciens en Algérie*. Paris: Imprimerie nationale, 1902.

Guechi, Fatima Zohra. "Du "nasab" au "laqab:" héritages controversés." In *Constantine: une ville, des héritages*, edited by Fatima Zohra Guechi, 31–75. Constantine: Média Plus, 2004.

——. "*Mahkama* Records as a Source for Women's History: The Case of Constantine." In *Beyond the Exotic: Women's Histories in Islamic Societies*, edited by Amir El-Azhary Sonbol, 152–61. Syracuse, NY: Syracuse University Press, 2005.

Guéno, Vanessa. "S'identifier à l'aube de l'état civil (*nufûs*): les justiciables devant le tribunal civil de Homs (Syrie centrale) à la fin du XIXe siècle." *Revue des mondes musulmans et de la Méditerranée* 127 (July 2010): 193–211.

Guha, Ranajit. *Dominance Without Hegemony: History and Power in Colonial India*. Cambridge, MA: Harvard University Press, 1997.

Guha, Sumit. "The Politics of Identity and Enumeration in India c. 1600–1990." *Comparative Studies in Society and History* 45, no. 1 (2003): 148–67.

Guignard, Didier. *L'Abus de pouvoir dans l'Algérie colonial: Visibilité et singularité*. S.l.: Presses universitaires de Paris Ouest, 2010.

——. "Conservatoire ou révolutionnaire? Le sénatus-consulte de 1863 appliqué au régime foncier d'Algérie." *Revue d'histoire du XIXe siècle* 41, no. 2 (2010): 81–95.

——. "Le diptyque *propriété et société* en Algérie et ses retouches successives (XIXe–XXIe siècles)." In *Propriété et société en Algérie contemporaine: Quelles approches?*, edited by

Didier Guignard, 7–42. Aix-en-Provence: Institut de recherches et d'études sur le monde arabe et musulman, 2017.

——. "Les inventeurs de la tradition 'melk' et 'arch' en Algérie." In *Les acteurs des transformations foncières autour de la Méditerranée au XIXe siècle*, edited by Didier Guignard and Vanessa Guéno, 49–93. Paris: Karthala, MMSH, IREMAM, 2013.

Guiral, Pierre. *Marseille et l'Algérie, 1830–1841.* Gap: Éditions Ophrys, 1957.

Gutton, Jean-Pierre. *Établir l'identité: L'identification des Français du Moyen Âge à nos jours.* Lyon: Presses universitaires de Lyon, 2010.

Hacking, Ian. *The Taming of Chance*. Cambridge: Cambridge University Press, 1990.

Haddad, Mouloud. "Les maitres de l'Heure: Soufisme et eschatologie en Algérie coloniale (1845–1901)." *Revue d'histoire du XIXe siècle* 41 (2010): 49–61.

Haddadou, Mohand-Akli. *Dictionnaire toponymique et historique de l'Algérie*. Tizi-Ouzou, Algeria: Achab, 2012.

——. "Les couches diachroniques du vocabulaire berbère." In *Trames de langues: Usages et métissages linguistiques dans l'histoire du Maghreb*, edited by Jocelyne Dakhlia, 353–67. Paris: Maisonneuve and Larose, 2004.

——. *Recueil de prénoms amazighs.* Algiers: Haut-Commissariat à l'Amazighité, 2003.

Halbwachs, Maurice. *On Collective Memory*, translated by Lewis A. Coser. Chicago: University of Chicago Press, 1992.

Hall, Bruce S. *A History of Race in Muslim West Africa, 1600–1960.* Cambridge: Cambridge University Press, 2011.

Halpérin, Jean-Louis. *L'impossible code civil.* Paris: Presses universitaires de France, 1992.

Hammond, Andrew. *Popular Culture in the Arab World: Arts, Politics, and the Media.* Cairo: American University in Cairo Press, 2007.

Hanley, Sarah. "Engendering the State: Family Formation and State Building in Early Modern France." *French Historical Studies* 16, no. 1 (Spring 1989): 4–27.

Hanley, Will. *Identifying with Nationality: Europeans, Ottomans and Egyptians in Alexandria.* New York: Columbia University Press, 2017.

——. "What Ottoman Nationality Was and Was Not." *Journal of the Ottoman and Turkish Studies Association* 3, no. 2 (2016): 277–98.

Hannoum, Abdelmajid. *The Invention of the Maghreb: Between Africa and the Middle East.* Cambridge: University of Cambridge Press, 2021.

Hanssen, Beatrice. "Language and Mimesis in Walter Benjamin's Work." In *The Cambridge Companion to Walter Benjamin*, edited by David S. Ferris, 54–72. Cambridge: Cambridge University Press, 2004.

Harbi, Mohammed. *L'Algérie et son destin: croyants ou citoyens.* Paris: Arcantère, 1992.

——. *Une vie debout.* Vol. 1: *Mémoires politiques, 1945–1962.* Paris: Découverte, 2001.

Hardwick, Julie. *Family Business Litigation and the Political Economies of Daily Life in Early Modern France.* Oxford: Oxford University Press, 2009.

Harris, Roy, and Talbot J. Taylor. *Landmarks in Linguistic Thought.* 2nd ed. Hoboken, NJ: Taylor & Francis, 1997.

Hart, David. "An Awkward Chronology and a Questionable Genealogy: History and Legend in a Saintly Lineage in the Moroccan Central Atlas, 1397–1702." *Journal of North African Studies* 6, no. 2 (Summer 2001): 95–116.

Hassett, Dónal. *Mobilizing Memory: The Great War and the Language of Politics in Colonial Algeria, 1918–39.* Oxford: Oxford University Press, 2019.

Hayes, Julie Candler. "Translation and the Transparency of French." *Translation Studies* 5, no. 2 (2012): 201–16.

——. *Translation, Subjectivity, and Culture in France and England, 1600–1800.* Stanford, CA: Stanford University Press, 2009.

Hegyi, Ottmar. "Reflejos del multiculturalismo medieval: los tres alfabetos para la notación del iberorromance." *Nueva Revista de Filología Hispánica* 30, no. 1 (1981): 92–103.

Heller-Roazen, Daniel. *The Enemy of All: Piracy and the Law of Nations.* New York: Zone Books, 2009.

Henry, Jean-Robert. "L'identité imaginée par le droit: de l'Algérie coloniale à la construction européenne." In *Cartes d'identité: comment dit-on "nous" en politique?*, edited by Denis-Constant Martin, 41–63. Paris: Presses de la Fondation nationale des sciences politiques, 1994.

Herlihy, David, and Christiane Klapisch-Zuber. *Tuscans and Their Families: A Study of the Florentine Catasto of 1427.* New Haven, CT: Yale University Press, 1985.

Hess, Andrew C. *The Forgotten Frontier: A History of the Sixteenth-Century Ibero-African Frontier.* Chicago: University of Chicago Press, 1978.

Heuer, Jennifer. *The Family and the Nation: Gender and Citizenship in Revolutionary France, 1789–1830.* Ithaca, NY: Cornell University Press, 2005.

Higert, Emilia. "Noms propres: prédicat de dénomination et traductibilité sont-ils inconciliables?" In *Sens, formes, langage: Contributions en l'honneur de Pierre Frath*, edited by René Daval, Emilia Hilgert, Thomas Nicklas, and Daniel Thomières, 201–21. Reims: ÉPURE, 2014.

Hirschberg, Haim Zeev. *A History of the Jews in North Africa*, translated by M. W. Eichelberg. 2nd ed. Leiden: Brill, 1974.

Hoffman, Katherine E. "Purity and Contamination: Language Ideologies in French Colonial Native Policy in Morocco." *Comparative Studies in Society and History* 50, no. 3 (2008): 724–52.

Hough, Carole, ed. *The Oxford Handbook of Names and Naming.* Oxford: Oxford University Press, 2016.

Howells, Robin. "The Eighteenth-Century *Conte*." In *The Cambridge History of French Literature*, edited by William Burgwinkle, Nicholas Hammond, and Emma Wilson, 369–77. Cambridge: Cambridge University Press, 2011.

Hull, Isabel V. *Absolute Destruction: Military Culture and the Practices of War in Imperial Germany.* Ithaca, NY: Cornell University Press, 2005.

——. *A Scrap of Paper: Breaking and Making International Law During the Great War.* Ithaca, NY: Cornell University Press, 2014.

International Federation of Library Associations and Institutions. *Names of Persons: National Usages for Entry in Catalogues.* 4th ed. Munich: Saur, 1996.

Irvine, Judith T. "Subjected Words: African Linguistics and the Colonial Encounter." *Language and Communication* 28 (2008): 323–43.

Ittmann, Karl, Dennis D. Cordell, and Gregory Maddox, eds. *The Demographics of Empire: The Colonial Order and the Creation of Knowledge.* Athens: Ohio University Press, 2010.

Jansen, Jan C. *Erobern und Erinnern: Symbolpolitik, öffentlicher Raum und französischer Kolonialismus in Algerien, 1830–1950.* Munich: Oldenbourg, 2013.

Jaouad, Hédi A. *Browning Upon Arabia: A Movable East.* Cham: Springer, 2018.

Jarvis, Jill. *Decolonizing Memory: Algeria and the Politics of Testimony.* Durham, NC: Duke University Press, 2021.

Jay, Martin. *The Dialectical Imagination: A History of the Frankfurt School and the Institute of Social Research, 1923–1950.* Berkeley: University of California Press, 1973.

Jenni, Alexis. *L'Art français de la guerre.* Paris: Gallimard, 2011.

Jiménez, Mónica A. "Puerto Rico Under the Colonial Gaze: Oppression, Resistance and the Myth of the Nationalist Enemy." *Latino Studies* 18 (January, 2020): 27–44.

Jomier, Augustin. *Islam, réforme et colonisation: une histoire de l'ibadisme en Algérie, 1882–1962.* Paris: Éditions de la Sorbonne, 2020.

Julien, Charles-André. *Histoire de l'Algérie contemporaine.* Vol. 1: *La conquête et les débuts de la colonisation (1827–1871).* 3rd ed. Paris: Presses universitaires de France, 1986.

Kafka, Ben. *The Demon of Writing: Powers and Failures of Paperwork.* New York: Zone, 2012.

Kafka, Franz. "Before the Law." In *Kafka's Selected Stories*, edited and translated by Stanley Corngold, 68–69. New York: Norton, 2007.

Kaiser, Wolfgang. "Asymétries méditerranéennes: présence et circulation de marchands entre Alger, Tunis et Marseille." In *Les Musulmans dans l'histoire de l'Europe.* Vol. 1: *Une intégration invisible*, edited by Jocelyn Dakhlia and Bernard Vincent, 417–42. Paris: Albin Michel, 2004.

Kalbī, Ibn al-. *Ǧamharat an-nasab: das genealogische Werk des Hišam Ibn Muḥammad al-Kalbī*, edited and translated by Werner Caskel and G. Strenziok. 2 vols. Leiden: Brill, 1966.

Kalman, Samuel. "Unlawful Acts or Strategies of Resistance? Crime and the Disruption of Colonial Order in Interwar French Algeria." *French Historical Studies* 43, no. 1 (February 2020): 85–110.

Karpat, Kemal H. *Ottoman Population 1830–1914: Demographic and Social Characteristics.* Madison: University of Wisconsin Press, 1985.

Kateb, Kamel. *Européens, "Indigènes" et Juifs en Algérie, 1830–1962: représentations et réalités des populations.* Paris: Institut national d'études démographiques, 2001.

Kateb Yacine. *Nedjma*, translated by Richard Howard. Charlottesville: University of Virginia Press, 1991.

Khalidi, Tarif. *Arabic Historical Thought in the Classical Period.* Cambridge: Cambridge University Press, 1994.

Khan, Geoffrey. "An Arabic Legal Document from the Umayyad Period." *Journal of the Royal Asiatic Society* 4, no. 3 (November 1994): 357–68.

Khanna, Ranjana. *Algeria Cuts: Women and Representation, 1830 to the Present.* Stanford, CA: Stanford University Press, 2008.

Khatibi, Abdelkebir. *Le blessure du nom propre.* Paris: Denoël, 1974.

——. *Love in Two Languages*, translated by Richard Howard. Minneapolis: University of Minnesota Press, 1990.

——. *Maghreb pluriel.* Paris: Denoël, 1983.

Kilito, Abdelfattah. *Thou Shalt Not Speak My Language*, translated by Waïl S. Hassan. Syracuse, NY: Syracuse University Press, 2008.

——. *The Tongue of Adam*, translated by Robyn Creswell. New York: New Directions, 2016.

Kisaichi, Masatoshi. "Three Renowned 'Ulamā Families of Tlemcen: The Maqqarī, the Marzūqi and the 'Uqbānī." *Journal of Sophia Asian Studies* 22 (2004): 121–37.

Kister, M. J., and M. Plessner. "Notes on *Caskel's Ǧamharat an-nasab*." *Oriens* 25/26 (1976): 48–68.

Kitouni, Hosni. "L'indigènisation de l'Algérien." Ms., 2017. https://www.academia.edu/11040218/LETAT_CIVIL_DES_INDIGENES_ALGERIENS.

——. *La Kabylie orientale dans l'histoire: pays des Kutama et guerre colonial.* Algiers: Casbah, 2013.

Klein, Martin. *Slavery and Colonial Rule in French West Africa.* Cambridge: Cambridge University Press, 1998.

Kleinberg, Ethan. "Just the Facts: The Fantasy of a Historical Science." *History of the Present* 6, no. 1 (Spring 2016): 87–103.

Kleinberg, Ethan, Joan Wallach Scott, and Gary Wilder. "Theses on Theory and History." *History of the Present* 10, no. 1 (2020): 157–65.

Koehler-Derrick, Gabriel, and Melissa M. Lee. "War and Welfare in Colonial Algeria." *International Organization* 77 (Spring 2023): 263–93.

Kolla, Edward James. *Sovereignty, International Law, and the French Revolution.* Cambridge: Cambridge University Press, 2017.

Komska, Yulia, Michelle Moyd, and David Gramling. *Linguistic Disobedience: Restoring Power to Civic Language.* Cham: Palgrave Macmillan, 2019.

Korman, Sharon. *The Right of Conquest: The Acquisition of Territory by Force in International Law and Practice.* Oxford: Oxford University Press, 1996.

Koskenniemi, Martti. *To the Uttermost Parts of the Earth: Legal Imagination and International Power, 1300–1870.* Cambridge: Cambridge University Press, 2021.

Kossmann, Maarten. *The Arabic Influence on Northern Berber.* Leiden: Brill, 2013.

Kossmann, Maarten, and Ramada Elghamis. "Preliminary Notes on Tuareg in Arabic Script from Niger." In *The Arabic Script in Africa Studies in the Use of a Writing System*, edited by Meikal Mumin and Kees Versteegh, 79–90. Leiden: Brill, 2014.

Kouidri, Mohammed. "Colonisation, indépendance et développement humain en Algérie: quel bilan?" *Insaniyat* [online], 65–66 (2014). https://journals.openedition.org/insaniyat/14852.

La Jonquière, Clément de. *L'Expédition d'Égypte, 1798–1801.* 5 vols. Paris: Charles-Lavauzelle, 1899–1907.

Lacan, Jacques. "The Function and Field of Speech and Language in Psychoanalysis." In Jacques Lacan, *Écrits: A Selection*, translated by Bruce Fink, 31–106. New York: Norton, 2002.

——. *On the Names-of-the-Father*, translated by Bruce Fink. Cambridge, UK: Polity, 2013.

——. *The Seminar of Jacques Lacan*, Book III: *The Psychoses, 1955–1956*, edited by Jacques-Alain Miller, translated by Russell Grigg. New York: Norton, 1993.

LaCapra, Dominick. *History and Criticism.* Ithaca, NY: Cornell University Press, 1985.

——. *History in Transit: Experience, Identity, Critical Theory.* Ithaca, NY: Cornell University Press, 2004.

——. "Trauma, Absence, Loss." *Critical Inquiry* 25, no. 4 (Summer 1999): 696–727.

Lacheraf, Mostefa. *Des noms et des lieux: mémoires d'une Algérie oubliée.* Algiers: Casbah, 1998.

Lapierre, Nicole. *Changer de nom.* Paris: Stock, 1995.

Laplante, Benoît. "From France to the Church: The Generalization of Parish Registers in the Catholic Countries." *Journal of Family History* 44, no. 1 (2019): 24–51.

Laporte, Jean-Pierre, Rachid Oulebsir, Tahar Hamadache, Salem Chaker, and Jean-Pierre Brun. "Olivier (La culture de l'olivier, de l'Antiquité à la Kabylie Contemporaine)." In *Encyclopédie berbère.* Vol. 35: *Oasitae-Ortaïas*, edited by Salem Chaker (2013). http://journals.openedition.org/encyclopedieberbere/2812.

Larcher, Pierre. "Le nom propre dans la tradition grammaticale arabe." In *Les non-dits du nom: Onomastique et documents en terres d'Islam, mélanges offerts à Jacqueline Sublet*, edited by Christian Müller and Muriel Roiland-Rouabah, 303–18. Beirut: Presses de l'IFPO-IRHT, 2013.

Laredo, Abraham I. *Les Noms des Juifs du Maroc: essai d'onomastique judéo-marocaine.* Madrid: Instituto B. Arias Montano, 1978.

Laroui, Abdallah. *A History of the Maghrib: An Interpretive Essay*, translated by Ralph Manheim. Princeton, NJ: Princeton University Press, 1977.

Larzul, Sylvette. "Les manuels de langue arabe des débuts de l'Algérie coloniale (1830–1871)." In *Manuels d'arabe d'hier et d'aujourd'hui: France et Maghreb, XIXe–XXIe siècle*, edited by Sylvette Larzul and Alain Messaoudi, 57–78. Paris: Bibliothèque nationale de France, 2013.

Laurens, Henry. *Les Origines intellectuelles de l'expédition d'Égypte: l'orientalisme islamisant en France, 1698–1798.* Istanbul: Isis, Institut français d'études anatoliennes, 1987.

——. *Orientales I: Autour de l'expédition d'Égypte.* Paris: CNRS Éditions, 2004.

Laurens, Henry, Charles C. Gillispie, Jean-Claude Golvin, and Claude Traunecker. *L'Expédition d'Égypte: 1798–1801.* Paris: Seuil, 1989.

Laurent, Franck. *Victor Hugo face à la conquête de l'Algérie.* Paris: Maisonneuve et Larose, 2001.

Lawson, Edwin D. "Personal Naming Systems." In *The Oxford Handbook of Names and Naming*, edited by Carole Hough, 169–98. Oxford: Oxford University Press, 2016.

Lazali, Karima. *Colonial Trauma: A Study of the Psychic and Political Consequences of Colonial Oppression in Algeria*, translated by Matthew B. Smith. Medford, MA: Polity, 2021.

Le Cour Grandmaison, Olivier. *Coloniser, exterminer: sur la guerre et l'État colonial.* Paris: Fayard, 2005.

Le Mée, René. "La réglementation des registres paroissiaux en France." *Annales de démographie historique* (1975): 433–77.

LeComte, Jeanne Glennon. "The Pharaon Family." Levantine Heritage. http://www.levantineheritage.com/testi88.htm.

Lecuit, Émeline, Denis Maurel, and Duško Vitas. "La traduction des noms propres: une étude en corpus." *Corpus* 10 (2011): 201–18.

Leder, Stefan. "Nasab as Idiom and Discourse." *Journal of the Economic and Social History of the Orient* 58 (2015): 56–74.

Lefebvre-Teillard, Anne. *Le nom, droit et histoire.* Paris: Presses universitaires de France, 1990.

Leibovici, Sarah. *Chronique des Juifs de Tétouan, 1860–1896.* Paris: Maisonneuve et Larose, 1984.

Leibring, Katharina. "Given Names in European Naming Systems." In *The Oxford Handbook of Names and* Naming, edited by Carole Hough, 199–213. Oxford: Oxford University Press, 2016.

Lekéal, Farid. "Justice et pacification: de la Régence d'Alger à l'Algérie: 1830–1839." *Histoire de la justice* 1, no. 16 (2005): 13–30.

Lem, Stanislaw. *Solaris*, translated by Joanna Kilmartin and Steve Cox. San Diego: Harvest Harcourt, 1987.

Lentz, Thierry. *Savary: le séide de Napoléon.* Paris: Fayard, 2001.

Leonard, Jacques. "Médecine et colonisation en Algérie au XIXe siècle." *Annales de Bretagne et des pays de l'Ouest* 84, no. 2 (1977): 481–94.

Leopold, Joan, ed. *Prix Volney Essay Series.* Vol. 1A: *The Prix Volney: Its History and Significance for the Development of Linguistic Research.* Vol. 1B: *The Prix Volney: Its History and Significance for the Development of Linguistic Research.* Dordrecht: Kluwer Academic, 1999.

Lesbaupin, Louis. "Thierry de Fougeray, un condottière au XIXe siècle." *Annales de la Société d'histoire et d'archéologie de l'arrondissement de Saint-Malo* (2008): 113–32.

Lespès, René. "L'origine du nom française 'd'Alger' traduisant 'El Djezaïr.' " *Revue africaine* 67 (1926): 80–84.

Leuwers, Hervé. "Révolution et guerre de conquête: Les origines d'une nouvelle raison d'État (1789–1795)." *Revue du Nord* 75, no. 299 (January–March 1993): 21–40.

Levi, Giovanni. "Les usages de la biographie." *Annales: économies, sociétés, civilisations* 44, no. 6 (1989): 1325–36.

Lévi-Strauss, Claude. *Tristes Tropiques*, translated by John and Doreen Weightman. New York: Penguin, 1973.

Lewis, Mary Dewhurst. *Divided Rule: Sovereignty and Empire in French Tunisia, 1881–1938.* Berkeley: University of California Press, 2014.

Lexique des règles typographiques en usage à l'Imprimerie nationale. 5th ed. Paris: Imprimerie nationale, 2002.

Likaka, Osumaka. *Naming Colonialism: History and Collective Memory in the Congo, 1870–1960.* Madison: University of Wisconsin Press, 2009.

Lodge, R. Anthony. *French: From Dialect to Standard.* London: Routledge, 1993.

——. "Molière's Peasants and the Norms of Spoken French." *Neuphilologische Mitteilungen* 92, no. 4 (1991): 485–99.

Loitron, Matthieu. "Quelle politique démographique pour l'Algérie coloniale?" In *L'Invention des populations: biologie, idéologie et politique*, edited by Hervé Le Bras and Sandrine Bertaux, 177–200. Paris: Odile Jacob, 2000.

Lopez, Jean-Marc. "Naissance de l'Algérie." *Pieds-Noirs d'hier et d'aujourd'hui* 94 (October 1998): 20–21.

Loualich, Fatiha. "Emancipated Female Slaves in Algiers." In *Subalterns and Social Protest: History from Below in the Middle East and North* Africa, edited by Stephanie Cronin, 200–209. London: Routledge, 2008.

Love, Stephanie V. "The Poetics of Grievance: Taxi Drivers, Vernacular Placenames, and the Paradoxes of Post-Coloniality in Oran, Algeria." *City and Society* 33, no. 3 (2021): 422–43.

Lovejoy, Paul. "Olaudah Equiano or Gustavus Vassa—What's in a Name?" *Atlantic Studies* 9, no. 2 (2012): 165–84.

Low, Michael Christopher. *Imperial Mecca: Ottoman Arabia and the Indian Ocean Hajj*. New York: Columbia University Press, 2020.

Maalouf, Amin. *Leo Africanus*, translated by Peter Sluglett. New York: New Amsterdam, 1992.

Maclean, Marie. *The Name of the Mother: Writing Illegitimacy*. London: Routledge, 1994.

Madigan, Daniel A. *The Qur'ân's Self-Image: Writing and Authority in Islam's Scripture*. Princeton, NJ: Princeton University Press, 2001.

Maghraoui, Yamina. "Genèse de la francisation des patronymes algériens entre 1875 et 1885 dans la ville de Mostaganem." *Actes des colloques de la Société française d'onomastique* 15 (2013): 207–10.

Mahmood, Saba. *Politics of Piety: The Islamic Revival and the Feminist Subject*. Princeton, NJ: Princeton University Press, 2005.

Mahmoudi, Amar. "De l'usage des prénoms rares des hautes plaines de l'ouest algérien. Frenda, Ain Dheb, Medrissa, El Bayadh, Labiod Sidi Cheikh." In *Des noms et des noms: état civil et anthroponymie en Algérie*, edited by Farid Benramdane, 39–44. Oran: CRASC, 2005. https://pnr.crasc.dz/index.php/fr/les-pnr/39-des-noms-et-des-noms%E2%80%A6,-%C3%A9tat-civil-et-anthroponymie-en-alg%C3%A9rie.

Maier, Charles. *Once Within Borders: Territories of Power, Wealth, and Belonging Since 1500*. Cambridge, MA: Harvard University Press, 2016.

Malti-Douglas, Fedwa. "The Interrelationship of Onomastic Elements: *Isms*, *Dîn*-Names and *Kunyas* in the Ninth Century A.H." *Cahiers d'onomastique arabe* (1981): 27–55.

Mann, Gregory. "What Was the 'Indigénat'? The 'Empire of Law' in French West Africa." *Journal of African History* 50, no. 3 (2009): 331–53.

Marçais, Philippe. *Textes arabes de Djidjelli*. Paris: Presses universitaires de France, 1954.

Marcus, Abraham. *The Middle East on the Eve of Modernity: Aleppo in the Eighteenth Century*. New York: Columbia University Press, 1989.

Marglin, Jessica M. *Across Legal Lines: Jews and Muslims in Modern Morocco*. New Haven, CT: Yale University Press, 2016.

——. "Citizenship and Nationality in the French Colonial Maghreb." In *Routledge Handbook of Citizenship in the Middle East and North* Africa, edited by Roel Meijer, James Sater, and Zahra Baba, 45–60. New York: Routledge, 2020.

——. "Extraterritoriality and Legal Belonging in the Nineteenth-Century Mediterranean." *Law and History Review* 39, no. 4 (November 2021): 679–706.

——. *The Shamama Case: Contesting Citizenship Across the Modern Mediterranean*. Princeton, NJ: Princeton University Press, 2022.

——. "Written and Oral in Islamic Law: Documentary Evidence and Non-Muslims in Moroccan Shari'a Courts." *Comparative Studies in Society and History* 59, no. 4 (2017): 884–911.

Margouma, Mansour. "La toponymie algérienne: lecture préliminaire de la dénomination de l'espace." *Esprit critique: Revue internationale de sociologie et de sciences sociales* 11, no. 1 (Winter 2008). http://194.214.232.113/publications/1101/esp1101article08.pdf.

Martin, B. G. *Muslim Brotherhoods in Nineteenth-Century Africa.* Cambridge: Cambridge University Press, 1976.

Massignon, Louis. *The Passion of al-Hallāj: Mystic and Martyr of Islam.* Vol. 3: *The Teaching of al-Hallāj*, translated by Herbert Mason. Princeton, NJ: Princeton University Press, 1982.

Matar, Nabil. *British Captives from the Mediterranean to the Atlantic, 1563–1760.* Leiden: Brill, 2014.

——. *Mediterranean Captivity Through Arab Eyes, 1517–1798.* Leiden: Brill, 2021.

——. *Turks, Moors, and Englishmen in the Age of Discovery.* New York: Columbia University Press, 1999.

Mauger, Gérard. "Violence." In *Abécédaire de Pierre Bourdieu*, edited by Jean-Philippe Cazier, 203–7. Mons: Sils Maria, 2006.

Mbembe, Achille. *Critique of Black Reason*, translated by Laurent Dubois. Durham, NC: Duke University Press, 2017.

——. *Necropolitics.* Translated by Steve Corcoran. Durham, NC: Duke University Press, 2019.

———. *On the Postcolony.* Berkeley: University of California Press, 2001.

McCants, William F. *Founding Gods, Inventing Nations: Conquest and Culture Myths from Antiquity to Islam.* Princeton, NJ: Princeton University Press, 2012.

McDougall, James. *History and the Culture of Nationalism in Algeria.* Cambridge: Cambridge University Press, 2006.

——. *A History of Algeria.* Cambridge: Cambridge University Press, 2017.

——. "A World No Longer Shared: Losing the *Droit de Cité* in Nineteenth-Century Algiers." *Journal of the Economic and Social History of the Orient* 60 (2017): 18–49.

McKeown, Adam M. *Melancholy Order: Asian Migration and the Globalization of Borders.* New York: Columbia University Press, 2008.

Memmi, Albert. *The Albert Memmi Reader*, edited by Jonathan Judaken and Michael Lejman. Lincoln: University of Nebraska Press, 2021.

Meouak, Mohamed. *La langue berbère au Maghreb médiéval.* Leiden: Brill, 2015.

——. "Langue arabe et langue berbère dans le Maghreb médiéval: notes de philologie et d'histoire." *Al-Andalus-Maghreb* 13 (2006): 329–35.

——. "Les méthodes biographique et prosopographique: leur application pour l'histoire sociale d'al-Andalus (milieu IIe/VIIIe-fin IVe/Xe siècles)." *Mélanges de la Casa de Velázquez* 28, no. 1 (1992): 191–208.

Merle, Isabel. "De la 'légalisation' de la violence en contexte colonial: le régime de l'indigénat en question." *Politix* 17, no. 66 (2004): 137–62

——. "La construction d'un droit foncier colonial: De la propriété collective à la constitution des réserves en Nouvelle-Calédonie." *Enquête* 7 (1999): 1–21.

——. "Retour sur le régime de l'indigénat: genèse et contradictions des principes répressifs dans l'empire français." *French Politics, Culture and Society* 20, no. 2 (2002): 77–97.

——. Review of *De l'indigénat*, by Olivier Le Cour Grandmaison. *Genèses* 86 (March 2012): 149–53.

Messaoudi, Alain. *Les arabisants et la France coloniale: savants, conseillers, médiateurs, 1780–1930.* Lyon: ENS éditions, 2015.

——. "Orientaux orientalistes: les Pharaon, interprètes du sud au service du nord." In *Sud-Nord; cultures coloniales en France (XIX-XX siècles)*, edited by Colette Zytnicki and Chantal Bordes-Benayoun, 243–55. Toulouse: Privat, 2004.

——. "Pharaon." In *Dictionnaire des orientalistes de langue française*, edited by François Pouillon, 758–60. Paris: IISMM, Karthala, 2008.

——. "Renseigner, enseigner: Les interprètes militaires et la constitution d'un premier corpus savant 'algérien' (1830–1870)." *Revue d'histoire du XIXe siècle* 41 (2010): 97–112.

Messick, Brinkley. *The Calligraphic State: Textual Domination and History in a Muslim Society.* Berkeley: University of California Press, 1992.

——. *Shari'a Scripts: A Historical Anthropology.* New York: Columbia University Press, 2018.

Meynier, Gilbert. *L'Algérie révélée, la guerre de 1914–1918 et le premier quart du XXe siècle.* New ed. Saint-Denis: Bouchène, 2015.

Mézin, Anne. *Les consuls de France au siècle des Lumières (1715–1792).* Paris: Ministère des Affaires Étrangères, 1997.

Millard, Éric. "Le rôle de l'état civil dans la construction de l'état." In *Mélanges en l'honneur du Doyen F.-P. Blanc.* Perpignan and Toulouse: Presses Universitaires de Perpignan et Presses Universitaires de Toulouse 1 Capitole, 2011.

Minawi, Mostafa. *The Ottoman Scramble for Africa: Empire and Diplomacy in the Sahara and the Hijaz.* Stanford, CA: Stanford University Press, 2016.

Mitchell, Timothy. *Rule of Experts: Egypt, Techno-Politics, Modernity.* Berkeley: University of California Press, 2002.

Modiano, Patrick. *Family Record,* translated by Mark Polizzotti. New Haven, CT: Yale University Press, 2019.

Mohammadi, Adeel. "The Ambiguity of Maternal Filiation (nasab) in Early and Medieval Islam." *Graduate Journal of Harvard Divinity School* 11 (Spring 2016). https://projects.iq.harvard.edu/hdsjournal/ambiguity-maternal-filiation-nasab-early-and-medieval-islam.

Montana, Ismael M. *The Abolition of Slavery in Ottoman Tunisia.* Gainesville: University Press of Florida, 2013.

——. "The *Bori* Colonies of Tunis." In *Slavery, Islam and Diaspora*, edited by Behnaz A. Mirzai, Ismael M. Montana, and Paul E. Lovejoy, 155–67. Trenton, NJ: Africa World Press, 2009.

Morlet, Marie-Thérèse. *Dictionnaire étymologique des noms de famille.* Paris: Perrin, 1991.

Morray, David. *An Ayyubid Notable and His World: Ibn al-ʿAdīm and Aleppo as Portrayed in His Biographical Dictionary of People Associated with the City.* Leiden: Brill, 1994.

Morrison, Toni. *Beloved.* New York: Penguin, 1987.

Moses, Dirk. *The Problems of Genocide: Permanent Security and the Language of Transgression.* Cambridge: Cambridge University Press, 2021.

Müller, Christian, Muriel Roiland, and Jacqueline Sublet. "Method of Arabic Onomastics." Introduction to the online database *Onomasticon Arabicum.* http://onomasticon.irht.cnrs.fr.

Nabulsi, Karma. *The Traditions of War: Occupations, Resistance, and the Law.* Oxford: Oxford University Press, 1999.

Naït-Zerrad, Kamal. *L'officiel des prénoms berbères.* Paris: Harmattan, 2003.

Natural Resources Canada, "Resolutions Adopted at the Eleven United Nations Conferences on the Standardization of Geographical Names." https://unstats.un.org/unsd/ungegn/documents/RES_UN_E_updated_1-11_CONF.pdf.

Nawas, John A. "Biography and Biographical Works." *Medieval Islamic Civilization: An Encyclopedia.* Vol. 1, edited by Josef W. Meri, 110–12. New York: Routledge, 2006.

Newell, Stephanie. *The Power to Name: A History of Anonymity in Colonial West Africa.* Athens: Ohio University Press, 2013.

Niort, Jean-François. *Homo civilis: contribution à l'histoire du Code civil français, 1804–1965.* 2 vols. Aix-en-Provence: Presses universitaires d'Aix-Marseille, 2004.

Nizard, Alfred. "Droit et statistiques de filiation en France: Le droit de la filiation depuis 1804." *Population* 32, no. 1 (1977): 91–122.

Noiriel, Gérard. "The Identification of the Citizen: The Birth of Republican Civil Status in France." In *Documenting Individual Identity: The Development of State Practices in the Modern World,* edited by Jane Caplan and John Torpey, 28–48. Princeton, NJ: Princeton University Press, 2001.

——. "Socio-histoire d'un concept: Les usages du mot 'nationalité' au XIXe siècle." *Genèses* 20 (1995): 4–23.

Noiriel, Gérard, Ilsen About, Henriette Asséo, and Peter Becker, eds. *L'identification: genèse d'un travail d'État.* Paris: Belin, 2007.

Nouschi, André. *Enquête sur le niveau de vie des populations rurales constantinoises de la conquête jusqu'en 1919.* 2nd ed. Paris: Bouchène, 2013.

Nyrop, Kristoffer. *Grammaire historique de la langue française.* 4 vols. Copenhagen: Gyldendal, 1899–1925.

O'Conner, Michael. "The Berber Scripts." In *The World's Writing Systems,* edited by Peter T. Daniels and William Brights, 112–19. Oxford: Oxford University Press, 1996.

Offen, Karen. *The Woman Question in France, 1400–1870.* Cambridge: Cambridge University Press, 2017.

Offerlé, Michel. "Les noms et le nombre: individualisation et anonymisation de l'électeur." In *L'écriture du nom propre,* edited by Anne-Marie Christin, 253–66. Paris: Harmattan, 1998.

Oualdi, M'hamed. *A Slave between Empires: A Transimperial History of North Africa.* New York: Columbia University Press, 2019.

Ould-Braham, Ouahmi. "À propos de l'ouvrage pédagogique de Belkassem ben Sedira: le *Cours de langue kabyle* (1887)." *Études et documents berbères* 2, no. 42 (2019): 7–44.

Ould-Ennebia, Karim. "Histoire de l'état civil des Algériens: Patronymie et acculturation." *Revue maghrébine des études historiques et sociales* 1 (September 2009): 5–24.

Ozavci, Ozan. *Dangerous Gifts: Imperialism, Security, and Civil Wars in the Levant, 1798–1864.* Oxford: Oxford University Press, 2021.

Pal, Maia. *Jurisdictional Accumulation: An Early Modern History of Law, Empires, and Capital.* Cambridge: Cambridge University Press, 2021.

Pandolfo, Stefania. *Knot of the Soul: Madness, Psychoanalysis, Islam.* Chicago: University of Chicago Press, 2018.

Panzac, Daniel. *Barbary Corsairs: The End of a Legend 1800–1820.* Translated by Victoria Hobson and John E. Hawkes. Leiden: Brill, 2005.

Parks, Robert. "Local-National Relations and the Politics of Property Rights in Algeria and Tunisia." PhD diss., University of Texas at Austin, 2011.

Patterson, Orlando. *Slavery and Social Death: A Comparative Study.* Cambridge, MA: Harvard University Press, 1982.

Pellegrin, Arthur. *Essai sur les noms de lieux d'Algérie et de Tunisie, étymologie, signification.* Tunis: S.A.P.I., 1949.

——. "Noms de toponymie africaine: les noms de lieux empruntés au règne animal." *IBLA, Revue de l'Institut des belles lettres arabes* 12 (1949): 77–80.

Pensky, Max. *Melancholy Dialectics: Walter Benjamin and the Play of Mourning.* Amherst: University of Massachusetts Press, 1993.

Perego, Elizabeth M. *Humor and Power in Algeria, 1920 to 2021.* Bloomington: Indiana University Press, 2023.

Perrin, Delphine. "Identité et transmission du lien national au Maghreb: étude comparée des codes de la nationalité." *L'Année du Maghreb* 3 (2007): 479–97.

Pervillé, Guy. "Comment appeler les habitants de l'Algérie." *Cahiers de la Méditerranée* 54 (June 1997): 55–60.

Peterson, Joseph W. *Sacred Rivals: Catholic Missions and the Making of Islam in Nineteenth-Century France and Algeria.* Oxford: Oxford University Press, 2022.

Petry, Carl F. *The Civilian Elite of Cairo in the Later Middle Ages.* Princeton, NJ: Princeton University Press, 1981.

Piazza, Pierre. *Histoire de la carte nationale d'identité.* Paris: Jacob, 2004.

Pitts, Jennifer. "Liberalism and Empire in a Nineteenth-Century Algerian Mirror." *Modern Intellectual History* 6, no. 2 (2009): 287–313.

Plarier, Antoine. "Le Banditisme rural en Algérie à la période coloniale (1871–années 1920)." PhD diss., Université de Paris I, Sorbonne, 2019.

Poizner, Annette. *Clinical Graphology: An Interpretive Manual for Mental Health Practitioners.* Springfield, IL: Thomas, 2012.

Porter, Theodore M. *The Rise of Statistical Thinking, 1820–1900.* Princeton, NJ: Princeton University Press, 1986.

Poughon, Jean-Michel. *Le code civil.* 2nd ed. Paris: Presses universitaires de France, 1995.

Powers, David S. *The Development of Islamic Law and Society in the Maghrib:* Qāḍīs, Muftīs *and Family Law.* New York: Routledge, 2016.

——. "Inheritance." In *Oxford Bibliographies in Islamic* Studies, edited by Andrew Rippin. Oxford: Oxford University Press, 2015. https://www.oxfordbibliographies.com.

——. *Law, Society, and Culture in the Maghrib, 1300–1500.* Cambridge: Cambridge University Press, 2002.

Prochaska, David. *Making Algeria French: Colonialism in Bône, 1879–1920.* Cambridge: Cambridge University Press, 1990.

Proust, Marcel. *Remembrance of Things Past*, translated by C. K. Scott Moncrieff and Stephen Hudson. Vol. 2. Hertfordshire, UK: Wordsworth, 2006.

Qashī, Fāṭima al-Zahra. "Shahūd al-'Adala fī Qusnṭīnīyat al-Qran al-Tāsa'a 'Ashr." *Insaniyat* 35–36 (2007): 57–76.

Rabinbach, Anson. "Between Enlightenment and Apocalypse: Benjamin, Bloch and Modern German Jewish Messianism." *New German Critique* 34 (Winter 1985): 78–124.

Raman, Bhavani. *Document Raj: Writing and Scribes in Early Colonial South India.* Chicago: University of Chicago Press, 2012.

Rancière, Jacques. *The Ignorant Schoolmaster: Five Lessons in Intellectual Emancipation*, translated by Kristin Ross. Stanford, CA: Stanford University Press, 1991.

Randeraad, Nico. *States and Statistics in the Nineteenth Century: Europe by Numbers*, translated by Debra Molnar. Manchester, UK: University of Manchester Press, 2010.

Raven, James. "The Oxford Dictionary of National Biography: Dictionary or Encyclopaedia?" *Historical Journal* 50, no. 4 (December, 2007): 991–1006.

Régent, Frédéric. "Structures familiales et stratégies matrimoniales des Libres de Couleur en Guadeloupe au XVIIIe siècle." *Annales de démographie historique* 2 (2011): 69–98.

Remaoun, Hassan, and Ahmed Yalaoui. "In memoriam, à notre collègue Abdelkader Djeghloul (1946–2010)." *Insaniyat* 51–52 (2011): 17–20.

Rey, Alain, ed. *Dictionnaire historique de la langue française.* New ed. 3 vols. Paris: Le Robert, 2019.

Rey-Goldzeiguer, Annie. *Le Royaume arabe: la politique algérienne de Napoléon III, 1861–1870.* Algiers: Société Nationale d'Edition et de Diffusion, 1977.

Ricci, Ronit. *Islam Translated: Literature, Conversion, and the Arabic Cosmopolis of South and Southeast Asia.* Chicago: University of Chicago Press, 2011.

Ridouane, Rachid. "Tashlhiyt Berber." *Journal of the International Phonetic Association* 44, no. 2 (2014): 207–22.

Riley, Denise. *"Am I That Name?" Feminism and the Category of "Women" in History.* Minneapolis: University of Minnesota Press, 1988.

——. *The Words of Selves: Identification, Solidarity, Irony.* Stanford, CA: Stanford University Press, 2000.

Robcis, Camille. *The Law of Kinship: Anthropology, Psychoanalysis, and the Family in France.* Ithaca, NY: Cornell University Press, 2013.

Roberts, Hugh. *Berber Government: The Kabyle Polity in Pre-Colonial Algeria.* London: Tauris, 2014.

——. "La Kabylie à la lumière tremblotante du savoir maraboutique." *Insaniyat* 16 (2002): 99–115.

Roberts, Sophie B. *Citizenship and Antisemitism in French Colonial Algeria, 1870–1962.* Cambridge: Cambridge University Press, 2017.

Robinson, Chase F. *Islamic Historiography.* Cambridge: Cambridge University Press, 2003.

Robinson, Majied. "Prosopraphical Approaches to the *Nasab* Tradition: A Study of Marriage and Concubinage in the Tribe of Muḥammad, 500–750 CE." PhD diss., University of Edinburgh, 2013.

Rosanvallon, Pierre. *Le Sacré du citoyen: Historie du suffrage universel en France.* Paris: Gallimard, 1992.

Rosenthal, Franz. *A History of Muslim Historiography.* Leiden: Brill, 1968.

——. *Knowledge Triumphant: The Concept of Knowledge in Medieval Islam.* Leiden: Brill, 1970.

Roudinesco, Elisabeth. *Jacques Lacan: An Outline of a Life and History of a System of Thought*, translated by Barbara Bray. New York: Columbia University Press, 1997.

Rouighi, Ramzi. *Inventing the Berbers: History and Ideology in the Maghrib.* Philadelphia: University of Pennsylvania Press, 2019.

——. *The Making of a Mediterranean Emirate: Ifrīqiyā and Its Andalusis, 1200–1400.* Philadelphia: University of Pennsylvania Press, 2011.

Ruedy, John. *Modern Algeria: The Origins and Development of a Nation.* Bloomington: Indiana University Press, 1992.

Rule, John C., and Ben S. Trotter. *A World of Paper: Louis XIV, Colbert de Torcy, and the Rise of the Information State.* Montréal: McGill-Queen's University Press, 2014.

Ruti, Mari. *The Singularity of Being: Lacan and the Immortal Within.* New York: Fordham University Press, 2012.

Saada, Emmanuelle. *Empire's Children: Race, Filiation, and Citizenship in the French Colonies*, translated by Arthur Goldhammer. Chicago: University of Chicago Press, 2012.

——. "La loi, le droit et l'indigène." *Droits* 43, no. 1 (2006): 165–90.

Sahlins, Peter. *Boundaries: The Making of France and Spain in the Pyrenees.* Berkeley: University of California Press, 1989.

——. *Unnaturally French: Foreign Citizens in the Old Regime and After.* Ithaca, NY: Cornell University Press, 2004.

Said, Edward W. *À contre-voie: mémoires*, translated by Brigitte Caland and Isabelle Genet. Paris: Serpent à plumes, 2002.

Saïdi, Kamel. *La nationalité algérienne: décryptage d'une identité confisquée.* Paris: Publisud, 2015.

Saidouni, Nacereddine. *Le waqf en Algérie à l'époque ottomane: XIe–XIIIe siècles de Hégire, XVIIe–XIXe siècles.* 2nd ed. Kuwait City: Awaqf Public Fondation, 2009.

Sainte-Marie, Alain. "La province d'Alger vers 1870: l'établissement du douar-commune et la fixation de la nature de la propriété en territoire militaire dans le cadre du Sénatus Consulte du 22 Avril 1863." *Revue de l'Occident musulman et de la Méditerranée* 9 (1971): 37–61.

——. "Législation foncière et société rurale: l'application de la loi du 26 juillet 1873 dans les douars de l'Algérois." *Études rurales* 57 (January–March, 1975): 61–87.

Santner, Eric. *On the Psychotheology of Everyday Life: Reflections on Freud and Rosenzweig.* Chicago: University of Chicago Press, 2001.

Sari, Djilali. *La Dépossession des fellahs, 1830–1962*. Algiers: Société nationale d'édition et de diffusion, 1975.

Saussure, Ferdinand de. *Course in General Linguistics*, translated by Roy Harris. London: Bloomsbury, 2013.

Schimmel, Annemarie. *Islamic Names*. Edinburgh: Edinburgh University Press, 1989.

——. *And Muhammad Is His Messenger: The Veneration of the Prophet in Islamic Piety*. Chapel Hill: University of North Carolina Press, 1985.

Schöck, Cornelia. *Adam im Islam: ein Beitrag zur Ideengeschichte der Sunna*. Berlin: Schwarz, 1993.

Schoolcraft, Ralph W. *Romain Gary: The Man Who Sold His Shadow*. Philadelphia: University of Pennsylvania Press, 2002.

Schreier, Joshua. *Arabs of the Jewish Faith: The Civilizing Mission in Colonial Algeria*. New Brunswick, NJ: Rutgers University Press, 2010.

——. *The Merchants of Oran: A Jewish Port at the Dawn of Empire*. Stanford, CA: Stanford University Press, 2018.

Schroeder, Jeanne Lorraine. *The Four Lacanian Discourses or Turning Law Inside-Out*. London: Birkbeck Law Press, 2008.

Scott, Cynthia Lyles. "A Slave by Any Other Name: Names and Identity in Toni Morrison's *Beloved*." In *Toni Morrison's* Beloved, edited by Harold Bloom, 195–202. New York: Bloom's Literary Criticism, 2009.

Scott, James C. *Seeing Like a State: How Certain Schemes to Improve the Human Condition Have Failed*. New Haven, CT: Yale University Press, 1998.

Scott, James C., John Tehranian, and Jeremy Mathias. "The Production of Legal Identities Proper to States: The Case of the Permanent Family Surname." *Comparative Studies in Society and History* 44, no. 1 (January 2002): 4–44.

Scott, Joan Wallach. *Only Paradoxes to Offer: French Feminists and the Rights of Man*. Cambridge, MA: Harvard University Press, 1996.

——. *The Politics of the Veil*. Princeton, NJ: Princeton University Press, 2007.

Sebag, Paul. *Les noms des juifs de Tunisie: origines et significations*. Paris: Harmattan, 2002.

Sebti, Abdelahad. "Au Maroc sharifisme citadin, charisme et historiographie." *Annales: économies, sociétés, civilisations* 41, no. 2 (March–April 1986): 433–57.

Sekula, Allan. "Dismantling Modernism, Reinventing Documentary (Notes on the Politics of Representation)." *Massachusetts Review* 19, no. 4 (Winter 1978): 859–83.

Sessions, Jennifer E. *By Sword and Plow: France and the Conquest of Algeria*. Ithaca, NY: Cornell University Press, 2011.

Sharkey, Heather J. *A History of Muslims, Christians, and Jews in the Middle East*. Cambridge: Cambridge University Press, 2017.

Shatzmiller, Maya. *The Berbers and the Islamic State: The Marīnid Experience in Pre-Protectorate Morocco*. Princeton, NJ: Markus Wiener, 2000.

Shryock, Andrew. *Nationalism and the Genealogical Imagination: Oral History and Textual Authority in Tribal Jordan*. Berkeley: University of California Press, 1997.

Shuval, Tal. *La ville d'Alger vers la fin du XVIII*e *siècle: population et cadre urbain*. Paris: CNRS, 1998.

——— "The Ottoman Algerian Elite and Its Ideology." *International Journal of Middle East Studies* 32, no. 3 (August 2000): 323–44.

Siblot, Paul. "Nomination et production de sens: le praxème." *Langages* 31, no. 127 (1997): 38–55.

Sifou, Fatiha. "La protestation algérienne contre la domination française: plaintes et pétitions (1830–1914)." PhD diss., Université de Provence, 2004.

——. "Les premières réactions politiques algériennes face à la conquête française (1830–1834)." *Majala al-'Ulūm al-Insāniya* 6, no. 1 (2017): 35–51.

Singham, Shanti Marie. "Betwixt Cattle and Men: Jews, Blacks, and Women, and the Declaration of the Rights of Man." In *The French Idea of Freedom: The Old Regime and the Declaration of Rights of 1789*, edited by Dale K. Van Kley. Stanford, CA: Stanford University Press, 1994.

Slyomovics, Susan. *Monuments Decolonized: Algeria's French Colonial Heritage.* Stanford, CA: Stanford University Press, 2024.

——. *The Performance of Human Rights in Morocco.* Philadelphia: University of Pennsylvania Press, 2005.

Smith, Andrea L. "Citizenship in the Colony: Naturalization Law and Legal Assimilation in 19th Century Algeria." *Political and Legal Anthropology Review* 19, no. 1 (May 1996): 33–49.

Solleveld, Floris. "Lepsius as a Linguist: Fieldwork, Philology, Phonetics, and 'the Hamitic Hypothesis.'" *Language and History* 63, no. 3 (2020): 193–213.

Sosa, Antonio de. *An Early Modern Dialogue with Islam: Antonio de Sosa's Topography of Algiers (1612)*, edited by María Antonia Garcés, translated by Diana de Armas Wilson. Notre Dame, IN: Notre Dame University Press, 2011.

Soufi, Fouad. "Famille, femmes, histoire: notes pour une recherche." *Insaniyat* 4 (1998): 109–18.

Soulaimani, Dris. "Writing and Rewriting Amazigh/Berber Identity: Orthographies and Language Ideologies." *Writing Systems Research* 8, no. 1 (2016): 1–16.

Spellberg, Denise A. *Politics, Gender, and the Islamic Past: The Legacy of 'A'isha bint Abi Bakr.* New York: Columbia University Press, 1994.

Spivak, Gayatri Chakravorty. *A Critique of Postcolonial Reason: Toward a History of the Vanishing Present* (Cambridge, MA: Harvard University Press, 1999).

——. *Outside in the Teaching Machine.* New York: Routledge, 1993.

Sriraman, Tarangini. *In Pursuit of Proof: A History of Identification Documents in India.* New Delhi: Oxford University Press, 2018.

Stein, Sarah Abrevaya. *Saharan Jews and the Fate of French Algeria.* Chicago: University of Chicago Press, 2014.

Steingass, Francis. *Arabic-English Dictionary.* New Delhi: Asian Educational Services, 2005.

Steinmetz, George. "Bourdieu's Disavowal of Lacan: Psychoanalytic Theory and the Concepts of 'Habitus' and 'Symbolic Capital.'" *Constellations* 13, no. 4 (2006): 445–64.

Stern, Karen B. *Inscribing Devotion and Death: Archeological Evidence for Jewish Populations of North Africa.* Leiden: Brill, 2008.

Stigler, Stephen M. *The History of Statistics: The Measurement of Uncertainty before 1900.* Cambridge, MA: Harvard University Press, 1986.

Stirk, Peter M. R. *The Politics of Military Occupation.* Edinburgh: Edinburgh University Press, 2009.

Stroomer, Harry. "Three Tashelhiyt Berber Texts from the Arsène Roux Archives." *Studies in Slavic and General Linguistics* 33 (2008): 389–97.

Sublet, Jacqueline. "Dans l'Islam médiéval, nom en expansion, nom à l'étroit: L'exemple d'Ibn Fuwaṭî." In *L'écriture du nom propre*, edited by Anne-Marie Christin, 117–34. Paris: Harmattan, 1998.

——. "La prosopographie arabe." *Annales: économies, sociétés, civilisations* 25, no. 5 (1970): 1236–39.

——. *Le Voile de nom: Essai sur le nom propre arabe.* Paris: Presses universitaires de France, 1991.

——. "Noms de guerre, Algérie 1954–1962." In *Actas del XII Congreso de la U.E.A.I., (Málaga, 1984)*, 687–96. Madrid: Huertas, 1986.

Surkis, Judith. *Sex, Law, and Sovereignty in French Algeria, 1830-1930.* Ithaca, NY: Cornell University Press, 2019.

Szajkowski, Zosa. "The Reform of the *État-Civil* of the French Jews During the Revolution of 1789." *Jewish Quarterly Review* 49, no. 1 (July 1958): 63–83.

Taïeb, Jacques. *Juifs du Maghreb: noms de famille et société.* Paris: Cercle de généalogie juive, 2004.

Taithe, Bertrand. "Algerian Orphans and Colonial Christianity in Algeria 1866–1939." *French History* 20, no. 3 (2006): 240–59.

——. "Missionary Hubris in Colonial Algeria? Founding and Governing Christian Arab Villages 1868–1930." In *Christian Missions and Humanitarianism in the Middle East, 1850-1950 Ideologies, Rhetoric, and Practices*, edited by Inger Marie Okkenhaug and Karène Sanchez Summerer, 133–54. Leiden: Brill, 2020.

Temimi, Abdeljelil. *Le Beylik de Constantine et Ḥâdj 'Aḥmed Bey, 1830-1837.* Tunis: Revue d'histoire maghrébine, 1978.

Tengour, Ouanassa Siari. "Constantine, 1887: des notables contre la 'naturalisation.'" In *Historie de l'Algérie à la période coloniale, 1830-1962*, edited by Abderrahmane Bouchène, Jean-Pierre Peyroulou, Ouanassa Siari Tengour, and Sylvie Thénault, 235–38. Paris: Découverte, 2014.

Terem, Etty. *Old Texts, New Practices: Islamic Reform in Modern Morocco.* Stanford, CA: Stanford University Press, 2014.

Thénault, Sylvie. "Le 'code de l'indigénat.'" In *Historie de l'Algérie à la période coloniale, 1830-1962*, edited by Abderrahmane Bouchène, Jean-Pierre Peyroulou, Ouanassa Siari Tengour, and Sylvie Thénault, 200–206. Paris: Découverte, 2014.

——. "Interner en République: le cas de la France en guerre d'Algérie." *Amnis: revue d'études des sociétés et cultures contemporaines Europe/Amérique* 3 (2003). https://journals.openedition.org/amnis/513?lang=en.

Thompson, Elizabeth. *Colonial Citizens: Republican Rights, Paternal Privilege and Gender in French Syria and Lebanon.* New York: Columbia University Press, 2000.

Thomson, Ann. *Barbary and Enlightenment: European Attitudes Towards the Maghreb in the 18th Century*. Leiden: Brill, 1987.

Thorvaldsen, Gunnar. *Censuses and Census Takers: A Global History*. London: Routledge, 2018.

Tillion, Germaine. *My Cousin, My Husband: Clans and Kinship in Mediterranean Societies*. Translated by Quintin Hoare. London: Saqi, 2007.

Tilmatine, Mohand. "Du Berbère à l'Amazighe: de l'objet au sujet historique." *Al-Andalus-Maghreb* 14 (2007): 225–47.

Todd, David. *A Velvet Empire: French Informal Imperialism in the Nineteenth Century*. Princeton, NJ: Princeton University Press, 2021.

Tolan, John, Henry Laurens, and Gilles Veinstein. *Europe and the Islamic World: A History*. Princeton, NJ: Princeton University Press, 2012.

Toledano, Ehud R. *As If Silent and Absent: Bonds of Enslavement in the Islamic Middle East*. New Haven, CT: Yale University Press, 2007.

——. *Slavery and Abolition in the Ottoman Middle East*. Seattle: University of Washington Press, 1998.

Tolédano, Joseph. *Une histoire de familles: les noms de famille juifs d'Afrique du Nord des origines à nos jours*. Jerusalem: Ramtol, 1999.

Triomphe, Pierre. *1815: La Terreur blanche*. Toulouse: Privat, 2017.

Trumbull IV, George R. *An Empire of Facts: Colonial Power, Cultural Knowledge, and Islam in Algeria, 1870–1914*. Cambridge: Cambridge University Press, 2009.

Turbet-Delof, Guy. *L'Afrique barbaresque dans la littérature française aux XVIe et XVIIe siècles*. Geneva: Droz, 1973.

——. "Notes lexicologiques sur la désignation de certaines collectivités ethniques ou géographiques d'Afrique du Nord." *Le Français moderne* 2 (April 1970): 151–54.

Udovitch, Abraham L., and Lucette Valensi. "Communautés juives en pays d'Islam: identité et communication à Djerba." *Annales: économies, sociétés, civilisations* 35, nos. 3–4 (May–August 1980): 764–83.

——. *The Last Arab Jews: The Communities of Jerba, Tunisia*. New York: Harwood Academic, 1984.

Valensi, Lucette. "Eusèbe de Salle." In *Dictionnaire des orientalistes de langue française*, edited by François Pouillon, 859–60. Paris: IISMM and Karthala, 2008.

——. *Mardochée Naggiar: Enquête sur un inconnu*. Paris: Stock, 2008.

——. *Tunisian Peasants in the Eighteenth and Nineteenth Centuries*, translated by Beth Archer. Cambridge: Cambridge University Press, 1985.

Van Den Avenne, Cécile. *De la bouche même des indigènes: échanges linguistiques en Afrique colonial*. Paris: Vendémiaire, 2017.

Vaughan, Megan. *Creating the Creole Island: Slavery in Eighteenth-Century Mauritius*. Durham, NC: Duke University Press, 2005.

Verskin, Sara. *Barren Women: Religion and Medicine in the Medieval Middle East*. Berlin: De Gruyter, 2020.

Versteegh, Kees. "Grammar and Logic in the Arabic Grammatical Tradition." In *History of the Language Sciences: An International Handbook on the Study of Language from the*

Beginnings to the Present. Vol. 1, edited by Sylvain Auroux, E.F.K. Koerner, Hans-Josef Niederehe, and Kees Versteegh, 300–306. Berlin: de Gruyter, 2000.

Viennot, Éliane. *L'âge d'or de l'ordre masculin: la France, les femmes et le pouvoir, 1804–1860*. Paris: CNRS éditions, 2020.

Vismann, Cornelia. *Files: Law and Media Technology*. Translated by Geoffrey Winthrop-Young. Stanford, CA: Stanford University Press, 2008.

Vries, Jan de. "Population." In *Handbook of European History 1400–1600: Late Middle Ages, Renaissance and Reformation*. Vol. 1: *Structures and Assertions*, edited by Thomas A. Brady Jr., Heiko A. Oberman, and James D. Brady, 4–9. Leiden: Brill, 1994.

Wagner, Esther-Miriam. *Linguistic Variety of Judaeo-Arabic in Letters from the Cairo Genizah*. Leiden: Brill, 2010.

Wahnich, Sophie. "Declaring Peace on Earth." In *France in the World: A New Global History*, edited by Patrick Boucheron, Nicolas Delalande, Florian Mazel, Yann Potin, Pierre Singaravélou, and Stéphane Gerson, translated by Teresa Lavender Fagan, Jane Kuntz, Alexis Pernsteiner, Anthony F. Roberts, and Willard Wood, 441–47. New York: Other Press, 2019.

——. *L'Impossible citoyen: l'étranger dans le discours de la Révolution*. Paris: Albin Michel, 1997.

Weber, Samuel. *Benjamin's-abilities*. Cambridge, MA: Harvard University Press, 2008.

——. "Introduction to the 1988 Edition." In Daniel Paul Schreber, *Memoirs of My Nervous Illness*, edited and translated by Ida MacAlpine and Richard A. Hunter, vii–liv. Cambridge, MA: Harvard University Press, 1988.

Wehr, Hans. *A Dictionary of Modern Written Arabic (Arabic-English)*. 4th ed., edited by J. Milton Cowan. Urbana, IL. Spoken Language Services, 1994.

Weil, Patrick. *How to Be French: Nationality in the Making Since 1789*, translated by Catherine Porter. Durham, NC: Duke University Press, 2008.

Weiss, Gillian. *Captives and Corsairs: France and Slavery in the Early Modern Mediterranean*. Stanford, CA: Stanford University Press, 2011.

White, Joshua M. *Piracy and Law in the Ottoman Mediterranean*. Stanford, CA: Stanford University Press, 2017.

Wieviorka, Michel, and Philippe Bataille, eds. *La France raciste*. Paris: Seuil, 1992.

Wilson, Stephen. *The Means of Naming: A Social and Cultural History of Personal Naming in Western Europe*. London: University College London Press, 1998.

Wright, Marcia. *Strategies of Slaves and Women Life-Stories from East/Central Africa*. New York: Lilian Barber Press, 1993.

Wrigley, E. A., and R. S. Schofield. *The Population History of England 1541–1871: A Reconstruction*. Cambridge: Cambridge University Press, 1989.

Wuilbercq, Émeline. "Algérie: changer de nom pour tier un trait sur le passé colonial?" *Jeune Afrique* (31 January 2014). https://www.jeuneafrique.com/165948/societe/alg-rie-changer-de-nom-pour-tirer-un-trait-sur-le-pass-colonial/.

Yacono, Xavier. "La Régence d'Alger en 1830 d'après des commissions de 1833–1834." *Revue de l'Occident musulman et de la Méditerranée* 2 (1966): 227–47.

Yermeche, Ouerdia. "L'état civil algérien: genèse d'un processus redénominatif." *Publications PNR du CRASC* (2005): 19–29.

——. "Le patronyme algérien: essai de catégorisation sémantique" In *Nomination et dénomination des noms de lieux, de tribus et de personnes en Algérie*, edited by Farid Benramdane and Brahim Atoui, 61–82. Oran: Centre de recherché en anthropologie sociale et culturelle, 2005.

Žižek, Slavoj. *The Sublime Object of Ideology*. London: Verso, 1989.

Zonabend, Françoise. "Le Nom de personne." *L'Homme* 20, no. 4 (October–December, 1980): 7–23.

Index

Page numbers in italics indicate figures.

'Abd al-Qādir, Amīr, 27, 124, 136
Abdelcader-ben-Het-Nedjar, 97
Aboccaja, Rosine Calfon, 87
"Abū" (father of), 41
Abū Ḍarba, Aḥmad bin Ismā'īl (Ahmed Bouderba), 13, 112, 114–20, 140, 260n111; loophole closing for, 124–27; loophole for, 120–24, *122*
Abu-Lughod, Lila, 45
Abu Shadi, Ahmed Zaki, 269n117
Accursed Share, The (Bataille), 167
acquired nickname. *See Cognomen*
Adam (biblical figure), 19–22, 31, 38, 216n18
Africa Commissions, 33, 36
Afroasiatic language family, 56
agency, 97, 120; Althusser on, 107; *état civil* and, 66; identity and, 13, 110, 117
Ageron, Charles-Robert, 258n83
aghas, 109
ahālī al-qabā'il (people of the tribes), 102, 107
Aïn Beida, 193
Algeria. *See specific topics*
Algeria, country name origins and colonization, 27–39
Algérianité (Algerianness), 2
Algerian names, 132–34; converting to French letters, 135–48, *142*. *See also specific topics*
Algerianness. *See Algérianité*
Algerian State. *See* État Algérien
Algerian War and Revolution, 5, 9
Algérie, 27–28, 33, 37, 96, 222n93
"Algériens," 30, 101–2
Algiers, occupation of, 27
alienation, 6, 7, 108
'Alī ibn al Ā'raj, 50–51
alphabet: Arabic, 138, 144; French, 138, 139, 141; International Phonetic, 138; standard, 138
Alsatian Jews, 134
Althusser, Louis, 106–8, 253n40
Amara, Noureddine, 244n85
Amrane-Minne, Djamila (Danièle Minne), 5–6
'Amushās tribe, 187, 277n97

anachronism of the name "Algerian," 29
ancient Greek language, 29
Anderson, Benedict, 207
Angioli, Marianna, 82
animals, 51, 57, 158
apostasy (*irtidād*), 133, 168
Appeals Court of Algiers, 174
Aquilina, Joseph, 82
Arab Bureau, 132, 135
Arabic alphabet, 138, 144
Arabic-French conversion standards, 134–48; conversion table, *142*. *See also* transcription and transliteration
Arabic language, 23, 140; Judeo-Arabic, 55; Latinization of, 145; medieval, 29; for Muslims, 55
Arabic linguistics, 229n35
Arabic names, 3, 23, 30, 41, 52, 121, 180; Berber names and, 57; Bulliet on, 42; classical model, 41–44, 61; for Muslims, 57–58, 61; for patronyms, 83; phonemes of, 113; technical shortcomings of, 43; toponyms and, 25
Arab Kingdom of Napoleon III, 133
Arabo-centrism of name conversion, 136
Arabo-Islamic names, 179; classical, 12, 41–44
Arendt, Hannah, 171
Arkoun, Mohammed, 20
aseklu n timmarewt. *See* family tree
asmā' al-ḥusnā, al-. *See* "most beautiful names"
Asmā' al-Sharīfa. *See* Nobel Names
assimilation, 3, 83; as "civil fusion," 132–33; of Algeria's political and legal institutions, 165–69; for Muslims, 166
Atoui, Brahim, 10
Aubignosc, Louis Philibert Brun d', 100
authoritarianism, 165
Awlād 'Abd al-Nūr confederation, 187
ayant droit (claimant), 162, 174–77, 191, 199
Azzoug family, 190
Babel-17 (Delany), 40, 65
babies, naming of, 45–46
Bahloul, Joëlle, 61, 64
Bakhtin, Mikhail (word with a loophole), 124
Baouche genealogical tree, *188*, 188–89
Baqara, al- (sura), 20
"Barbaresques," 101–2
Bartolo, Magdelaine, 82
Bataille, Georges, 160
Beaussier, Marcelin, 135–36, 264n39
Bedouins, 103–6
Beloved (Morrison), 15
Belsey, Catherine, 277n90
Ben Abu, Angel, 91
Ben Ahmed, Seddik, 155
Ben Ali, Moustafa, 53
Bénavente, Marie Joséphine Victoire, 82
Ben Bella, Ahmed, 5
Ben Cheneb, Mohammed, 141
Ben Djeriou, Mohamed, 154
Ben Ferhat, Hezîa bent Haida ben Braham ben Ahmed Khodja, 198, 200
Benjamin, Walter, 19–21, 217n27
Benkrerech, Richard Mohammed, 178–79
Ben Mihoub, Fatima bent Mohammed, 188
Ben Mohammed, Ali ben Larbi, 193
Benmounah, family, 194–97
Benramdane, Farid, 4, 10
Ben Sedira, Belkacem, 140–41
Benton, Lauren, 34, 35
Berber (language) *See* Tamazight
Bey, Ḥajj Aḥmad, 92
biblical names, 62
bin al-Ḥajj, Sīdī Aḥmad, 44
bin Mūsā, Sayyid Aḥmad bin Ibrahim, 47, 112
bin Qadūr, Sh'aban, 184
bin Slīman, Ḥuwa bint Muḥammad, 183–84
"bint" (daughter of), 41, 58
bint Abi Bakr, 'Ā'isha, 51

birth certificates, 37
"Black/Dark Decade" (*Décennie Noire*, ca. 1991–2002), 207
Blais, Hélène, 25
Bleu-Blanc-Rouge (French flag color ideals), 2
Bodichon, Eugène, 94–95
Bodin, Jean, 39, 67
Boët, Jean Louis Maurice, 193, 278n116
Bonaparte, Napoleon, 12, 70–74, 83, 98, 116, 126; in Egypt, 25; *état civil* and, 69; "wherever the flag flies" and, 95
Bône, *état civil* in, 90–95
Bontems, Claude, 222n93
Borgos, Maria Rosario, 85
Bori societies, Tunisia, 56
Bouderba, Ahmed. *See* Abū Ḍarba, Aḥmad bin Ismā'īl
Bouderba, Ismaël, 140
Boudin, Jean-Christian-Marc, 93–94
Bourdieu, Pierre, 8–9, 22, 214n38
Bourmont (General), 102
Bozzo, Antoine, 196–97
Brahmia, Fatima, 193
Bresnier, Louis-Jacques, 135, 145–46
Breton names, 131
"broomstick marriages," 67
Brubaker, Rogers, 244n85
Bugeaud (Governor General), 26–27
Bulliet, Richard, 42
Bū Mā'aza, 52–53
Bū Sitta, 52

caïds, 109
Calvo, Carlos, 35
Camus, Albert, 5
Capeletti, Jean-Baptiste, 17
capital, cultural, 150
capital punishment, 243n72
Caprioli, Octavio, 82
Catholic Church, 26, 67, 75–76, 125, 129
Celtic language, 131
Chachoua, Kamel, 59–61
chains of nasabs (*silsilat al-nasab*), 43
Chais, Anne, 75
Chaker, Salem, 5, 57, 157
Chambre of Peers, 35
Charles X (King), 78–79, 243n65
Cheese and the Worms, The (Ginzburg), 16
Cheriguen, Foudil, 10
children, naming of, 45–46, 157
cholera, 93
Christelow, Allan, 197
Christianity, 19, 122, 178; Catholic Church, 26, 67, 76–77, 125, 129; Judeo-Christian tradition, 20; Protestants, 67, 75–76, 170
citizenship, 88, 133; and état civil, 68, 170; and legal assimilation of Muslim, 165–69
civil marriage, 68, 88, 172
civil pensions, 163
civil registration, 164, 194–200
civil rights, 170. See also *rights*
claimant. See *ayant droit*
classical Arabo-Islamic names, 12, 41–44
clochardisation culturelle. *See* "cultural homelessness"
coercion, 8
Cognat, Jacques, 103, 105
Cognomen (acquired nickname), 128
Cole, Joshua, 68–69
collective names, 99
collective nouns, 102
Collège Impérial Arabe-Français, 140
colonialism, 9–10, 12–13, 85–86, 94, 104, 162. *See also* precolonial naming
colonial legal regime, 169–74
colonial names, 7, 40, 83–86, 96
colonial toponyms, 27
colonial trauma, 206
colonization. *See specific topics*
Colonna, Fanny, 17
commissaire de l'état civil. *See* registrar
Commission of Sciences and Arts, 141

common nouns, 222n100, 224n126
concubinage, slavery and, 194–96
Congress of Vienna, 78
"conquest by names," 27
consanguineous marriages (parallel cousin marriage), 197
conscription, 163
consent, marriage and, 171
consonants, 47, 59
Constitution of Algeria (1963), 7
Convention of 1830, 125
Corbin, Alain, 17
corsairs, 75, 98
Corsica, 32, 36
couleur sonore. *See* "sound of color"
court. *See mahakma*
creation narratives, 18–20
Crémieux, Adolph, 166
Cremieux Decree (1870), 88
Crimean War, 132
cultural capital, 150
"cultural homelessness" (*clochardisation culturelle*), 213n26

Dakhlia, Jocelyne, 56, 104, 259n97
Dan, Pierre, 30
Daoud, Kamel, 1, 5
"Dark/Black Decade" (*Décennie Noire*, ca. 1991–2002), 207
Darman, Isaac, 184, 185
daughter of. *See* "bint"
Davis, Natalie Zemon, 123
death, in *état civil*, 90–95
Decazes, Élie, 35–36
Décennie Noire, ca. 1991–2002. *See* "Black/ Dark Decade"
"Declaration of Peace to the World" (1790), 74
decolonization, 5, 10
deconstruction, 18
Defoe, Daniel, 39
De Gaulle, Charles, 28
Delany, Samuel R., 40, 65
Democratic and Popular Algerian Republic. *See* République Algérienne Démocratique et Populaire
demography, 68–69, 106; état civil as source of racialized data, 92–95, and genocide, 94–95, 94n137
Dents du destin, Les (Makouta-Mboukou), 40
deputies. *See Khulafā'*
Derrida, Jacques, 15, 23, 228n19
Desan, Suzanne, 68
deux langues. *See* "two tongued"
Deval, Alexandre, 99
Deval, Pierre, 98–99
disappropriation, 5
dispossession, 39
divorce, 68, 171
Djeghloul, Abdelkader, 5, 109
Djerbal, Daho, 29
Djeriou, Louise, 155
Djeriou, Seddik ben Ahmed, 155
Djeriou, Zakia Seddik, 155
Dolly, Charles, 132, 134
Don Juan (Molière), 146
Dopigez, Abbé, 103
doubled signature, 123
Drici, Amor, 182–85
droit musulman, 196
Dumas, Alexandre, 52–53
Dumasy, François, 88
Durand, Célestine, 115–16, 118, 126–27, 140

Eco, Umberto, 261n3
École des Langues Orientales, 140
École des Lettres d'Alger, 141
École Normale Primaire d'Alger/ Bouzaréah, 140
Egypt, 25, 70, 78–79, 83, 116
embassy exterritoriality, 71–72
empty lands. *See terra nullius*
endonyms, 23–24
Enlightenment, the, 119–20

Esmeralda (fictional character, *The Hunchback of Notre Dame*), 53
estate name (*nom de terre*), 151
État Algérien (Algerian State), 23
état civil (vital statistics system), 4, 11, 67–73, 116, 133–34, 160–64, 201; agency and, 66; Algeria beginning of, 74–80; *ayant droit* and, 174–77; calculation of legal subject, 66–67; changing names and, 180–86; registration and exclusion, 194–200; colonial legal regime and threats to, 169–74; colonial names and, 83–86; colonization and, 80–83; death and race in, 90–95; family break up, 174–77; French Revolution and, 12–14, 169; genealogical trees and, 181, 186–92, *188*, *190*, *191*; history of, 67–69; Jews and Muslims in, 86–90; large families and, 192–94; legal assimilation and, 165–69; patronymics and, 177–80; pejorative names and, 153; sovereignty and, 69–74, 76–77; race in, 90–95; registration and exclusions, 194–200. *See also* citizenship; women; "wherever the flag flies"
État civil: Inventaires (Grangaud, M.), 128
"état civil of the natives," 161–62, 164, 174, 178, 199–200, 203, 208
ethnonyms, 102
European language supremacy, 145
existing toponyms, 25
exonyms, 24
Eyriès, Thérèse, 84

family names, 121, 149–51, 163, hereditary, 129; Jewish, 62
family relationships, 14
family size, 176–77, 188–89, 192–94
family tree (*aseklu n timmarewt*; *shajara al-nasab*), 160–61, 176. *See also* genealogical trees
"fanaticism" and Arabic language, 145
Fanon, Frantz, 1, 7–8, 158
Faruq, Marie Joanny Charles, 84
father (*ism al-ab*), 43
father of. *See* "Abū"
fatwa (legal opinion), 167–68, 273n32
Fellag, Mohand Saïd, 15; on names, 158–59
Feraoun, Mouloud, 45
feudalism in Algeria, 172–73
Filus, David, 87
First World War, 19–20, 27, 107, 162
Foucault, Michel, 248n121
France. *See specific topics*
France-Algeria exhibition match (2001), 2
Francis I (King), 237n7
Francocentric names, 83–84
Franco-Prussian War, 73, 107
French alphabet, 138, 139, 141
French letters, Algerian names converting to, 135–48, *142*
French names, modernization of, 128–32
Frenchness, 2
French Revolution, 6, 32, 129, 161; *état civil* and, 12–14, 169; Muslims in, 116; noble names during, 151; personal names and, 128, 132; territorial expansion and, 74

Gabeau, Charles, 136–37, 139, 141, 143–44, 148
Gaga, Mohammed ben El Hadj Ahmed, 53–54
Gambia, 16
gender: Jewish names and, 63–64; prejudice, 185; ratio, 198–99
genealogical name. *See nasab*
genealogical trees, 161, 176, 181, 186–92, *188*, *190*, *191*, 202
Genesis (biblical story), 20–21
genocide. *See* demography
Gérardin, Prosper, 100
Germany, 73–74, 107
Ghabrial, Sarah, 172, 244n84
Ginzburg, Carlo, 16–17

Giovanné, Enrico, 81
given name. See *ism*
Godechot, Jacques, 240n45
Gohier, Louis-Jérôme, 169–70
Goitein, S. D., 51–52
Goux, Angélique, 129
Gramsci, Antonio, 9
grandes familles. See large families
grandfather (*ism al-jadd*), 43
Grangaud, Isabelle, 88
Grangaud, Michelle, 128
great-grandfather (*ism ab al-jadd*), 43
Great Survey for Algeria, 33
Greek language, ancient, 29
Grégoire, Jean-Stanislas, 81
Group of Experts on Geographical Names (UNGEGN), 23–24
Gsell, Stéphane, 28
Guechi, Fatima, 50
Guerroudj, Abdelkader, 5
Guerroudj, Djawad (Gilbert Minne), 5
Guerroudj, Nassima (Catherine Minne), 5
Guerroudj, Tewfik (Claude Minne), 5
Guha, Ranajit, 9

Haddadou, Mohand-Akli, 10
Hague Regulations of 1907, 239n33
Haiti, 32, 115
Halbwachs, Maurice, 209
Ḥallāj, Manṣūr al-, 21
Ḥamadī, Ḥuwa, 184–86, 200
Hammadi family, 189, 191
Hanley, Will, 242n56
Harbi, Mohammed, 7
hegemony, and symbolic violence, 9, 35
hereditary family names, 129
heteroglossia, onomastic, 55–59
hijāb al-ism. See "veiling name"
Histoire de Barbarie (Dan), 30
history and names, 16–18
homonyms, 18, 130
honorific name. *See* teknonym
Horkheimer, Max, 20
ḥubūs. See religious endowments
Hugo, Victor, 53, 232n78
Hunchback of Notre Dame, The (Hugo), 53

Ibn 'Abdallah, Ḥusayn, 122
Ibn 'Abdallāh, Muḥammad, 52
Ibn Bādīs, 'Abd al-Ḥamīd, 168
Ibn Badīs, Sharīf ibn Makkī, 175, 184, 196
"ibn"/"bin" (son of), 41, 58, 62
Ibn Khaldun, 136
Ibnou Zakri, Mohammed Saïd, 59–61, 65
Ibshīhī, Muḥammad ibn Aḥmad al-, 49, 51
identity, 12, 206; agency and, 13, 110, 117
imperialism, 119
India, 9
indigénat (indigenous penal code), 169
indigène (native), 102, 104–6, 161
indigenous penal code. *See indigénat*
inheritance, 14, 131, 168; Islamic law on, 164, 192; marriage and, 82; for women, 197–98
International Phonetic Alphabet, 138
interpellation (Althusser), 106–8
irtidād. See apostasy
Islam, 19, 121, 167. *See also* Muslims
Islamic calendar, 46
Islamic family law, 154
Islamic inheritance law, 164, 192
Islamic law, 170, 175, 186, 192, 194–97, 208
Islamic reform movement, 168
ism (given name), 41, 45–46, 61
ism ab al-jadd. See great-grandfather
ism al-ab. See father
ism al-jadd. See grandfather
issues de l'immigration, 1
Iveton, Fernand, 5

Jacotot, Joseph, 145
jāmi' masjid. See mosques
Jansen, Jan, 27
Jay, Martin, 217n27
Jayjalī, Faṭṭūm bint Muḥammad bin 'Azzūz al-, 50

Jenni, Alexis, 2
Jewish family names, 62
Jewish names, 61–64
Jews, 130–31, 167, 175; Alsatian, 134; in *état civil*, 86–90; Maghribi, 62
job applications, 2
Journal officiel, 6
Judaism, 19
Judeo-Arabic language, 55
Judeo-Christian tradition, concept of, 20
Julien, Charles-André, 31, 258n83
July Monarchy, 119
Jumhūriyya al-Jazā'iriyya al-Dīmuqrāṭiyya al-Sh'abiyya al-, 23
juste milieu, 119

Kabylia, 9, 55, 59–61, 137
Kafka, Franz, 165
Kant, Immanuel, 74
Kateb, Kamel, 198
Katshāwa, 125–26
khaṭṭ al-yad (signature), 110
khodja. *See* secretary
Khulafā' (deputies), 22
kinship authority, 208
kinship group, Latin name for. *See Nomen*
Kitouni, Hosni, 6–7, 153, 155, 162
Kleiber, Georges, 23
Klein, Martin, 16
Knox, Robert, 95
Kroualedi, Fatma, 3
kunya. *See* teknonym

Lacan, Jacques, 205, 208; Bourdieu and, 214n38; Judeo-Christian tradition and, 20; "Name-of-the-Father" and, 204, 212n11; *parlêtre* and, 9
Laguerra, Ambrosio, 82–83
land, 148–53; *terra nullius*, 28
language, 120; Afroasiatic family, 56; ancient Greek, 29; Berber, 55–59, 140–41, 264n40; Celtic, 131; domination of, 20; European language supremacy, 145; Judeo-Arabic, 55; metalanguages, 147; prejudices, 145; purity, 147; quasi-names and, 101–6; Romance, 56, 62; social being and, 19; sub-Saharan African, 56, 145; Tamazight, 136; violence of, 8. *See also* Arabic language
laqab sobriquets, 50
Larcher, Émile, 172–73
Laredo, Abraham Isaac, 62, 64
large families (*grandes familles*), 192–94
Larrera de Morel, Jean de Dieu Laurent, 196–97
Latinization, of Arabic, 145
Law for Equality of Opportunity (31 March 2006), 2
Lazali, Karima, 206–7
Lefebvre-Teillard, Anne, 131
legal opinion. *See* fatwa
Leo Africanus, 122–23
Lepsius, Richard, 138
Lewis, Mary, 244n85
Liet, Sophie, 145
Life of an Unknown, The (Corbin), 17
lingua franca, 56, 259n97
linguistics: Arabic, 229n35; structure, 18
locus regit actum (the place governs the act), 70–71, 73, 76, 81, 172
Louis-Philippe, duc d'Orleans, 26, 79, 130
Louis XVI (King), 76, 170

Mabroka, 91–92
Mac Guckin de Slane, William, 136–37, 139, 141, 143–44, 148
Macron, Emmanuel, 29
Madigan, Daniel, 217n35
Maghrib, 45
Maghribi Jews, 62
mahakma (court), 184–86
Makouta-Mboukou, Jean-Pierre, 40, 65
male-centered social or symbolic order, 185
male longevity, 177, 189

malicious (pejorative) names, 13, 50–54; Warnier Law and, 153–57
Malo, Abel, 25
Malta, 81
Mamelouks, 116
Marcus, Abraham, 43
Marglin, Jessica, 83, 244n85
marital status, 43
marriage, 83, 88, 92; "broomstick," 67; civil, 68, 89, 172; consanguineous, 197; consent and, 171; inheritance and, 82; for Muslims, 150, 173–74; proof of, 173
Masqueray, Émile, 52
Massignon, Louis, 21
master registers (*registres-matrices*), 66, 88, 161–63, 174, 176, 181, 199
maternal *nasabs*, 227n14
Mbembe, Achille, 4, 248n121
medieval Arabic language, 29
Melian Dialogue, 11
Memmi, Albert, 7
Merle, Isabelle, 169
Messaoudi, Alain, 140, 148
Messick, Brinkley, 110
metalanguages, 147
Meursault Investigation, The (Daoud), 1, 5
military, 163, 239n33; Algeria as military colony, 165, 169
Ministry of Foreign Affairs, 81, 98
Ministry of War, 31, 36–37, 93, 98, 100, 127, 165
Minne, Catherine (Nassima Guerroudj), 5
Minne, Claude (Tewfik Guerroudj), 5
Minne, Danièle (Djamila Amrane-Minne), 5–6
Minne, Gilbert (Djawad Guerroudj), 5
misogyny, 171
Mitchell, Timothy, 8
Mochón, Estefanía Valenzuela, 112
modernity, 20, 180
modernization, of French names, 128–32
Modiano, Patrick, 282n16
Molière, 146
Moniteur algérien, Le (newspaper), 36–37, 81
Moniteur universel, Le (newspaper), 32
monotheistic traditions, 18–19
Montlosier, Comte de, 36
Moor Party, 109
Morocco, état civil, 201
Moroccan Jewish names, 64
Morrison, Toni, 15
mosques, congregational (*jāmi' masjid*), 125
"most beautiful names" (*al-asmā' al-ḥusnā*), 21
mother of. *See* "Umm"
mother of the child. *See umm al-walad*
mothers, 43
Muḥammad (Prophet), 44–47, 51, 60, 63, 161
Muqrani Revolt, 148
Muslims, 29, 116, 161, 170, 207; apostasy and, 133, 168; Arabic language for, 55; Arabic names for, 57–58, 61; assimilation for, 166; in Bône, 90–91; Catholicism and, 26; conscription for, 163; deaths of, 94–95, 106; in *état civil*, 4, 14, 86–90, 92, 161, 172, 180; "état civil of natives" and, 178; first, 51; in first registers, 86–90; inheritance for, 164, 192; Jews and, 63; legal status of, 173; marriage for, 150, 173–74; mosques for, 125; personal status for, 167, 171, 173–74; population figures and, 94; religious endowments, 33

nafs (soul or self), 167
Naggiar, Mardochée (Mordecai Naggiar), 17, 122
Nahrawānī, Abū al-Faraj al-Mu'āfā ibn Zakariyyā' al-, 42–43
name is a sign, the. *See Nomen est omen*
namenlos (nameless), 22

"Name-of-the-Father," Lacanian concept of, 204, 212n11
Name of the Rose, The (Eco), 261n3
names. *See specific topics*
name changes, procedures for, 16, 130, 180–86
Napoleon Bonaparte. *See* Bonaparte, Napoleon
Napoléon I, 151
Napoleonic Code, 69, 73, 238n16
Napoleonic wars, 72
Napoléon III, 133, 135, 148, 166
naqma or *naqwa*, 157–58
nasab (genealogical name), 41, 43–44, 58, 157, 163, 180, 205, 227n14
National Assembly, 166, 196
nationality, 133, 169, 244n85
native. *See indigène*
naturalization, 168
necropolitics, 248n121
Nedjma (Kateb), 203–8
Netter, Jacqueline, 5
"New France," 24
Nobel Names (*Asmā' al-Sharīfa*), 46
Noiriel, Gérard, 68
nom à particule. See seigneurial names
nom de famille, 4
nom de terre. See estate name; seigneurial names
Nomen, Latin name of kinship group, 128
Nomen est omen (the name is a sign), 6
Norès, Edmond, 154
norms: French, 12, 14, 130; onomastic, 40; symbolic violence and, 9
northwest Africa, 17, 25, 29–30; precolonial naming across, 44–50; toponyms in, 24

Oedipus, 205
Old Testament, 130
olive trees, 160
"On Language as Such and on the Language of Man" (Benjamin), 19
onomacide, concept of, 4
onoma nullius (unnaming Algerians), 97–101
onomastic brutalism, 3
onomastic decolonization and research of Algerian scholars, 10
onomastic heteroglossia, 55–59
onomastic norms, 40
On the Name (Derrida), 15
Orléans, Henri d', 27
otherness, 6
Ottoman Empire, 12, 30, 33, 56, 70, 72, 76–79
Oualdi, M'hamed, 122, 244n85
Out of Place (Said), 255n60

"pacification," 105
Pallicière, Catharina, 81
Paradis, Jean-Michel Venture de, 140
parallel cousin marriage. *See* consanguineous marriages
paranyms, 33
parler petit nègre (Fanon), 158
parlêtre (Lacan), 9
Pāshā, Ḥusayn, 101
patriarchy, 9, 150
patrilineal line, 43
patronyms, 14, 108, 149–50, 163, 176–83, 186–88, 202; as patriarchal sign, 129–31
Patterson, Orlando, 16
pejorative (malicious) names, 13, 50–54; Warnier Law and, 153–57
Pensky, Max, 19
people of the tribes. *See ahālī al-qabā'il*
Perez, Françoise-Catherine-Virginie, 81
Perpetual Peace (Kant), 74
personal forename. *See Praenomen*
personal status (*statut personnel*), 86, 167
Pervillé, Guy, 29
Peterson, Joseph, 179
Pharaon, Joanny, 84–85, 116, 140
phonemes, 113, 138
phonetics, 146

physical violence, 7, 22, 24, 106
Pinagot, Louis-François, 17
place governs the act, the. *See locus regit actum*
polysemy, 54
Pontecorvo, Gillo, 241n46
Poor Man's Son, The (Feraoun), 45
possessions (legal concept), 32–38, 75, 223n111, 224n126
possessions françaises dans le nord de l'Afrique, les, 32, 36, 79
postcolonial studies, 18
power: names and monotheistic traditions 18–22; social being and, 19; symbolic, 8, 16, 202, 204; of words, 36
practical jokes, 153
Praenomen (personal forename), 128
precolonial naming, 40, 65; across northwest Africa, 44–50; Arabic names and, 44–54; Berber/Tamazight names and, 55–61; Ibnou Zakri and, 59–61; Jewish names and, 61–64; malicious names and, 50–54; onomastic heteroglossia and, 55–59
private endowment (*waqf al-ahlī*), 197
proper nouns, 222n100, 224n126
property: law, 14, 148; owners, 87–88; relations, 34; rights, 133, 187
Protestants, 67, 75–76
protests, in France (2005), 1–2
Proust, Marcel, 16, 38
psychoanalysis, 18. *See also* Lacan
psychopathology, 7
"public knowledge," 163

Quasimodo (fictional character, *The Hunchback of Notre Dame*), 53
quasi-names, 101–6
Qur'an, 20–21, 38, 47, 50, 60

race: in *état civil*, 90–95; slavery and, 195
Races of Men, The (Knox), 95
racism, 1, 3
Raḥmāniyya Sufi center, 49
Raimbert, Jean-Dauphin, 99
Rancière, Jacques, 145
reclaiming of names, 5
Régis, Max, 29, 221n83
registrar (*commissaire*), 175
registration, civil, 164
registres-matrices. See master registers
religious endowments (*ḥubūs* or *waqf*), 197
Rémusat, Henri, 103
République Algérienne Démocratique et Populaire (Democratic and Popular Algerian Republic), 23
resistance dialogue, names in, 106–9
res nullius, 34
Revolution of 1830, 31, 79
rights, 86; civil, 170; exclusion of Muslims, 132–33, 150, 161, 165–74; property, 133, 187
Riley, Denise, 13
riots. *See* protests
Robinson Crusoe (Defoe), 39
Romance languages, 56, 62
Roman Empire, 128
Roman law, 34
Rouis, El Hadj ben Moussa bou, 154
royal ordinance (22 July 1834), 31

Sabbatier, J., 104
Sacy, Antoine Silvestre de, 140, 145
Sahnoun family, 190–91
Said, Edward, 255n60
Saint-Cyr, M. de, 130
Saint-Domingue, 32
sans nom patronymique. See "Without Patronymic Name"
Saussure, Ferdinand de, 18
Savary (General), 126–27
Sayyid (title), 48
Scientific Commission of Algeria (est. 1839), 141, 143
Second Republic (1848–1852), 165

Second World War, 102, 201, 209
secretary (*khodja*), 175
seigneurial names (*nom à particule*; *nom de terre*), 129, 148–53, 177
self. *See nafs*
Sénatus-Consulte, 133, 166, 187
Senegal, 16
settler colonialism, 94
Sha'bān petition, 114, 117, 127
shajara al-nasab. *See* family tree
Shakespeare, William, 4, 277n90
Sifou, Fatiha, 109
signatures, 109–14, *111*; graphologists and, 127
signs, violence of, 8
silsilat al-nasab. *See* chains of nasabs
"Sister Republics," 70
slavery, 16, 195, 196, 197, 280n130
Slavery and Social Death (Patterson), 16
SNP. *See* "Without Patronymic Name"
"social atom," 17
social being, 19
social categories, 107
son of. *See* "ibn"/"bin"
soul. *See nafs*
"sound of color" (*couleur sonore*), 2
sovereign names, 18–24
Spain, 81, 126
Spanish Hapsburgs, 30
Spanish Reconquista, 121
Spellberg, Denise, 51
Stamp Paid (fictional character, *Beloved*), 15
standard alphabet, 138
Staouëli, 180
statut personnel. *See* personal status
Steinmetz, George, 214n38
Stranger, The (Camus), 5
Straumann, Benjamin, 34–35
subjectivity, 7–10, 123–24, 133
Sublet, Jacqueline, 41
sub-Saharan African languages, 56, 145
sujet de droit, 133
Surkis, Judith, 172, 267n87, 273n25
surnames. *See* family names
symbolic identification, 253n44
symbolic power, 8, 16, 202, 204
symbolic structures, 21–22
symbolic violence, 7, 8–10, 22, 214n29
Syria, 25

Tabet, Messaouda, 88–89
Ṭahṭāwī, al-, 44, 140
Takitount, genealogical trees of, 186–92, *188*, *190*, *191*
Tamazight etymology, 10
Tamazight language, 55–59, 140–41, 136, 264n40
Tamazight names, 3, 13, 25, 55–61, 136–37, 180
teknonym (*kunya*, honorific name), 41, 49
terra nullius (empty lands), 28
territorial acquisitions, 35
territorial expansion, wars of, 74
Th'ālibī, Sīdī 'Abd al-Raḥman al-, 46
Thibaudeau, Antoine, 70
Thierry-Dufougeray, Florent, 99–100
Third Republic, 148, 166
Thomson, Ann, 98
Thon, Joseph, 85
Thon, Louise Elisabeth Africa, 85, 93
Thucydides, 11
titles, 48, 112, 129
toponyms: Arabic names and, 25; colonial, 27; existing, 25; in northwest Africa, 24
transcription, 138, 144, 146
translation, 146
translation, country names, 23–24
transliteration, 138
trauma, colonial, 206
Treaty of Ryswick (1697), 32
Treaty of Versailles (1768), 32
tréma marks, 139
Tripoli, 78

Tunisia, 56, 62, 78, 115, 122 ; état civil in, 201
Turbet-Delof, Guy, 29, 30
"two tongued" (*deux langues*), 53–54

Udovitch, Abraham, 63
Ūfiyya tribe, 125
"Umm" (mother of), 41
umm al-walad (mother of the child), 195–96
Underground Railway, 15
UNGEGN. *See* Group of Experts on Geographical Names
"Universal-Bibliothek," 20
Universal Exposition (1889), 52
universalism, 120

Valée (Governor General), 26
Valensi, Lucette, 17, 63, 122, 197
Van den Boogert, Maurits H., 242n58
Vanture, Jean Louis, 75
"veiling name" (*hijāb al-ism*), 21
Véroelé, Claude, 75
violence, 11, 162; of language, 8; physical, 7, 22, 24, 106; quasi-names and, 101–6; slavery and, 195; symbolic violence, 7, 8–10, 22, 214n29
vital statistics system. *See état civil*
Vocabulaire, 137, 141, 178–80
Volney, Comte de, 25, 120, 145
vowels, 47, 139

waqf. See religious endowments
waqf al-ahlī. See private endowment
war making, 74
Warnier Law (1873), 148; and topographic surnames, 150–53, 155
wars: Algerian War and Revolution, 5, 9; Crimean, 132; Franco-Prussian, 73, 107; Napoleonic, 72; of territorial expansion, 74; World War I, 19–20, 27, 107, 162; World War II, 102, 201, 209
Weil. Patrick, 244n85
"wherever the flag flies" (état civil and French sovereignty) 71–73, 74, 77, 95
White Fathers missionary society, 178–79
white supremacy, 150, 164
Wieviorka, Michel, 2
"Without Patronymic Name" (*sans nom patronymique*, SNP), 164, 208
women, 14, 45, 59; exclusion from family with état civil, 197–200; inheritance law for, 197–98; Kabyle, 9; titles for, 48–49
words, power of, 36
World Cup (1998), 2
World War I, 19–20, 27, 107, 162
World War II, 102, 201, 209
Wretched of the Earth, The (Fanon), 1

Yacine, Kateb, 203–8
Yemen, 110
Yermeche, Ouerdia, 10, 214n29

Zaynab, Lālla, 49
Zaytuna University, 141
Zeraffa, Joseph, 88–89
Žižek, Slavoj, 253n44

GPSR Authorized Representative: Easy Access System Europe, Mustamäe tee 50, 10621 Tallinn, Estonia, gpsr.requests@easproject.com

www.ingramcontent.com/pod-product-compliance
Lightning Source LLC
LaVergne TN
LVHW041627060925
820435LV00016B/119
* 9 7 8 0 2 3 1 2 1 6 0 1 2 *